RESEARCH AGENDAS IN THE
SOCIOLOGY OF EMOTIONS

SUNY Series in the Sociology of Emotions
Theodore D. Kemper, Editor

RESEARCH AGENDAS
in the
SOCIOLOGY OF EMOTIONS

THEODORE D. KEMPER, EDITOR

STATE UNIVERSITY OF NEW YORK PRESS

Published by
State University of New York Press, Albany

© 1990 State University of New York

Printed in the United States of America

For information, address State University of New York Press,
90 State Street, Suite 700, Albany, NY 12207

Library of Congress Cataloging-in-Publication Data

Research agendas in the sociology of emotions / Theodore D. Kemper,
editor.
    p. cm.
Papers presented at the American Sociological Association
Convention, Chicago, 1987.
    ISBN 0-7914-0269-X. — ISBN 0-7914-0270-3 (pbk.)
    1. Emotions—Sociological aspects—Congresses. 2. Social
psychology—Methodology—Congresses.   I. Kemper, Theodore D., 1926–
. II. American Psychological Association. Convention (1987 :
Chicago, Ill.)
HM291.R44   1990
302'.072—dc20   89–26193
                                                        CIP

10 9 8 7 6 5 4 3 2 1

Contents

v

part one

INTRODUCTION

1.

Themes and Variations in the Sociology of Emotions

Theodore D. Kemper

Like the basic elements of matter, intellectual fashions have a finite half-life. For a generation, the cognitive perspective dominated the social sciences. Simply as style, it seemed appropriate for a post-industrial, Boolean age that is automated, computerized, and founded on higher and higher refinements in organizational rationality. Although countervailing ideologies flourished in the popular realm—in New Age movements, the drug culture, cultist spiritual enterprises—most social scientists staked their theoretical fortunes on examining their subjects' cognitions. Emotions were relegated to the fringes of scientific work, the property of quasi-scientific disciplines such as psychoanalysis and cultural anthropology, although emotions were often unwittingly smuggled in under such rubrics as attitudes, charisma, and social class identity. Among philosophers, too, emotions remained of interest, a troublesome feature of the troublesome mind-body problem.

But with the inevitable cresting of a virtually exclusive interest in cognition and its problems—this is an instance of the exhaustion of the possibilities of Kuhnian "normal science"—emotion has reemerged as a legitimate and interesting topic of inquiry. The beginning of the current attention to emotions among sociologists illustrates the oft-cited principle that new knowledge emerges when the intellectual climate favors it. That this is not tautology is shown by the fact that usually, unbeknown to each other, several investigators commence work on the new topic at about the same time. Possibly the most famous instance of this was the simultaneous work of Charles Darwin and Alfred Wallace, both of whom arrived at approximately similar conclusions concerning the evolution of species through environmental selection.

In the sociology of emotions, 1975 was the watershed year: Arlie Russell Hochschild (1975) published an article on emotions in a feminist collection; Thomas Scheff organized the first session on emotions at the American Sociological Association meetings in San Francisco; and Randall

3

Collins (1975) theorized a central place for emotions in the microdynamics of stratification in his book *Conflict Sociology*. Of course, lead time on all such work is considerable, therefore we may date the turn to emotions from the early 1970s. Why just then? It is tempting to speculate that sociologists were responding to the *Zeitgeist* of the decade of the 1960s, with its attack on linear logic, its emphasis on the importance of expressiveness, and its concentrated focus on the self.

By the end of the 1970s, there were also the first and second books specifically devoted to emotions by sociologists (*A Social Interactional Theory of Emotions* [Kemper, 1978a], and Scheff's *Catharsis in Healing, Ritual and Drama* [1979]); the appearance of an article on emotions in a special issue of *The American Sociologist* devoted to new theoretical approaches (Kemper, 1978b); and the dynamizing articles in the *The American Journal of Sociology* by Shott (1979) and by Hochschild (1979). At the brink of the 1980s, the sociology of emotions was poised for developmental take off. And indeed it has, centered in the recruitment of many new participants and publications, and culminating in the successful organization of a section on emotions in the American Sociological Association.

This work arises from the section's first two thematic sessions, presented at the 1987 meetings of the American Sociological Association in Chicago. I proposed as a theme for those sessions: Research Hypotheses in the Sociology of Emotions. True to the spirit of all collective undertakings, the title was revised to *Research Agendas in the Sociology of Emotions*, with Candace Clark and Steven Gordon as organizers and chairs of the sessions.

The origin of the theme was the idea that, given the nascent status of the emotions sub-field in sociology, it would be useful for some of those with developed theories to present both an overview of their position and a program of research that would help to elaborate and test the theory they espoused. A research-oriented approach would enable interested scholars and students to see where they themselves might fit in the sociological study of emotions.

Although each contribution here stands on its own merit in exploring a specific theoretical facet of the sociology of emotions, each also, by design or by default, partakes of a particular choice, option, or alternative that is available in social scientific work today. These choices are organizing matrices for thought and for research. They aid implicitly (and often unconsciously) in assembling certain ideas and, as certainly, in precluding others. Some of the alternatives are simply that; others contest the terrain between them, fighting, one might say, for the soul of the sociology of emotions and for the allegiance of students and scholars who might be attracted to it. As one opts for one or another side of each of the alternatives, one achieves a definite position that comprises a metatheory over and above the substantive core of one's work. I shall discuss these alternatives now and where the contributions fit. (N.B. Some contributions will appear under a single rubric, others under several, as dictated by the content of the contribution.)

Micro Versus Macro. Sociology began as the study of society, with major attention to social institutions—family, polity, economy, religion, and so forth—and how their shape and form determine stability or instability, progress or decay, justice or injustice, in society as a whole. The great early thinkers, including Comte, St. Simon, Marx, Durkheim, Spencer, Weber, Simmel, Mannheim, Cooley, and Mead confronted these grand themes in original works that carved out the first scientific analyses of society.

But, despite their main concern with macro and evolutionary or historical issues, these thinkers also treated micro questions. Individual happiness, suicidal despair, alienation, conscience, religious fervor, the nuances of love, self-regard—all found a place in early sociological work. Society and the individual, so seamlessly mitered together by Cooley, were indeed obverse to each other. But the growth of knowledge and its complexity also promoted the specialization and segregation of scholarly interests into either macro or micro-sociology questions and careers. However, today, more self-consciously than before, sociologists are examining the micro-macro mix and the nexus between them. Randall Collins (1981), who helped initiate the new interest in micro-macro analysis presents here a synthesis of his approach, in which some of the central processes of macro-sociology— social order, conflict, and stratification—are seen to rest on the long unappreciated micro-level foundation of emotion.

For Collins, social order is Durkheimian solidarity and moral commitment. These emerge in the course of "interaction rituals" at the micro level, when two or more actors focus on a common activity. In the proper circumstances, a common mood is experienced, and this leads to a sense of unity among the actors, as in Durkheim's analysis of religious rituals in small face-to-face groups. Conflict, too, rests on a foundation of emotion, in as much as it involves a mobilization of sentiments of anger toward carriers of opposing social interests. Both solidarity and conflict perspectives are joined in Collins' micro-macro analysis of stratification.

Collins views stratification in terms of two dimensions, namely, power and status (see also Kemper, this volume). Power rituals are interactions structured by the division of roles into order-givers and order-takers, mainly in large-scale organizations, which Collins sees as the principal arena of modern stratification systems. Although these actors participate with different goals and interests, crucially a common mood of shared emotions arises nonetheless. Because of their dominance, order-givers derive "emotional energy" from the interaction—their interests have been satisfied, their commands obeyed. On the other hand, order-takers frequently experience loss of emotional energy. Their interests are being neglected, their wishes ignored.

Status rituals, which are somewhat independent of the power-based rituals, are interactions that involve membership inclusion or exclusion, centrality or peripherality of location in the interaction sphere, cosmopolitanism or localism of one's network of interaction partners. In Collins' view, these respectively increase or diminish emotional energy.

Broadly speaking, these interaction patterns provide a foundation of emotional resources for participation in further interactions, therefore Collins' idea of "interaction ritual *chains,*" which cumulate across time and space to constitute the macro structure of stratification. Successful interactions in the power-status spheres breed enthusiasm, confidence, and a sense of meaningful affiliation with the groups in which emotional energy was gained. Unsuccessful interactions in the power-status spheres breed depression, embarrassment, and alienation from the group and its interests. Collins sees such emotions as anger, fear, elation, and the like, as short-term resultants that emerge from especially frustrating or especially pleasing pulses of interaction that punctuate the long-term pattern of greater or lesser emotional energy.

Like Collins, Michael Hammond examines macro social organization—especially stratification systems—from a micro perspective. Taking an evolutionary view, he contends that, as a species, we have an inbuilt need for dependable, long-term affective gratification. Hammond's argument, which advances by a series of heuristic, logical surmises, considers what social strategies are likely to be adopted to ensure what he calls "affective maximization."

In the paradigmatic case, individuals are confronted with choices among possible sources of affective maximization. These may be persons, objects, experiences, and so forth. Hammond reasons that to be able to choose efficiently among these requires some knowledge about them. This would prompt the emergence of an information scheme that would differentiate among possible choices according to their potential for providing affective maximization. Logically, this would lead to a classificatory matrix through which individuals could become aware of all their possible choices, for example, at a very simple level, the differentiation of fruits into oranges, apples, plums, peaches, and so forth, and humans into male and female, old and young, short and tall, and so on.

But, Hammond suggests, an even more efficient system would be to create a *hierarchically* differentiated classification, so that potentially gratifying objects are ordered according to a scale of preference, established by the cumulated prior experiences of others—in our examples: plums, peaches, oranges, and apples, and males and females, old and young, tall and short *in that order.* Applied to human actors, who are, of course, the fundamental source of affective maximization, this preferential scheme provides the rudiments of a stratification system, since some characteristics would be ranked as more desirable than others. These might include specific somatic, motivational, and performance attributes as well as ascriptive qualities such as gender, ethnicity, family origin, and the like. Hierarchical differentiation in the manner just described not only ranks persons, objects, roles, and experiences according to how desirable they are for purposes of affective maximization, but also, in regard to persons and roles, ranks their control of opportunities to obtain affective maximization.

Now, early in history, Hammond reasons, when groups were small, this hierarchically differentiated preference system would have led to very little hardship, in as much as there was scant economic surplus to distribute disproportionally among the stratified population. But with growth in scale and the introduction of technological complexity, increasingly large surpluses were appropriated in such a manner that those at the low end of the hierarchy experienced considerable deprivation. Hammond suggests that in these circumstances a new form of differentiation was likely to, and did, emerge, especially for the benefit of those who were ranked low in the existing preference order. This involved the hierarchical differentiation of *time:* the future can be designated as the repository of a superior level of affective maximization, either in this life or in a postulated hereafter. Belief systems are now invoked to alleviate the burden of inadequate affective resources in the present. In essence, cognitive management is applied to the mending of emotional distress. (This theme resounds in the work of Hochschild and Thoits, this volume).

Within this framework, Hammond is able to argue against sociobiological propositions concerning inbuilt genetic bases for stratification. Rather, he postulates an initial human condition—the need for affective maximization—and conjectures what forms of social organization might be most likely to emerge to attain the affective goal. The human emotional matrix, then, shapes social organization in order to facilitate the pursuit of affective goals.

Thomas Scheff here approaches the micro-macro issue through shame and pride, which he sees as the linchpins of social control. Following Darwin, McDougall, and Cooley, Scheff proposes that individuals engage in more or less perpetual emotional monitoring of the sentiments of approval or disapproval of self that are presented by others. Individuals not only cognize others' reactions, but also react emotionally with either pride (for approval) or shame (for disapproval). These emotions operate in somewhat gyroscopic fashion to guide the individual along a socially prescribed path. Cumulating this effect across the whole society provides a micro-basis for a macro-effect, namely, the general pattern of conformity that prevails in society. Social order is thus constructed by aggregating the total of individual cases of experience of pride and shame.

Scheff poses an important question: If shame and pride are so crucial to the maintenance of social order and so pervasive, why don't we see these emotions manifested more often? Relying mainly on the work of psychologist Helen Block Lewis, who did intensive microanalysis of verbatim psychotherapy protocols, Scheff proposes that indeed both shame and (by implication) pride are present, only they are masked, sometimes even from those who are experiencing these emotions. Lewis argued that shame, specifically, can be disguised and unacknowledged in two forms: "overt, undifferentiated shame," which includes painful feelings, blushing, lowered gaze, low-volume stammering speech, among the major signs; and "bypassed shame," which is marked by covert symptoms, such as obsessive, repetitive thought. Scheff regards both these as so prevalent that they may massively contaminate many situations in which actors experience critical evaluation from others, for example children vis-à-vis parents; students vis-à-vis teachers; even nations vis-à-vis nations.

Norman Denzin, too, takes a macro view in relation to emotion. Focusing on movies and television, he offers a semiotic reading of dramas about alcohol and alcoholism. Denzin discovers an underlying emotional logic in these productions in which cultural and societal definitions of class and gender provide the subtext for the manifest emotions of the characters. As vehicles of culture transmission, film and TV dramas define proper and legitimate emotions and serve to shape individuals' desires and self-definitions so that they can experience the affects that society deems proper for them.

Steven Gordon explicitly links micro and macro through his employment of the classical social structure and personality paradigm. In that tradition, which also includes culture and personality studies, elements of macro organization or culture were linked across the society-individual gap to personality dispositions (often Freudian in origin), or to concepts such as "national character." Gordon proposes that social structure and culture may differ in how they affect emotions: the former more influential on behavioral and motivational aspects of emotion, while the latter may have greater effect on the quality, intensity, object, and setting of emotion. From the social structure perspective, Gordon poses questions about what specific elements affect emotion; (a) whether it is better to look at structural effects on emotion content, or at abstract elements of emotion; (b) what intermediate structures operate to translate macro structures into micro effects; (c) how structural change in society ultimately leads to change in the emotions that are socially relevant; and (d) about the cultural relativity of emotion paradigms (for example, emotions are considered internal events by most Americans, but social relational nexi in the Southwest Pacific).

Gordon distinguishes between *emotion*, which he proposes is a response based on inborn, undifferentiated bodily arousal, and *sentiment*, which he defines as a socially-learned composite of bodily sensations, gestures, and cultural meaning connected with a social relationship, and provided with a cultural label. This definition fosters a perspective on emotions (sentiments) that stresses their social, as opposed to biological, origin. Entailed are such matters as their (a) long-term character (in contrast to the relatively short time span of emotions more closely linked to the biological); (b) the social constraints that structure emotional situations even in the absence of underlying physiological response; and (c) how social fiat overrides the physiological in dictating change in emotion. Gordon proposes three processes by which emotions are transformed into sentiments: *Differentiation*, which elaborates the raw emotional materials into highly nuanced and complex patterns that are coordinated with social variability; *Socialization*, which entails the social processes, including rewards and punishments, and modeling, by which culture members learn about emotional experience; and *Management*, which allows social determination through normative interventions that bring emotions into line with social prescriptions. Conclusively, in regarding the micro-macro link, Gordon focuses attention on the analytic possibilities in both directions—not only how societal structure affects emotions, but also how emotions affect societal structure.

Quantitative Versus Qualitative Methods. Can emotions be measured and quantified? Or are emotion phenomena only qualitative? Lynn Smith-Lovin and David Heise answer unequivocally yes to both questions. When approached through their Affect Control Theory, emotions have both quantitative and qualitative aspects. Their model does not "split a difference," but, rather, formulates the emotions question in a way that embraces both approaches. Smith-Lovin and Heise have calculated the numerical values of certain underlying meanings of common language terms for behaviors, identities, objects, and emotions. Given that a certain situation reflects a certain meaning, they are able to predict the emotions that are likely to be felt in the situation. That is, they predict a set of numerically valued meanings, to which specific, common language emotion terms have been found plausibly to correspond.

Smith-Lovin and Heise base their meaning analysis on the three commonly found dimensions of the Semantic Differential method. These are: (a) *evaluation* (how good or pleasant something is); (b) *potency* (how powerful or strong something is); and (c) *activity* (how aroused or active something is). All the items of a culture—including objects, actions, roles, and emotions—can be rated according to the three dimensions. In essence this produces a profile of the culture in terms of evaluation (E), potency (P), and activity (A). Consensual ratings were obtained from culture members who provided numerical scores for each item and the average ratings of an item on the three dimensions comprise the meaning of the item.

Heise's and Smith-Lovin's affect control theory holds broadly that actors behave so as to maintain their fundamental identities. Thus, if a Father Kisses a Child, the action conforms to the culturally sanctioned meaning of the Father identity. However, if a Father Abuses a Child, this does not confirm the Father identity. In such cases of discrepancy between behavior and identity, an emotion will be experienced—which emotion depends on the degree of discrepancy—and is determined in the affect control model by calculating the degree of departure of the untoward act from the normal pattern for the given identity. Degree of departure means how far the away the EPA ratings of the discrepant act are from the EPA ratings of acts that are normal for the given identity. According to the theory, and somewhat counterintuitively, the actor will seek to return to a state of harmony with the fundamental identity at issue, and will tend to choose a subsequent act that will attain the harmony. Failing this, there can be a shift in identity. Therefore, if the abusive Father does not retrieve his fundamental identity through reparative or loving action, he will necessarily rethink his identity (or observers will rethink it) to bring it into conformity with his conduct. In this process, emotion provides a signal that there is a discrepancy to be mended, or an identity to be reformulated. Whether dealing with identities, behaviors, or emotions, the affect control model works through the EPA values of the specific behaviors, identities, and so forth, and produces new values according to what the actor is likely to do. The new values are then translated through the dictionary of EPA profiles of culture items into discrete identities, behaviors, roles, and emotions.

In addition to Smith-Lovin and Heise, the other sociologists of emotion who have collected empirical data (and discuss it here) are Arlie Russell Hochschild, Peggy Thoits, and Candace Clark. Their approach to emotions is mainly qualitative. But some of their work is done with meta-emotional concepts, such as emotion management techniques (see Thoits, this volume) and these lend themselves to quantification, as in Thoits's frequency counts of different management strategies by gender and other attributes.

Positivism Versus Anti-Positivism. One of the major intellectual debates in the social sciences today is between positivists and anti-positivists. In general, the positivist view is that emotions can be examined as more or less objective phenomena, determined by certain social structural and interactional conditions. Both the conditions and the emotions are susceptible to measurement that is often, though not always, quantitative. Positivist investigators frequently seek covariance patterns between social structures and interaction patterns, on the one hand, and the emotions that are hypothesized to ensue, on the other. Furthermore, emotion is examined in its physiological as well as its social, cognitive, and expressive aspects, in order to pursue a complete theory of emotion.

Per contra, non- or anti-positivists argue against the possibility of treating emotions as objective, measurable phenomena. Emotions are considered cognitive constructions that have no reality aside from the mental processes that allow the individual to perceive situations that normatively demand certain emotional responses. Positivists and anti-positivists ordinarily differ also in their sources of intellectual inspiration. Positivists are devotees, mainly, of the natural sciences, in which so much progress has been achieved in the cumulation of knowledge, whereas anti-positivists are often inspired by philosophy, which does not seek to cumulate knowledge, but to set forth the conditions under which knowledge can be accumulated, that is, rules of epistemology.

In this work, the positivist view is represented mainly by Theodore Kemper, who proposes that social structures give rise to specific emotions—at least modally—and that a sociology of emotions must also accommodate the physiological underpinnings of emotions. The idea that social structures determine specific emotions is based on the notion that we are phylogenetic inheritors of a set of primary emotions—fear, anger, joy, and depression—(Kemper, 1987) that serve evolutionary adaptive needs, and that there are certain environmental contingencies to which these emotions are responsive. For humans, the major environmental contingencies in contemporary society are social. Therefore the vicissitudes of social relations determine emotions—unless society intervenes normatively to require a different outcome. When it does so, it runs the risk of distorting emotional life—as when it tampers with sexuality, or seeks to repress deprived and resentful populations, or insists on emotional wholeheartedness when the heart is still broken (see Thoits, this volume).

According to a very comprehensive body of results from a number of disciplines, emotional outcomes of interaction can be predicted from a model that centers on the social dimensions of power and status. Power and status interactions directly produce emotions. Fundamental to the model is the idea that actors necessarily interpret their and others' power and status positions subjectively. Notwithstanding, this usually leads to a consensual judgment. Should this not be the case, further interaction usually makes it clear. The positivist argument here is that regardless of phenomenal differences from culture to culture in what constitutes power and status, and what one judges to be a "good" outcome or a "bad" one, once the judgment is made, the phylogenetically adaptive emotions will ensue when certain power and status outcomes occur in interaction.

Denzin here asserts a vigorous anti-positivist view. He proposes a sociology of emotions project that ignores the conventional science approach, which would be (a) to treat emotion as a variable, (b) undertake cross-cultural studies, (c) develop the history of particular emotions, and (d) examine the association between emotions and standard sociological categories such as social class, gender, ethnicity, and so forth. Denzin's ultimate anti–positivist dictum opposes efforts to build a theory of emotions, whether grand or middle range.

Rather, Denzin would have sociologists of emotions study what he calls "emotionality," which is, for him, the *Ding an Sich*. This would include how emotion is structured as a lived experience, the forms of emotional feeling and intersubjectivity, violent emotions, temporality and emotions, epiphanies and shattering emotions (which have the effect of bringing about decisive changes in lives) among other questions. While these problems clearly emerge from phenomenology, from which Denzin derives his perspective, other questions he proposes may share some common ground with positivist approaches, for example cultural constraints on emotionality, the relation of emotions to self and biography, and differences in emotionality according to gender—notwithstanding that the research approaches are likely to differ. For example, Denzin endorses using the self as a datum and field of investigation, a highly unlikely resource for positivist investigators.

To be judicious in the debate about positivism is both a desideratum and difficult. The difficulty is that the positions often appear both polar and preemptive, as if there were no middle ground. Indeed, in an important sociological sense, there is none, for to endorse one side of the debate is to sponsor careers that cater to it and snuff out those that do not. Reduced to fundamental terms, it is Weberian-style conflict between competing status groups, each under the banner of a preemptive claim. Readers must either choose sides, or wisely refuse to do so, in order to create a syncretic field of study that incorporates the best of both approaches.

Political Economy of Emotions. Another axial difference in contemporary sociology centers on whether a problem is examined apart from its historical rootedness, or whether the historical context, particularly the mode of production, is analytically central to the problem. This issue is a variation on the positivist-anti–positivist theme, and stems from Marx. Although virtually all sociologists today acknowledge a debt to Marx's analysis of the social relations that underlie and determine the patterns of daily life, and of the importance of social structures of stratification, only some apply Marx's specific analysis of political economy. Political economy in this sense involves the way different groups in society are positioned in relation to the mode of production, how the basic constituents of life—from the earning of a livelihood to the experiences of desire and pleasure—are related to the organization of technical and social elements involved in the production of society's goods and services. Marx's main analysis was of capitalism, hence the political economy approach today mainly locates problems for sociological analysis in that setting.

Denzin treats the problem of emotions as rooted fundamentally in issues of political economy (he describes it as the domain of work), along with those of gender, and class. These structures are historical, in this case "post-modern," and they have "cultural" effects; that is, they provide a set of meanings embodied in cultural productions, such as movies and television, that set forth models of action and emotionality. But these reflect the political economy of postwar, late Capitalist America, whose elements, according to Denzin, include: (a) bureaucratization, which organizes individuals into compartmentalized roles and interaction opportunities; (b) commodification, which translates all human interests, including desire, sexuality, and eroticism, into marketable goods; (c) mass-mediated reality, which removes individuals from direct encounters with the world, but overloads the senses with pseudoreality; and (d) the deconstruction of (that is, concentrating extreme skepticism on) major, sustaining "myths," such as those of the value of science, the prevalence of freedom, and the efficacy of democracy.

Denzin seeks no "theory" of emotions, but rather to understand how emotionality is "lived" in such a world. This approach allows him to examine the cultural productions of our time (here, mainly, films about alcoholism), not in terms of manifest plot, but as strictures about the limits of emotion and reason in the very specific society that gives them life. Viewers' needs and emotional selves are shaped by these films. They learn how to be, and what it means to be, emotional in a particular historical moment of the productive process, in particular sites where particular emotions are endorsed as suitable and desirable. Following Louis Althusser, Denzin argues that the social relations of emotionality in the media are "ideological," not the real relations that prevail, and which must be examined.

Hochschild too works in the arena of political economy. One of her main concepts is emotional labor, which she defines as the emotion work that one must do as part of one's job. Emotion work is brought into play when what one feels is discrepant from the "feeling rules" proposed by society, or self. Emotions must then be managed to bring them into line with feeling rules. Hochschild proposes that this can be done by such methods as surface acting, or by deep acting. In the former, one puts on the expressive visage or body stance of the emotion, in the hope of stimulating the authentic feeling. In deep acting, one resorts to more profound strategies, such as modifying bodily or mental states, designed to evoke an emotion more in line with feeling rules.

Hochschild's analysis of the emotional labor of airline flight attendants provides insight into the way emotions have become a commodity, sold along with one's labor power in capitalist society. She contends that nearly a third of men's work and about half of women's work requires emotional labor. These workers are constrained to adjust their emotions according to the feeling rules set down by their employers, rather than feeling the emotions they would normally feel in the circumstances. Hochschild's main concern here is with the political economy of gender, to which I turn now.

Gender Analysis. Possibly the most important development in recent sociology is the emergence of gender as a central analytic category. Although gender has not been absent from empirical studies, where data are often analyzed separately by male and female, the current status of gender is entirely different. Based on feminist analyses of the presuppositions of many theories and theorists, the new consideration of gender stratification takes it to be as important as stratification by economic criteria. The emerging labor force of women workers and women managers of organizations has derailed older notions of superordination and role segregation between the sexes.

In the study of emotions, gender is a particularly significant differentiation. Apart from conventional ignorance that holds women to be more "emotional" than men, there is the fact that male and female hormonal processes differ, hence this may differentiate degree and type of affect. For example, in the domain of aggression—emotional precursor, anger—higher levels of male testosterone, which have been tied to aggression or dominance-seeking—may determine different rates of anger. But social and cultural shaping and repression have affected the ease with which women express anger. In addition, traditional patterns of social organization, which have focused women's attention on caring roles in the family and community, may also affect the threshold of anger in women, and their styles of coping with it (see Thoits, this volume). The task of gender analysis is to untangle this knot of biological and social components, not only with respect to anger, but all emotions.

Hochschild here analyzes what might be thought of as a gender economy, where men and women act on the basis of their fundamental gender ideologies, which are justifications for the maintenance or change of social relations between the sexes. Focusing on two-job families that also have a young child, Hochschild applies her notion of feeling rules and emotion work to the problems the couples face in the management of the complex fit between work roles and child care, which Hochschild imaginatively refers to as the "second shift."

Gender ideologies among these couples divide into traditional (husband should work, wife mainly stay at home to do child care), egalitarian (both husband and wife should work and share responsibilities equally for child care), and transitional (something in between the first two). When husband and wife have discrepant ideologies, the stage is set for powerful emotions. Hochschild examines the emotional pathways that are used in developing a gender strategy, as she calls it, for change. Wives who desire their husband to be more egalitarian need to muster their indignation so they can distance themselves from their positive feelings for their husband, as they prepare to confront him over the issue of sharing the work of the second shift; or they must deal with the resentment and depression that follow from accommodation to their husband's resistance to change by diminishing their work involvements; or they must shed their embarrassment over the shabby results of their indifferent housekeeping, if that expedient was used to economize on time to allow a full commitment to the job; or they must find ways to cope with or avoid guilt over the resort to cutting back on time spent with the child, when this solution was deemed the necessary one.

Male emotional pathways were particularly marked when they resisted their wife's demand for a more egalitarian arrangement. Often the male gender strategy went to almost ludicrous lengths to reduce the need for wife's contributions to his comfort—any sacrifice to avoid the need to contribute to the work of the second shift.

Thoits employs gender as a fundamental analytic category in her effort to evaluate techniques for emotion management. She finds that in the face of a distressing emotional experience, women and men choose different emotion management strategies. Women tend to seek catharsis experiences and social support, try to see the situation differently, and gain perspective by writing about the distress in diaries, letters, poetry, and the like, while men tend to try thinking through the troubling situation, engaging in hard exercise, or simply accepting their distress. This invites subsequent analysis of techniques of socialization and of social structural differences between men and women that might lead to the differences in emotional management strategies. (Denzin, Clark, and Gordon in this volume also examine emotions through a gender lens.)

Managing Versus Accounting for Emotions. Indisputably the most popular perspective in the sociology of emotions deals with how emotions are managed. This contrasts with the approach that attempts to account for emotions, for example, Collins, who attributes a common emotional mood to those who engage in interactional rituals together, or emotional energy to those located in order-giving positions in the social structure; or Kemper, who hypothesizes that specific emotions follow from gain or loss of either power or status in social interaction. One reason for the popularity of the management approach is its compatibility with a generally anti–positivist stance, derived in particular, here, from symbolic interactionism. In the version propounded by Blumer (1969), that sociological approach demurs on the possibility of relating variables (such as power and status) to emotions. (We shall meet this position again below in the section on prediction versus description.)

The management approach to emotions is based on the foundations developed and elaborated by Hochschild, Thoits, Gordon, and Clark. First, emotions are socially constructed. This means that emotions are not irrevocable, biologically-guided, natural phenomena that simply happen to people. Rather, they are amenable to social direction, enhancement, and suppression. Second, social construction is mainly accomplished via norms or feeling rules that inform individuals about which emotion is suitable in which situation. A considerable part of emotion socialization in childhood is devoted to specific tuition, to opportunities to observe models, and to incidental learning of emotion norms. These norms apply not only to proper and improper emotions, but also provide behaviors, expressions, and labels for emotions. Third, the social constructionist position asserts that emotions can be managed. This means that when a deviant emotion is experienced, the individual who is cognizant of the norms can take measures to reintegrate his or her emotional experience with the normative requirement. We have already seen in Hochschild's position that in various occupations, emotion management is one of the principle requirements, since the job itself consists mainly of emotional self-presentation.

Thoits here explains in some detail how management of emotions can be accomplished. First, she postulates that emotion is understandable as a complex consisting of situational cues, physiological reactions, expressive gestures, and an emotion label. These are interlinked in such a manner that changing one of these elements has a potential domino effect on the others. Thoits further postulates two modes of emotion management:

behavioral and cognitive. That is, those who find they are emotionally deviant and want to accommodate to the relevant emotion norms, may work on the four emotion elements either through behavior change or cognitive change.

Behaviorally, one may change situational cues by leaving the situation, or by rearranging it, for example, by getting someone else to leave. One may change one's physiology by breathing more slowly, or by charging up one's system through a bout of heavy exercise, or by ingesting drugs. One may change expressive gestures directly, by masking them with the gestures of the proper emotion, or by exaggerating them, or by refusing to be expressive at all. (The final category, involving behavior and the emotion label is null.)

Cognitively, according to Thoits, one can change the situation by reinterpreting it, or by reflecting that it will soon end, or by focusing on either positive or negative characteristics of the other actors in the situation. One can apply cognitive leverage to physiology by monitoring and concentrating on one's physiological signs, from pulse rate to palmar perspiration. Finally, one can relabel the emotion in the light of other considerations, for example, by tracking how the situation continues to unfold and finding evidence of different intent in one's interaction partner(s).

Emotion management (of both own and others' emotions) is also the focus of Clark's exploration here into the micropolitics of emotion. Clark wishes to explain how people come to know, defend, or extend their "place," in social relationships. Place is an individual's composite rank vis-à-vis another on the dimensions of power, status, and distance (or intimacy). It stands for what an individual may claim or assume as a "right" in interaction with others who, in turn, have their place and its rights. Place encompasses etiquette, vocabulary, the proxemics of space, even touch. Those with higher place operate more freely in these modes; those with lower place are more constricted.

According to Clark, although social interaction directly establishes one's place, one's place claims are limited by the self-concept, which may dictate more or less place as proper or deserving. But emotions also have a hand, for they operate in a number of ways to determine the place one claims, and the methods by which the claims are made. First, emotion serves a signal function with respect to place, for example, to act in an embarrassing manner directly affects one's place in the interaction.

Second, emotion is a place-marker, both intrapersonally as well as interpersonally. In the former mode, emotion demarcates one's place, as in the example of embarrassment, above; or one's emotions can make one pliant to the sometimes egregious place claims of others, as in cases of victims—an abused spouse, a concentration camp inmate—identifying with the aggressor. In the interpersonal mode, emotions are often the message of a place claim addressed to others, alter-casting them for certain responses, for example, rage to reduce another's place, love to induce them to elevate one's own.

Clark proposes five ways in which emotions can be used as tactical weapons in the micropolitics of claiming or maintaining place. First, expressing negative emotions to another or withholding positive emotions is intended to induce the other's fear, or shame, hence put the other "one down." Second, expressing positive emotions to another, or withholding negative emotions, is intended to induce the other's liking or solidarity sentiments. Third, controlling another's level of emotional arousal, as for example, making the other lose his or her "cool," while remaining calm and collected oneself is intended to "displace" the other. Fourth, eliciting the other's feeling of loyalty and obligation assures that the other will not reduce one's own place. And last, one can patronize the other, by expressing positive emotions that mark one's own superiority and the other's inferiority, as for example, expressing sympathy for a superior, or pointing out the other's problems. According to Clark, these tactics of emotional micropolitics serve to create and maintain hierarchy in social relations.

Affect Control Theory not only seeks to predict emotions but also is premised on management of emotions. Indeed, Heise and Smith-Lovin can generate predictions about when emotion management is likely to occur, namely, when behavior has led to a transient identity that is at odds with the fundamental identity of the actor. They are also able to predict specific management actions in the given situation. These are not conceived as management in the manner of Thoits, since they apply only in the given situation of identity discrepancy, and are not identifiable as general management techniques.

Prediction Versus Description. The beginning of all theory is description. This is necessarily the case, since without an aggregate of coherently presented details, there would be nothing to theorize about. Description promotes the generation of concepts. Linkages between concepts may be observed, even if only tentatively. And theory, as conventionally understood, consists of a set of linked concepts, that is, statements of how concepts are related to each other, for example, unjustified loss of status produces anger. For those who affirm the value of predictive theory, there is no alternative but to start with description.

The debate here is whether description can be set aside at some point and more formal operations can be undertaken, such as creating theoretical propositions and testing hypotheses. Here the paths among various approaches to the sociology of emotions diverge sharply. Although the issue partakes somewhat of the positivist-anti–positivist polarity (e.g., Denzin favors only description), most positivist-oriented investigators recognize the importance of description. Smith-Lovin, whose work with Affect Control Theory (ACT), represents a relatively high level of positivist application, is nonetheless eager for descriptive studies by which to augment the domain that is susceptible to ACT analysis. Similarly, Thoits, whose approach to emotions is quantitative as well as qualitative, here presents the details of a number of descriptive studies that evoke important questions for her. Through relatively simple inquiries about emotional deviance directed to male and female respondents, she is able to address questions about gender that it would be hard to develop without the descriptive data. She can see immediately whether there are gender differences in the amount and type of emotional deviance and in strategies to cope with it. The descriptive percentages then can lead to theoretical surmises as to why the genders differ in these matters. At some point this leads to a test of predictive hypotheses.

Gordon, Hochschild, and Clark also shun the predictive approach in favor of description. To some extent this is due to their sense that insufficient data exist for the formulation of theoretical propositions. But their approaches, which owe something to Symbolic Interactionism, also derive from it the premise that we cannot know in advance how individuals will construct their lines of action, therefore, to seek predictive theory is inherently problematic. If, in addition, one considers cross-cultural and historical variations, as Gordon does, a predictive theory is unlikely.

Per contra, Kemper proposes that at the proper level of abstraction prediction is not only possible, but can lead to a cumulative science of emotions. Following the argument of Willer and Webster (1970), Kemper chooses power and status as universal dimensions of interaction at the level of "theoretical constructs" that can lead to prediction across a broad span of social conditions. Therefore, regardless of the particular setting or culture, Kemper predicts that arbitrary deprivation of status leads to anger. Culture may "play" with this, and attempt to convert it into something else, and indeed may manage to do so, but this is after the fact, namely, after anger has been initiated. (Here Hochschild would say that her "interactive" model is better able to explain the ensuing management of emotion. Indeed, although Hochschild's model embraces the frequently evolving nature of emotional experience, it does not contradict the original proposition concerning the initial instigation of anger in the relational condition of status loss.)

Collins, too, offers a predictive theory in that in his formulation the structural relations between order-givers and order-takers are seen to result in certain emotions. These cumulate or dissipate emotional energy in a manner that leads to a chain of relatively successful or unsuccessful future interactions.

While Hammond's evolutionary theory would seem to offer few opportunities for prediction in the time-bound present, in fact, it generates numerous predictions about current relationships among social structure, emotion, and the physiological substrate of emotion.

Biosocial Versus Social Construction. The final issue separating different approaches in the sociology of emotions to be considered here entails the role of biological and physiological influences. Related also to the positivist-anti–positivist debate, this issue reaches deep into the origins of sociology as a discipline. In *The Division of Labor in Society*, Durkheim (1933), pitted sociological analysis firmly against biological explanations of human conduct. Indeed, to establish sociology as a viable scientific discipline it was vital that biology not preempt the social. In *The Rules of Sociological Method*, Durkheim (1938) erected another barrier against biological intrusion by affirming that "social facts must be explained only by other social facts." Since then, biological initiatives have languished in sociology. Nor have biological approaches fared any better under the banner of sociobiology, a theoretical position that cavalierly preempts sociological explanation by locating the origins of a great deal of social organization in the genes. This argument has been thoroughly rejected by sociologists. (Readers can find the arguments pertinent here in Caplan, 1978.)

In the sociology of emotions, the confrontation of the biological and the social is both more focused and more heated than in most other sociological subfields. Virtually every sociologist of emotions acknowledges a physiological substrate to emotions. The debate turns on how important it is. Gordon denies its significance for the sociology of emotions, affirming rather that the sociologically interesting emotions—he calls these sentiments—are socially constructed derivatives of raw emotional arousal. Therefore, if anger is raw emotion, social mechanisms create sentiments of annoyance, rage, bitterness, and jealousy. According to Gordon, it takes social construction and emotional culture to make these variants possible.

Hochschild prefers an "interactive" approach, in which physiological reactions are a part of the emotion complex, but subject to a significant degree of social management. Indeed, for Hochschild as for Thoits, one strategy for managing emotional deviance is to activate or suppress bodily arousal.

In the controversy over the role of the physiological, sociologists of emotions have paid particular attention to the work of Stanley Schachter and Jerome Singer (1962). These psychologists purportedly found that emotions could be rendered theoretically in a two-factor model: cognition of a situation in conjunction with *undifferentiated* physiological arousal. The supposed fact of undifferentiated arousal allowed some sociologists of emotions to conclude that the physiological substrate was therefore unimportant. Recent experimental findings as well as analyses of the results of work based on the Schachter and Singer paradigm have cast considerable doubt on their view (for review of the arguments see Kemper, 1981; 1987; and Gordon, this volume). Hence, the way may be open to a judicious reexamination of the links between sociological and physiological processes in the formation of emotion.

Kemper has argued most strongly for such a link, based on a body of psychophysiological data that fosters the integration of the two quite distant levels of analysis. He argues that a complete theory of emotion must ultimately deal with the fact that emotion is biologically rooted, and regardless of the degree of social conversion, construction, or management, the interface between the two must be illuminated.

CONCLUSION

It should be apparent from this review of metatheoretical issues in the sociology of emotions that the field is extremely broad, and accessible from virtually any sociological persuasion. (See table 1.1 for a synoptic view of the several metatheoretical issues reviewed here and the location of each of the contributors to this volume with respect to them.) It can be argued that the reproduction of some of the major conflicts and controversies of the sociological macrocosm in the subdisciplinary microcosm of the sociology of emotions is a warrant not of fracture, but of opportunity. The diver-

TABLE 1.1
Location of Contributors on Metatheoretical Issues

	Macro	Quanti-tative	Positi-vist	Politi-cal Econ.	Gender	Manage-ment	Predic-tion	Biolo-gy
Clark					+	+		
Collins	+		+	+			+	+
Denzin	+		+	+				
Gordon	+					+		
Hammond	+		+				+	+
Hochschild				+	+	+		
Kemper			+				+	+
Scheff	+	+						
Smith-Lovin Heise		+	+			+	+	
Thoits		+'			+	+		

sity of approaches all devoted to a discrete phenomenon augurs well for the attainment of knowledge in sufficient breadth and depth to potentiate a remarkable synthesis. Although some staunch defenders of their paradigms may reject any concourse with other paradigms, the future is usually wiser than the past in being able to see precisely those channels of integration between different approaches that too fervent practitioners could not see earlier.

Different eras in scientific and intellectual work also have at their core a different ethos. The present period is one of deconstruction, in which no paradigm is credible as more worthy than another. This breeds isolation and a fortress mentality among different theoretical persuasions. In the mode of Weber's (1958) analysis of the consequences of Calvinist anxiety in *The Protestant Ethic and the Spirit of Capitalism*, we may say that the deconstructive demiurge has fastened a paralyzing anxiety on all approaches. To ward off the concern that one's own paradigm may be worthless, one demeans the others. To maintain confidence in one's own perspective, one resists linkages with others that do not pass ideological muster. Some of the most careful description of these competitions between competing scientific perspectives can be found in the volume on "grid" and "group" by Douglas (1982).

But *Zeitgeists* do change and, perhaps, with the approaching millennium—a symbolic occasion of some moment even in an ultra-rational age—there may be a turn toward synthesis, a classical period of reassessment and integration of diverse knowledge. These periods of intellectual assimilation seem to follow periods of upheaval and heterodoxy, whether in the political or intellectual domain, whether in art or science. In this sense, there can be no permanent revolution. Having achieved their proximate goals, the revolution must subside. Weber (1947) gave us this idea in his notion of the routinization of charisma.

We may look forward to such routinization in the sociology of emotions, but not yet. First the battles may intensify, but we must trust that as new cohorts of students and scholars enter this field, in their understandable efforts to establish their own intellectual identity they will abandon the stale confrontations of their seniors and mentors. From their vantage point they will know much more than we do now, and those now *doing* the sociology of emotions should be inspirited by this.

REFERENCES

Blumer, Herbert. 1969. *Symbolic Interaction*. Englewood Cliffs, N.J.: Prentice-Hall.

Caplan, A. L. 1978. *The Sociobiology Debate: Readings on Ethical and Scientific Issues*. New York: Harper and Row.

Collins, Randall. 1975. *Conflict Sociology*. New York: Academic.

———. 1981. "On the Microfoundations of Macrosociology." *American Journal of Sociology* 86:984–1014.

Douglas, Mary. 1982 (Ed.) *Essays in the Sociology of Perception*. London: Routledge and Kegan Paul.

Durkheim, Émile. 1933. *The Division of Labor in Society*. Translated by George Simpson. New York: Macmillan.

———. 1938. *The Rules of Sociological Method*. Translated by Sarah A. Solovay and John H. Mueller. Chicago: University of Chicago Press.

Hochschild, Arlie Russell. 1975. "The Sociology of Feelings and Emotions." Pp. 280–307 in *Another Voice*, edited by Marcia Millman and Rosabeth Moss Kanter. Garden City, N.Y.: Doubleday.

———. 1979. "Emotion Work, Feeling Rules and Social Structure." *American Journal of Sociology* 85:551–75.

Kemper, Theodore D. 1978a. *A Social Interaction Theory of Emotions*. New York: Wiley.

———. 1978b. "Toward a Sociology of Emotions: Some Problems and Some Solutions." *The American Sociologist* 13:30–41.

———. 1981. "Social Constructionist and Positivist Approaches to the Sociology of Emotions." *American Journal of Sociology* 87:336–62.

———. 1987. "How Many Emotions Are there? Wedding the Social and the Autonomic Components." *American Journal of Sociology* 93:263–89.

Schachter, Stanley, and Jerome Singer. 1962. "Cognitive, Social, and Physiological Determinants of Emotional State." *Psychological Review* 69:379–99.

Scheff, Thomas J. 1979. *Catharsis in Healing, Ritual and Drama*. Berkeley and Los Angeles: University of California Press.

Shott, Susan. 1979. "Emotion and Social Life: A Symbolic Interactionist Analysis." *American Journal of Sociology* 84:1317–34.

Weber, Max. 1958. *The Protestant Ethic and the Spirit of Capitalism*. Translated by Talcott Parsons. New York: Scribner.

———. 1947. *The Theory of Social and Economic Organization*. Translated by A. M. Henderson and T. Parsons. New York: Oxford University Press.

Willer, David, and Murray Webster, Jr. 1970. "Theoretical Concepts and Observables." *American Sociological Review* 35:748–57.

part two

EMOTIONS AND SOCIAL MACRO PROCESSES

2.

Stratification, Emotional Energy, and the Transient Emotions

Randall Collins

Emotion potentially occupies a crucial position in general sociological theory. As we attempt to be more precise and more empirical about sociological concepts, we find that many of the most important rest to a considerable extent upon emotional processes.

Durkheim raised the fundamental question of sociology: What holds society together? His answer is the mechanisms that produce moral solidarity; and these mechanisms, I suggest, do so by producing emotions. Parsonian sociology, which took the most reified, agentless side of Durkheim, put the argument in equivalent terms: Society is held together by values. But values, to the extent that they exist—and leaving open the issue of how far they are shared, and under what conditions—are cognitions infused with emotion. On the conflict side of sociological theory, Weber's central concepts also imply emotion: (a) the legitimacy that underlies stable power, (b) the status group ranking by which stratification permeates everyday life, and (c) the religious world views that motivated some crucial periods of economic action. When we attempt to translate any of these concepts into observables, it is apparent that we are dealing with particular kinds of emotions. Marx and Engels are perhaps farthest away from theorizing about emotional processes; in their models, everything is structural (even alienation, which for Marx is an ontological relationship, not a psychological one). But it is apparent that in Marxian analyses of class mobilization and class conflict, emotion must play a part—whether it is the mutual distrust within fragmented classes that keeps them apart (Marx 1852/1963), or the solidarity that dominant classes have and that oppressed classes acquire only in revolutionary situations. In these respects, Marx and Engels' conflict theory comes close to a dynamic and non-reified version of Durkheim's themes.

These are some reasons why the sociology of emotions should be brought into the central questions of sociology. What holds a society together—the "glue" of solidarity—and what mobilizes conflict—the energy of mobilized groups—are emotions; so is what operates to uphold stratification—hierarchical feelings, whether dominant, subservient, or resentful. If we can explain the conditions that cause people to feel these kinds of emotions, we will have a major part of a core sociological theory. There is of course a structural part of such a theory, and a cognitive part, but the emotional part gives us something essential for a realistic theory on its dynamics.

Let me put the issue in another way. The classic sociological theories mentioned above implicitly concern emotions, but they do not usually refer to them explicitly. This is because our theories have a macro primacy, or at least deal with social life at a level of considerable abstraction and aggregation. We are told of something called "legitimacy," or worse yet, "values," floating somewhere in a conceptual sky beyond the heads of real people in ordinary situations. If we attempt a micro-translation of sociology—not necessarily an absolute micro-reduction, but a grounding of macro-concepts in real interactions across the macro-grid of time, space and numbers—we are led to see the importance of emotional processes. In other words, the micro-translation of macro concepts (like those discussed above) yields us emotion.

Unfortunately, this is not what classic (and even modern) microtheories have stressed. Mead and symbolic interactionism emphasize process, emergence, and cognition; Schutz and phenomenology emphasize routine and cognition; the exchange theory emphasizes behaviors and payoffs; the expectation states theory again stresses cognition. Emotion of course could be brought into these theories, but it is central to none of them. But there are two crucial versions of micro-sociology that do not have to be pressed very far to yield us the central micro-dynamics of emotion as a social process—a process that will serve us for unpacking the macro-sociological issues mentioned at the outset.

The first of these is what I call "Interaction Ritual Theory." The term is Goffman's (1967). But Goffman, like everyone else, speaks of emotion only in passing. He focuses on the structure of micro-interaction, on its constraints and levels, on the interplay between its subjective and objective components. The crucial thing to see is that Goffman is applying Durkheimian theory to micro-situations: he is concerned with how ritual solidarity is generated in the little transient groups of everyday life, at the level of the encounter. These "natural rituals" (as I would call them) are equivalent to the formal rituals Durkheim analyzed—religious ceremonies in aborigine tribes, patriotic rituals in the modern state—which produce sacred objects and moral constraints. Goffman broadened Durkheim in a way that shows how social order is produced on the micro-level: that is to say, all over the map, in transient situations and local groups, which may well be class-stratified or otherwise divided against each other, instead of in the reified Durkheimian way (which Parsons followed) in which it seems to be "Society" as a whole that is being integrated.

Goffmanian analysis of Interaction Ritual, then, is the analysis of a wide-ranging and flexible mechanism, which produces pockets of moral solidarity, but *variously* and *discontinuously* throughout society. It helps us to connect upwards to the macro-structure, especially via stratification. And it connects downward to the micro-details of human experience and action, because rituals are made with emotional ingredients, and they produce other sorts of emotions (especially moral solidarity, but also sometimes aggressive emotions) as outcomes. I will make considerable use of the Durkheimian/Goffmanian model of rituals in my stratification theory of emotions.

We see emotions in another important version of micro-sociology. Garfinkel's ethnomethodology, at first sight, seems to be pitched on a different level. With its concern for the construction of mundane reality, and its heavy use of phenomenological abstractions, it seems to be essentially a cognitive theory. Cicourel (1973) even called his own version "Cognitive Sociology." Nevertheless, I want to suggest that ethnomethodology reveals emotion at its core. Garfinkel's most important contribution is to show that humans have intrinsically limited cognitive capabilities, and that they construct mundane social order by consistently using practices to *avoid* recognizing how arbitrarily social order is actually put together. We keep up conventions, not because we believe in them, but because we studiously avoid questioning them. Garfinkel (1967) demonstrated this most dramatically in his "breaching" experiments, in which he forced people into situations that caused them to recognize indexicality (i.e. that they rely on tacit acceptance of what things mean contextually) and reflexivity (that there are infinite regresses of justifying one's interpretations). Interestingly enough, the reactions of his subjects were always intensely emotional. Usually it was an emotional outburst: (becoming red in the face, blurting out "You *know* what I mean! Do you want to have a conversation or don't you?") Sometimes it was depression, bewilderment, or anger at having been put in a situation where they constructed a reality they later discovered to be false. In short, when people have to recognize that they are tacitly constructing their social worlds, and in an arbitrary and conventional way, rather than simply reacting to a world that is objectively there, they show intense negative emotions.

I suggest that Garfinkel's breaching experiments reveal something very much like Durkheim's world. In this case, conventional social reality is a sacred object; Garfinkel's experiments, violating the sacred object, call forth the same effects as would violating a ritual taboo for a tribal member, desecrating the Bible for a Christian, or defaming the flag for a patriot. In Durkheim's theory, moral sentiments attach to sacred objects. When they are violated, this positive sentiment of moral solidarity turns negative, into righteous anger directed against the culprit. Just so in Garfinkel's experiments: there is outrage against the violator of everyday cognitive conventions. Garfinkel's strategy parallels Durkheim's: to show the conditions that uphold a social fact by revealing the opposition that occurs when it is broken. Durkheim used suicide and crime as means of highlighting the social solidarity that is their opposite; Garfinkel extended the method to reality-construction as a whole.

Ethnomethodology's lack of explicit focus on emotions is misleading. One could well say that everyday life reality-construction is an emotional process, and that the emotions that uphold reality come forth in intense form when the social reality is broken. Furthermore, Garfinkel has shown that human cognition is limited; social order cannot be based on rational, conscious agreement. (Durkheim, 1893/1964, argued the same, but in the context of criticizing utilitarianism.) If cognition does not hold society together, then, what does? Garfinkel tends to leave this on the level of cognitive practices (mostly borrowed from Schutz); but it is a peculiar form of cognition, cognitive practices for how to get by without too much cognition. Ethnomethodology seems to have an mysterious x-factor underlying social order, which the very notion of indexicality prohibits us from probing. But let us take the plunge anyway: leave the cognitive plane, and recognize the x-factor as emotion.

DISRUPTIVE AND LONG-TERM EMOTIONS: OR "DRAMATIC" EMOTIONS AND EMOTIONAL ENERGY

This analysis forces us to widen our conception of emotion. Our ordinary usage refers to emotions as experiences that are, for the most part, sudden and dramatic. "Don't be so emotional" is advice predicated on this conception. The famous emotions are the most dramatic ones: fear, terror, anger, embarassment, joy, and so forth. Some people and some cultures are regarded as too "unemotional" (note for example the currently trendy disparagement of "WASP" culture). But both Goffman and Garfinkel force us to see there are also emotions that are undramatic; they are long-lasting, underlying tones or moods, that permeate social life. Garfinkel's mundane reality, for example, is characterized by the feeling—I stress that this is a feeling rather than an explicit cognition—that "nothing out of the ordinary is happening here." This is an uninteresting emotion, from the point of view of the actor but, if Garfinkel is right, considerable work went into producing that feeling of ordinariness, and into keeping ourselves from see-ing that work itself. Mundane reality is a "members' accomplishment."

In Goffman and Durkheim, the ordinary-life, long lasting feelings are somewhat more apparent. These theories stress solidarity, feelings of mem-bership, and in Goffman's case, feelings about one's self. These are, if ev-erything goes well, smoothly persistent sentiments, though they may have an "up" feeling tone, or a "down," depressed tone in some important cases, as I will demonstrate. Once we think about them, we readily accept these as part of the larger realm of emotion. Solidarity feelings, moral sentiment, the enthusiasm of pitching oneself into a situation, or being carried along by it; and at the other end, depression, alienation, embarrassment—these are recognizably longer lasting kinds of emotions. Garfinkelian mundanity is merely a generic emotional quality at the middle of the plus-minus scale.

My point is not to enter into terminological controversy. It would be useless for us to define emotions in such a way that we can only talk about the dramatic, disruptive emotions; whatever we call them, we must also be able to talk about the long-term emotional tones, even the ones that are so calm and smooth as not to be noticed. In theoretical terms, it is the long lasting ones (which I discuss below as emotional energy) that are of greatest importance. But I will also attempt to show that the dramatic, short-term emotions are explainable against the backdrop of the long-term emotions.

INTERACTION RITUAL (IR) AND EMOTIONAL ENERGY (EE)

The basic model of ritual interaction (IR) that I derive from Durkheim has the following elements:

1. A group of minimum size two assembled face-to-face. The sheer physical presence of human animals in the same place is a precondition for the emotional and cognitive processes that follow.
2. Focus of attention upon the same object or activity, and mutual aware-ness of each other's attention. Collective formalities, such as a church service or political protocol, are important only because they are one easy way to focus common attention. But any circumstances in everyday life that focus attention in this way (Goffman, 1967, cites ordinary con-versations as an example) have the effect of producing a ritual situation. The crucial feature is that individuals become caught up in a group ac-tivity, in which they are mutually aware of what each other is doing. This makes the group itself the focus of attention, as a transindividual reality, influencing members from outside while permeating their con-sciousness from within.

3. Members share a common mood. It is inessential what emotion is present at the outset. The feelings may be anger, friendliness, enthusiasm, fear, sorrow, or many others. This model posits an emotional contagion among the persons present, for they are focussing attention on the same thing and are aware of each other's focus; they become caught up in each other's emotions. As a result, the emotional mood becomes stronger and more dominant; competing feelings are driven out by the main group feeling. On the ultra-micro level, this seems to happen by the process of rhythmic entrainment physiologically (Chapple, 1981; McClelland, 1985). That is to say, activities and emotions have their own micro-rhythm, a pace in which they take place. As the focus of interaction becomes progressively more attuned, the participants anticipate each other's rhythms, and thus become caught up "in the swing of things" (Wohlstein and McPhail, 1979; Warner, 1979; Warner et al., 1983; Gregory, 1983). Participants feel sadder in the course of a successful funeral, more humorous as part of a responsive audience at a comedy show, more convivial during the build-up of a party, more engrossed in a conversation as its rhythms become established.

4. The outcome of a successful build-up of emotional coordination within an interaction ritual is to produce feelings of solidarity. The emotions that are ingredients of the ritual (in no. 3 above) are transient; the outcome however is a long-term emotion, the feelings of attachment to the group that was assembled at that time. Thus, in the funeral ritual the short-term emotion was sadness, but the main "ritual work" of the funeral was producing (or restoring) group solidarity. The emotional ingredients of a party may be friendliness or humor; the long-term result is the feeling of status group membership.

I refer to these long-term outcomes as "emotional energy" (EE) (Collins, 1981). This is a rather undifferentiated term, that includes various components. The most important component, I suggest, is very energy-like. It is a continuum, ranging from a high end of confidence, enthusiasm, good self-feelings; down through a middle range of lesser states, and to a low end of depression, lack of initiative, and negative self-feelings. Emotional energy is like the psychological concept of "drive" (e.g. in Hull's system), but it has a specifically social orientation. High emotional energy is a feeling of confidence and enthusiasm for social interaction. It is the personal side of having a great deal of Durkheimian ritual solidarity with a group. One gets pumped up with emotional strength from participating in the group's interaction. This makes one not only an enthusiastic supporter of the group, but also a leading figure within it. One feels good with the group, and is able to be an energy-leader, a person who stirs up contagious feelings when the group is together.

At the low end of the emotional energy continuum, the opposite is the case. Low emotional energy is a lack of Durkheimian solidarity. One is not attracted to the group; one is drained or depressed by it; one wants to avoid it. One does not have a good self in the group. And one is not attached to the group's purposes and symbols, but alienated from them.

There are more differentiated variants of emotional energy as well, besides this up/down, high/low in solidarity and enthusiasm. We will see below there are two major dimensions of stratification (power and status) that produce specific qualities of emotional energy. But while we are considering the main, generic level of emotional energy, I will mention one more Durkheimian feature. Emotional energy is not just something that pumps up some individuals and depresses others. It also has a controlling quality from the group side. Emotional energy is what Durkheim (1912/ 1954) called "moral sentiment": it includes feelings of what is right and wrong, moral and immoral. Individuals, who are full of emotional energy, feel like good persons; they feel righteous about what they are doing. Persons with low emotional energy feel bad. Though they do not necessarily interpret this feeling as guilt or evil (that would depend on the religious or other cultural cognitions available for labelling their feelings), at a minimum, they lack the feeling of being morally good persons, which comes from enthusiastic participation in group rituals.

These feelings of moral solidarity can generate specific acts of altruism and love; but there is also a negative side. As Durkheim pointed out, group solidarity makes individuals feel a desire to defend and honor the group. This solidarity feeling is typically focussed on symbols, sacred objects (like a tribal totemic emblem, a Bible or Koran or other holy scripture, a flag, or a wedding ring). One shows respect for the group by participating in rituals venerating these symbolic objects; conversely, failure to respect them is a quick test of nonmembership in the group. It appears that individuals who are already members of the ritual group are under especially strong pressure to continue to respect its sacred symbols. If they do not, the loyal group members feel shock and outrage, that is their righteousness turns automatically into righteous anger. In this way, ritual violations lead to persecution of heretics, scapegoats, and other outcasts.

5. Rituals shape cognitions. The main objects or ideas that were the focus of attention during a successful ritual become loaded with emotional overtones. Those ideas or things become symbols; whatever else the ideas may refer to on the mundane level, there is also a deeper,

Durkheimian level on which symbols invoke membership in the group that charged them up with ritual significance.

It is in this way that society gets inside the individual's mind. Our lives consist of a series of interactions, some of which generate more ritual solidarity than others. (This is what I refer to as "interaction ritual chains.") The high-solidarity rituals give individuals a store of cognitions that they carry around with them, and use to think and communicate with. Whenever someone thinks in terms of concepts that were the focus of a successful interaction ritual, they are subjectively reinvoking the feelings of membership in that group. We are, to speak in the idiom of Symbolic Interaction, imagining society in our minds; it would be more accurate, however, to say that we feel the emotions of social solidarity in the various ideas with which we think. This helps explain why persons who derive emotional energy from group interactions continue to have emotional energy even when they are alone. They are pumped up with emotional energy because of a successful interaction; this energy gets attached to ideas, and thinking those ideas allows these individuals to feel a renewed surge of socially-based enthuasism.

I have couched this on the positive side, in terms of persons with high emotional energy. The same would apply on the negative side as well. Persons with low emotional energy lack the charge of ideas with solidarity; and their ideas may even be charged with antipathy to particular groups. (We shall see how this fits situations of group stratification.) This carries over into their subjective lives; they are depressed even when they are alone, and their thoughts move away from the symbols of groups that make them depressed. Thus, emotionally-charged symbols motivate individuals when they are away from ritual encounters.

STRATIFIED INTERACTION RITUALS:
POWER RITUALS AND STATUS RITUALS

The model of interaction rituals gives us the general process of interaction. IR's themselves are variable, insofar as rituals can be successful or unsuccessful: that is, how much focus and emotional contagion actually takes place, and therefore, how strongly the participants become attached to membership symbols. This will depend on a number of conditions: (a) ecological factors, which allow or force groups to come together, and in what size and frequency; (b) motivational factors, which affect how attractive particular kinds of interactions are for particular individuals; and (c) material resources which individuals use to put on the staging of rituals, that is, the material props for focussing attention and for generating certain kinds of emotions to begin with. Variations in these conditions lead us to the stratification of interaction.

Power Rituals. What I am calling the dimension of power is all those factors that bring together individuals who are unequal in their resources such that some give orders and others take orders. This is an interaction ritual, insofar as it involves focusing attention on the same activity, and becoming aware of each other's involvement; it has a shared emotional focus, which builds up as the ritual successful proceeds. (As always, it is also possible that the ritual will not proceed successfully, that it will break down into avoidance or conflict; however, let us deal with that variant separately.) The focus of a power ritual is the process of giving and taking orders. As many organizational studies show (especially the classic studies of informal work groups, many of which are used as an empirical base by Goffman, 1959), the order-takers do not necessarily carry out the bosses' orders; for that matter, the bosses do not always expect them to do so, or even know very clearly what they want done. But the crucial item of attention is showing respect for the order-giving process itself. Order-givers are in charge of a Goffmanian frontstage performance; they take the initiative in it and, if they are successful, they uphold the organizational chain of command. For this reason, the order-giving classes have a Goffmanian "frontstage personality"; they are attached to their frontstage roles. In Durkheimian terms, order-givers get emotional energy from dominating in power-rituals; and their ritual stance makes themselves loyal to the symbols of the organization. Their cognitions are of the "official" sort (see evidence summarized in Collins, 1975: 62–87).

People who are order-takers participate in these rituals in a different way. They are required to take part: whether by the raw coercion of military force (as in the army, a prison camp, or in feudal/aristocratic societies), or by the slightly more long-range coercion of a paycheck, fines and privileges, or chances of promotion wielded by bosses, teachers, and other persons in authority. The situation of taking orders, of being coerced, is in itself alienating. But persons subject to authority usually cannot evade it directly; their resistance usually occurs in non-ritual situations, when they are out of the direct surveillance of an order-giver: for example in Goffmanian backstages where they criticize or ridicule their bosses, or in their normal work routine in which they put in a perfunctory performance. In this sense, the order-taking classes have a "backstage personality."

Order-takers nevertheless are required to be present at order-giving rituals, and are required to give at least "ritualistic" assent at that moment. They and their boss mutually recognize each other's position, and who has the initiative in the ritual enactment. Thus, power rituals are an asymmetrical variant on Durkheimian interaction rituals. There is a focus of attention, on the order-giving process. But the emotions that are invoked are constrained; there is a tone of respect, of going along with what the order-giver is demanding. The more coercive and extreme the power differential, the more emotional contagion there is. The medieval peasant, or the child who is being beaten, are forced to put themselves into a state of compliance, of going along with what the master/parent/authority figure wants. It is a coerced focus of attention; the order-taker has to try hard to anticipate what the order-giver wants. Conversely, the order-giver uses coercion precisely in order to feel this mastery over the subordinate's mind, to "break their will." (Cf. my analysis of torture, in Collins, 1981a.) Less coercive forms of order-giving have correspondingly less powerful ritual effects.

According to this theory, a successful order-giving ritual coerces a strong mutual focus of attention, and produces strongly shared emotion. But it is a heavily mixed emotion. Insofar as there is successful role-taking on both sides (and that is at the core of any successful ritual), the order-giver feels both his/her own sentiment of mastery, and the order-takers' feelings of weakness. On the other side, the order-taker has a mixture both of his/her own negative emotions—weakness/depression, fear—and the mood of the dominator, which is strong emotional energy, dominance, and anger. I propose that this is why persons, who are severely coerced (concentration camp inmates, marine corps recruits, beaten children), tend on one level to identify with the aggressor, and will enact the aggressor's role when possible in the future. They have an emotional complex of fear and anger, although situationally the fear side is dominant when they are taking orders. Conversely, I propose that order-givers, who use extreme coercion, acquire sado-masochistic personalities, because of the role-taking that goes on, thus blending anger/dominant feelings with a sense of the fear and passivity that they invoke in their subordinates.

Power rituals thus produce complex emotions. Order-givers and order-takers share the dominance/anger/fear/passivity complex, but in very different proportions. They also share an orientation toward dominant symbols, but again with a different blend of emotions. Order-givers identify themselves with the sacred objects of their organization; they respect these symbols as ideals, and are foremost in requiring other people to kowtow to them too. This is the conservatism of dominant classes, their self-appointed motivation as upholders of tradition, as restorers of law and order, and righteous uprooters of heretics and deviants.

Order-takers, on the other hand, have an ambivalent attitude toward the dominant symbols. They are alienated from these symbols, and privately speak and think of them cynically, if they can get away with it (see evidence summarized in Gans, 1962: 229–262). Thus, the modern working class is generally alienated from the business ideals of their bosses, and army troops ridicule the rhetoric of their commanders. These symbols become, so to speak, negative sacred objects; when and if rebellion is possible, a suddenly liberated order-taking class wreaks vengeance on the symbols that it formerly had to bow to. (Kids without career chances in the academic system, who are forced order-takers in schools, thus tend to acts of vandalism and other forms of "deviance," directed precisely at the "sacred objects" in whose name they are subordinated: Cohen, 1955.) It is also possible that order-takers hold the dominant symbols in a kind of superstitious respect, that is, if they are so tightly coerced that there is little opportunity for distancing themselves, no backstages into which they can retreat from their masters' surveillance, they are ritually forced to show respect for the sacred symbols at all times. Thus arises the "loyal retainer" mentality, found among long-time servants and peasants (and in a different context, among children who are strongly coerced by their parents, but also strongly controlled, and given no opportunities to rebel). The difference between these two kinds of order-takers' attitudes depends primarily upon ecological structures: whether coercive control is continuous, or allows breaks into backstage privacy.

I have schematically outlined two polar types of participation in power rituals: order-giving and order-taking (formally stated in Collins, 1975: 73–5.) But power-rituals are a continuum. There are several kinds of positions in the middle between the extremes: persons who are order-transmitters, who take orders from some above them and give orders to others below; I suggest that these individuals tend to blend the order-givers and order-takers culture into a narrow and rigid "bureaucratic personality."

There is another kind of midpoint between extremes: the person who neither gives nor takes orders, but who interacts with others in egalitarian exchanges (Collins, 1975: 74). Analytically, this is a point on the power dimension on which there is effectively no power; therefore, the effects of order-giving and order-taking are both neutral. In order to explain what will happen at this neutral level of power, we must turn to the status dimension.

Status Rituals. I am using the term "status" in an sense that is slightly different from ordinary. Status sometimes is used as a general term for hierarchical differences of all kinds. But here I want to restrict it to something close to what Weber meant by *stand*, or the word translated as "status group." The fundamental feature here is belonging or not belonging. This too is a continuum; in everyday life, it appears as popularity vs. unpopularity.[1]

This dimension of membership vs. nonmembership is analytical, in the sense that any individual (and any interaction) can be classified both as to where it stands in terms of status membership, and in terms of power inequality. That means that every individual, and every interaction, is producing both status membership effects, and power effects. The power effects, however, might be zero, if there is no order-giving and order-taking in that situation; on the other hand, even extreme situations of order-giving also have a status dimension, insofar as the group is assembled and some membership feelings are being generated.

In what ways can individuals differ in their status participation? There are several subdimensions here. First consider how the ritual situation itself is structured. How much does the individual participate? Is he/she always there, always taking part in the interaction rituals, always a member of the group? Or is he/she isolated, never or rarely a member? Along that continuum, we can see people who are on the fringes of the group, just barely members, barely participating; others are nearer to the core, while at the center is the sociometric star, the person who is always most intensely involved in the ritual interaction. This person is the Durkheimian participant of the highest degree, and should be subject to the strongest effects of ritual membership that we examined above: emotional energy, moral solidarity, and attachment to group symbols. At the other end, there is the Durkheimian nonmember, who receives no emotional energy, no moral solidarity, and no symbolic attachments.

Every individual may be calibrated somewhere along this dimension, from central participant to outsider. We could measure how often and how centrally they participate in membership rituals, and give them a score on their overall Durkheimian solidarity or their "social density of interaction." My hypothesis is that this correlates with emotional energy and moral sentiments.

There is another subdimension of status group participation. In what kinds of groups does one participate? It may be always the same group; in this case we get local solidarity. According to Durkheimian theory, this should produce strong attachment to reified symbols, literal-mindedness, and a strong barrier between insiders and outsiders. There is high conformity within the group, along with strong distrust of outsiders and alien symbols.

At the other end of this subdimension, there is participation in a loose network consisting of many different kinds of groups and situations. This is a cosmopolitan network structure. The Durkheimian theory predicts the result will be more individualism, more relativistic attitudes towards symbols, and more abstract rather than concrete thinking. Stated in terms of emotions, this implies that persons in cosmopolitan networks have relatively weak feelings of conformity to group symbols, emotional coolness of tone, and general trust in a wide range of interactions. When symbols are violated or ritual procedures go badly, the members of tight, localized groups respond with anger and fear (especially if rituals are backed up by coercion on the power dimension). Can there be ritual violations in loose cosmopolitan groups, where there is less intensity and conformity? Yes, because there can be violations of the appropriately casual and sociable tone of interaction. Goffman (1959, 1967) concentrated most of his analysis upon situations of cosmopolitan interactions, and depicted just such violations and their sanctions. Following Goffman, I would suggest that persons in these situations respond by amusement to minor ritual violations by others, and with embarrassment, contempt, and a desire to exclude perpetrators of more serious violations of the sociable order. The persons who commit these Goffmanian sacrileges feel anxiety and embarrassment.

This, then, is my set of hypotheses about how the various dimensions of interaction ritual affect emotions. By way of summary, let us recapitulate the model, first in terms of the effects on long-term emotions (emotional energy), and then in their effects on short-term, transitory emotions.

EFFECTS ON LONG-TERM EMOTIONS:
EMOTIONAL ENERGY (EE)

The IR chain model, as previously stated, proposes that individuals acquire or lose emotional energy in both power and status interactions. Order-givers gain EE, order-takers lose it; successful enactment of group membership raises EE, experiencing marginality or exclusion lowers it. Further, the amount of EE gained by status group membership is weighted by the ranking of the group one has participated in (as conveyed by the membership connotations of the symbols that were used in that encounter). This is to say, status groups can be additionally ranked by the power of their members in the larger society; there are communities made up of upperclass order-givers, of working-class order-takers, and so forth; here the membership community can also carry an indirect reflection of the power relations, even when they are "off duty." Successfully using high-status symbols in an encounter both generates local solidarity, and a feeling of high rank; whereas successfully generating solidarity in a low-ranking group generates less EE. Interaction rituals are connected in chains over time, with the results of the last interaction (in emotions and symbols) becoming inputs for the next interaction. Thus, EE tends to cumulate (either positively or negatively) over time.

"Emotional energy", however, is rather general metaphor that needs to be unpacked. I believe that there is a general component, an overall level of being "up" or "down." But this is an overflow of more specific emotional energies. Emotional energy is specific to particular kinds of situations; it is a readiness for action, which manifests itself in taking the initiative in particular sorts of social relationships or with particular persons.[2] Thus, there is EE specific to power situations—expecting to dominate, or be dominated; as well as an EE specific to status situations—expecting to be a central member, or a marginal one, or not to be accepted at all. Furthermore, these emotional energies tend to be specific to particular networks and groups, or particular kinds of them: some persons feel full of confidence and initiative in a party of professional acquaintances, but not in a sexual situation; some feel confidence in a business negotiation, but not a political one.

People move through the chain of encounters that make up their daily lives on an up-and-down flow of EE: They are more attracted towards certain situations than others, and sometimes feel disinterest or repulsion. In each situation as it unfolds, their own emotional and cultural resources, meshing or failing to mesh with those of the people they meet, determine to what extent the IR will be successful and unsuccessful. These outcomes, in turn, raise or lower EE. The end result is motivation to repeating those sorts of encounters with particular persons and to avoid them with others.

Emotional energy manifests itself both physically and psychologically, but its underlying basis—the form in which it is "stored," so to speak—is probably not as energy per se. EE has some cognitive component; it is an expectation of being able to dominate particular kinds of situations, or to enact membership in particular groups. The cognitive side of this is that symbols (particularized memories as well as generalized ideas or emblems) have emotional energy attached to them, in the sense that the symbols call forth a high or low degree of initiative in enacting social relationships using those symbols. But this is not a process of conscious calculation, of the actor thinking "I will get a good feeling of power or status if I interact with so-and-so."[3] Instead, certain symbols come to mind, or appear in the external environment, and spark off propensities (positive or negative) for social action. The "expectation" may work on a subconscious level. It is an anticipation of being able to coordinate with someone else's responses, of smoothly taking their role in the ongoing flow of the interaction, and thus anticipating the build-up of emotional force that goes on within a successful IR. The process of "rhythmic entrainment" of the ultra-micro aspects of interaction is the mechanism by which emotional contagion occurs within a successful interaction. Thus, there is a very fine-grained, micro-anticipation that happens within the interaction itself (on a level down to fractions of a second), as well as a more long-term expectation of being able to enter into such micro-coordination with particular kinds of people. "Emotional energy" exists as a complex of these kinds of expectations, a priming for successful ritual interaction in particular settings.

The low end of EE is depression, manifested in withdrawal, both from expressiveness and activity. Depression may be a more complex process than high EE.[4] I hypothesize that experience at the low end of the power dimension brings depression: low energy, and loss of motivation. But this may happen only when order-takers experience a strong degree of uncontrollability; when their lack of control is only moderate, they may typically respond by anger, that is, by a temporary increase in the output of EE, as vigorous reactance against the situation that is controlling them (Frijda, 1986: 290).

Negative experience on the status dimension, however, may have a different effect. I suggest that failure of membership in a group ritual brings a degree of depression commensurate with the social failure. Kemper (1978) however argues that low status may bring anger as well as shame. Scheff (1987a, 1987b) argues that exclusion from membership brings shame, which may produce a spiral with rage (i.e. anger). I would regard shame as a form of low EE, with the specific cognitive component directed towards one's social image (i.e. social membership) in a particular group. Anger occurs when there is an abrupt negative change in expected social membership feelings, that is, it is a short-term emotion due to the disruption of expectations; the long-term effect of membership loss is nevertheless depression. Hence, there is no long-term increase in vigor of the sort that angry reactance brings for moderate levels of put down on the power dimension, that is, when there are a structural opportunities for mobilizing rebellion.[5]

The main long-term emotional energies resulting from stratified interaction, then, are: (a) high levels of enthusiasm, confidence, and initiative, resulting from either power or status situations; (b) low levels of the same (i.e. depression, shame), resulting again from either power or status; (c) anger, which results from moderate levels of negative experience (I believe, largely on the power dimension, although possibly on the status dimension as well), particularly in situations where there are sufficient possibilities of fighting back. There is one other long-term emotional disposition: the amount of trust or distrust of other people. At the trust end of the continuum, this simply manifests itself as high EE, willingness to take initiative towards certain social situations. At the distrust end, it comes out as fear of particular situations. I suggest that distrust/fear is attached to particular structural configurations, namely, distrust of those who are outsiders to the local group; it is the result of the structural subdimension of status group interaction, in which there is tight local closure of group boundaries.

SHORT-TERM OR DRAMATIC EMOTIONS

Most research on emotion has focussed on the short-term, dramatic emotions: the "phasic" rather than the "tonic," the outbursts that disrupt the ongoing flow of activity (Frijda, 1986: 2, 4, 90). My argument is that the short-term emotions are derived from the baseline of emotional energy; that it is against the backdrop of an ongoing flow of emotional energy that particular disruptive expressions are shaped. Surprise, for example, is an abrupt reaction to something that rapidly and severely interrupts the flow of current activity and attention. This is also the general pattern of more important short-term emotions.

The positive emotions become intense largely because of a contagious build-up during an interaction ritual. This is the case with enthusiasm, joy, and humor: all of these build up in social situations as the result of a successful ritual. Psychological analysis tends to take these emotions from the individual viewpoint. For example, joy is explained as the result of the momentary expectation of success in some activity (Frijda, 1986: 79). This is sometimes true; but I am suggesting that joy and enthusiasm are particularly strong when an assembled group is collectively experiencing this expectation or achievement of success (e.g., fans at a game). Further, the group itself by successful emotional contagion can generate its own enthusiasm (which is what a party does).

These kinds of positive emotional outbursts are relatively short and temporary in their effects. They happen against a baseline of previous emotional energy; for a group to establish this kind of rapport, its members need to have previously charged up some symbols with positive attraction, so that these symbols can be used as ingredients in carrying out a successful ritual. A previous cumulation of emotional energy is thus one of the ingredients in making possible the situational build-up of positive emotion. Frequently, the positive emotions (joy, enthusiasm, humor) are generated by a group leader, an individual who takes the focus, who is able to propagate such a mood from their own stores of emotional energy. Thus, this individual serves as a kind of battery for group emotional expressiveness. Persons who occupy this position in IR chains are what we think of as "charismatic." In general, personality traits are just these results of experiencing particular kinds of IR chains. (This is true at the negative end as well, resulting in depressed, angry, and arrogant persons, etc.)

Love and sexual passion (especially the latter) also are situationally generated emotions. They are most intense when there is an emotional contagion within the group (usually a very small group of two persons), focusing on precisely this emotion. Again, the previous experience in IR chains (in this case, especially interactions that constitute a sexual marketplace) determine the baseline of emotional energy, which is available to be aroused in this way.

The negative short-term emotions are even more clearly related to the baseline of emotional energy.

Anger is generated in several ways. Psychologically, anger is often regarded as the capacity to mobilize energy to overcome a barrier to one's ongoing efforts (Frijda, 1986: 19, 77). This means that the amount of anger should be proportional to the amount of underlying effort; that is, the amount of emotional energy one has for that particular project. High emotional energy may also be called "aggressiveness," the strong taking of initiative. This can have the social effect of dominating other people, of lowering their emotional energy, and of making them passive followers. This implies that there is a connection between the generic quality of high emotional energy—especially the EE generated in power situations—and the expression of the specific emotion of anger.

The disruptive form of anger, however, is more complicated. That is because anger in its intense forms is an explosive reaction against frustrations. Truly powerful persons do not become angry in this sense, because they do not need to; they get their way without it. For a powerful person to express anger is thus to some extent an expression of weakness. However, persons who are powerful can afford to become angry; their power-anger is an expression of the expectation that they will get their way against the obstacle. In the case of a social obstacle—the willful opposition of some other person—it is an expression of their confidence that they will be able to mobilize an enforcement coalition to coerce that person into compliance, or to destroy their resistance. Thus, previous stores of EE determine when and how someone will express explosive anger.[6]

The most violent expression of anger occurs when one feels strong in overcoming a strong frustration. If the provocation itself is overwhelmingly strong, the feeling is fear, not anger. A prior build-up of fear, which is eventually mastered by winning a conflict, thus tends to result in an outburst of anger at just the moment of feeling sure of the victory. Violent atrocities in warfare tend to happen in this kind of situation. (For examples and analysis, see Collins, 1989.)

Persons who are weak do not manifest anger in the same way. I suggest it is only when they have enough resources to be able to mount some resistance (or at least some social privacy, a separate social circle in which they can utter symbolic threats) that weak persons, order-takers, have anger. This follows from the principle that the core of anger is the mobilization of energy to overcome an obstacle. It is only when there are enough social bases of support to generate EE that one can react to a frustration (in this case, being dominated) by mobilizing anger. Persons who are too weak (i.e. structurally they lack resources or space in which to mobilize any other socially based EE), do not react to being dominated by anger, but by depression.

In between these two situations there are selective outbursts of anger. This is the targeted anger that individuals feel against particular other persons. I suggest that this occurs because these individuals are structural rivals in the market of social relationships, for example, two women competing for the same man, or two intellectuals competing for the same audience. Here one does not feel angry against someone who is stronger than oneself (rebellious anger), nor against someone weaker (dominance anger); rather, this is a case of someone frustrating one's own projects. The anger here is not really "personal"; there is no role-taking (as in the dominance/subordination forms of anger) although the target is a person, and the underlying structure is a social one; it is only an accident that the obstacle to one's goals happens to be a person.

Another especially Durkheimian form of short-term emotion is *righteous anger*. This is the emotional outburst, shared by a group (perhaps led by particular persons who act as its agents) against persons who violate its sacred symbols. It is group anger against a heretic or scapegoat. Such anger only happens when there is a previously constituted group; one can predict that righteous anger is proportional to the amount of emotional charge of membership feelings around particular symbols. The amount of such charge, in turn, is highest where the group has high social density and a local (rather than cosmopolitan) focus. Where the group networks are diffuse and cosmopolitan, on the other hand, I suggest that the short-term emotion felt at disruption is embarrassment on behalf of the disrupter—that is, resulting in status exclusion, unwillingness to associate with that person, rather than a violent ritual punishment to restore symbolic order.

Righteous anger is not very well understood, despite its great importance in political sentiments as well as dynamics of local communities (scandals, witch-hunts, political hysterias). The theoretical difficulty is understanding just how this kind of anger relates to the power and status dimensions of group structure. In the Durkheimian model, it seems to be the group in general, and all its adherents, who are outraged at the violation of its symbols. But I suspect that anger, and therefore violence as a punishment (burning a witch or heretic at the stake, throwing drug dealers or gamblers or abortionists in jail) is related to the power dimension, since the use of violence is the ultimate sanction of power. To explain righteous anger, we seem to need the power and status dimensions in conjunction. That is, where the status group structure is dense enough and locally closed enough so that there is a strong sense of group membership, attached to reified symbols; this ritual community has a power hierarchy within it, which regularly exercises coercive threats to enforce obedience to orders; under these circumstances, ritual violations (violations of membership symbols on the status dimension) are taken as a threat to the power hierarchy as well.

Righteous anger is a particularly intense emotion because it is expressed with a strong sense of security: individuals feel that they have the community's support, and not merely in a loose sense. Righteous anger is an emotion that is an evocation of the organized network that has been previously established to use violence. Persons who feel righteous anger are evoking their feeling of membership in an enforcement coalition.

As evidence, I would point to the fact that the most violent punishments for ritual deviance (witch-burning, public tortures and executions in medieval patrimonial states; violent atonement for taboo violations in tribal societies) occur where the political agents are both highly coercive in their ordinary operations, and are active in enforcing group cultures (Collins, 1981a; Douglas, 1966, 1973). Heresy trials and violent ritual punishments have disappeared precisely to the degree of the separation of church and state; it is where these spheres (the power hierarchy and the status community) are fused that righteous anger is most prevalent. In some degree, however, the political hierarchy still remains the focus of status rituals, that is, claims to be a community as well as an organization for wielding power. This makes it possible to mobilize deviance-hunting as a form of status intrusion into the political sphere, even in relatively differentiated modern societies. And it is advocates of a return to the fusion of community with polity who are most strongly involved as "moral entrepreneurs" in modern deviance-hunting. (Such advocates seem to come from the localized sectors of modern society, especially the remnants of traditional and rural communities; in addition, the attempt of socialist regimes to recreate this same kind of collective solidarity helps explain their concern for rituals of conformity.)

Fear is another short-term negative emotion. The most intense and briefest forms of fear are those that most sharply disrupt activities; at the extreme, intense fear experience is next to a startle response. Crying is an expression of fear in a more complex sense: it is a social call for help in distress. Adults do not cry very much because their horizon widens out. Instead of relatively short-term and simply physical threats or discomforts, the most important form of fear becomes fear of social consequences; however, fear of being coerced or fear of social exclusion, are more long-term experiences. Furthermore, since the problem is itself the social situation, crying (which is a communication of helplessness) is subordinated by more complex adjustments of EE. One cannot usually so readily call on others for sympathy, if one is being coerced or excluded.[7] Crying, as a form of emotional communication, is upstaged by more direct emotional response in the form of fear and avoidance.

In social relationships, fear is basically a response to someone else's anger. It is an anticipatory emotion, the expectation of being hurt. Thus, it is most directly related to long-term emotional energy deriving from subordination on the power dimension. It occurs in similar circumstances to depression, but it has a more confrontational structure. Where depression is a withdrawal of EE (i.e. withdrawal of attention from particular activities), fear is a kind of social cringing before the consequences of expected actions. It is socially a more complex emotion than either anger or depression. Depression can be regarded as kind of sinking of EE levels because of the bludgeoning effects of negative social situations; fear is a negative anticipation of what will happen, which assumes enough EE to take some initiative, or at least remain alert to situations that carry social dangers. Hence, one can experience fear of status loss (membership exclusion), as well as fear of power coercion. On the power dimension, fear is probably mobilized together with anger, in cases where a person is able to mobilize anger, but has low confidence in being able to win positive results from its expression.   •

TRANSFORMATIONS FROM SHORT-TERM EMOTIONS INTO LONG-TERM EMOTIONAL ENERGY

The results of various short-term emotional experiences tend to flow back into the long-term emotional makeup, which I have called "emotional energy." Emotional energy, though, does not have to depend upon the dramatic emotions; situations of uncontested domination or belonging add to one's store of confidence and sense of attraction towards particular kinds of situations; undramatic feelings of subordination and unpopularity have similar negative effects. The dramatic short-term emotions also spill over, though it is an unexamined question whether their very quality as dramatic makes them more important for long-term emotions, or brackets them as a sort of exception. In the case of positive short-tern emotions (joy, enthusiasm, sexual passion), it seems likely that these experiences should build up the store of EE, although perhaps in a very situation-specific way (i.e. one becomes attached to repeating just those situations with particular partners).

In the case of negative emotions, there is a long-standing clinical tradition that sees traumatic situations as the major determinant of long-term social and psychological functioning. Particular experiences of intense anger, fear, or shame are regarded as controlling one's whole subsequent functioning. This may well be true, to a degree; however, it should be seen against the background of the overall level of emotional energy. A person who generally has favorable, if undramatic, experiences on the power and status dimensions of their everyday interactions, will likely get over an episode of extreme anger, fear, or shame. I suggest it is only when the individual's overall "market position" of interactions is on the negative side that particularly intense dramatic experiences are stored up and carried over as "traumas," especially in highly charged memories of the sort that Freudian therapy is designed to ventilate.

Scheff (1987a) proposes a model with a more social micro-mechanism than the Freudian: There is a shame/rage cycle in which an individual who experiences a shaming situation feels rage against the perpetrator, which can lead to further conflicts; these typically have unsatisfactory outcomes, resulting in further shame and rage. Rage at oneself can also become part of a self-reflective loop, intensifying this process. Scheff presents evidence that the traces of previous emotional arousals, especially anger, can remain at an unconscious, trace level; that there are unconscious shame behaviors that are manifested in the micro-details of interactions. I think, though, that Scheff has chosen a sample of cases in which these shame/rage cycles are well established; however, he has not considered the cases in which the cycle does not occur or terminates quickly. That is to say: Scheff concentrates on social relationships among individuals who are relatively equally matched, who are at the middle levels of dominance and popularity, such that they can continue long cycles of shaming and raging at each other. More extreme differences in power would not allow a conflictual cycle to go on; and if persons are not confined to the same network of status interactions (i.e. their market possibilities are more open) they may cut short a shame cycle by leaving that interaction and finding another where the resource lineups may be different.

QUESTIONS FOR FURTHER RESEARCH

I have formulated the principles of this general model of interaction rituals by considering the dimensions that seem to be involved in Durkheim and Goffman's discussions of ritual interaction. Above, I have suggested how the micro-mechanisms I have posited are congruent with experimental evidence, especially on rhythmic coordination between interactants. The IR model itself needs to be explicitly tested, especially for its effect upon emotional solidarity. This could be done either experimentally or in a natural setting, provided that before-and-after measures (or preferably continuous measures) of emotional intensity were available. The unobtrusive measures described below could be of use.

Testing the IR Model. The most important test is to show that there is a circular relationship between the amount of focus of mutual attention, the amount of coordination of activity (especially micro-coordination on an unconscious level), and the build-up of a common emotion. As indicated, it does not matter which emotion is involved at the outset—happiness, grief, conversational enthusiasm, and so forth—the model predicts that if the conditions of focus and mutual coordination exist, the shared emotional intensity will build up correspondingly. A further part of the model to be tested involves the after effects of a successful ritual (i.e., an interaction that evoked this shared emotion): the participants should come away with enhanced EE, and they should have favorable emotional attachment to symbols generated within that interaction.

The emotional effects of power and status rituals are specific applications of the more general IR theory. The theories of power and status rituals that I have spelled out above are congruent with a good deal of empirical research that was carried out for other purposes, but relatively little has been done explicitly attempting to test these principles. In none of this is emotion treated very explicitly, but only sometimes in passing, while the main focus has been on the cultural and behavioral consequences of stratification. The multidimensional theory that I presented in *Conflict Sociology*, (Collins, 1975) was in part derived to fit the empirical generalizations found in stratification research up to that time, and to make them congruent with the observations upon which Dahrendorf (1959) and Goffman (1959) drew in building their theories. Subsequent research also fits some of my predictions regarding class cultures.

A weakness of the literature on social class is that it has mostly used crude conceptualizations of its independent variables. Unidimensional schemes (as used by Gans, 1962, 1967, in his field research, as well as Bourdieu, 1979/1984, and virtually everyone else) leave one not knowing which factor (power or status rituals) is really operating on the micro-level. Worst of all are scales that combine different measures (education, income, occupational prestige, etc.) as if they were all indicating some underlying dimension called "stratification." This is searching for a myth, and it washes out the actual grid of causal processes that distribute people across several dimensions of the social landscape. Occupational prestige scales are perhaps the least desirable way of measuring stratification, because they are tied to the realm of vague ideologies rather than actual work experiences. (For instance, "professor" ranks quite high, but if the same person is identified as "sociologist," he/she drops about fifteen points (see Treiman, 1977); if they are identified as "assistant professor in a junior college" they drop still further.) Jencks (1985) showed that public ideas about vaguely specified occupations hide most of the variation even in what people actually think is a good job. Therefore, a measure of stratification ought to deal with what people actually do in their work experience, not with what other people think about them.

We have squeezed most of the juice out of the standard census demographic categories as independent variables, but cling to them because they are easy to measure. What is needed is to measure explicitly the power and status dimensions of people's work and other social experience, as it actually happens. Only Bernstein (1971–75) has paid much attention to micromeasures of situational behavior, but only for the dependent variables (speech codes), while relying on crude global measures of the independent variables (social class). The work of Kohn's group (Kohn, 1977; Kohn and Schooler, 1983) is perhaps closest to measuring the operative conditions within work situations. Their measure—closeness of supervision—is an indicator of the order-giving/order-taking dimension, although it only extends from a neutral point down to the order-taking side; it still lacks a measure of degrees of dominance on the order-giving side. Closeness of supervision may also indicate the social density factor, a dimension of status group structure. Kohn's other principal independent variable, complexity of work, appears related to the diversity of communications, i.e., the other structural dimension of status communities, but mixes the social complexity of a job with the complexity of a material task.

In general, I would interpret Gans (1962, 1967, 1971, Bourdieu (1979/1984), and Bernstein (1971–75) as showing the effects of the social network dimension; Rosabeth Kanter's (1977) comparison of secretaries, women managers, blocked-mobility men managers, and upwardly moving men managers is another version of the power dimension.

In the realm of independent variables, I would strongly advocate that network position be brought into the standard sociological toolbox. Burt (1982) has shown that people's network position has an important effect on the way they behave and on their cognitions; there is a good deal of work (Laumann, 1966; Laumann and Pappi, 1976) that describes difference in network positions of members of different social classes. Although this work is mainly interested in macro processes, such as community power structure, as dependent variables, an equally significant payoff should exist for explaining micro-variables, the attitudes and behaviors of individuals—including their emotions. Network position should be a good measure of the status structure, including both the condition of social density of interaction, and the cosmopolitan/local distinction.

Testing Power and Status Effects on Emotions. What is needed is a multivariate design, measuring independently the amount of order-giving and order-taking that happens in one's daily life; the amount of time in the presence of other people versus alone; the amount of diversity of communications/focus of attention. This could be done by interviews, though a better measure would be observational. Possibly a compromise would be to get people to keep a diary of these items over a period of time. Continuous observation is difficult in practical terms, but periodic sampling of different kinds of work situations might be just as good.

The general theory of stratification I have formulated has as dependent variables the cognitions, behaviors, and emotions of individuals. As indicated, there is much more available research bearing, at least inferentially, on the effects of everyday life power and status rituals upon cognitive culture than upon emotions. For specific purposes of developing the IR theory of emotions, it would be necessary to measure explicitly the emotions in these ritual situations. This measurement needs to be done for both long-term emotions (emotional energy), and the short-term, disruptive emotions.

Measuring Emotional Energy. Since methodologies for studying the short-term, dramatic emotions are more widely known, I will concentrate here on the problem of measuring EE. My argument, that EE builds up or declines over a series of interaction rituals, depending upon the ups and downs of one's experiences of power and status, is inferential. There is little direct evidence for it. Mazur and Lamb (1980; see also Kemper, 1990) have shown that power experience has some continuing effects upon hormone levels. Heise (1979, 1987), using pencil and paper studies of hypothetical events, shows that social actions change the affectual loadings of various categories of persons along power and status dimensions (as well as on a general dimension of activation, which may be equivalent to the underlying dimension of my EE). Heise postulates that chains of real-life interactions are motivated by ongoing shifts in these affect levels.

In order to measure shifts of EE in real-life situations, it would be desirable to follow people's experiences across a chain of interactions. A long-term design would be necessary. Possibly this could be constructed in a laboratory situation lasting several days; observation in natural conditions would also be desirable, especially to estimate how long emotional effects of interactions may last. I suspect, however, that the time-decay of emotional energy, if it is not reinvested and reinforced by subsequent interactions, may be less than a few days.

For independent variables, we would measure experiences of order-giving, order-taking, and egalitarian interaction; the social density of interaction (amount of focus, amount of emotional contagion); and the variety (cosmopolitanism/localism) of interaction patterns. For the dependent variable—a measure of EE—it would be best to use unobtrusive measures. Here are some possibilities:

Voice. The amount of confidence, initiative, and dominance (high EE) vs. apathy, withdrawal, depression (low EE) may be measurable by the style rather than content of talk. Recordings of voice samples in particular kinds of interactions may be measured for: (a) loudness of tone; (b) speed of talking; (c) fluidity, hesitation pauses, and (d) false starts. One of the best indicators may be the latency of speech: the amount of time in delay between and end of one speaker's turn, and the start of another. Ability to get the floor, vs. incidence of contested speech turns, may be another indicator. It may also be possible to find measures of EE by a micro-analysis of the sound wave frequencies on subliminal levels. (See Scherer, 1982, 1985, for studies of the emotional dimensions of recorded speech.)

Eyes. Eye contact, dominating or avoiding mutual gaze is another possible measure of EE (see Mazur, et al., 1980; Mazur, 1986). However, this perhaps applies more to the power dimension of EE than to the status dimension.

Facial expression. Ekman and Friesen's (1975/1984, 1978) manual shows the ways that emotions are expressed in the several zones of the face. Ekman's work (1984) also indicates which zones are most easily controlled by deliberate efforts to mask emotions, while other zones tend to express spontaneous emotions. The limitation of this method is that it has focussed primarily on the dramatic, disruptive emotions. But facial measures of EE could perhaps be developed, both for high EE (confidence, enthusiasm) and low EE (apathy, depression).

Bodily Postures and Movements. Ekman (1984; also O'Sullivan et al., 1985) has also considered bodily movements as emotional expression, and indicated the extent to which the body is controllable in masking emotions. Again, we need to consider bodily measures of high and low EE, as well as the dramatic short-term emotions. Since high EE is social confidence and dominance, it should be manifested in movements towards other people, especially movements that take the initiative and that lead to rhythmic coordination. Low EE, conversely, should show movements and postures of withdrawal, and low initiative. Depending upon the amount of compliance vs. rebellion, low EE persons in a social situation should show either a pattern of following other's nonverbal leads; or a freezing of movement; or (in the case of conflict at moderated levels of EE) a rapid or jerky alternation between orienting toward and away from the others.

A combination of several of these measures—voice, face, bodily posture and movement—could be studied simultaneously. The result of such multi-measure studies would likely show us which measures are redundant, and which are most highly correlated with long-term patterns (i.e. with the flow of EE across situations). After a series of such studies, we could concentrate on the most efficient measures of EE.

Other Hypotheses to Test. I have suggested tests of the basic mechanism of interaction ritual itself, and of the hypothesized effects on emotions of order-giving, order-taking, and the social density and diversity of interaction networks. There are many ramifications here that need investigation, including specific topics like the righteous anger produced by ritual violations of symbols generated in communities of high social density; the carryover between dramatic and undramatic short-term emotions into long-term emotional energies; and the reverse, in which long-term emotional energies provide the baseline for short-term emotions. These elementary processes, too, could eventually be integrated with the more complex conditions set forth in Kemper's (1978) theory of emotions.

A PAYOFF FOR MACRO-SOCIOLOGY

Once good measures of EE, and its various subdimensions, are available, a further step is possible: to carry out unobtrusive emotion surveys. The sociologist could sample a population of people across situations, much as we now sample attitudes (usually abstracted from situations). This would give a map—a dynamic map, over time—of the emotional ecology of society. One might analogize it to an emotional weather map. Such a sampling of emotional patterns on the micro-level, when aggregated, tells us about the emotional patterns of the macro-structure. This in turn should give us a measure of the dynamic factors involved in macro processes of economic life, politics, cultural movements—indeed, the whole range of concerns of traditional macro-sociology. An accurate view of the macro-structure, stripped down to its skeleton of micro-situations linked together in time and space, would reveal waves of emotion, attached to cognitions and motivating physical behavior, flowing across social space. We would then be in a position to test theories of how emotional energies operate both to stably reproduce social structure, and to energize the dynamics of conflict and change.

NOTES

1. My usage is similar to Kemper's (1978), except Kemper wishes to stress that groups are almost always unequal in status, whereas I conceive status groups as capable of being completely independent of each other. One group of friends (or coreligionists, or ethnic members) can be more or less oblivious to another clique; I confine "status" to the internal structure of each group, leaving open the question of whether the various groups have any ranking in relation to each other. Kemper also goes on to define "status" as rank given to individuals voluntarily, a willingness

to comply without being forced, so that Kemper's power vs. status is the difference between enforced compliance and voluntary compliance. I agree that there is such a thing as voluntary compliance, but I would regard this as a transformation of status into power, of using status resources—that is, the emotional energy and sacred symbols that come from status rituals—in order to get compliance in practical situation, that is, in the realm of power. Instead, I confine "status" relations to the "horizontal" dimension of being included or excluded, from purely sociable, nonutilitarian activities. The sociologically most important variation in status group structure is its shape as a network, especially its density and the degree of cosmopolitanism or local closure of the network around particular individuals. As we shall see, these differences in "horizontal" structure of groups allow us to make predictions of the emotions that flow from a Durkheimian model of the forms of group solidarity.

2. Frijda (1986: 13, 71) describes emotion as a felt but latent action tendency; a readiness for contact with the environment at the high end, and at the low end disinterest and apathy.

3. Sometimes certain persons may have this kind of self-conscious deliberation; but that is the result of special circumstances, probably much previous experience in moving through hyper-complex "cosmopolitan" networks, together with many ups and downs in the power/acceptance (status) dimensions.

4. I am leaving aside complexities on the physiological level, where several different components of hormonal and neural systems are apparently involved. In physiology generally, specific states of emotional arousal are due more to the balance between various systems rather than to the activation of some system by itself. See also Frijda (1986: 39) on both simple and complex varieties of depression.

5. Kemper's theory has the additional complication that he postulates anger (as well as shame) resulting from situations in which an actor feels he/she is shortchanged in status, vis-à-vis someone else. That is, Kemper deals with the more complicated situation of comparisons between the status one thinks oneself (and someone else) ought to get, and what they actually get. I prefer to begin the explanation from a simpler and, I believe, more fundamental process: the emotions that derive from dominating or being dominated, being a member or a nonmember. The Kemper theory adds not only expectations from past experience, but also a moral judgment as to the propriety of the outcome compared to some valued ideal. The two theories may be congruent, in the following respects. I propose that experiences in power situations, and in status-membership situations, result in increases or decreases in emotional energy. EE itself involves expectations for future situations; but the IR mechanisms, which produce EE in the first place, are, so to speak, first-order mechanisms of emotional production. Emotional energy becomes an ingredient in allowing future situations to occur, and in determining their emotional outcomes. The expectations that are important in Kemper's model may be regarded as situationally-specific arousals of EE. Kemper's theory seems to me to explain a second-order quality of emotions, those that arise from violation or confirmation of

expectations. Both types of mechanisms may be operating in the same situation, for instance, there can be depression from non-acceptance in a status group (my hypothesis of first-order effects), and anger from one's assessment of this non-acceptance as unjust (Kemper's second-order effects).

Kemper adds further complexities, including the attribution as to the agent responsible for the experience (one's self, other persons, impersonal forces). I would suggest that these cognitions themselves are explainable (at least in part), by the Durkheimian theory of social density (including Douglas' 1966, 1973, "grid" and "group" model). Blaming oneself only occurs when there is a relatively differentiated group structure producing categories of individual agency and responsibility; blaming impersonal forces (e.g. magic) or taboo violations, are cultural actions generated by particular kinds of group structures. Thus, an individual's prior experience in living within particular kinds of network structures should affect what agency they perceive as operative in their immediate situations, and will shape specific emotions along the lines Kemper proposes.

6. Notice that dominant individuals may deliberately provoke weaker persons to become angry, for example, the game of trading insults found among youth gangs (at one time called "the dirty dozens"). This is a game to humiliate weak persons, who are goaded into expressing anger, but are unable to back it up by a show of physical dominance. This is playing on the underlying principle that strong persons keep their cool; when they do rise to anger, they express it in such a powerful form as to drastically penalize anyone who is its victim.

7. Thus crying, like anger, tends to occur in a relatively "realistic" manner; it is most often expressed in situations in which it has a chance of accomplishing its end.

References

Bernstein, Basil. 1971–75. *Class, Codes, and Control.* London: Routledge and Kegan Paul.

Bourdieu, Pierre. 1979–1984. *Distinction: A Social Critique of the Judgement of Taste.* Cambridge: Harvard University Press.

Burt, Ronald S. 1982. *Toward a Structural Theory of Action.* New York: Academic Press.

Chapple, Eliot D. 1981. "Movement and sound: the musical language of body rhythms in interaction." *Teacher's College Record* 82:635–648.

Cicourel, Aaron V. 1973. *Cognitive Sociology.* New York: Free Press.

Cohen, Albert K. 1955. *Delinquent Boys: The Culture of the Gang.* New York: Free Press.

Collins, Randall. 1975. *Conflict Sociology: Toward an Explanatory Science,* New York: Academic Press.

———— 1981."On the Micro-foundations of Macro-sociology." *American Journal of Sociology* 86:984–1014.

———— 1981a. "Three Faces of Cruelty: Toward a Comparative Sociology of Violence." In *Sociology Since Midcentury: Essays in Theory Cumulation.* N.Y.: Academic.

———— 1989. "Sociological Theory, Disaster Research, and War." In Gary Kreps (ed.), *Social Structure and Disaster: Conception and Measurement.* University of Delaware Press.

Condon, William S., and W. D. Ogston. 1971. "Speech and body motion synchrony of the speaker-hearer." in D. D. Horton and J. J. Jenkins,(eds.), *Perception of Language.* Columbus, Ohio: Merrill.

Dahrendorf, Ralf. 1959 *Class and Class Conflict in Industrial Society.* Stanford: Stanford University Press.

Douglas, Mary. 1966. *Purity and Danger. An Analysis of Concepts of Pollution and Taboo.* London: Routledge and Kegan Paul.

Douglas, Mary. 1973. *Natural Symbols.* Baltimore: Penguin Books.

Durkheim, Émile. 1893/1964. *The Division of Labor in Society.* New York: Free Press.

———— 1912/1954. *The Elementary Forms of the Religious Life.* New York: Free Press.

Ekman, Paul. 1984. "Expression and the Nature of Emotion." In Klaus R. Scherer and Paul Ekman (eds.), *Approaches to Emotion.* Hillsdale. N.J.: Lawrence Erlbaum.

Ekman, Paul, and Wallace V. Friesen. 1975–1984. *Unmasking the Face. A Guide to Recognizing Emotions from Facial Clues.* Palo Alto: Consulting Psychologists Press.

———— 1978. *The Facial Action Coding System (FACS).* Palo Alto, California: Consulting Psychologists Press.

Frijda, Nico H. 1986. *The Emotions.* Cambridge: Cambridge University Press.

Gans, Herbert J. 1962. *The Urban Villagers.* New York: Free Press.

———— 1967. *The Levittowners.* New York: Random House.

Garfinkel, Harold. 1967. *Studies in Ethnomethodology.* Englewood Cliffs, N.J.: Prentice-Hall.

Goffman, Erving. 1959. *The Presentation of Self in Everyday Life.* New York: Doubleday.

———— 1967. *Interaction Ritual.* New York: Doubleday.

Gregory, Stanford W. Jr. 1983 "A Quantitative Analysis of Temporal Symmetry in Microsocial Relations." *American Sociological Review* 48:129–135.

Heise, David R. 1979. *Understanding Events. Affect and the Construction of Social Action.* New York: Cambridge University Press.

———— "Affect Control Theory: Concepts and Model." *Journal of Mathematical Sociology* 13: 1–33.

Jencks, Christopher. 1985. Unpublished paper.

Kanter, Rosabeth M. 1977. *Men and Women of the Corporation.* New York: Basic Books.

Kemper, Theodore D. 1978. *A Social Interactional Theory of Emotions.* New York: Wiley.

———— 1990. "Testosterone, Social Structure, and Male Sexuality." In *Social Structure and Testosterone: Essays in the Socio-Bio-Social Chain.* New Brunswick, N.J.: Rutgers University Press.

Kempton, Willet. 1980. "The rhythmic basis of interactional micro-synchrony." In Mary R. Key (ed.), *The Relationship of Verbal and Nonverbal Communication.* New York: Mouton.

Kendon, Adam. 1970. "Movement coordination in social interaction." *Acta Psychologica* 32:1–25.

Kohn, Melvin L. 1977. *Class and Conformity.* Chicago: University of Chicago Press.

Kohn, Melvin L., and Carmi L. Schooler. 1983. *Work and Personality.* Norwood, N.J.: Ablex.

Laumann, Edward O. 1966. *Prestige and Association in an Urban Community.* Indianapolis: Bobbs-Merrill.

———— 1973. *The Bonds of Pluralism.* New York: Wiley.

Laumann, Edward O., and Franz U. Pappi. 1976. *Networks of Collective Action. A Perspective on Community Influence Systems.* New York: Academic Press.

Marx, Karl. 1852–1963. *The Eighteenth Brumaire of Louis Bonaparte.* New York: International Publishers.

Mazur, Allan. 1986. "Signaling Status through Conversation." Syracuse University.

Mazur, Alan, E. Rosa, M. Faupel, J. Heller, R. Leen, and B. Thurman. 1980. "Physiological aspects of communication via mutual gaze." *American Journal of Sociology* 86:50–74.

Mazur, Alan, and Theodore A. Lamb. 1980. "Testosterone, status, and mood in human males." *Hormones and Behavior* 14:236–246.

McClelland, Kent. 1985. "On the Social Significance of Interactional Synchrony." Dept. of Sociology, Grinnell College.

O'Sullivan, Maureen, Paul Ekman, Wallace Friesen, and Klaus Scherer. 1985. "What you say and how you say it: the contribution of speech content and voice quality to judgments of others." *Journal of Personality and Social Psychology* 48:54–62.

Scheff, Thomas J. 1987a. "The Shame-Rage Spiral: A Case Study of an Interminable Quarrel." In Helen B. Lewis (ed.), *The Role of Shame in Symptom Formation*. Hillsdale, N.J.: Lawrence Erlbaum Associate.

———— 1987b. "Shame and Conformity: the Deference-Emotion System." In *Micro-Sociology: the Analysis of Discourse*. Hawthorne, N.Y.: Aldine.

Scherer, Klaus R., and Paul Ekman (eds.). 1984. *Approaches to Emotion*. Hillsdale, N.J.: Erlbaum.

Scherer, Klaus R. 1982. "Methods of Research on vocal communication." In Klaus R. Scherer and Paul Ekman (eds.), *Handbook of Methods in Nonverbal Behavior Research*. New York: Cambridge University Press.

———— 1985. "Outline of a Workshop on Vocal Affect Measurement." Annual Meeting, International Society for Research on Emotion.

Treiman, Donald J. 1977. *Occupational Prestige in Comparative Perspective*. New York: Academic Press.

Warner, Rebecca M. 1979. "Periodic rhythms in conversational speech." *Language and Speech* 22:381–96.

Warner, Rebecca M., T. B. Waggener, and R. E. Kronauer. 1983. "Synchronization cycles in ventilation and vocal activity during spontaneous conversational speech." *Journal of Applied Physiology* 54:1324–1334.

Wohlstein, Ronald T., and Clark McPhail. 1979. "Judging the presence and extent of collective behavior from film records." *Social Psychology Quarterly* 42: 76–81.

3.

Affective Maximization: A New Macro-Theory in the Sociology of Emotions

Michael Hammond

The sociology of emotions is a new micro area of inquiry, but it can also stimulate macro-theoretical work. Indeed, the sociology of emotions can produce models as grand as any in the history of social theory. Affective maximization is one such model. It postulates that the patterning of social and idea structures in certain ways will increase the likelihood of positive affective arousal for individuals. Furthermore, since this patterning is sensitive to conditions of social scale, the specific social and idea structures that are most likely to emerge vary in a non-random manner. These changes offer a new view of human social evolution.

The basic argument is that as a species we are constructed to seek positive emotional arousal. This drives us to prefer experiences where such arousal can be had. It also leads us to erect certain social and idea structures, that is, if they provide us with positive arousal. These structures differentiate individuals (or objects, places, occasions, etc.) according to attributes that are hierarchically ranked for their arousal potential. Which attributes are chosen for this kind of hierarchical differentiation depends on such factors as how much information is required to establish, for example, the status of an individual with respect to the attribute. Sex or age are low information attributes, while godliness requires a great deal of information. Social scale and technology also affect the manner in which social differentiation will occur. These hinder or encourage the concretization, or material embodiment, of the kinds of differentiations that are adopted, and they also affect the time frame that is used to organize social commitment to the differentiation scheme. For example, this-worldly and other-worldly temporal differentiation is an important variable in the organization of social schemes for affective maximization. Through postulating a species need for affective arousal, we can address a great many questions about social organization and social evolution.

The logic of the model is somewhat similar to that used in neuro-chemistry. Scientists have discovered that the reason certain opiates "work" is that their chemical structure mimics the structure of naturally occurring chemicals in the brain. These opiates are able to unlock an existing key to arousal in the nervous system. Furthermore, these opiates sometimes increase the amount of such arousal. In the affective maximization case, certain social and idea structures can mimic patterns of affective arousal and can offer greater guarantees of arousal. With such guarantees, individuals find it most attractive to create these structures.

There are three parts to this model: (a) a consideration of the general structural pattern that affective attachments are likely to take; (b) an analysis of how social differentiation might mimic this pattern; and (c) an outline of the consequences of this symmetry for the evolution of social differentiation. The formal steps in this model are numbered consecutively, one through twenty-four, with descriptive sections inserted to expand and highlight the logic.

THE BASIC PATTERN OF HIERARCHICAL DIFFERENTIATION

First, let us engage in a thought experiment and try to imagine, without any reference to a social structure, what would be the most likely pattern to emerge from individuals seeking certain types of affective arousal. The logic would be something like this:

1. Individuals will seek actions marked by non-distressful, positive arousal. From both qualitative studies and research on human brain lateralization, neurochemistry, and other aspects of affective physiology, we know that humans are biologically wired for such arousal, and that it is virtually impossible to suppress (See Davidson, 1984; Tucker, 1981; Schwartz, 1987; Schwartz et al., 1981; Kemper, 1987; Hammond, 1987b, 1988 for a discussion of the physiology of this arousal).

    Emotions on the negative side of this spectrum, such as fear and anger, are often an unavoidable by-product of strong positive arousal. For instance, a threat to a beloved object could lead to such emotions. Or they can serve as arousal intensifers by mixing with positive emotions, such as in the case of the mixture of fear and joy in many religious rituals. However, there is little evidence that such negative emotions are sought after for themselves. Rather, the positive side of the affective spectrum is a general source of motivation.

2. Except perhaps in early infancy, extensive instinctual guidelines for arousal do not exist. Nor are there significant instinctual programs for

most other aspects of human life. In comparison with other species, instinctual impoverishment marks humanity.

3. Given instinctual impoverishment and our extensive cognitive capacities, human beings can manipulate their worlds to increase the likelihood of positive arousal.

4. Given the profound physiological attractiveness of positive arousal, individuals will try to shape their worlds, consciously or unconsciously, to evoke a strong pattern of such arousal. Whether or not this affective project results in a pattern that is as strong as is physiologically possible depends upon the circumstances of an individual. Strength of arousal is denoted by the intensity, frequency, and security of arousal. Security of arousal is defined in terms of the likelihood of stable long-term arousal. The pursuit of such a pattern is called "affective maximization."

5. Affective maximization is a compelling motivational principle and individuals will pursue it even in the face of major negative consequences. Emotional arousal can rarely be mobilized exclusively for affective maximization, and maximization efforts may well fall short of an ideal amount; but efforts to maximize positive arousal are prevalent in all individuals. However, to seek affective maximization does not necessarily mean a quest for "happiness," at least in the sense of a cheerful contentedness. Indeed, a search for happiness may or may not be a good maximization strategy. This is also the case for the pursuit of hedonistic pleasure.

6. In the quest for affective maximization, individuals will seek affective attachment. Attachment is a tie marked by recurring affective arousal attributable to individuals, ideas, objects, or whatever. Attachment increases the likelihood of positive arousal by virtue of the continuity of past, present, and potential future arousal. Given that history, the separation from or loss of such a tie is felt negatively.

It is most elegant and parsimonious to postulate a need for arousal itself, and to demonstrate that other needs, such as a need for attachment, or as we shall see below, a need for status, can be deduced from it. However, it could be that the wiring of the human central nervous system is not so elegant. The alternative theoretical path is to postulate an innate need for attachment, and then to argue that affective arousal is crucial to the motivational dynamics of such attachments. In either case, analysis of the need for attachment comes to focus on affective arousal, and the rest of the affective model follows as set out below.

7. Instinctual guidelines to specify attachments do not exist, hence, many potential ties exist.

8. Since human affective ties are not heavily imprinted, once a bond is established it is not necessarily locked in and unbreakable. Instead, human ties are precarious and must be reinforced if they are to endure.

9. Given the precariousness of all human affective ties—death or change of heart by others are always possible—an efficacious long-term strategy of affective maximization would be to create multiple ties, rather than a single tie whose disintegration would be excessively painful.

10. Human physiological capacity for affective arousal is finite. This means that intense arousal can only be occasional; otherwise physiological debilitation sets in. This limitation also means that only a few affective ties can be maintained at any given time; many potential ties must be ignored (Wellman, 1988, pp. 42–45). Since attachments marked by deep arousal in the past are likely to provide such arousal in the future, unequal bonding is a probable maximization strategy. Although this strategy decreases the total number of bonds, some strong bonds are likely to be forged. This pattern is called "uneven attachment." It creates social boundaries that are marked by the unequal allocation of affective weight among both potential and actual ties. Thus, uneven attachment produces differentiation.

11. In the pursuit of affective maximization, hierarchical differentiations that rank order the desirability of certain affective ties are more efficient than non-hierarchical distinctions. Hierarchies increase the appeal of certain ties and decrease the appeal of others. They are a powerful framework in terms of the utilization of scarce time and information in the process of creating uneven attachment. For example, attachments could initially be selected randomly with no differentiation among potential ties. Lacking an a priori ranking of potential attachments in terms of characteristics believed to increase the chances that the tie would flourish affectively, individuals would be constrained to choose from among potential attachments on a random basis. Although random bonds would certainly produce some positive arousal and might even produce some striking ties, they would not be as likely to produce as much arousal over time as would be fostered by an a priori selection code contained in a scheme of hierarchical differentiation.

FIRST SUMMARY

Altogether, the most efficient affective maximization strategy for individuals is to pursue multiple, uneven attachments framed by hierarchical differentiation of the attributes of candidates for affective ties. Deep affective arousal is possible without these structural elements, but it is also less secure. Each of these elements adds a non-random aspect to arousal. The more of these elements present, the greater the likelihood of long-term, deep arousal. Assuming a preference for affective maximization, individuals should seek to make use of as many of these structural elements as possible.

COGNITIVE AND TIME CONSTRAINTS

Given the utility of hierarchical differentiation as a means of generating affective attachments, two developments of the differentiation scheme are likely to emerge. The first is the use of some low-information criteria for evaluating potential or actual attachments. The second is the embodiment of the differentiation criteria to make attachment boundaries more concrete and tangible. Both of these developments are rooted in the limitations in individual cognitive capacity to process information relevant to the making of bonds, and limitations in time available for forging affective ties.

Information about the attribute of ties is crucial for creating and maintaining unequal attachments. For example, male-female differentiation requires relatively little information since the external physiological differences are easy to identify. In contrast, differentiation based on individual achievements requires a great deal of information. Differentiation with high information is appealing because it can be more subtly shaped around specific characteristics of individuals. However, if all affective ties were necessarily based on high information, physiological limitations in human cognitive capacities for information processing would decrease the number of possible bonds and, thereby, the overall security of arousal. On the other hand, if some ties were based on low-information, the number of ties and the security of arousal would increase. Thus, in their pursuit of affective maximization through multiple ties, individuals will be disposed to mix high-information and low-information ties.

Limitations in capacity for information processing are also linked to a more general limitation in the time available to any individual to devote to affectively laden ties. Since time is a finite resource, whatever would make for a more efficient use of it in the pursuit of arousal would be most appealing. Embodiment is one such element. It aids affective arousal by providing tangible and/or sensible means by which to experience and express an attachment. Embodiments such as physical objects and rituals of spoken words and movements give concrete form to arousal and increase the likelihood of arousal over time by aiding the reexperience of the affective tie. Unembodied ties are more chancy. Arousal remains unstructured and while spontaneous, essentially unpredictable, since there are no exterior objectifications to cue arousal. Overall, because embodied ties reduce time and information demands for attachments, they have a greater probability of

producing arousal. Therefore, virtually all attachments are likely to be embodied to some degree.
This logic produces the next two steps in the model:

12. Given individual limitations in time and information processing capacity, individuals will mix low-information and high-information ties in the pursuit of affective maximization.
13. Given these same limitations, individuals will also seek to embody their ties in order to increase the likelihood of arousal.

SOCIAL DIFFERENTIATION

This existential matrix for differentiation has nothing to do per se with the kinds of social differentiation with which we are familiar, for example, social class, gender, race, and so forth. However, the pursuit of affective maximization creates the linkage. Social differentiation offers something special in this quest. It can mimic the basic existential pattern of hierarchical differentiation described above. It can also offer the possibility of increasing arousal probabilities.

First, social differentiation can increase the efficiency of selecting ties for uneven attachment. More ties, or ties with a greater likelihood of long-term arousal, are possible for the same investment of time and energy. Second, social differentiation can decrease the precariousness inherent in human bonding. Thus, individuals will be predisposed to create structures of social differentiation. Metaphorically, it might be said, these structures "cause" themselves to be created.

Let us return to the neurochemical metaphor proposed at the outset. If opiates affect us because their chemical structure mimics naturally occurring chemicals in the brain, might it be the case that certain social structures mimic the pattern that is most likely to emerge from "naturally" occurring affective pursuit? In addition, since human instinctual poverty and the availability of complex cognitive tools jointly necessitate and enable us to shape our worlds to a degree unparalleled in any other species, would we not create those social structures if they enhanced the likelihood of positive affective arousal?

The logic in such a possibility would be this:

14. Given the precariousness of emotional ties to specific individuals, one maximization strategy would be to mix some specific ties with some that are not linked' to specific persons. These broader attachments, such as to gender groups, occupational specializations, ethnic commu-

nities, or the like offer a great deal of long-term security of arousal even if some, or all, personal ties are broken.

15. Lacking any preexisting schemes for selecting ties for affective maximization, individuals must choose their attachments on the basis of whatever information they can collect about the characteristics of potential attachments. This would lead to the construction of highly idiosyncratic classifications of potential ties. But these individually created classifications would require a major investment of time and energy. On the other hand, were there a preexisting classification system, developed by others out of their own emotional experience, individuals could use it to develop more ties, and ties that would likely be more secure, for the same investment of time and effort. Therefore, in the pursuit of affective maximization, the use of non-idiosyncratic and preexisting classifications of potential ties is highly likely.

16. Given its value as a preexisting classification for uneven attachment, social differentiation is an almost irresistible framework within which to pursue affective maximization. Social differentiation divides a population: in terms of sex, kinship, race, occupation, and so forth. Social differentiation can also divide any other potential candidates for uneven attachment, such as ideas, objects, places, and so forth. The distinction between the sacred and the profane is an archetypal example of the social differentiation of ideas. On the grounds cited, some social differentiation will emerge in every human population.

17. In pursuit of affective maximization, hierarchical differentiation is more efficient than non-hierarchical differentiation. Therefore, most, if not all, social differentiation is likely to be hierarchically structured. That is, socially differentiated attributes are also likely to be ranked in terms of their desirability.

18. Also, as we have seen above, hierarchical differentiations that are embodied are likely to be more effective in guaranteeing long-term arousal than purely abstract categorizations. Embodiments help to make the categories more real by giving them a manifest and tangible expression that can facilitate arousal and attachment.

19. Embodiments marked by social inequality are particularly efficacious in terms of establishing uneven attachment. Social inequality is the unequal distribution of social resources such as prestige, power, and wealth. It can aid the pursuit of affective maximization in several ways: (a) Inequality itself can be an affectively attractive end. It is one type of hierarchical difference, based upon differential concentration of various social resources. These may be sought directly for their arousal potential, for example, in the positive arousal gained by celebrities from the deference and attention provided by their audiences.

(*b*) Inequality can reinforce activities that already have affective appeal. A person might find intrinsic satisfaction in such activities as hunting, writing, or performing. But if the activity resulted in the acquisition of other valued social resources, for example, wealth, power, or recognition, the affective weight of the activity would increase. These social resources may not have determined the original choice to pursue the activity, but they can serve as an appealing bonus.

(*c*) Inequality can aid the selection of affective attachments by decreasing the number of ties a person is likely to consider. It does this by highlighting the desirable, embodied attributes of some potential ties, and distancing many others because they lack these attributes. Without such hierarchical differentiation as expressed in the embodiments of social inequality, individuals might well face an anomie of choice, in which there are no well-defined reasons to commit one's emotional fervor to one potential tie or another.

(*d*) Inequality can serve to enhance attachment by providing a bridge to other affective foci. For example, similarity of status might lead to friendship or mate selection. There is indeed evidence for both homophily and homogamy with respect to such an indicator of inequality as social class. Inequality could also be a pillar for a strong sense of self-esteem, and this could become a base with which to create many other ties.

(*e*) Inequality can be a means to acquire or forge other affective ties. It may provide access to desirable objects or services. Or it could enable pursuit of other arousing actions, such as special sexual opportunities, or other hedonistic quests. In such cases, inequality need not be valued so much for its own sake, but rather as a means to some other affective goal.

Either as a means or an end, there can be a physiological appeal to inequality. This is not because it is an innate need, as some researchers have suggested (e.g., Collins, 1975; Madsen, 1985; McGuire, et al., 1983), but because inequality can increase the likelihood of secure affective arousal. However, even if one postulates that there is an innate need for status, and that affective arousal is a key part of the motivational dynamics of that need, then the logical focus again returns to the problems of generating affective arousal, and the remainder of the formal model continues as presented below.

At least for some part of a population, inequality can serve as one means to affective maximization. Every individual in a population does not have to pursue inequality. Some might settle on other kinds of embodied hierarchical differentiation. But in a population as a whole, inequality is simply too useful a type of such differentiation, and some individuals will try to create such structures in their quest for secure affective arousal.

Inequality is unlikely to be the only vehicle used for arousal, because no single strategy is likely to guarantee the best overall result. As suggested above, a mixed strategy for evoking arousal is generally more effective. For example, some social differentiation, such as an ethic, religious, or nationalist boundary, might be shared by a population and be the basis for common arousal in ritual. This homogeneity would be rooted in a common arousal history and provide a background against which to frame other day-to-day activities.

At the same time, these shared differentiations can be mixed with other hierarchical boundaries that create a degree of heterogeneity within the group. For example, there might be male-female or economic differentiation. An exclusive use of such heterogeneity-creating boundaries could produce so little in common within a population that opportunities for affective investment and maximization could be destroyed. Therefore, a mixture of homogeneity- and heterogeneity-creating boundaries is the most probable pattern to appear in terms of affective maximization. It is sometimes an uncomfortable mix, as individuals are pulled in two different directions, but the benefits of such a strategy are likely to outweigh the costs.

TIME AND SOCIAL DIFFERENTIATION

A last general aspect of social differentiation must be noted. This is the element of time. Time can become a basis for affective weighting and a means of increasing the likelihood of arousal. In terms of the affective maximization model, there are two postulates in regard to time:

20. Given their greater potential for security of arousal, social differentiations with temporal extension, that is, they endure in predictable form, are more appealing than those that emerge, change, or disappear randomly. Temporal extension may take the form of perfect eternality, in which past, present, and future are fixed and unchanging; or the pattern in question may be subject to change over time, to a greater or lesser degree. Temporal extensions are potentially appealing affectively under two conditions: first, if they are organized hierarchically; second, if they are presented as having a strong probability that the processes they involve will continue, that is, that change or non-change be non-random and consistent.

21. In the case of temporal extensions involving change, expected differences between past, present, and future can be hierarchized so that individuals invest in them emotionally. Temporal differentiation is de-

fined as a framework in which the future is expected to be better than the present. For example, the future, whether on earth or elsewhere, can be used as a basis for positive affective arousal. As we shall see below, the probability of using temporal differentiation as a means of affective maximization grows as social scale increases and other means of maximization are eroded.

To recapitulate, the most likely structure of any social differentiation will be a temporally extended, embodied, and hierarchical rendering.

SOCIAL SCALE, DIFFERENTIATION, AND INEQUALITY

Although many frameworks of differentiation are structurally equivalent, they are not operationally equivalent, because their affective appeal is tied to conditions of social scale. Scale affects whether different frameworks for affective maximization can be maintained over time among more than a few individuals. Scale is a measure of likely rates of interaction and information exchange among members of a population. These in turn are indicators of the problems that individuals will face and the means available to them for affective maximization.

It is still useful to define scale approximately as Durkheim (1893) did: size and concentration of population; and complexity of technology, especially for communication and transportation. In this sense, even a small country whose population is concentrated in large cities has greater social scale than a large country whose population is dispersed over myriad small settlements. The scale of the smaller country would be even greater if it used more elaborate technologies than the larger country, because these are a key measure of the likely movement and exchange of information between members of a population, and of the means they are likely to have to create social differentiation.

The sensitivity to scale of affective maximization is tied to individual limits of both time and cognitive capacity to obtain and process information. As noted earlier, both the time that individuals can devote to affective attachments, and the information that they can carry about concerning them, are finite. In general, there is likely to be some interaction among the elements that define scale—average interaction time and information availability—and the type of social differentiation that is adopted.

As scale increases, average interaction time decreases, therefore available information about specific others is likely to decrease as well. This affects the type of social differentiation that is most useful in guiding individual choices for affective maximization. But the relation between scale and differentiation is complex. It depends on how information is used to establish criteria for social differentiation, and on the variable costs of the different criteria that are selected. These connections have different implications at different social scales. First we will discuss information processes, then the costs of selecting differentiation criteria according to their information requirements.

Information is crucial in regard to two aspects of social hierarchies: first, defining and evaluating differences; and second, selecting the types of embodiment that mark these differences. Social differentiation depends on information about differences worth taking into account. It is likely that at least some of these differences will require very little information. Indeed, the differentiation itself constitutes the vehicle by which the information is conveyed. Easily visible or otherwise perceivable differences such as sex, age, race, or language are examples of the kind of differentiation that requires very low amounts of information. In one form or another, differentiations of this kind are likely to emerge in all human populations.

Information is also crucial in regard to the types of embodiment that accompany social differentiation. For example, differentiation is often embodied in the unequal distribution of key social resources such as prestige, wealth, or power. However, these different inequalities vary in the amount of information they require. Prestige ranking requires more information than ranking according to material wealth, which is generally manifest and easy to observe. Power differentiation would seem to fall between wealth and prestige in information demands.

But different types of inequality have different social costs. Although high in information requirements, prestige is least costly to individuals. On the other hand, while economic inequality is least demanding in requiring information, it is potentially most costly to individuals in other ways. Differences in material wealth affect such vital matters as health, reproduction, and mortality much more directly than prestige differences. Power inequality can be expected to lie between the two extremes in terms of cost for at least some part of a population. Thus, if prestige is unequally distributed, but economic and political resources are equally distributed, then the costs of inequality would be minimum.

Given the high negative costs, extensive economic and political inequality almost inevitably arouse opposition from those who are deprived or disadvantaged. At larger social scales, the ability of the opposition to overthrow the dominant economic and power elites depends on their adopting many of the organizational techniques of those they oppose. This is because, at the larger social scales, the elites have more resources at their call with which to produce larger, and organizationally more complex, units of control. To oppose them successfully also requires larger, more complexly organized counterforces. Thus, not only does larger scale make more inequality possible, it also limits the chances for successful opposition in the name of a return to less stringent patterns of inequality.

At larger social scales, opposition often succeeds more in the pattern of the "circulation of elites," or it changes sometimes into other forms, such as temporal differentiation. For example, in the face of massive irremediable inequality, individuals may shift their affective focus to hopes for a better life in the next world. At smaller scales, resistance to efforts at extreme economic or political inequality is more likely to succeed. The elites do not have such powerful organizational resources to protect themselves with, and the opposition does not require a build-up of the same level of organization of counterforces.

We may conclude from this that the most likely pattern of social differentiation to appear first, historically, and to last the longest, would have had low amounts of inequality, especially of the kind with major negative effects, that is, economic and political inequality. At the small social scales of our early history, other forms of low-information differentiation, such as sex and age, and high-information differentiation like prestige would still have been effective in uneven attachment. The argument can be summarized in propositional form.

22. In the pursuit of affective maximization, individuals will seek some hierarchically differentiated social ties that are relatively low in information demands.
23. In pursuit of affective maximization under conditions of varying social scale, individuals construct social differentiations with interaction and information levels consonant with their own available time and cognitive capabilities. The pattern of change in types of differentiation is part of the larger pattern of human social evolution.
24. Changes in social scale create different levels of interaction and information available for affective attachment. As social scale increases, given the finite capacities of individuals, the average amount of interaction time* and detailed information shared by all individuals in a population decreases. This means that it is more probable that political and economic inequality will emerge, since these affective boundaries require on average less information and interaction among members of a population.

In terms of the model, as developed to this point, major economic and political inequality should emerge relatively late historically. There is no instinct to pursue these types of inequality, nor are they "functionally necessary" so that a society may ensure that the "best and the brightest" are somehow slotted into the "most important" social positions. In small, dispersed populations, certain individuals or groups might be affectively aroused by the prospect of extreme social differences and might even attempt to erect such differences. However, as long as other forms of hierarchical differentiation, such as prestige ladders in terms of age, sex, or individual achievement, were available, and offered much the same guarantee for arousal and uneven attachment, it is less likely that efforts at creating extreme inequality would succeed. In small populations with their high personal interaction rates, other forms of differentiation could provide ample opportunity for affective boundary formation.

For example, a sexual division of labor—males hunt and females gather—could provide one social boundary for activities that could be loaded affectively. For males, hunting could provide considerable positive arousal, but it would most likely be considerably damped if the economic products of hunting were distributed inequitably. The affective pull of hunting would be greatest if all hunters shared equally. Similarly, post-hunt rituals, for example, campfire camaraderie, would also be diminished by a pattern of inequitable distribution. Over all, then, economic inequality would erode the potential for positive arousal available in hunting for most male members of the population. *Mutatis mutandis*, the same logic would also apply to female emotional investment in their economic activities. In conditions of stringent inequality of benefit from economic activity, individuals would have to seek other arenas in which to obtain positive arousal. For this reason, economic inequality would be strongly resisted in small societies where such alternatives might be restricted, for example, by technological limitations.

CRITERIA FOR SOCIAL DIFFERENTIATION IN SMALL SCALE SOCIETIES

Based on the requirements of the affective maximization model, we may project some possible criteria for social differentiation that would be likely in small scale societies. First, because they require very low-information, are age and sex. These are manifest, unambiguous qualities by which individuals can recognize each other for purposes of creating boundaries for affective arousal. In one form, and to one degree, or another, these criteria are universal, and claim attention not only in small scale, but also in large societies as well.

Kinship is another highly likely vehicle for affective maximization in small-scale cultures. Ordinarily, the newborn's need for intense care produces a non-random pattern of interaction between the biological mother and infant. A highly efficient strategy for affective maximization would be to continue building upon this relationship, rather than to abandon it and start anew with another tie. The same logic would apply to maintaining affective relations with brothers and sisters. Later in life, these provide a basis upon which to continue to allocate affective ties.

Since sexual activity and positive affective arousal are linked in our species, and since sexual activity and reproduction are also connected, the affective arousal also links with the reproductive result. Therefore, the biological father of the newborn might also be caught up in the same non-random, affectively laden patterns; as might too, by extension, the father's brothers or sisters. By similar extension, if the biological father is not available, mother's brother can serve as a social father, a fictive parent in biological terms, but a very real relative in terms of a positive affective tie.

Because it is so readily available as a basis for differentiating potential affective attachments, kinship is an important aspect of virtually all such cultures. This is not because there is some innate, or genetic, motivation to affiliate with kin, but rather that kinship classifications regularly emerge as a by-product of the pursuit of affective maximization.

Another criterion for affective maximization in the conditions of small social scale is the hierarchical division between the sacred and the profane. When divine sanction is applied to existing social boundaries, it gives them an unusually solid degree of temporal permanence. If existing social arrangements have relatively low negative costs, this temporal permanence is appealing. The invocation of the divine is the most likely vehicle for such permanence, making the social boundaries eternal categories with an other-worldly foundation.

Finally, in small-scale cultures, there could be many status ladders that were well-known to all individuals. Hunting achievements, "gathering" knowledge, healing skills, entertainment capacities, fecundity, negotiating sensitivity, and so forth—all could serve as bases for inducing affective arousal. Indeed, as one anthropologist noted in an admittedly romantic summary, everybody could be famous (Murphy, 1978, p. 240), because the special qualities of many individuals could be easily recognized in a social world small enough for such reciprocal knowledge to exist. With positive arousal potential rooted in age, sex, kinship, religious ceremonies, and multiple status ladders, it is no wonder that these small worlds are not "hard driving" cultures pushing constantly to manufacture new arousal opportunities.

THE CONSEQUENCES OF INCREASING SCALE

When social scale increases, new problems emerge in securing affective maximization. Average interaction time and the amount of reciprocal information among individuals decline. The likelihood increases that individuals will require more extreme forms of hierarchical differentiation to stake out their affective boundaries.

One strategy would be to concentrate affective attention on material objects. These are manifest and tangible, and they require less interaction time and reciprocal information than would investments in non-material interests, for example, in other people. A second strategy would be to turn to economic inequality, either as an affective and in itself, or as a means of acquiring material possessions. Importantly, the appeal of this strategy is not because there is a deep and powerful need for economic inequality wired into the species, or that it is functionally necessary to motivate individuals with special talents to take on special roles. Instead, this appeal of inequality emerges as a by-product of specific historical conditions in which the pursuit of affective maximization requires a new focus and sharpening due to an increase in social scale.

Although some arousal could be attained by sharing the increased material production among everyone, given the technological limitations on production, at least in the early stages of growth in social scale, such a distribution would provide much weaker boundaries than an alternative strategy in which a few receive a lot of the economic benefits. Although most are deprived of much chance of affective investment in material objects by the second strategy, it clearly provides maximization opportunities for the elites who enjoy the unequal concentration of material goods. In larger scale societies, elites also benefit from the organizational dynamics described above that limit the opportunities of opposition groups seeking to avoid such expanded inequality.

After lengthy historical experimentation with extensive inequality systems, other hierarchies were created to try to overcome the limitations of these systems. One was to add a hierarchy of temporal differentiation in which the future was promised to be better for the deprived groups than the present. In the early historical development of societies at larger social scale, future-oriented solutions were scarcely susceptible to realization, due to the limited technologies of material production. Therefore, the major temporal differentiations were other-worldly. A rich future could be differentiated from the impoverished present, but only after death. In the face of massive material inequality, the appeal of such a radical temporal hierarchical differentiation can be, and still remains, enormous. The affective guarantees it offers can be as great as the this-worldly guarantees offered in smaller scale social worlds. Thus, we can see why idea systems marked by this temporal quality would emerge and spread.

THE LOGIC OF INDUSTRIALIZATION

As long as technology was limited, other-worldly appeals could flourish. But with technological enhancement and more surplus production, temporal differentiation could be firmly anchored to this world. A surplus production system that could consistently produce massive amounts of material goods would make it possible for the relentless flow of such goods to serve as a form of hierarchical differentiation for affective purposes. This could decrease somewhat the pressures to use inequality as the primary means of social differentiation. With such a level of production, extensive inequality would not be the only secure means to acquire material possessions. Also, by constantly providing "new and improved" goods, an aspect of temporal differentiation could be added, making it possible for many to look forward to new arousal possibilities that the new goods would provide in the future. This could also decrease the reliance on inequality as the primary means to assure change and variety within the lifetime of an individual.

When the first massive surplus production system erupted in the industrialization of Western Europe, it was soon able to tap tremendous affective potential. After only a few centuries, this solution to the problem of how to generate embodied hierarchical differentiation for affective arousal has swept around the world. Although economic inequality could not be eliminated totally, for it is too affectively appealing a means of hierarchical differentiation in a large scale culture, the relative weight of economic inequality as a form of differentiation could decline within industrialized countries.

Once again, material goods have a deep affective appeal not because we are innately wired to desire ever more of such goods, any more than the attraction of inequality is rooted in an innate need for it. Instead, the affective appeal of the material is its ability to provide a framework of uneven attachment in large scale social settings. The greater the capacity of a system to produce these goods, the wider the affective appeal.

A barrage of material goods and services is not the only alternative means of hierarchical differentiation for affective attachment that industrialized societies can offer. An idea system like science can both fuel the production process and also offer a highly appealing affective framework (Hammond, 1987b). In modern natural science, new theories that improve upon previous work are generated at an almost frenzied pace. This science is the most temporally differentiated idea system in history. Even a few years without new theories is considered too long to mark a truly hot scientific field. Similarly, the social sciences, the arts, and the humanities are marked by a steady stream of new ideas hierarchically differentiated as better than past ideas. A range of subcultures also offers an array of new and special affective experiences, transcendental or otherwise. The ease of divorce and remarriage encourages maximizing arousal by changing marriage partners. All of these alternatives are structurally symmetrical in that they introduce an element of temporal change as a focus for affective weighting. Each may be affectively appealing to some, and thereby decrease somewhat the potential fixation on massive material and political inequality as the most secure means of this-worldly affective maximization.

Finally, to state that there is an affective maximization logic in these many historical changes is not to assert that somehow this guarantees human happiness or fulfillment. There will be many cases in which just the opposite occurs. Indeed, in a population as a whole, affective maximization guarantees a great deal of unhappiness, especially in larger cultures where low-information affective boundaries, such as economic inequality, are so appealing. Also, an obsession with this-worldly temporal differentiation creates an atmosphere of change that is both exhilarating and distressing, especially for those who are left behind in the rush to the new.

Indeed, if individuals were not affective maximizers, then life in many industrial cultures would be almost idyllic by the standards that other species might use to judge the quality of their existence, such as secure food supply. In these cultures, many might be physically secure, but that is not sufficient for affective maximizers. If humans were content with physical security and lower affective arousal levels, large-scale cultures might look very different, but that simply is not the way the species appears to be wired. Either in terms of comparing one's condition to others, the distributive justice problem, or in seeking new areas for affective focusing, the resolution of the affective problem is ultimately impossible with finite physiological tools in large-scale social worlds.

Altogether, industrialization represents the latest in the long series of human social creations that try to deal with the problems of affective maximization in the face of growing social scale. It represents the furthest development in what can be understood as the two master trends of social evolution, increasing material embodiment and increasing temporal differentiation in our hierarchies for affective attachment.

A RESEARCH AGENDA IN AFFECTIVE MAXIMIZATION

Regardless of its macro-historical implications, the affective maximization model would be useful if only as a descriptive framework. Therefore, research could begin with the gathering of qualitative reconstructions by individuals of the patterns in their affective attachments. How do individuals actually distribute their affective ties? Do they use hierarchical classifications in this distribution as postulated above? Do they embody their attachments in different ways? What do they see as their most likely affective arousal situations? By gathering such individual reconstructions, it should be possible to provide a test of the conceptual bases of the model.

Research could also focus on the prediction that different cultures use different hierarchies to evoke similar affective arousal. If this is the case, there should be some similar physiological markers for such arousal. For example, there should be some physiological parallels between other-worldly religious arousal in preindustrial cultures and this-worldly economic arousal in industrial cultures. There is a fair amount of qualitative literature concerning arousal in both of these historical situations, and the descriptions of arousal would be interesting to compare. Or, by drawing upon the research tradition of Ekman and others (Ekman, Friesen, and Ellsworth, 1982), facial expressions in these various activities might be used to analyze affective states. For example, we have many facial expressions in the arts of the preindustrial worlds, and these could be compared with the results we get by the many pictorial techniques we have today, for example, photographs, movies, and television. Thus, researchers might look for indications of arousal in capitalistic economic activities that appear to have the same mixture of elation and fear often present in religious arousal in nonindustrialized cultures. Or ritual combat in modern sports and primitive warfare (where the actual risk of death or serious injury was minimal), could be compared in the search for similar arousal states.

Research might focus on the prediction that within the same culture, different means could be used for the same affective ends. Like market activities, athletic competitions in our culture are generally patterned hierarchically in terms of winners and losers. Arousal states in these activities might be compared to the arousal associated with the generation of hierarchically differentiated ideas among scientists and other intellectuals. The extensive literature on creativity and competition in the arts, the sciences, and sports might be reviewed in terms of this model. Physiological similarities might be found as individuals use different hierarchically structured activities to pursue the same type of affective arousal. If no such similarities were found, then it would indicate that there are major motivational impulses at the root of humanity's attraction to hierarchies other than affective maximization.

Generally, it would be useful to investigate the physiological markers of the relationship between hierarchical differentiation and affective arousal. Some of this kind of work has been done with athletic competition (Biersner, McHugh, and Rahe, 1981; Mazur and Lamb, 1980), and with differentiation in social status (Madsen, 1985; McGuire, Raleigh, and Johnson, 1983). Henry (1986) suggested that religious arousal invites such research into its physiological underpinnings. Other possibilities would in clude examining arousal in concert performers and audiences, for this is a situation in which individuals expressly seek arousal changes. Fortunately, a technological revolution in neurochemistry is greatly facilitating access to human physiological states. Applying these research techniques to the measurement of socially situated affective arousal should hasten the articulation of the physiology and sociology of emotions.

If different affectively based hierarchies draw upon the same physiological resources, and if these resources are finite, then as opportunities for arousal increase in certain areas, they would be likely to decrease in others. For example, we might look for an inverse relationship between religious excitation and social class, assuming that, as individuals rise in class, they have more opportunities for materially embodied hierarchical differentiation in this world. If these economic opportunities actually provide greater guarantees of arousal over time, and if these secular and religious differentiations draw upon the same physiological resources, then upward mobility should result in a reallocation of affective resources, and a decline of interest in the practices of other-worldly arousal. On the other hand, if these two different arousal hierarchies draw upon very different physiological resources, then there is little physiological reason why one should decrease as the other increases.

Another example of such logic would be that since certain drugs mimic some of the physiological consequences of positive arousal, the epidemiology of these drugs should be related to the opportunity structures for certain forms of hierarchical differentiation. Where entry to these structures is denied or restricted, due, for example, to economic or racial barriers, there should be a predisposition to seek alternative means of arousal, for example, in drugs. After all, if we are all "addicted" to frameworks of hierarchical differentiation as a means to increase the likelihood of certain arousal states, then other forms of addiction might be more likely to occur if access to culturally approved forms is restricted.

Similarly, if opportunity structures affect probabilities of long-term arousal, then age should be an important variable. For instance, at age twenty, arousal can be expected to be more similar among individuals, because individuals, who might be lower in economic status, still have other means of hierarchical differentiation, such as physical prowess. However, at midlife, physical strength declines such that strategies that do not rely on prowess offer more long-term opportunity for successful hierarchical differentiation, and arousal patterns might be expected to show more affective variation. For example, there might be a differential decline in sexual arousal, a common indicator of overall arousal interests. Individuals who relied more on physical characteristics as an affective focus might be expected to have a greater decline than individuals with higher economic status, in part because those who successfully focused on economic accumulation are still deriving affective reinforcement out of hierarchical success in another part of their lives. Indeed, one consequence of social inequality is that it limits the maximization possibilities of some individuals and enhances that of others. Over decades of individual lives, there should be observable consequences of such differential opportunity.

Difference in sexual arousal would not be due to the fact that economic or political power is an aphrodisiac, as some have suggested, but rather because it is a form of successful hierarchical differentiation. We are not innately wired for power, but since power takes the general form of this differentiation, it can be very appealing and result in measurable changes in sex hormones associated with arousal, for example, testosterone. (See Mazur and Lamb, 1980; Kemper 1990). In extremely small-scale cultures, where ample alternative means of secured arousal are available, power is likely to be a rare phenomenon in comparison with large-scale cultures where secure means are not as widely available.

The affective maximization model could also be used to reexamine the "magic numbers" literature in the social sciences. Magic numbers refer to the idea that there are certain numerical tipping points beyond which certain social forms become more or less difficult to create or maintain. Both Plato and Aristotle used such numbers in their analysis of the appropriate size of a democratic polis. Magic numbers have also been applied to the study of friendship networks, organizational size, committee effectiveness, and community coherence (Fischer, 1982; Sale, 1980; Johnson, 1982; Luhmann, 1982). These are often intuitively appealing, but their underlying causal basis has not been well specified. Although some have attempted explanations in terms of cognitive limitations in the human capacity to process information, I have shown (Hammond, 1986) that these models provide no motivational base to account for the numbers. The affective maximization model provides such a base to explain why numbers have the effects they do. Growing numbers do not just produce technical problems of coordinating larger groups. These numbers also produce motivational problems among affectively maximizing individuals with finite cognitive and affective capacities.

Finally, the affective maximization model invites a restudy of the research on social patterns marked by both universality and tremendous historical variation. Male-female social differentiation, kin calculation, assortative mating, and incest avoidance are examples. In any species other than Homo sapiens, the universality of such patterns would invite a direct genetic explanation. But the historical variation is so great that it is problematic how to account for it. Classical sociobiologists such as E. O. Wilson, David Barash, and Robert Trivers explain these patterns genetically.

However, the range of variation in the data has called into question one or another aspect of their explanations (Lopreato, 1984, Chapter 9; Thiessen and Gregg, 1980; van den Berghe, 1980; Sahlins, 1977). The affective maximization model may be helpful in disentangling these issues, because of its greater ability to cope with historical variation while still postulating the emergence of certain patterns.

For example, in analyzing the likely patterns of hierarchical differentiation in small-scale cultures, a reinterpretation of the emergence of male-female differentiation was presented earlier in this chapter. Given its potential contribution to affective maximization, it was seen to be highly likely, but not innate in the sense that humans were specifically wired for male-female ranking. It is simply a readily available and low-information boundary in subdividing a population for uneven attachment. The research question then becomes, what historical variation might be expected in such a boundary as social scale changes?

Even in foraging cultures, females might oppose such differentiation and ranking. However, like all opposition groups, they are' also caught up in the logic of affective maximization, and must then offer another means of low-information hierarchical differentiation. This would not be easy to do at a low level of productive technology. With industrialization and the gradual accumulation of alternative means of low information hierarchical differentiation, for example, material accumulation, male-female differentiation should lessen in importance. However, it is not likely to disappear, since male-female differentiation remains a readily available, low-information allocation hierarchy that is simply too useful to some members of a population, especially to those who cannot fully share in the material differentiations available in high-technology cultures. For instance, it should be more prevalent in recent immigrant communities from nonindustrialized lands or in long-standing poor communities, and it should decrease as socioeconomic status increases and other means of hierarchical differentiation become more available.

Similarly, I argued above that kinship calculation was virtually inevitable in small-scale cultures as a means of affective maximization, but that it was not innate. The research question here is what historical variation would be likely from such a perspective? In terms of macro-analysis, it is plausible that groups using kin logic as a basis for affective ties would have a greater likelihood of surviving than groups that did not. In addition, the use of kin for affective ties should decline as other means of differentiation become available. The rule would be: the greater the number of such alternatives, the less important kin calculation is likely to be, especially in an extended form beyond a few very close ties linked to reproduction.

Due to interaction in early life, kinship can often provide affective ties for later life that have a better chance of providing positive emotional arousal than ties without such a personal history. However, there are bound to be many instances when early interaction is more negative than positive, or when early ties simply do not carry over into later life. If few other means of affectively secure differentiation exist in a culture, then the best strategy would be to stick with kinship as a key principle even though certain specific relationships may be problematic. As more opportunities for differentiation become available, then the best strategy is to use kinship more selectively, and to cut ties when they are not affectively rewarding. Thus, kinship is more likely to be important in foraging cultures, or in systems marked by hyper-inequality and socially generated scarcity, because both systems have a limited range of social differentiations to secure arousal.

CONCLUSION

Altogether, the affective maximization model provides a new link between the physiological and sociological. By focusing analysis on the scale sensitive qualities of affective arousal, a new macro-theory can be constructed using arousal as a key part of the micro-motivational dynamics of other needs, such as an attachment need and a status need, or arousal can be seen as a crucial need in itself. This model provides a new perspective on the ancient question of why individuals can become addicted to certain social and idea structures. Also, by linking micro- and macro-analysis, it deals with historical change in these structures and demonstrates that they both have the same long-term master trends of increasing material embodiment and temporal differentiation. Claude Lévi-Strauss once remarked that the reason certain social and idea structures appear is that they are "good to think." Perhaps sociologists of the emotions can show that equally important is that they are "good to feel."

REFERENCES

Biersner, Robert J., William McHugh, and Richard Rahe, 1981. "Biochemical Variability in a Team Sports Situation." *Journal of Human Stress* 7:12–17.

Collins, Randall. 1975. *Conflict Sociology.* New York: Academic Press.

Davidson, R. J. 1984. "Hemispheric asymmetry and emotion." Pp. 39–57 in *Approaches to Emotion*, edited by K. R. Scherer and P. Ekman. Hillsdale, New Jersey: Erlbaum.

Durkheim, Émile. 1893 (1964). *The Division of Labor in Social Life.* New York: Free Press.

Ekman, Paul, Wallace Friesen, and Phoebe Ellsworth. 1982. "What Emotion Categories or Dimensions Can Observers Judge from Facial Behavior?" Pp. 39–

55 in *Emotion in the Human Face*, 2d ed. Edited by Paul Ekman, Cambridge: Cambridge University Press.

Fischer, Claude S. 1982. *To Dwell Among Friends*. Chicago: University of Chicago Press.

Hammond, Michael. 1986. "Finite Human Capacities and the Pattern of Social Stratification." In *The Knowledge Society*, G. Bohme and N. Stehr (eds.). Dordrecht: D. Reidel Publishing.

——— . 1987a. "Evolution and Emotions." *Sociology of Emotions Newsletter*. 2(2): 2–3.

——— . 1987b. "The Role of Desire in the Social Psychology of Science." Presented at the Sociology of Science Yearbook Conference, University of Colorado, Boulder.

——— . 1988. "Affective Maximization and Structural Mimicry: A New Theory of Human Social Evolution." Presented at the annual meeting of the American Sociological Association, Atlanta.

——— . Forthcoming. "Differential Attachment and Human Social Evolution." In *The Sociophysiology of Social Life*. Edited by Patricia Barchas. New York: Oxford University Press.

Henry, James P. 1986. "Religious Experience, Archetypes, and the Neurophysiology of Emotions." *Zygon*. 21:47–74.

Johnson, Gregory. 1982. "Organizational Structure and Scalar Stress." Pp. 389–421. In *Theory and Explanation in Archaeology*. Edited by C. Renfrew. New York: Academic Press.

Kemper, Theodore D. 1987. "How Many Emotions are There? Wedding the Social and the Autonomic Components." *American Sociological Review*. 93:263–289.

——— . 1990. "Social Structure, Testosterone, and Male Sexuality." In *Social Structure and Testosterone: Essays in the Socio-Bio-Social Chain*. New Brunswick, NJ: Rutgers University Press.

Lee, Richard. 1979. *The Kung San*. Cambridge: Cambridge University Press.

Lopreato, Joseph. 1984. *Human Nature and Biocultural Evolution*. Boston: Allen and Unwin.

Luhmann, Niklas. 1982. *The Differentiation of Society*. New York: Columbia University Press.

Madsen, Douglas. 1985. "A Biochemical Property Relating to Power Seeking in Humans." *American Political Science Review*. 64:448–457.

Mazur, Allan, and T. D. Lamb. 1980. "Testosterone, Status, and Mood in Human Males." *Hormones and Behavior.* 14:236–246.

McGuire, Michael, M. Raleigh, and C. Johnson. 1983. "Social Dominance in Adult Male Vervet Monkeys II. Behaviour-Biochemical Relationships.: *Social Science Information.* 21:311–328.

Murphy, Robert. 1978. "Reply to Gerald Berreman's Scale and Social Relations." *Current Anthropology.* 19:239–240.

Sahlins, Marshall. 1972. *Stone Age Economics.* Chicago: Aldine.

———. 1977. *The Use and Abuse of Biology.* London: Tavistock.

Sale, Kirkpatrick. 1980. *Human Scale.* New York: Coward, McCann, and Geoghegan.

Schwartz, Andrew. 1987. "Drives, Affects, Behavior, and Learning." *Journal of the American Psychoanalytic Association.* 35:467–506.

Schwartz, G. E., D. Weinberger, and J. Singer. 1981. "Cardiovascular Differentiation of Happiness, Sadness, Anger, and Fear Following Imagery and Exercise." *Psychosomatic Medicine.* 43:343–364.

Thiessen, D. D. and B. Gregg. 1980. "Human Assortative Mating and Genetic Equilibrium." *Ethology and Sociobiology.* 1:111–140.

Tucker, D. M. 1981. "Lateral Brain Function, Emotion, and Conceptualization." *Psychological Bulletin.* 89:19–46.

van den Berghe, Pierre L. 1980. "Incest and Exogamy." *Ethology and Sociobiology.* 1:151–162.

Wellman, Barry. 1988. "Structural Analysis: From Method and Metaphor to Theory and Substance." Pp. 19–61 in *Social Structures: A Network Approach.* Edited by Barry Wellman and S. Berkowitz, Cambridge: Cambridge University Press.

part three

POLITICAL AND GENDER ECONOMY OF EMOTIONS

4.

On Understanding Emotion: The Interpretive-Cultural Agenda

*Norman K. Denzin**

> *The only thing a social, and cultural phenomenology of the emotions has a right to postulate at the outset is the fact of interaction itself. Basic to interaction are the thoughts and feelings that persons have of themselves while interacting. I interact, I think, and I Feel.*
>
> Paraphrase of William James, 1890/1950, Vol. 1, p. 224

> *[The feelings of the person] are ways of acting, thinking, and feeling that present the noteworthy property of existing outside the individual consciousness*
>
> Durkheim, 1895/1964, p. 2

> *The emotions and experiences of previous generations weigh on the consciousness and the lives of each succeeding generation*
>
> Paraphrase of Karl Marx, 1852/1983, p. 312

INTRODUCTION

My intention is to offer a framework for the cultural, and interpretive study of emotionality. The present statement draws on my earlier phenomenological analysis of emotional understanding (Denzin, 1984), my recent work on the alcoholic self and the recovering alcoholic (Denzin, 1987a, 1987b), and an ongoing study of film and the American alcoholic (Denzin, 1988a, 1988e). I shall first outline the major terms and assumptions that organize this work, then discuss how it is being implemented in empirical studies dealing with film and the American alcoholic, and close with a discussion of directions for future research.

.

A NOTE ON THEORY AND METHOD

It is not my intention to produce a theory of the emotions or to offer a methodology for testing propositions or hypotheses derived from a theory. Rather I offer an interpretive framework for understanding how emotions, as individual and cultural phenomenon, are experienced in everyday life. The following arguments are central to my position:

1. Emotion must be studied as lived experience.
2. The essential features of emotion must be isolated and described.
3. Emotion must be understood as a process that turns on itself, elaborates itself, and has its own trajectory.
4. The phenomenological understanding and interpretation of emotion will not be causal. It will be descriptive, interpretive and processual. Variables, factors and causal agents will not be sought (Denzin, 1984, p. 11).
5. Any interpretation of emotion must be judged by (a) its ability to bring emotional experiences alive, and (b) its ability to produce understanding of the experiences that have been described (Denzin, 1988d).
6. The phenomenological interpretation of emotional experiences must be cultural and historical.

BACKGROUND ASSUMPTIONS

Consider the following discourse. It is taken from Raymond Carver's (1982) short story, "What We Talk About When We Talk About Love." Two couples are sitting at a kitchen table drinking gin and tonics and talking about their past experiences with the men and women they have loved.

> Terri said the man she lived with before she lived with Mel loved her so much he tried to kill her. Then Terri said, 'He beat me up one night. He dragged me around the living room by my ankles. He kept saying, "I love you, I love you, you bitch." He went on dragging me around the living room. My head kept knocking on things . . . What do you do with love like that?' (Carver, 1982, p. 138).

Terri's husband, Mel comments on this man:

> The man threatened to kill me . . . I'd get a call in the middle of the night and have to go to the hospital at two or three in the morning. It'd be dark out there in the parking lot, and I'd break into a sweat before I could even

get to my car. I never knew if he was going to come up out of the shrubbery or from behind a car and start shooting. I mean, the man was crazy (Carver, 1982, pp. 138, 141).

Now consider the following statement written by a sixteen-year-old, black, high school freshman. He is describing how movies affect his emotions.

Many times I have gone to see a love picture. Sometimes I would find myself dreaming that I was the player and not one of the fans . . . I'd dream of making love to some beautiful girl like Greta Garbo, Clara Bow. Sometimes I would think of them so much until I'd go home and dream about them. I remember taking my girl to the movies to see a love play . . . While sitting in the show I had my arms around my girl . . . I could feel her tremble sometimes when certain things occurred . . . I'd do the same thing. When we left the show we were in a daze. We talked about that picture for two or three weeks. *We would make love to each other like the actors in the show did* (Blumer, 1933, p. 113, italics added).

A white, twenty-two-year-old college senior comments on how passionate love films affected her:

Norma Talmadge was my favorite as a screen lover, she possessed such a wistful love appeal. The love-making in the pictures sets up a fantasy-love scene in which I am the heroine. It decidedly makes me want to be kissed and fondled. Going out with boys after a romantic love picture I would let them kiss me (Blumer, 1933, p. 112).

Emotional experiences, such as those described in Carver's short story, and by Blumer's students, connect persons to others (see Clough, 1988, for a critical feminist reading of Blumer's materials, and Sklar, 1975 for criticisms of the politics involved in Blumer's project). These experiences are shaped by the culture-making institutions of a society (e.g. the movies), by the gender stratification system, or the relations between the sexes, and by the political economy (work) of everyday life (Lefebvre, 1971/ 1984). The rather voluminous literature on the sociology of the emotions does not contain any serious and sustained phenomenological, interpretive treatment of these kinds of emotional experiences (Denzin, 1984, p. vii; see for example Kemper 1978; Hochschild, 1983; Scheff, 1983). Students of emotions have not examined how persons experience emotion, how they feel emotions, how they define their emotions (e.g., what is love), or how they share their emotions with others. Nor is there an interpretive framework that would locate emotional experiences, such as those recounted by

Blumer's moviegoers, within their broader structural and cultural contexts in modern and postmodern (pre- and post-World War II) society. As a consequence, the cultural worlds of lived emotional experience have not been studied in depth or detail. This article attempts to fill this void.

THE PHENOMENOLOGICAL PERSPECTIVE: TERMS AND THESES

Feelings are sensations of the lived body. The lived body is the locus of the person's feelings. It provides the point of reference for emotional experiences. It has the four-fold structure: (1) it is the physical body, (2) the body felt from within by the person, (3) the body as it acts and is seen by others, and (4) the body as is expresses the self for the person (Denzin, 1984, p. 111). Emotion refers to self-feelings. Self-feelings are sequences of lived emotionality (Denzin, 1984, p. 3). They have a three-fold structure: (1) a sense of feeling or experiencing an emotion, for example, fear; (2) a sense of the self feeling the feeling; and (3) a revealing of the inner, moral meaning of this feeling for the self (Denzin, 1985, p. 224; Heidegger, 1975/1982, p. 137). A brief discussion of each of these dimensions is required (See Denzin, 1985, p. 227).

First, self-feelings involve the feelings of feelings and the sensations that accompany an emotion. For example, Mel's fear involved breaking out in a sweat and feeling some of the fear in this way. Second, self-feelings refer to the reflective, self-awareness that an emotion is being felt. Blumer's black high school freshman could feel himself trembling as he watched certain scenes on the movie screen. In this second aspect of self-feeling, the person applies the feeling that is felt to him- or herself. Mel would break out in sweat and apply his feeling of fear to who he was as he walked across the parking lot. The students in Blumer's study felt themselves to be lovers as they watched passionate love scenes in the movie theatre. Third, self-feelings, when defined and felt, reveal inner self-meanings to the person. That is, they feel and see themselves as lovers, persons who are afraid, or who are being battered by their husbands, and so on. Self-images arise out of self-feelings. They are experienced with *emotional associates,* that is, with persons who are implicated in the subject's world of emotional experience.

Emotionality refers to the process of being emotional. Being emotional locates the person in the world of social interaction with others. It involves the lived body and the three structures of self-feeling just discussed. When an emotion is experienced it is termed a "lived emotion." There are four forms of lived emotion: (1) sensible feelings of sensations, (2) feelings of the lived body, (3) intentional value-feelings, and (4) moral feelings of the self.

Sensible feelings are sensations felt in the lived body. Pain or hunger are examples. Others cannot directly share in the experiencing of sensible feelings. When Terri's head banged against things in the living room, she felt the sensible feeling of pain. Feelings of the lived body often build on sensible feelings, but they are not located in a particular part of the body. Words like sorrow, fear, sadness, despair, or intense anger describe feelings of the lived body. Terri felt fear toward her husband, and she felt this fear throughout her body, just as Mel was afraid of this man. Intentional value-feelings are feelings about feelings, like Blumer's students watching screen lovers and learning how to be lovers themselves. Intentional value-feelings are feelings about feelings, like wanting to be in love with another person, and attempting to put that love in place. With this form of lived emotion the person literally intends to have a feeling about an experience, or another person. Feelings of the self and the moral person (see below) reference the feelings the person has about him- or herself as a moral being. These feelings may draw on intentional value-feelings, but they are given a particular stamp of uniqueness by each person.

Emotional practices structure lived emotion. Emotional practices are embodied, embedded actions (i.e., drinking, watching a film, working, lovemaking, eating, cooking, playing, exercising). Emotional practices are connected to, and produce, sensible feelings, feelings of the lived body, intentional value-feelings and feelings of the moral person. They produce anticipated and unanticipated alterations in the person's inner and outer streams of emotional experience (Denzin, 1984, pp. 281–282). Blumer's students, for example, went to movies so as to learn how to be lovers. They were learning an emotional practice.

Emotional practices are gender specific, and are molded by the ideological structures of domination and gender stratification of society. Recall Terri's first husband. He loved her so much he tried to kill her. He dragged her around the living room by the ankles. This emotional practice, or set of actions, reflected how he attempted to dominate and control her. Emotional practices are codifed in social and cultural texts that signify and represent the emotional relations between men and women in intimate, friendly, and marital relationships. The twenty-two-year college senior, quoted above, learned how to be kissed and fondled by watching the movie star Norma Talmadge. She let young men kiss her the way she saw Norma Talmadge being kissed on screen. Film, a culture-making institution, (see discussion below), shaped her emotional, love-making practices. When they experience emotionality, persons build understandings of themselves and of others. Paradoxically, the interactional, cultural, public order of everyday life often structures and gives meaning to the inner worlds of deep emotional experience. (Consider, again, Blumer's high school students who went to movies to learn how to be lovers.) It is to this order, the realm of the cultural, that I turn next.

CULTURAL STUDIES AND THE STUDY OF EMOTIONALITY

I want now to offer a cultural-interpretive framework for the analysis of emotionality and intimacy in the postmodern period (see Mills, 1959; Hall, 1987; Grossberg, 1986). In so doing, I hope to move the sociology of emotions more directly into the field of cultural studies (see Mukerji and Schudson, 1986; Swidler, 1986; Williams, 1982). Basic to the framework that I will develop is the position that human emotionality is shaped by the ensemble of social relationships that bind human beings to one another. Emotionality is a relational phenomenon. (Marx, 1945–1846/1983, p. 157; Kemper, 1978). I shall focus my attention on the intimate relationship, and its effects on the emotional life of its participants.

I contend, after Simmel (1984, pp. 65–71) that love, emotionality, and intimacy are basic forms of existence and interaction in human society. I also assume that these forms of experience are objectified in culture and reproduced in cultural-making institutions. Culture, the shared resources and understandings persons draw upon when they act together (Becker, 1986, p. 13), is shaped by culture-making social structures, including those groups and those institutions explicitly oriented to the production of cultural meanings. Film is a culture-making institution. How films produce, create, define, and reify these cultural, emotional forms of experience demands study.

Indeed, a relational, interpretive sociology of emotionality in the postmodern period (since WWII) is inconceivable without an interpretive, interactionist sociology of the cinema (see Morin, 1984, p. 396; Steudler, 1987, p. 45). The present analysis extends Sklar (1975, p. 3), who argued that for the first half of the twentieth century the "movies were the most popular and influential medium of culture in the United States" (see also Room, 1983, p. 1). I suggest that this influence extends from the 1950s into and through the present decade in American life. (See Sklar, 1975, p. 316 who makes the same claim, while recognizing the important impact of television as a cultural-making institution in the last half of the twentieth century.)

The discussion will be organized as follows. First, I will offer a general, interpretive framework for implementing the cultural study of film and emotionality. Then I offer a discussion of the sociology of film and its relevance for the cultural study of emotionality and social relationships in the postmodern period. I am proposing four conceptual moves at the same time. First, the sociology of emotions must connect the emotions to the study of social relationships (see Hardesty, 1987, p. 248). Second, it must begin by focusing on specific, gendered relational forms, for example, marriage, family, and intimate relations. Third, the sociology of emotions must enter the field of cultural studies. Fourth, film is an excellent research site for the merger of these three concerns.

CULTURAL STUDIES, FILM, AND EMOTIONALITY

Five general theses organize my discussion. They deal with film and the cultural reading of emotionality and intimacy. The first thesis states that emotionality is shaped by culture-making institutions. More specifically, each of the forms of emotional experience discussed above—sensible feelings, feelings of the lived body, intentional value-feelings, and moral feelings of self—are influenced by cultural representations, especially filmic, of emotional experience.

In this respect, films have a double significance for the student of emotions. First, as Blumer (1933, p. 198) noted, the goal of a film is to "fascinate the observer and draw him [or her] into the drama . . . [T]he forte of motion pictures is their emotional effect." A film's meanings are emotional and rooted in the viewer's biography, that is, what he or she brings to the experiences depicted in the film. A film works to the degree that it creates an emotional relationship with the viewer. Second, the story that is told in a film is itself emotional, and involves larger-than-life, symbolic and imaginary representations of "real" life, emotional experiences (see Metz, 1982).

The second thesis argues that the emotional practices that are represented in film are gender specific, and are molded by the ideological structures of domination and gender stratification that exist in the social structure. These practices are codified in social and cultural texts that represent the emotional relations between men and women in intimate, friendly, and marital relationships.

The third thesis argues that it is necessary to study how culture-making institutions, including the news, the mass media, but especially film and television, ideologically represent love, desire, sexuality, intimacy, marriage, emotionality, and emotional bonding. A brief discussion of the terms intimacy, desire and sexuality is necessary.

INTIMACY

Intimacy refers exclusively to what each of two participants in a dyad give or show only to the other person and to no one else (Simmel, 1950, pp. 126–127). What is given includes secrets, self-revelations, personal gratitude, intense emotional understanding, subordination, abandon, love, and perhaps sexuality. Intimacy is a gendered production, involving the exchange of sexual self-identities, often drawn from the body of understandings that operate in the culture at large. The intimate relation is an interactional structure between two persons that displays the above features. It may be legally regulated, as in marriage; although all marriages are not intimate relationships (Simmel, 1950, p. 324).

Indeed, Hollywood has given a worldwide moviegoing public a number of classic male-female intimate film relationships: Laughton-Lancaster, Bogart-Bacall, Bogart-Bergman, Gable-Vivien Leigh, Gable-Monroe, Tracey-Hepburn, Hepburn-Wayne, Taylor-Burton, Hoffman-Streep, Redfield-Streep, Molly Ringwald-Anthony Michael Hall, and Madonna-Sean Penn, among others. The list is long and constantly being added to. The point is that Hollywood pairs male-female stars in intimate, but not always marriage relations, and these depictions become cultural representations of gendered intimacy in our society.

DESIRE AND SEXUALITY

Following Lacan (1977), Sartre (1943/1956), and Foucault, 1986, I contend that desire is that mode of consciousness, or self-awareness that seeks to realize and lose itself in its own self-centeredness. Desire is self-desire. It is insatiable. It is its own object. Yet it requires another for its realization, and in the process often commodifies the other, turning the he or she into an object of desire and pleasure. Desire can take many forms, including aesthetic, sexual, interactional, intimate, political, economic, and alcoholic. Desire stands at the center of any intimate relationship, for what is desired is self-realized through the intimacy offered by the other. Sexual desire, erotically and pornographically defined and represented, connects self and other in real and imagined embodied interactional states. Pleasure is sought in the body of the other, and this may take sadomasochistic, illicit, or voyeuristic forms.

Consider again the following statement given by one of the moviewatchers in Blumer's study. It draws together the above discussion of intimacy, love, desire, and sexuality

> Many times I have gone to see a love picture. Sometimes I would find myself dreaming that I was the player and not one of the fans . . . I'd dream of making love to some beautiful woman like Greta Garbo (Blumer, 1933, p. 113).

This viewer identified with the symbolic (Greta Garbo is a symbol of an ideal female lover) and imaginary (she is not the person she plays on the screen), stories told on the screen. He entered the film and became an on-screen lover. His emotions and self-understandings were shaped by his interactions with, and interpretations of these cultural representations of love, desire and sexuality. He dreamed of making love to this person. His emotional and sexual desire were awakened and shaped by this experience. His moviegoing experiences have shaped his intentional value-feelings concerning love, desire, and his relationship to women.

Returning now from this excursus on intimacy, desire, and sexuality, my fourth thesis about film and the cultural reading of emotionality is that the contemporary study of emotionality must be historical and culturally grounded in the postmodern, postwar period of American life (see Mills, 1959). This thesis implies two interrelated notions. First, attention must be given to the structures of late capitalism including commodification, bureaucratization, the production of mass-mediated realities, the decline in power of the metanarrative myths of truth, science, freedom, and democracy (Lyotard, 1984), and the rise of the simulacrum (Baudrillard, 1983a, p. 1), or the hyperreal (media) representations of real life experiences (see Mills, 1959, and Grossberg, 1986, p. 75).

Commodification means that everyday life in the postmodern world (Lefebvre, 1971/1984) is shaped by tendencies to turn persons and experiences into objects that can be purchased and consumed. Moviegoers pay money to be entertained, to have their fantasies fed, and to learn how to be lovers. The mass media mediate lived cultural experiences. They objectify and makes commodities out of the very experiences they represent to the viewing public. In so doing, the media create "needs" and desires that might not otherwise exist. As such, these institutions shape intentional value-feelings as well as moral feelings of self. Listen to Blumer's students:

Male, 17, white, high school senior. —One great desire that has risen from the movies has been the desire to own a car and to be able to go anywhere, anytime that I wanted. The movies have made me dislike restraint of any kind. They have also made me dislike work (Blumer, 1933, p. 159).

Female, 17, white, high school senior. —Fashionable pictures made me long for fine clothes. I could not see why my parents were not able to buy me all the clothes that I wanted (Blumer, 1933, p. 159).

Female, 15, Negro, high school freshman. —The movies often made me dissatisfied with my neighborhood, because when I see a movie, the beautiful castle, palace, stone and beautiful house, I wish my home was something like these (Blumer, 1933, p. 158).

Female, 16, white, high school junior. —One thing I must admit. When I go to a love or romance movie, I wish some sheiky looking fellow would fall in love with me (Blumer, 1933, p. 155).

On the basis of their moviegoing experiences, these individuals were led to challenge the schemes of life interpretation they inherited from their parents. They express dissatisfaction with their homes, their neighborhoods, the clothes they wear, the restraints in their lives, and even the need or desire to work. Their film experiences undermined certain American myths concerning tradition, parental knowledge, what is valued, and what is not valued. Their emotional definitions of self were shaped by the movies and the simulated reproductions of family life these films present. The films have created, or shaped subjects who do not fit into the lives they presently live.

A second implication embedded in the fourth thesis is that the affective formations and sites of emotional experience in the postmodern period (home, work, leisure, sexuality, sport, medicine, prisons, film, music, literature, televisions, schools, church, the court system), must be examined (See Foucault, 1980). Particularly, I argue that the researcher must study how film and movies represent these emotional sites; that is, the places of work, home, sexuality, leisure, and so on. Once these representational frameworks are identified, the emotional experiences that occur within them must be investigated.

These affective, or emotional sites are structured as "ideological state apparati" (Althusser, 1971, p. 165); that is, as places where concrete and imaginary individuals are constituted as subjects who have emotions, beliefs, and social relationships with others. In these sites, ideology—those beliefs about the way the world is and ought to be—operates. This ideology is multifaceted. It includes beliefs about gender, love, intimacy, sexuality, the value of work, family, religion, education, money, freedom, and other cultural ideals. This ideology represents "not the system of real relations which govern the existence of individuals, but the imaginary relation of those individuals to the real relations in which they live" (Althusser, 1971, p. 165; see also de Lauretis, 1987, p. 6).

There is an interaction between sites and ideology. Ideology shapes the representations of sites, for example, the presentation of beautiful lovers in castles. In turn, ideology molds the experiences that occur within sites, leading to the belief that certain kinds of experience can be found only in certain kinds of places, for example, persons can only be truly happy in a beautiful home where they wear beautiful clothes.

Film, as an ideological apparatus that represents imaginary relations between people, structures the meanings persons bring to the interactional sites they confront on a daily basis. Films show how concrete individuals are constituted as subjects who have particular emotional experiences in specific emotional sites. By so doing, films undermine, even as they support, underlying cultural beliefs concerning how emotionality is to be constructed, defined and experienced. That is, films present negative and positive emotionality. They connect these experiences to gendered, family, and intimate relations in concrete emotional sites. In so doing they mold the inner emotional life of the person.

The following statements from moviegoers illustrate and amplify these points.

RELIGION

> Male, 20, white, Jewish, college junior.—When I was sixteen years old, I saw the picture . . . The Ten Commandments . . . and from that time on I have never doubted the value of religion. The many, many hardships which my people went through for the sake of preserving our race were portrayed so vividly and so realistically that the feeling of reverence and respect for my religion was instilled in me (Blumer, 1933, pl 177).

Viewing this film helped to constitute this individual as a subject who believed in the value of his religion. This film help create a Jewish subject. His intentional-value feelings toward his religion were shaped by seeing this film. At the same time, his moral feelings of self were altered. This second point is even more evident in the following statement that speaks to how film shapes family experiences.

FAMILY

> Female, 16, white, high school junior.—I remember once I had trouble with my mother . . . I was very downhearted and thought how cruel they were to me. That night I went to the movies . . . [I]t hit the nail on the head. It concerned a girl who did not get along with her family and one who did. The one girl was so good that everyone loved her and her life was very happy. The other girl was not happy and people did not like her because she was not sweet, good and kind to her mother like the other girl. This made me think that I was just like the girl who was not good . . . so I went home that night with the intention of being as good as possible to my mother and trying to make family life as happy and pleasant as possible (Blumer, 1933, p. 174).

This woman's moviegoing experience gave her a set of ideals and emotional values concerning how she should relate to her family. The film presented two emotional types: a sweet girl and a bad girl. The woman identified with both types and attempted to fit her image of herself to the good, kind, and sweet girl. The film anchored an emotional definition of self to an emotional site, her family, and held forth an emotional ideal (intentional value-feeling, and moral'feelings of self), which she hope to attain for herself. The next person connected self to the workplace.

WORK

> *Female, 16, white, high school junior.*—I can remember very distinctly
> that when I was thirteen years old, I saw a moving picture in which the
> heroine was a very young, pretty girl. In school she had taken a business
> course and after working hard she had been promoted to the position of pri-
> vate secretary. To this very day I would like to be a private secretary. I used
> to sit and dream about what my life would be like after I had that position
> (Blumer, 1933, p. 169).

Here a woman dreams herself into an occupation and a work site, being a
private secretary. Her dream reinforces the gender stratification system. She
is a secretary, not a boss. She sees herself as a heroine in this work position. She has interiorized a moral picture of a self that mirrors women's
place in the larger social order.

My fifth and final thesis about culture, film and emotionality is that
emotional experiences are gender-specific and ideologically defined by the
larger cultural order. Within any emotional site there are typically two separate structures of emotional experience: masculine and feminine. These
emotional codes come together in the fields of sexuality and desire; that is
on the terrain of gendered sexual relationships (see Lacan, 1977; Simmel,
1984, pp. 102–132). These four terms (male, female, sexuality, desire) are
actualized in love, intimacy, friendship, and family.

Here is a male moviegoer commenting on how romantic films a affected his love life:

> *Male, 18, white, college sophomore.*—During my last two years of high school,
> I did a lot of dating. . . . My program or plan of campaign was, first, a
> movie, then a dance, then a slow dance home. When I first started taking
> girls out to the movies, I was impressed with the enormous number of fellows
> that put their arms around their date in the show and I became aware that
> heads already close got closer when love scenes were introduced. I tried the
> things I saw and was pleased with the results. A good love story was more
> inspiring on a date than a picture in which love was not the important ele-
> ment. . . . I didn't get a kick out of what appeared on the screen, but I did
> like the effect a love scene had on my dates (Blumer, 1933, p. 114).

This man's experiences speak to the masculine perspective within the male
culture that sees women as objects of sexual desire. Here are two women:

> *Female, 18, white, high school sophomore.*—As far as I can remember, I've never
> had a real hot date immediately after seeing a passionate picture. Perhaps its
> just as well that I didn't, for my sake anyway (Blumer, 1933, p. 133).

> *Female, 19, Negro, high school senior.*—About love-making from the movies I
> learned a good deal, although I wasn't brave enough to attempt to imitate

the love-making of Greta Garbo and others on my boy friends. Sometimes after we had seen a Greta Garbo movie, my boy friend would become so romantic that I had to send him home (Blumer, 1933, p. 113).

Movies are emotional sites, places where gendered conceptions of love, love-making, and sexuality are defined. These two women have found their place within the male-female sexual culture. There is a fit between these two cultures, as these quotes reveal. Men and women want the same thing from one another; that is they want an intimate, sexual relationship with a member of the opposite sex.

RECAPITULATION AND RESEARCH EXEMPLARS

A three part summary of the above argument may now be given. First, movies create emotional representations of self, sexuality, desire, intimacy, friendship, marriage, and family (see Blumer, 1933, p. 198). These representations draw upon the ideological structures of everyday life. They create a "politics of emotionality and feeling" (Grossberg, 1986, p. 73) that shapes real life, lived emotional experiences. This politics of feeling locates particular emotional experiences, work, love, romance, violence, in particular cultural activities and practices, for example, the family, schools, moviegoing, or the workplace. A politics of feeling addresses how cultural practices shape and empower personal experiences. At the same time, it examines how persons empower, or seize these practices and turn them to their own emotional ends. A politics of emotionality attempts to uncover how particular forms of emotionality (intentional value-feelings, feelings of the moral self, etc.) are structured by the emotional economy of everyday life (Grossberg, 1986, p. 74), that is, what forms of emotional experience are made available in what emotional sites?

Second, a politics of emotionality examines how persons shape, define, attempt to control, and experience their emotions within these sites. In addition to being framed by social, cultural, ideological, gender, and interactional factors, emotionality can be influenced by persons themselves (See Kemper, 1978). One way they attempt to manipulate their emotions is through the use of drugs. Seven of ten American adults drink alcohol, at least occasionally (Denzin, 1987a, p. 16). It is estimated that over 90 million Americans regularly use antihistimines, antianxiety drugs, smoke marihuana, or use cocaine (Straus, 1982, p. 140–141). Polydrug use is common; five of seven drinkers use more than one drug.

If the emotions are lived and experienced under the influence of drugs, then an interpretive, cultural analysis must establish (1) how drugs and alcohol shape lived, emotional experience in families, friendships, and intimate relationships, where love, sexuality, and desire come together (see Kemper, 1978); (2) establish how drugs, culturally, ideologically, and historically have become a part of the American way of being emotional; (3) examine the cultural representations of drug and alcohol use (and abuse), and the place of medicine, science, and industry in the prescription, creation, and production of these chemicals. Since the larger social structure makes these drugs available, the political economy of drug-taking intermingles with and shapes the political economy of emotionality.

Third, specific genres of film, including the family melodrama, women's films, social problems movies, and the alcoholism film (to be discussed below) focus explicitly on the intersection of drug induced emotional experiences and selfhood, marriage, family, and intimacy. An analysis of these films should contribute to a deeper understanding on how emotionality is experienced in the postmodern period. It is to this topic that I now turn.

I will first discuss film and the alcoholism film as a research site for the study of emotionality. Then I will take up the general problem of connecting cultural studies to the study of emotionality. This will address the thesis, discussed above, that the actual lived, emotional experiences of interacting individuals in this historical moment must be thickly described, interpreted, and related to the structural and cultural formations that surround and define them (see Hall, 1987, Denzin, 1984, 1986, 1987g, 1988d).

READING FILM

A film is a complex, emotional, narrative structure, that tells a story, while it depicts a version of social reality. Every film speaks to its historical moment, while it reflects the political economy of the larger society. A film may be read in a multitude of ways, including the interpretive stances of institutionalism, semiotics, psychoanalysis, Marxism, feminism, realism, and hermeneutics (See Deleuze, 1986; Huaco, 1965; Kracauer, 1960 and Andrew, 1984 for a review). I have proposed (Denzin, 1987c, 1987d) that any film may be read at two levels. The first I term "textual realism." At this level, the viewer asks what story does the film tell and how is its story told to the members of the viewing culture. The second level is "subversive." It asks how the film functions ideologically so as to tell its story in a way that reinforces the values and beliefs of everyday life. My main interest is in the second type of reading.

ALCOHOLISM FILMS AND THE STUDY OF EMOTIONALITY

Since the early 1900s, drinking, drunkenness, and alcoholism have played major and minor parts in American cinema. Between the years 1908 and

1989 Hollywood made at least 600 movies in which "one or more of the major characters were marked by inebriety [or] the character's drinking was presented as a problem with which the character self-consciously struggled" (Room, 1985, p. 1). At least twenty-eight such Hollywood films were made between 1945 and 1962 (Room, 1985, p. 1), and from 1980 to 1987 at least thirteen, some for television. The characters were presented as alcoholics, or as problem drinkers. They were invariably positioned within a marriage, or intimate relationship, which was damaged, if not destroyed by alcoholism.

Alcoholism films tell emotional stories about the lives of alcoholics. They anchor the character's emotionality in alcoholism, alcohol, and the alcoholic drinking act. These practices are located in the alcoholic marriage. Emotionality is presented in the films as an interactional phenomenon shaped by the "disease" of alcoholism. The signs and multiple meanings of alcohol, drinking, and alcoholism are built into the dramatic story that is told. These meanings are woven into the narrative of the film and into a set of emotional practices and social relationships the alcoholic has with others. These structures serve to make a point about the effects of these signs, that is, alcoholic drinking on human experience.

The films follow the biographical narrative form, and typically, but not always, move along two lines. First, they depict the rise to prominence, fall from grace, and gradual redemption of the alcoholic. During this trajectory the alcoholic may destroy those she (or he) is close to. Second, within the narrative structure of the film the alcoholic will be placed in a variety of situations where alcoholic, or uncontrolled drinking, surrender to alcoholism (giving up), collapse, recovery, being tested, relapsing, and then recovering again are presented.

The conclusion of the alcoholic film will locate the alcoholic in one of three situations: (1) he or she will still be drinking and die, or go insane as a result of alcoholism, as in the film *Under the Volcano*; (2) the alcoholic will have achieved sobriety either through will power (e.g., *The Country Girl*) or Alcoholics Anonymous (e.g., *Come, Back, Little Sheba*) and have attained his or her rightful place in family and society; or (3) sobriety will have been attained, but the alcoholic walks away from family and society, as in *Paris, Texas*, or, as in the case of the character Krysten, in *Days of Wine and Roses*. The resolution often differs, depending on gender. Males appear to find a place in work (e.g., *The Verdict*); women in A.A. or in treatment centers (e.g. *Life of the Party*, or *The Betty Ford Story*). Thus, women are fated to remain within the illness or disease called alcoholism, while males appear to be able to transcend their disease.

These films invariably position a cast of characters along the dimensions of sobriety and drunkenness, and controlled and uncontrolled sexuality. There will be a sober and then drunk, alcoholic, or problem drinker, who engages in controlled and then uncontrolled drinking. In the process, he or she falls from a respectable position in society. The fall corresponds to drunkenness and free, wild, tabooed sexuality. This individual will be contrasted to, an in control spouse, who signifies the respectability the film holds forth as a value. The alcoholic, in turn, is presented as a diseased individual driven to insanity, lewdness, voyeurism, and violence. Alcohol, as a signifier of released emotionality, is used as a vehicle for illuminating the more general problems of self control and social control in group life. Therefore, alcoholism can be read as is a metaphor for the destructive aspects of desire and sexuality in society. In this formulation, the alcoholic family becomes the metaphor for society-at-large. The alcoholic merges these two metaphors into the biographical story the film attempts to tell.

EMOTIONALITY IN THE ALCOHOLISM FILM

Elsewhere (Denzin, 1987e) I have proposed that four structures of experience shape the intimate relations that create and constrain emotionality in the alcoholism film. These are: (1) the alcoholic drinking act and the euphoric and depressive effects of alcohol on conduct; (2) the absence of alcohol and the negative effects of sobriety on intimacy in the relationship; (3) alcoholic drinking, desire and sexuality; and (4) negative emotions connected to the past.

These four structures erode and destroy the underlying positive, intimate, emotional foundations of the relationship. They turn the relationship into a nightmare of fear and violence. Alcohol masks self-feelings. It creates illusions of intimacy, and feeds into the self-destructive lines of interaction the partners have built up with one another. Drinking is typically presented as a catalyst for the sexual act. Relapses from sobriety are seen as being caused by the intimate emotions associated with sexuality.

In *Days of Wine and Roses*, for example, the two main alcoholic characters, Joe and Krysten, become sexually intimate only when they drink. Alcohol releases Krysten's emotional inhibitions. It appears to give Joe strength and courage to overcome his job insecurities. But as Joe and Krysten become more and more alcoholic in their drinking, they fight and argue and become violent. Their drinking, which initially drew them together, begins to destroy their marriage. They finally separate. Joe becomes sober in A A and Krysten moves back with her father. At one point, while intoxicated and living in a motel, she calls Joe for help. She is drunk and seduces Joe. As he gets into bed with her he begins drinking.

RECONCEPTUALIZING THE ALCOHOLISM FILM

Alcoholism films are, in fact, not about alcoholism. They are about the control of reason and emotion in society. Sobriety and alcoholism respectively signify rationality and irrationality, reason and emotion. When intoxicated, the alcoholic acts irrationally. When sober he or she conforms to the normative standards of everyday life. By locating alcoholism in the family, these films reproduce the dominant cultural ideology that makes each family responsible for its own problems. They also make the family the locus of the greatest amount of pain associated with alcoholism. At the same time, they reproduce cultural, gender stereotypes concerning drinking and self-control; women help men get sober, men don't sober up women. When women drink they become promiscuous. Alcohol releases sexuality and "intimate emotionality." The alcoholic family, or intimate relationship (e.g., *Eight Million Ways to Die*), becomes the emotional site where the politics of emotionality that operate in society at large are played out. When the alcoholic family, or alcoholic relationship is destroyed, or drastically altered because of the alcoholic's conduct, the film is making a statement about the failure of the family to contain its own problems. Alcoholism films, in a Durkheimian sense, reflect the moral, collective consciousness of the society. They state that society cannot tolerate wild, uncontained emotionality, free sexuality, or transgressions against the family, the primordial cultural institution. These films sacrifice individuals to save families. The alcoholic family becomes a metaphor for society, while alcoholism reflects a mode of emotionality society cannot tolerate. On the surface these films often tell a tale of recovery. Underneath they are making statements about the emotions and how they must be contained, at all cost, by society. I turn now to a general consideration of film and its relation to everyday life.

FILM, EVERYDAY LIFE, AND THE
CULTURAL STUDY OF EMOTION

Sociologists have been slow to use film (and photography) in their studies of society (see Becker, 1986, p. 229; see Denzin, 1988c, chpt. 9 for a review). Morin (1984), and Steudler (1987), following Barthes (1957/1972, p. 11), have challenged sociologists of everyday life to develop a sociology of film. I have attempted to take this challenge two steps further. First, I have suggested that the sociology of emotions, which is part of the sociology of everyday life (Douglas and Johnson, 1977; Kotarba and Fontana, 1984), must deal with the cultural representations of intimate, emotional relationships. This leads, secondly, to the analysis of a genre of Hollywood movies, the alcoholism film. In this way, I have attempted to move the sociology of emotions more directly into the field of cultural studies.

Films are simultaneously visual records of, and a part of, everyday life (Steudler, 1987, p. 46). These records and representations structure lived experience: they set fashion, keep tradition alive, record tabooed acts, and ceremonialize the sacred (see note two above). Films are interactional productions. They do not simply assert their truths, "rather we interact with them in order to arrive at conclusions" (Becker, 1986, p. 279). Films, as visual representations of society are both methods of research, and resources, or topics to be studied in their own right. In this essay, I have used them as tools for research, and not stressed how they are produced, structured, and given meaning by their creators (See Jarvie, 1970.).

Film expresses particular versions of the social imagination. Not only do films represent what is "immediately apparent in a given society" (Steudler, 1987, p. 46), but they also allow "the needs, desires and dreams of a period to be projected" into the realms of the social (Steudler, 1987, p. 46). Films, in this regard, are the perfect site for the Durkheimian analysis of society and culture. They encapsulate "the sensitivity, aspirations and dreams of societies in particular historical and sociological situations" (Morin, 1984, p. 402). They have become the repositories of the collective consciousness and subconsciousness of postmodern culture.

IDEOLOGY AND FILM

Films do not faithfully reproduce reality. A film "screens" and frames reality to fit particular ideological, or distorted images of real social relationships (Steudler, 1987, p. 46). Any film will be a site for the play of multiple ideological versions of reality. In Days of Wine and Roses, for example, these include: (1) differing views of AA and alcoholism; (2) contrasting images of sexuality, youth, and marriage; and (3) competing pictures of family and work. Sociological analysis must uncover the ideological distortions that are embedded with any film's text. How a culture-making institution functions can then be analyzed. As a film attempts to build its particular version of reality, in which one set of events is seen as naturally causing another, contradictions and inconsistencies will appear. (For example, why does Kristen, who values family, walk away from her husband and child?) A subversive reading of ideology attempts to uncover these inconsistencies, which lie within the "mythical" structure the film creates (see Barthes, 1957/1972, p. 11).

By representing multiple versions of reality, a film manages to reflect the very reality it distorts. That is, the contradictions and distortions that are represented are themselves drawn from the contradictions that exist in everyday life. Therefore, in the 1960s there were women alcoholics like Kristen who refused to join AA and in the 1950s there were housewives like Lola, in *Come back, Little Sheba,* who were regarded as failures by their neighbors and husbands. There were also women who recovered in AA, men who walked away from their families and rejected AA, and housewives who were not like Lola or Kristen. The distortions that film produces open up corners of everyday life "we had ended up forgetting—that had become, as it were, unfamiliar" (Steudler, 1987, p. 47). In opening up these corners of reality, and by exaggerating particular sets of experiences over others (i.e. the negative as opposed to the positive sides of recovery), films perpetuate stereotypes, fears, and anxieties that exist in the culture-at-large.

However, the visions of real life that the film projects are as valid, or as truthful as any other (Steudler, 1987, p. 47). Truth is always partial, incomplete, and based on a group's or individual's perspective (Becker, 1986, pp. 280–281). The statements that a film makes bear the stamp of the cultural, social, and economic contexts that surround the filmmaker's work. The film is also the product of teamwork, and of political economies of production, distribution, and consumption. Any film, in turn, builds upon patterns of meaning and action that exist in the society-at-large. In so doing, it modifies those patterns of meaning, and creates new experiences for viewers. In this way film creates the realities it reproduces on the screen.

A PROLEGOMENON FOR RESEARCH

It remains to offer an agenda for research that would join the cultural and the interpretive approaches to the study of emotionality. Culture-making institutions create emotional needs and fantasies, and often lead persons to judge their own lives in terms of the emotional fantasies given in these larger than life social texts. The actual connection between lived experiences and the cultural representations of those experiences must be established. What follows is a prolegomena for research, the beginning of a program given in the form of assertions. The focus is on film and television as culture-making institutions that shape lived emotional experiences.

FILM AUTOBIOGRAPHIES, CULTURAL REPRESENTATIONS, AND LIVED EXPERIENCES

The method of securing film autobiographies pioneered by Blumer in the 1930s (Blumer, 1933, pp. 203–207) needs to be reactivated, and fitted to the film and television watching experiences of special populations in the late 1980s. Blumer (1933, pp. 3, 204) asked individuals (481 college and junior college students, 583 high school students, 67 office workers, and 58 factory workers) to write movie "autobiographies." They were given a sheet of instructions, which included writing on the following items: (1) a history of the individual's interest in the movies, including what kind of pictures and movie stars were first, and currently liked, and with whom movies were usually seen; (2) how movies influenced the person's play, daydreams, emotions, and moods; (3) what was imitated from the movies, for example, mannerisms, gestures, ways of dressing, poses; (4) what was learned about love-making and how to behave with the opposite sex; (5) experiences with pictures of love and romance, for example, falling in love with a movie idol, writing love letters to movie favorites, practicing love scenes in play. In another study (Blumer and Hauser, 1933), Blumer asked a similar, but modified set of questions to juvenile delinquents in several Illinois prisons in order to explore whether movies influenced delinquent behavior.

SPECIAL POPULATIONS

Following Blumer's lead, special populations of film viewers should be studied. These would be social groups that are created by two general sets of processes: (1) the age, gender, ethnic, legal, and religious structures of society; and (2) the structures of emotional experience that produce specific groupings, for example, alcoholics and the children of alcoholic families. These populations should be studied in terms of their lived experiences and the cultural representations of these experiences as given in film and television.

For example, Davis (1988a, 1988b) extended Blumer's method. He showed two alcoholism films, *Days of Wine and Roses*, and *Under the Influence* to groups of student volunteers from alcoholic families, and interviewed them in groups concerning the meanings of these films.

Davis found that the students interpreted the films in terms of their unique family histories. If they had an alcoholic parent, who was still drinking, they strongly identified with the destructive effects of alcoholism on family life. If they had a parent who had recovered, they compared their family's recovery experiences with those depicted in the film. Davis's group interviews indicated that the meanings of the movies changed as the students' discussions took place. One student would mention something about the movie, and this would lead another to remember a family experience that the film had touched. In another study, using this type of special population, the experiences of recovering alcoholics were compared to the recovery experiences of alcoholics in specific films (see Denzin, 1987d). Many other possibilities for special populations research can be found. The emotional experiences of being a middle-class American teenager in love can be compared to the film representations of these experiences as given in the movies written and produced by John Hughes (*The Breakfast Club, Pretty in Pink, Sixteen Candles*). The lived experiences of female black family members from the South can be compared with Steven Spielberg's controversial film interpretation of Alice Walker's Pulitzer winning book, *The Color Purple*. The point of the above comparisons is to explore how these cultural representations mask, distort, and misrepresent the worlds of lived emotional experience.

THE POLITICAL ECONOMY OF EMOTION

Film and television produce structures of emotional experience. These texts imitate such intentional value-feelings and moral feelings of self as love, fear, hate, and guilt. MTV (Kaplan, 1988), and highly successful family comedies ("The Cosby Show," "Family Ties," "Growing Pains," see Ephron, 1988), reproduce mythical family structures that bear little relationship to real life in everyday American families. How they do this requires study.

I suggest that the postmodern politics of emotionality locates key emotional feelings in cultural texts that lie outside the person. Daily, the Cable news network bombards the viewer with news about the lives of troubled, pained, dying, starving, mutilated persons (see Barthelme, 1988). An "ecstasy of spuriously interpreted emotion" (see Baudrillard, 1983b) overflows these texts, while they are presented within a language that presumes true, emotional understanding.[1] A sense of false, and empty emotional identification is created.[2] Silent television viewers sit in the shadow of this news and judge their lives in terms of the emotional tragedies that didn't happen to them today.

The ways in which the political economy of emotion shapes forms of lived emotional experience (as described above)—sensible feelings, feelings of the lived body, intentional value-feelings, feelings of the moral self—need to be investigated in detail.

EMOTIONS UNDER THE INFLUENCE OF DRUGS

The cultural representations of emotions experienced "under the influence" of drugs need to be studied. Alcoholism movies, for example, depict various forms of "drinking comportment," often contrasting alcoholic and normal, social drinking. They connect this comportment to various emotional states, including being depressive, suicidal, hostile, violent, sexually attractive, humorous, creative, pitiful, playful, powerful, and self-content. These representations suggest that valued and de-valued emotional states can be achieved by using alcohol (see Denzin, 1988a; Herd, 1985; Room, 1983). Hollywood and television have created and maintained images of the "happy and sorrowful drunk," and the "skidrow" alcoholic. These images play into and shape the understandings the American public has of alcoholism, the alcoholic, and alcohol as a beverage, as opposed to a drug, and these too should be investigated.

THE DIS-EASES OF EMOTIONALITY AND VIOLENT EMOTIONALITY

The dis-eases of emotionality, from mental illness, to drug addiction, alcoholism, sexual, and family violence, and incest are culturally represented in film, television soap operas, and made for television psychodramas. Victims are presented as being emotionally traumatized, and offenders are presented as suffering from an emotional illness that is often explained in Freudian, psychodynamic, psychopathological terms (see Herd, 1985). Sociologists of emotion need to examine how these diseases and illnesses of the emotions are presented and defined in these cultural texts (see Flemming and Manvell, 1986). Often, these texts reproduce an individualistic, as opposed to a social explanation of mental illness, alcoholism, family violence, sexual abuse, and incest.

SHATTERING EMOTIONALITY

The violent emotions are recurring features in popular culture. Violence, murder, rape, torture, and sadomasochistic rituals are the stock and trade of MTV, *Miami Vice*, and the *Rambo* series (see Kaplan, 1988). These forms of violent emotionality are valued, and presented as forms of action that define and create positive human character. Heroes and villians are defined in terms of the masculine abilities to be honorably violent. By continuing to present and value violent emotional experiences, the popular culture contributes to the deep-seated violence that rests at the core of American society (Denzin, 1984, p. 168).

The popular culture emphasis on violent emotionality often proceeds on the assumption that shattering emotional experiences (e.g. rape, violent death, emotional rejections) turn lives around. Elsewhere (Denzin, 1988d), I have used the term "epiphany" to refer to these emotional moments when individuals experience a sudden revelation or insight into themselves and their relationships with others. These experiences leave indelible marks on human character and human relationships. Examples include being raped, being an incest victim, having a family member violently murdered, experiencing the sudden death of a child, going through an ugly divorce, and undergoing treatment for alcoholism or drug addiction.

Such experiences are often the subject matter of Hollywood film and television melodramas (e.g., *The Burning Bed, Chinatown, The Godfather, Kramer vs. Kramer, The Betty Ford Story*). These filmic texts embody a theory of human experience that presumes that shattering emotional experiences either turn lives around, or destroy them. Sociologists of emotion need to study these texts and to compare their representations of shattering emotional experiences with the experiences of real live people who have been raped, suffered incest, and so on.

CULTURAL REPRESENTATION OF VARIED RELATIONAL FORMS

If emotionality is a relational phenomenon, then the cultural representations of specific relational forms, including youth, peer, and work groups, male and female friendships, violent, alcoholic marriages, non-violent "happy" marriages must be examined. I have alluded to this point in the discussion above of family television shows, teenage movies, and alcoholism films. Films like *Butch Cassidy and the Sundance Kid, East of Eden, The Deer Hunter,* about male bonding and male friendship, could be compared to *Julia,* and *The Turning Point,* which deal with female friendships. The film representations of the gendered emotions that connect males to males and females to females could then be compared and contrasted. This leads to the next suggestion for research.

The different forms of emotional experience connected to these social formations, including competition, masculinity, femininity, love, sexuality, and desire must be interpreted. Do different codes of honor and emotional character exist in male as opposed to female relationships? How is the female expression and experiencing of emotionality represented in these relationships and how do these representations differ when the individual is male and the relationship is cross-gender?

FILM AS A RESEARCH SITE

I have argued throughout that sociologists must learn how to use and read film and television as research sites for the sociology of emotions. They must take seriously Simmel's assertion that the human emotions are objectified in culture and reproduced in culture-making institutions. To this end, sociological students of film, must learn how to do semiotic, subversive, feminist film readings. They must experiment with viewer film and television autobiographies. They must show how viewer interpretations of films are anchored in social relationships. The cultural approach to the study of emotionality will always be biographical, and hermeneutic. Its recurring challenge will be to connect the world of lived experiences to the cultural representations of those experiences. That connection will always be dialectical, negotiated, conflictual, ambiguous, open-ended, and interactional. Human freedom and novelty exist in these spaces between private lives and their public representations.

THEORY WORK IN THE SOCIOLOGY OF EMOTIONS

Finally, a cursory inspection of recent proposals concerning work in this field reveals concern for such matters as subcultural differences in emotions, cross-cultural, and historical comparisons in the study of the emotions, new macro-theoretical models, the emotional dimensions of social stratification, institutional areas and the emotions, emotions and the small group, emotions and sexuality, emotions and artificial intelligence theory.

I take exception to these proposals.[3] They display a tendency to turn the emotions into variables that can be measured and studied in first one and then another area of sociological specialization (e.g. organizations, stratification, small groups, racial and ethnic relations, the schools, work and occupations, the family).

In my vision of the emotion project, the above strategy moves the study of lived emotional experience off center stage and makes it part of the satellite system of ancillary theories that can be put to use in any substantive sociological area. This newly emerging field called the "sociology of emotion" must curb the desire to build quantitative, "middle-range" theories of the emotions. Indeed, lived emotional experiences cannot be meaningfully quantified. Theory building, whether middle-range, or otherwise, should not be a goal. Rather, we should be preoccupied with thickly describing and representing the problematic emotional experiences of the persons we study.

I envision our project as being one that interrogates human experience from inside. We must locate the human being within language and within emotionality. We must inquire into what kind of gendered emotional being this late postmodern period is creating. We should be doing work on the structures of emotional experience, on the forms of emotional feeling and intersubjectivity, on the violent emotions, on temporality and emotionality, on moments of epiphany and shattering emotionality, on self, biography and emotionality, on the cultural constraints on emotionality, on the diseases of emotionality that our late postmodern period valorizes, defines, treats, and cures.

In this project, the key experience we have access to is our own (see Sudnow, 1978, p. 154). We must work outward from our own biographies and troubles into those institutional sites where others, sharing our troubles, come together (see Mills, 1959; Ellis, 1988). In these sites, people do things together (Becker, 1986), including emotion work for themselves and others (Hochschild, 1983). Our methods must always be interpretive, phenomenological, critical, and biographical.

Keeping emotionality center stage means that we do not subvert our project by turning the emotions into variables. Nor do we ask how a focus on the emotions can fill out, or better inform traditionally established areas of sociological study. Our project should be emotionality: how emotionality, as a process, is lived, experienced and given meaning by interacting individuals. We challenge other sociologists to build with us a fuller, interactive picture of historically situated individuals, who, as emotional beings, experience and give meaning to their existence through the emotions they live and feel.

CONCLUSIONS

The sociology of the emotions must begin to study the cultural texts of the postmodern period. Films (and television) are critical cultural texts that await interpretation. These texts contain emotional representations that structure lived experience (Blumer, 1933). They take us back to family, parent-child relationships, and love and intimacy. And in them we witness a society, speaking to its members through its collective representations. Inherently conservative, film as a social institution thus keeps alive the deeper, inner core values of the cultural order (on these values see Shils, 1975). It is these values that persons draw upon when they judge their own lived emotional experiences. By studying these films and our reactions to them, we gain a deeper understanding of how a cultural industry shapes public and private consciousness.

I have suggested that a sociology of the emotions simultaneously requires a sociology of the intimate relationship and of film. The present study has indicated how the reading of films contributes to this goal. The family alcoholism film brings before us all the emotional experiences that any intimate relationship could ever hope to contain: sexuality, eroticism, tabooed acts, bad faith, violence, divided selves, twisted love, old dreams, absent father figures, dead children, alcoholic husbands and sick wives.[4]

Our understanding of emotionality and the intimate relationship can only benefit from a closer reading of those social texts which bring these alcoholic, and nonalcoholic relationships, always in larger-then-life form, in front of us. In the genre of film I have discussed, Hollywood forces us to confront alcoholics, alcoholism, alcoholic families, and alcoholic emotions. In these pictures some us find pictures of ourselves. Therefore, we study ourselves as we view and read these films. This is why the sociology of intimacy and emotion needs a sociology of film.

NOTES

*I would like to thank Theodore D. Kemper for his comments on earlier versions of this manuscript, especially for pushing me to develop the research agenda associated with my approach. I also thank Lawrence Grossberg for clarifying certain points concerning the concept politics of feeling.

1. Emotional understanding refers to the knowing and* comprehending, through emotional means, including sympathy and imagination, the intentions, feelings and thoughts expressed by another (Denzin, 1984, p. 282).

2. Emotional identification occurs when I identify myself with, or through the self of another person, and when I define my emotions in terms of the other's emotions.

3. In taking exception to this recent literature, I am not intending to take an "either/or" position. Ten years ago there was no sociology of emotion. It would be arrogant and ridiculous to presume that the framework I advocate is the only correct perspective to pursue in this new field of inquiry. In taking exception, I am, however, attempting to clearly separate my approach from that of others.

4. There are also, of course, positive experiences in intimate relationships.

REFERENCES

Andrew, Dudley. 1984. *Concepts in Film Theory.* New York: Oxford.

Alcoholic Anonymous. 1939, 1956, 1976. *Alcoholics Anonymous.* New York: Alcoholics Anonymous World Services.

Bateson, Gregory P. 1972a. "Double bind." In *Steps to an Ecology of Mind.* by Gregory Bateson. New York: Ballantine, pp. 271–278.

Bateson, Gregory P. 1972b. "The Cybernetics of Self: A Theory of Alcoholism," pp. 309–337 in *Steps to an Ecology of Mind,* by Gregory Bateson New York: Ballantine.

Barthes, Roland. 1957–1972. *Mythologies*. New York: Hill and Wang.

Barthelme, Frederick. 1988. "On Being Wrong: A Convicted Minimalist Spills Bean," *New York Times Book Review*, Sunday, 3 April, section 7:1, 25–27.

Baudrillard, Jean. 1983a. *Simulations*. New York: Semio(texte).

Baudrillard, Jean. 1983b. "Ecstasy of Communication," Pp. 126–134 in *The Anti-Aesthetic: Essays on Postmodern Culture*. Edited by Hal Foster. Port Townsend, WA: Bay Press.

Becker, Howard S. 1986. *Doing Things Together*. Evanston, Ill.: Northwestern University Press.

Bell, Daniel. 1960. *The End of Ideology: On the Exhaustion of Political Ideas in the Fifties*. New York: The Free Press.

Blumer, Herbert. 1933. *Movies and Conduct*. New York: The Macmillian Company.

Blumer, Herbert, and Philip Hauser. 1933. *Movies, Delinquency, and Crime*. New York: The Macmillian Company.

Cavell, Stanley. 1971. *The World Viewed: Reflections on the Ontology of Film*. New York: The Viking Press.

Cherlin, Andrew. 1983. "Changing Family and Household: Contemporary Issues from Historical Research." *Annual Review of Sociology* 9:51–66.

Clough, Patricia T. 1988. "The Movies and Social Observation: Reading Blumer's *Movies and Conduct*." *Symbolic Interaction* 11:85–97.

Cook, Jim, and Mike Lewington. 1979. *Images of Alcoholism*. London: British Film Institute.

Davis, Ed. 1988a. "Viewer's Interpretation of Films About Alcoholism." In *Studies In Symbolic Interaction*, Vol. 10. Norman. K. Denzin (Ed.). Greenwich, CN: JAI Press.

Davis, Ed. 1988b. "Making Sense of the News: A Phenomenological Interpretation of Viewer Place Identification." Dissertation in process, Department of Geography, University of Illinois at Urbana-Champaign.

de Lauretis, Teresa. 1984. *Alice Doesn't: Feminism, Semiotics, Cinema*. Bloomington: Indiana University Press.

de Lauretis, Teresa. 1987. *Technologies of Gender: Essays on Theory, Film, and Fiction*. Bloomington: Indiana University Press.

Denzin, Norman. K. 1988a. *Film and the American Alcoholic*. Hawthorne, NY: Aldine de Gruyter, forthcoming.

————. 1988b. *The Alcoholic Family.* Hawthorne, NY: Aldine de Gruyter, forthcoming.

————. 1988c. *The Research Act. 3/e.* Englewood Cliffs, N.J.: Prentice-Hall.

————. 1988d. *Interpretive Interactionism.* Newbury Park, CA: Sage.

————. 1988e. "Reading *Tender Mercies*: Two Interpretations." *Sociological Quarterly* 29: in press.

————. 1988f. "*Blue Velvet*: Postmodern Contraditions." *Theory, Culture and Society* 5:461–73.

————. 1987a. *The Alcoholic Self.* Newbury Park, CA: Sage.

————. 1987b. *The Recovering Alcoholic.* Newbury Park, CA: Sage.

————. 1987c. "Under the Influence of Time: Reading the Interactional Text." *The Sociological Quarterly* 28:327–340.

————. 1987d. "Reading Tender Mercies: Two Interpretations." Presented to the 1987 Annual Spring Symposium of the Society for the Study of Symbolic Interaction. Urbana, Illinois, 8 May.

————. 1987e. "Reading Intimacy in the Alcoholic Marriage: Case Studies from Film." Presented to the 1987 Annual Meetings of the Society for the Study of Symbolic interaction, Chicago, Illinois, 19 August.

————. 1987f. "Cultural-Interpretive Studies of Emotionality." Presented to the 1987 Annual Meetings of the American Sociological Association. Section on "Sociology of Emotions: Research Agenda for the Sociology of Emotions. Part I."

————. 1987g. "On Semiotics and Symbolic Interactionism," *Symbolic Interaction* 10:1–21.

————. 1986. "Postmodern Social Theory." *Sociological Theory* 4:194–204.

————. 1985. "Emotion as Lived Experience." *Symbolic Interaction* 8:223–240.

————. 1984. *On Understanding Emotion.* San Francisco: Jossey-Bass.

Deleuze, Giles. 1986. *Cinema 1: The Movement Image.* Translated by H. Tomlinson and B. Habberjam. London: Athlone Press.

Douglas, Jack. D., and John. M. Johnson (Eds.), *Existential Sociology.* New York: Cambridge University Press.

Durkheim, Émile. 1894–1964. *The Rules of Sociological Method.* New York: Free Press.

Ellis, Carolyn. 1988. "Accepting and Denying Death in the Doctor's Office." Presented to the 1988 Annual Meetings of the American Sociological Association, Atlanta, Georgia, 28 August.

Elsasser, Thomas. 1972. "Tales of Sound and Fury: Observations on the Family Melodrama." *Monogram* 4:2–15.

Ephron, Delia. 1988. "TV Families: Clinging to the Tried and Untrue." *The New York Times.* Sunday, June 26, section 2 (Arts & Leisure): 1, 10.

Flemming, Michael, and Roger, Manvell, 1986. *Images of Madness: The Portrayal of Insanity in the Feature Film* Cranbury, N.J.: Associated University Presses.

Foucault, Michel. 1986. *The Care of the Self: Vol. 3 of the History of Sexuality.* New York: Pantheon Books.

Foucault, Michel. 1980. *Power/Knowledge: Selected Interviews and Other Writings 1972–1977.* New York: Pantheon Books.

Gilmore, Thomas. 1987. *Equivocal Spirits: Alcoholism and Drinking in Twentieth-Century Literature.* Chapel Hill: University of North Carolina Press.

Gitlin, Todd. 1983. *Inside Prime Time.* New York: Pantheon Books.

Grossberg, Lawrence. 1986. "History, Politics and Postmodernism: Stuart Hall and Cultural Studies." *Journal of Communication Inquiry* 10:61–77.

Gusfield, Joseph. 1981. *The Culture of Public Problems: Drinking-Driving and the Symbolic Order.* Chicago: University of Chicago Press.

Gusfield, Joseph. 1963. *Symbolic Crusade: Status Politics and the American Temperence Movement.* Urbana, Ill.: University of Illinois Press.

Hall, Stuart. 1987. "Questions and Answers," forthcoming in, *Marxism and the Interpretation of Culture.* Edited by Cary Nelson and Lawrence Grossberg, Urbana, Il.: University of Illinois Press.

Hardesty, Monica. J. 1987. "The Social Control of Emotions in the Development of Therapy Relations." *The Sociological Quarterly* 28:247–264.

Harwin, Judith. and Shirley. Otto, 1979. "Women, Alcohol and the Screen." Pp. 37–50 in *Images of Alcoholism,* edited by Jim. Cook and Mike. Lewington. London: British Film Institute.

Herd, Denise. 1986. "Ideology, Melodrama, and the Changing Role of Alcohol Problems in American Films." *Contemporary Drug Problems.* Summer: 213–247.

Herd, Denise and Robin Room. 1982. "Alcohol Images in American Film: 1909–1960." *Drinking and Drug Practices Surveyor* 18:24–35.

Hochschild, Arlie Russell. 1983. *The Managed Heart.* Berkeley: University of California Press.

Huaco, George. A. 1965. *The Sociology of Film Art.* New York: Basic Books.

James, William. 1890–1950. *The Principles of Psychology.* New York: Dover.

Kaplan, E. Ann (Ed.). 1978. *Women in Film Noir.* London: British Film Institute.

Kaplan, E. Ann. 1988. *Rocking Around the Clock: Music Television, Postmodernism and Consumer Culture.* New York: Methuen.

Kemper, Theodore D. 1978. *A Social Interactional Theory of Emotions.* New York: Wiley.

Kinney, J. and G. Leaton. 1978. *Loosening the Grip: A Handbook of Alcohol Information.* Saint Louis: C. V. Mosby.

Kotarba, Joseph, and Andrea Fontana (Eds.). 1984. *The Existential Self in Society.* Chicago: University of Chicago Press.

Kracauer, Siegfried. 1960. *Theory of Film: The Redemption of Physical Reality.* New York: Oxford University Press.

Lacan, Jacques. 1977. *Ecrits: A Selection.* New York: W. W. Norton.

Lacan, Jacques. 1957–8. "Les Formations de L'inconscient." *Bulletin de Psychologie* 9:1–15.

Lefebvre, Henri. 1971–1984. *Everyday Life in the Modern World.* Translated by S. Rabinovitch, with a New Introduction by P. Wander. New Brunswick, New Jersey.: Transaction Books.

Levine, Harry. 1985. "The Birth of American Alcohol Control: Prohibition, the Power Elite, and the Problem of Lawlessness." *Contemporary Drug Problems* 12:63–115.

Levine, Harry. 1978. "The Discovery of Addiction: Changing Conceptions of Habitual Drunkenness in American History." *Journal of Studies on Alcohol* 39:143–174.

Maltins, Leonard. 1986. *TV Movies and Video Guide: 1987 Edition.* New York: New American Library.

Marx, Karl. 1852–1983. "From the Eighteenth Brumaire of Louis Bonaparte." Pp. 287–323 in *The Portable Karl Marx.* Edited by E. Kamenka. New York: Penguin Books.

Merleau-Ponty, Maurice. 1973. *The Prose of the World.* Evanston, Il: Northwestern University Press.

Merton, Robert. K. 1957. *Social Theory and Social Structure*. New York: The Free Press, revised edition.

Metz, Christian. 1982. *The Imaginary Signifier: Psychoanalysis and the Cinema*. Bloomington, Ind.: Indiana University Press.

Mitchell, Juliet. 1982. "Introduction—I. Pp. 1–26 in *Feminine Sexuality: Jacques Lacan and the Ecole Freudienne*. Edited by Juliet Mitchell and Jacqueline Rose. New York: Norton.

Mills, C. Wright. 1959. *The Sociological Imagination*. New York: Oxford.

Morin, Edgar. 1984. *Sociologie*. Paris: Fayard.

Mukerji, Chandra, and Michael Schudson. "Popular Culture." *Annual Review of Sociology* 12:47–66.

Riesman, David., Nathan Glazer, and R. Denny. 1953. *The Lonely Crowd*. New York: Doubleday Anchor Books.

Roffman, Peter. and Jim Purdy. 1981. *The Hollywood Social Problem Film: Madness, Despair, and Politics from the Depression to the Fifties*. Bloomington, Ind.: Indiana University Press.

Room, Robin. 1985. "Alcoholism and Alcoholics Anonymous in U.S. Films: 1945–1962: The Party Ends for the 'Wet Generation.' Presented to the Conference on Cultural Studies on Drinking and Drinking Problems," Helsinki, 24–28 September, 1985.

Room, Robin, 1983. "The Movies and the Wettening of America: The Media as Amplifiers of Cultural Change." Delivered to a colloquium on Representations de l'alcohol et de l'alcoolisme dans le cinema francais," 6–7 June 1983, Paris, France.

Sartre, Jean-Paul, 1943–1956. *Being and Nothingness: An Essay on Phenomenological Ontology*. New York: Philosophical Library.

Scheff, Thomas. J. 1983. "Toward Integration in the Social Psychology of Emotions." *Annual Review of Sociology* 9:333–354.

Shils, Edward. 1975. *Center and Periphery: Essays in Macrosociology*. Chicago: University of Chicago Press.

Simmel, Georg. 1984. *Georg Simmel: On Women, Sexuality and Love*. Guy Oakes, Editor and Translator. New Haven: Yale University Press.

Simmel, Georg. 1950. *The Sociology of Georg Simmel*. Translated and edited, with an Introduction by Kurt. Wolff. New York: The Free Press.

Sinclair, Andrew. 1964. *An Era of Excess: A Social History of the Prohibition Movement*. New York: Harper.

Sklar, Robert. 1975. *Movie-Made America: A Social History of American Movies.* New York: Random House.

Steudler, Francois, 1987. "Representations of Drinking and Alcoholism in French Cinema." *International Sociology* 2:45–59.

Straus, Robert. 1982. "The Social Costs of Alcohol in the Perspective of Change, 1945–1980." Pp. 134–148 in *Alcohol, Science and Society Revisited.* Edited by E. Gomberg, H. White, and J. Carpenter. Ann Arbor: The University of Michigan Press.

Sudnow, David. 1978. *Ways of the Hand: The Organization of Improvised Conduct.* Cambridge: Harvard University Press.

Swidler, Ann. 1986. "Culture in Action." *American Sociological Review* 51:273–86.

Wiley, Norbert. 1967. "America's Unique Class Politics: The Interplay of the Labor, Credit and Commodity Markets." *American Sociological Review* 32:531–541.

Williams, Robin. 1982. *The Sociology of Culture.* New York: Schocken Books.

Films

Come Back, Little Sheba. 1952. Director, Daniel Mann, Producer, Hal Wallis. With Burt Lancaster, Shirely Boothe, Terry Moore, Richard Jaeckel. Production Co., Paramount. 99 minutes. Screen Play, Ketti Frings, from the play by William Inge.

Days of Wine and Roses. 1962. Director, Blake Edwards, Producer, Martin Manulis. With Jack Lemmon, Lee Remick, Charles Bickford. Production Co., Warner Brothers. 116 minutes. Originally a television play by J. P. Miller.

5.

Ideology and Emotion Management:
A Perspective and Path for Future Research

Arlie Russell Hochschild

As I see it, the sociology of emotions is a name for a body of work that articulates the links between cultural ideas, structural arrangement, and several things about feelings: the way we wish we felt, the way we try to feel, the way we feel, the way we show what we feel, and the way we pay attention to, label, and make sense of what we feel. The sociology of emotions supplements and deepens theories about how people think or act. If as George Homans has suggested, we should bring men back into sociology, then we had better bring emotions back in with them. (Thoits forthcoming). A sociology of emotions offers a special vision of how we experience and appraise social settings, and of how emotions partly constitute what we think of *as* social settings. At our best, we are not simply adding a new dependent variable to the traditional roster. Nor are we just plowing up the terminological ground, using new words for what used to be referred to as "values" or "attitudes." We are theorizing all that becomes apparent when we make the simple assumption that what we feel is fully as important to the outcome of social affairs as what we think or do.

I have divided this essay into three parts. In the first, I have outlined three models of emotion, elucidated the interactional model, (which makes most sense to me) and described two concepts basic to my view of emotions, "feeling rules" and "emotion work." (Hochschild 1975; 1979; 1983).

This model of emotion and these concepts first took shape as I studied responses to some open-ended questions about emotions I posed to students in several classes at the University of California, Berkeley. (e.g., "Describe an instance in which you felt one thing but thought you should feel another.") These concepts became sharper as I interviewed flight atendants and observed Delta Airlines' Stewardess Training Center in Atlanta, Georgia. In the course of doing research on the emotional aspect of service work, as reported in my book, *The Managed Heart*, I chose flight attendants because I wanted to study service workers who do a great deal of "emotional labor," that is, the work of trying to feel the right feeling for the job. (By "emotion work" I refer to the emotion management we do in private life; by "emotional labor" I refer to the emotion management we do for a wage.) In an attempt to capture a range of types of emotion work, I contrasted the work of flight attendants, whose job is to be "nicer than natural," with the work of bill collectors, whose job is to be, if necessary, "nastier than natural." I argued that these two occupations represent the toe and the heel of the growing service sector in the American economy. At the toe of the economy are jobs that create a market for goods or services, deliver services, and call for enhancing the status of the customer. At the heel are the jobs that call for collecting on what's been sold and sometimes require deflating the status of the customer. Most work falls somewhere between these two extremes.

In the second part of this essay I have turned from emotional experience on the job to that in the family. I have described some aspects of my recent research on fifty two job couples reported in *The Second Shift* (1989). In this research, I have picked up some theoretical threads that were left hanging in the *Managed Heart*. For example, Delta Airlines' Stewardess Training Center proposed a set of feeling rules that formed the "underside" of their occupational ideology; they spelled out the emotional requirements for being a "good flight attendant." But how do we derive those feeling rules that apply to roles that are far more diffuse and personal, like the role of husband and wife, man and woman.

In the *Managed Heart*, I described how workers managed their feelings in troubling moments. It was an analysis of types of moments. But we can also ask by what principle do we manage our feelings over the course of a long string of moments? That is, how do we fit emotion management to *a line of action through time?* In the course of exploring these questions, I was led to the concept of "gender strategy," the emotional preparation it requires, and the emotional consequences that follow from it.

In the third part of this essay I have suggested some paths for future research about gender strategies, ethnic strategies, and class strategies. I have also outlined a series of questions about the ideological and organizational contexts of these strategies on the one hand, and their relations to the "real self" on the other.

Part I: An Emotion Management Perspective

We feel. But what is a feeling? Feeling is the term we use for more diffuse or mild emotions. Following Peggy A. Thoits (in this volume), I would define emotion as an awareness of four elements that we usually experience at the same time: (*a*) appraisals of a situation, (*b*) changes in bodily sensations, (*c*) the free or inhibited display of expressive gestures, and (*d*) a cultural label applied to specific constellations of the first three elements. We learn how to appraise, to display, and to label emotion, even as we learn how to link the results of each to that of the other. This is the definition of emotion. A feeling is an emotion with less marked bodily sensation; it is a "milder" emotion.

We can also speak of the function of emotion. Emotion functions like a sense. Indeed, it is a sense, and our most precious one. It is part of our sentient nature (Hochschild 1975). We feel just as we hear, or see, or touch. Like these other senses, emotion communicates information to the self. As Freud said of anxiety, feeling has a "signal function." It is hard to know for *sure* what is true about how we stand in the world. We continually guess. In this context of uncertainty, one important clue is how we feel. From feeling we discover our own apparent viewpoint on and relationship to the world. Feeling tells us "what-is-out-there-from-where-I-stand." A man seems tall if we see him from the ground. He is tall from where we stand. We infer from how tall he looks not only his height but also where we stand as we gauge it. Similarly, emotion tells us about the vis-à-vis. For example, a young man parts from a woman who is just a good friend, but suddenly finds himself devastated at her absence. Reflecting on this feeling, he pries out the unacknowledged idea that he loves or depends on her. Feelings are not the only clue to our relationship to the social world, but we often use them as a check.

Feeling is a sense, but what kind of a sense is it exactly? There are three models of emotion current in the growing social science literature on emotion: (*a*) the organismic, (*b*) the interactional and (*c*) the social constructionist. (For more on this see Gordon 1981). These models differ in how much importance they accord to social influence; the social constructionist accords most importance, the interactionist next most, and the organismic, the least importance. According to the organismic model, social influences enter in only to *elicit* feeling, and to *regulate* its expression. According to the interactional model, social factors influence emotion in these ways but they also do so in other ways as well. Social factors enter not simply before and after but interactively *during* the experience of emotion. There are more "points of social entry." For example, a careless driver smashes into a man's new car (a social influence elicits his anger.) He grows red in the face, and clenches his teeth, but doesn't ball his fist to punch (social factors regulate the owner's expression of anger.) This much the organismic model tells us. But to the interactionist, the whole social story has not been told. The owner of the damaged car can whip himself up into a further frenzy of rage, focusing on the newness of the car, the carelessness of the other driver, re-evoking his anger, and stirring it further.

Or, after a momentary flash of anger, he can focus on his image of himself as a man of maturity, probity, stature in the community. He may narrow his focus to the name and telephone number of the other driver's insurance company. In the form of feeling rules and emotion management, other social factors have helped to *shape* his feeling *as* he felt it (see Geertz 1959, Gordon 1985; Lazarus 1980, Shweder and Levine 1984; Shott 1979). In the second model, as in the first, biological factors enter in—there are nerves, hormones, and neurotransmitters—without these we would feel no emotion, just as without eyes we would not see. But social forces have given shape to the biological, have turned it into a strip of experience with a name, a history, a meaning, and a consequence of a certain sort.

According to the third social constructionist model of emotion, biology doesn't enter into emotion as a causative force at all. Feeling is entirely constituted by social influences. In the interactive model, biological factors emerge as "ingredients," which are socially shaped. In the constructionist model, all the ingredients are social. Gordon (1981) espoused this approach as especially useful for sentiments such as nostalgia and sympathy.

Probably some of the emotions, some of the time, fit the organismic model, and some of the emotions, some of the time, fit the social constructionist, but in my view most emotions, most of the time, fit the interactional model. For an initial formulation see "Models of Emotion: from Darwin to Goffman" in *The Managed Heart*, (1983, pp. 201–222).

The interactionist model points to a certain paradox; a feeling is what happens *to* us. Yet it is also what we do to make it happen. There is an ongoing stream of experience. We pay attention to a moment in it, or we don't. We name aspects of it or we let them go nameless. We evoke feeling or we suppress it. We sense that our feeling is inappropriate or we don't. We appraise the fit of feeling to feeling rule in this or that way, seeing how much our feeling fits our rule. The act of getting in touch with a feeling, allowing a feeling, even the act of acknowledging a feeling become part of an intricate process that makes the thing we get in touch with, allow, or acknowledge into the feeling as we know it. In managing feeling, we contribute to the creation of it.

We try to feel. But how can we try to feel? We may induce a light-hearted gaiety at a celebratory moment, or a respectful awe at a commemorative event. Some feelings we push out. Others we hold in, control, or prevent ourselves from acknowledging or expressing for more than a moment. We manage to feel and we manage to not feel.

This we can do, I have argued, by two basic methods. In surface acting, we change feeling from the "outside in." In deep acting, we change feeling from the "inside out." Let me briefly illustrate each method of emotion management with examples from my study of flight attendants. Using the first method, surface acting, we consciously alter outward expression of emotion in the service of altering our inner feeling. Our mental focus is on our slumped shoulder, bowed head, or drooping mouth. In surface acting, we do not simply change our expression; we change our expression in order to change our feeling. One flight attendant described her surface acting in this way: "If I pretend I'm feeling really up, sometimes I actually cheer up and feel friendly. The passenger responds to me as though I were friendly and then more of me responds back."

Using the second method, deep acting, we change our feeling by altering something more than surface appearance. There are several types of deep acting. In one type, bodily deep acting, we alter our feelings by changing our bodily state. For example, one flight attendant said, "Sometimes I purposely take deep breaths. I try to relax my neck muscles. Then I'm not so likely to take the guy (a drunken passenger who insults her) seriously." She detachs herself from the provocative encounter and becomes less angry.

Through another type of deep acting, we may change how we feel by prompting ourselves, or narrowing our mental focus to a particular image or point of reference. For example, one flight attendant said, "I may just talk to myself: 'Watch it. Don't let him get to you. Don't let him get to you. Don't let him get to you.' And I'll talk to my partner and she'll say the same thing to me. After a while the anger goes away." Another flight attendant said, "I discovered that this elderly couple had taken a lap dog on board. It's strictly against regulations but I let them do it provided the dog stayed on the woman's lap. Well, they let it walk up and down the aisle and the dog did a mess in the aisle. The man pushed his call button and demanded that I wipe it up. He said 'You're the help. You clean it up' And here I thought I was doing this sweet couple a favor. I was so shocked and so mad. But I held it in. I counted backwards—thirty minutes 'til we land, twenty-nine minutes, twenty-eight . . . I didn't blow up."

A third form of deep acting involves changing our feeling by deliberately visualizing a substantial portion of reality in a different way. This is the form of deep acting described by the famous Russian theater director, Constantin Stanislavski, in his book *An Actor Prepares* (1965). Using this method, the flight attendant changes her mental images and ideas in the hope of transforming her feelings, and, incidentally, her outer expression of them too. For example, one flight attendant said, "I try to remember that if he's drinking too much, he's probably scared of flying. I think to myself, 'He's like a little child.' Really that's what he is, and when I see him that way, I don't get mad that he's yelling at me. He's like a child yelling at me then." (Hochschild 1983:35–55). Thoits (1985 and this volume) has further improved our understanding of how people change their feelings by changing various components of feeling.

In everyday life, we manage feelings through surface and deep acting. In this sense, we are all flight attendants. Each time we manage feeling, we engage, as flight attendants do, in a series of momentary acts. Like the tiny dots of a Seurat painting, the micro-acts of emotion management can compose, through repetition and change over time, a movement of the entire form of a feeling. A feeling has changed. We have done emotion work.

The importance of emotion management lies not only in our success at it, for we often fail miserably, but also in the continual homage we pay to the social conventions of affective life. The exact way in which we "hold" feeling—how loose, how tight, how reluctant, how keen—is important in itself as a way to understand that easy to miss moment when culture most powerfully affects what we think we should feel, what we try to feel, and sometimes what we feel.

EXPRESSION RULES AND FEELING RULES

We often try to appear to feel amused, pleased, sad, and in doing so we follow *expression rules*. These are the unarticulated ground rules of social interaction most appreciatively exposed in the works of Erving Goffman. For Goffman, (1956; 1961) rules of interaction were the general traffic regulations of social life. Embedded in these were rules that referred specifically to the display or masking of feeling.

We also try to feel actually amused, pleased, sad, and in doing so we follow *feeling rules*, which are rules about what feeling is or isn't appropriate to a given social setting. We might say, "I should feel more grateful to him than I do, given all he's done for me." Or, "I should feel happier at my good news." Feeling rules tell us how joyous, angry, jealous, grateful, or loving in a given sort of company, at a given time or place, we *ought* to feel.

Feeling rules are not simple yes-no norms. They are more like "zoning regulations" that demarcate how much of a given feeling, held in a given way, is crazy, unusual but understandable, normal, inappropriate, or almost inappropriate for a given social context. Feeling rules govern how deeply we should feel, and for how long. According to a feeling rule, we can be off or on in our timing, and in the duration, or intensity of our feeling. As Thoits (1985) points out, we may also be "on" or "off" in the target of our feelings, as when a person feels romantic love for his or her psychotherapist, or fury at an infant. At the same time, most feeling rules leave room for certain lapses, departures, and ambivalences. One working mother I interviewed, a hardworking executive who had primary care of her three and six-year-old childen, was called into her boss's office. He joyously congratulated her on her promotion to a job with much more challenge and pay but also much longer hours. Well-wishers gathered around to share her joy. She described her feelings: "I said thank you to everyone. I tried to act happy and part of me was happy. But driving home that night I could feel myself sinking into a deep depression that lasted a month. I could not take that new job. No way, not and keep my family and marriage together. Given what I had to pass up, it was normal to get depressed, but not normal to get *that* depressed."

Feeling rules establish zones that mark off degrees of appropriateness, or understandability of a feeling. We can visualize these zones by conceiving of emotion lines dividing these zones. By an "emotion line" I mean an imaginable series of emotional reactions to a series of instigating events. Take a person's notion to what, in a series of provocations, might rightly call for an angry response. A flight attendant I interviewed for *The Managed Heart* described her anger line this way:

> Now if a man calls out to me, "Oh, waitress," I don't like it. I'm not a waitress. I'm a flight attendant. But I know that sometimes they just don't know what to call you and so I don't mind. But if they call me "honey," or "sweetheart" or "little lady" in a certain tone of voice, I feel demeaned, like they don't know that in an emergency I could save their little chauvinistic lives. But when I get called "bitch" and "slut" I get angry. And when a drunk puts his hands right between my legs—I mean good God!

The airline envisioned a different anger line for its front line workers. This worker noted wryly:

> Now the company wants to say, look that's too bad. That's not nice. But it's all in the line of public contact work. I had a woman throw hot coffee at me, and do you think the company would back me up? Would they write a letter? Bring a suit? Ha! Any chance of negative publicity and they say, "No." They say for me not to get angry at this. It's a tough job and part of the job is to take this abuse in stride.

The worker and the company had very different ideas about how much anger should go with the hot coffee incident. To the worker, the hot coffee incident was an insult; she had a right to feel indignant. To the company, the hot coffee incident was the everyday stuff of public contact work, and a flight attendant was paid good money to cope with it.

There are different kinds of emotion lines. We develop jealousy lines, love lines, sadness lines—notions of how much it would take of certain provocative events to inspire just how much "appropriate" feeling. Societies and subcultures, families and individuals vary in their ideal emotion lines, that is, notions about what series of feelings constitute "reasonable" responses to a series of events. Our emotion lines are connected by underlying orientations to feeling, which vary by culture and subculture. The individual's emotional response to a line of provocative events is a clue to how he or she zones emotions. What is a temperate zone in one subculture may be tropical in another.

If we don't apply feeling rules to ourselves, others may gently remind us of them. They may express concern for us ("is everything all right?") so as to signal what expression of ours seems inappropriate to them. If we seem "off" in our feeling, they may express surprise or puzzlement: "Why are you depressed? You've just passed your exams." Of if we don't seem to feel enough, they may give us permission to feel more, "I know how you must feel; just let it out."

Most of the time, we become aware of feeling rules when we or others have feelings that are *wrong*. Rarely do we say to ourselves, "Ah, now that's the right feeling." People differ in their comfort with emotional deviance. Some quickly acknowledge an inappropriate feeling, and agonize over the interpretation and repair of it while others easily tolerate prolonged states of emotional deviance.

Both the content of feeling rules and the seriousness with which they are taken probably varies from one social group to another. Some cultures may exert more control on the outer surface of behavior, allowing freedom to actual feelings underneath. Such cultures may focus on the expression rules that govern surface acting. Other cultures may exert relatively more social control on the inner emotional experience, focusing on feeling rules that govern deep acting. (Hochschild 1983, 56–76).

Expression and feeling rules are integral to what Gordon (1981; 1988) has called "emotional culture." In addition to feeling rules, emotional culture includes beliefs about emotions (such as "love lasts forever" or "a person can die of grief"). It includes notions about how we should attend to, codify, appraise, manage, and express feelings. Emotional culture is reflected in advice books, films, religious tracts, psychiatric theory, and law (e.g., what constitutes a crime of passion.) Thus, the study of emotion leads us, on the one hand, from emotions to emotion management, emotion rules, and emotional culture. On the other hand, it leads us to the social structures that pin a person into his or her immediate social world, and to the influences of that social world, which evoke the emotions a person feels (Kemper 1978 and this volume).

PART II: EMOTIONAL PREPARATION AND CONSEQUENCES OF GENDER STRATEGIES

My study of emotion and feeling rules in the world of service workers left me with a number of questions. What is the link between ideology (or culture) and feeling rule? In my study of service workers, I found that flight attendants were invited to internalize the company-sponsored occupational ideology, and its rules about how workers should feel in a variety of trying situations. But in private life, outside the context of a company training program, how is ideology related to feeling rules and to feelings? In my interviews with flight attendants and bill collectors, I collected moments of emotional labor, classified them, and related them to their occupational context. But in private life, it is not so clear what principle guides individual moments of emotion management. People differ in how they manage feeling. Research by Thoits (1988 and this volume) suggests that men and women, Catholics, Protestants, and agnostics prefer different methods of emotion management. Thoits points to the different ways these groups are socialized to cope with feelings that don't fit feeling rules. But this finding poses the question: Do men and women subscribe to different feeling rules? If so, how are these rules connected to gender ideologies?

These questions led me, in my next research project, to focus on the gender ideologies of men and women, and the emotional culture associated with them. I wanted to know how actors put together gender ideology, feelings, and action. How are thought and feeling related to what Swidler (1986) called a "strategy of action," a persistent way of ordering action through time. For example, are there emotional strategies that prepare the ground for the behavioral strategies men and women pursue in combining work and family life? If so, what are they? What are the emotional costs and benefits of each?

I moved from a focus on occupational roles, in which the ideology comes with the job to a focus on marital roles, in which partners bring with them similar or conflicting gender ideologies, and notions of what a husband and wife owe to and deserve from, each other. In *The Managed Heart*, I focused on various kinds of feeling rules and emotion management. In *The Second Shift* I focus on how actors prepare their feelings for a long-term line of action. In *The Managed Heart* I looked at the emotional costs service workers suffer when they do and do not manage on the job emotions. In *The Second Shift* I explore the emotional costs of gender strategies.

I interviewed fifty married couples, in which both partners worked at full-time jobs and also cared for children under the age of six. I interviewed their babysitters and, for comparative purposes, a variety of other kinds of couples; I also did field observations in the homes of ten families.

With the growth of the two-job marriage, we have seen a parallel and related rise in divorce. I wanted to focus on one source of tension in the two-job couple, the question of how to divide the housework and child care, or what I call the "second shift." Who does how much? How does each partner feel about it? I wanted to get a closer look at the link between each one's notion of fairness on this matter, and harmony between them.

All these couples face a shortage of time and the abundance of demands that emerge when two people face four tasks—his job, her job, caring for the children and tending the home. In every couple, the woman felt a conflict between work and home more keenly than the man did. But the second shift often became emotionally loaded for both. Some husbands, who did little work at home, felt guilty; their wives felt frustrated and resentful. But reactions varied widely, depending on each partner's gender ideology, how strongly each felt about it, and how each aligned ideology and feeling with his or her course of action.

GENDER IDEOLOGIES AND FEELING RULES

The gender ideologies of these men and women fell into three main types; (a) traditional, (b) egalitarian and (c) transitional. Implicit in each ideology were rules about how one should feel about one's work outside and inside the home. Traditional men and women felt a woman's place was in the home even though she might have to work, and that a man's place was at the workplace even though he might have to help at home. Many traditional women talked as if they were being gracious to help support the family, help they reserved some right to resent giving (since earning money wasn't their job). Correspondingly, many traditional husbands felt that by doing housework they were doing their wife a favor for which their wife should feel grateful. In addition, traditional women did not believe it was right to identity with their paid jobs, or to love their work, though some guiltily did. And traditional men did not wish to identify themselves too closely with women's work at home, though again, some did.

The egalitarian man or woman felt that husbands and wives should share both the paid and unpaid work. The wife was supposed to identify with her work, and to feel her career mattered as much as her husband's (though some egalitarian women didn't really feel theirs did). The egalitarian husband was supposed to feel that his role as householder and parent mattered as much as his wife's (though some didn't feel theirs did).

The transitional man or woman adhered to a mix between the traditional and egalitarian ideology: he or she believed it was good for the wife to work full-time outside the home, but it was also her responsibility to do most of the work at home. It was her right to care about and enjoy her paid work. She was supposed to have an identity outside the home. But she didn't have a right to feel angry at a husband who didn't help much, since her husband wasn't supposed to have an identity equivalent to hers inside the home. Nor, if he didn't help at home, did the transitional husband feel obliged to feel very much guilt. Those were the feeling rules.

Traditionals were a small minority among both men and women, and of the rest, more women were egalitarian and more men were transitional. Thus, men and women often applied different feeling rules to what they actually felt about work and home.

EMOTIONAL ANCHORS TO IDEOLOGY AND FEELING RULES

Quite apart from differences in the content of gender ideology and feeling rules, I began to be impressed by the different ways individuals *hold* ideology. A few traditionalists railed passionately against the ERA, abortion, and the economic need for a wife to work, as if a vital moral order were endangered. Others stated the same beliefs matter-of-factly. Some men also seemed to be egalitarian "on top" but traditional "underneath." This led me to explore the feelings that infused people's ideologies, and to ask how actors care about their beliefs. Passionately? Nonchalantly? Angrily? Hopelessly? Fearfully?

I had to revise my earlier model, according to which feeling rules were something that governed feelings, and were not themselves the object of feelings. In those cases in which people didn't seem to care much about their ideology or the feeling rules it implied, the old model remained: "feeling rule versus feeling." But in the case of passionate or ambivalent ideologies, I had to stop to explore what lay behind feeling rules.

The underlying feelings of some people seemed to reinforce their surface ideology, while those of other people seemed to subvert it. Some underlying feelings seemed traceable to "cautionary tales"—important episodes from a person's past that carried meaning for the future. For example, one passionate traditionalist, an El Salvadoran daycare worker married to a factory worker, spoke vehemently against the ERA, comparable worth, abortion rights, and anything that would detach a woman's identity from the home. Reinforcing her gender ideology was her urgent desire to avoid the terrible struggles of her mother, a single mother whose husband abandoned her and her baby (the respondent) because she was "too dominating." The message of this cautionary tale of abandonment seemed to be: submit to your man and he won't leave you. The gender ideology of some passionate egalitarians seemed fueled by a dread born of a different cautionary tale: a mother who became a "doormat" to her husband, lacked self-esteem and felt depressed.

Often the feeling reinforcing a person's gender ideology seemed to derive from the combined influence of a cautionary tale from the past and a situation in the present. For example, a Black forklift driver, a father of three, firmly resisted the entreaties of his wife, a billing clerk, to help with housework and childcare. Even if his wife worked full-time, he strongly felt housework wasn't a "man's" job. He felt more strongly about this than other men I interviewed who were in his situation, and shared his point of view. His cautionary tale also concerned an early loss; as a three-year-old, his mother had left him in the care of his aunt, not to return until he was twenty. Now, against his wife's will, it seemed he was trying to keep control of her by urging her to detach herself from work and the idea of economic self-sufficiency, and to center her attention at home. The cautionary tales of the daycare worker and the forklift driver suggest biographic clues to the emotional anchors of gender ideology.

In other cases, the underlying feeling seemed to subvert the surface ideology. Consider the example of John Livingston, a white businessman who had been on the brink of divorce and had sought marriage counseling only a few months before I interviewed him. He described a childhood of extreme neglect in an Irish working-class family, a reclusive father and workaholic mother; she was a waitress during the week, and took an extra job selling ice cream on weekends. He spoke of how much it meant to him to be married and to "finally communicate with somebody."

Ideologically, John was an egalitarian. His mother had "always worked"; he had always expected his wife to work and was "all in favor of sharing" the provider and homemaker roles in his own marriage. But when their daughter Cary was born, his feeling rules became harder to follow. After Cary's birth, John very distinctly felt his wife withdraw from him. As he put it, "I felt abandoned, you might say, and angry." When his wife returned to a demanding job, he resented it bitterly. As he explained:

> Maybe I was jealous of Cary because for the six years before she was born, I was the most important person to Barbara. For several months while she was working those long hours, I would come home and spend most of the night with Cary, which was okay. But I *resented* Barbara not being there. I wanted a few minutes to myself. Then I felt Cary was being cheated by her not being here. And I wanted Barbara to spend more time with me! So I withdrew. I didn't want to complain, to make her feel guilty about working long hours. But I resented it.

John believed Barbara should be engrossed in her work. At the same time he felt furious that she was. His feeling rule clashed with his feeling. Since it was John's habit to withdraw when he was angry, he withdrew. His wife grew upset at his withdrawal, creating a painful marital deadlock which, through their long hours at work and caring for Cary (supermom and superdad strategies), they were avoiding.

Like John, many working parents seemed to be either egalitarian on top and traditional underneath, or traditional on top and egalitarian underneath. Times of rapid economic and cultural change may well create more complicated relations between acknowledged and unacknowledged feelings, between apparent ideologies and their emotional anchors.

EMOTIONAL PATHWAYS OF GENDER STRATEGIES

We not only adopt ideologies and feeling rules aboout dividing the work at home, we pursue gender strategies—persistent lines of feeling and action through which we reconcile our gender ideology with arising situations. Thus, our acts of emotion management are not randomly distributed across situations and time; they are guided by an ideologically informed aim. This aim is to sustain a certain gendered ego-ideal, to be, for example, a "cookies-and-milk mom" or "a career woman" or some mix of the two, or neither. And this aim also sustains a certain ideal balance of power and division of labor between husband and wife. If we understand ourselves not simply as people but as pursuers of gender strategies, and if we attune ourselves to the feeling rules that guide them, we can see a certain pattern in how feelings clash with rules, and in what feelings need managing. Often our gender strategy corresponds to what we consider our "real self." Who—as a man or a woman—we are trying to be fits who we think we really are. We may also find our gender strategy curiously at odds with our "real self." We may be only vaguely aware or totally unaware of our gender strategies and of the conflicts they pose for our "true self."

A gender strategy is a "strategy of action" in the sense in which Ann Swidler has used this term (1986, p. 283; also see Goffman 1969). It is a strategy of behavior, a certain kind of conscious or unconscious plan for what to do. But a gender strategy is also a strategy of emotion, in the sense that we actively evoke and suppress various feelings in order to clear a preparatory emotional pathway to our actions (see Thoits 1985). We try to change "how we feel" to fit "how we must feel" in order to pursue a given course of action.

In the way they divided housework and childcare and in the way they felt about this and about each other, the two-job couples I studied reflected long-term gender strategies. A few working mothers had always shared the work at home with their husbands and worked to maintain this arrangement (a strategy of stabilized equity). But those who had not always shared, pursued one of two strategies. They pressed their husbands to do more work at home, or they didn't. Wives who tried to get their husbands to do more at home pressed in an active, direct way—by persuasion, reminding, argument, or sometimes by a you-share-this-work-or-else showdown (a strategy of active change). Other wives pressed their husbands in passive or indirect ways; they "played dumb" or got "sick"; they called on their husband to take on a larger load at home. Or through passive ways, some women increased the cost of not helping out by emotionally isolating their husbands or losing sexual interest in them because they were "too tired" (a strategy of passive change).

Other working mothers kept most of the responsibility and work of the home for themselves. They became "supermoms," working long hours at their jobs, and keeping their children (who napped during in the afternoon at daycare) up late at night to give them attention. Some working mothers reduced their time, effort and sometimes commitment to their job, their housework, and even to their children and husband. Or they managed their conflict by some combination of cuts.

To prepare the way for her behavioral strategy, the working mother may create a certain "emotional pathway" for it. She may try to feel what it would be useful to feel in order to follow her strategy of action. For example, a few women confronted (or almost confronted) their husbands with an ultimatum; "either you share the responsibility for tasks at home with me or I leave." To go through with this showdown, they had to rivet their attention on the injustice of the unfair load they carried and dwell on its importance to them. They distanced themselves from all they would otherwise feel for their husband and suspended their empathy for his situation. They steeled themselves against his resistance. One working mother described how she approached her husband:

> I'd had it. I was wiped out. And he was getting his squash game in like before the baby came. So I steeled myself. I prepared myself. I told him, "This can't go on." If he hadn't said yes, I was ready to get very mad. I figured if he couldn't show me that consideration, he didn't love me. I'd had it. I mean marriages end like this.

Other working mothers avoided steeling themselves by working through indirect means, developing incompetencies at home, so as to draw their husbands into the work at home by "needing help" paying the bills or driving a car. Their task was to maintain self-esteem by distancing themselves from the helpless image they had cultivated. Working mothers who cut back on their hours of work often prepared themselves for this move beforehand by trying to suppress or alter their feelings about work, and its meaning for their identity. Despite this anticipatory emotional work, one highly successful businesswoman with an MBA who quit her job to consult part-time felt naked in public without the status shield of her professional role. As she explained it, "I used to be so gung-ho at work. But I just decided I had to put that aside while my kids are young. It was much harder than I thought, though, expecially when I'm walking in the supermarket and other people just think I'm a housewife. I want to shout at them, "I have an MBA! I have an MBA!."

Other working mothers clung to their work commitments but relinquished their former concern about how the house should look or how meals should taste. Interpreting the look of the house as a personal reflection on themselves, women pursuing traditional gender strategies felt embarrassed when the house looked messy. On the other hand, egalitarian women often *tried* not to care how the house looked, some even priding themselves on how little they noticed the mess, how dirt no longer "got to them," how far beyond embarrassment they were.

More important than cutting back on housework, working mothers sometimes also resolve their conflict by cutting back on the time and attention they give their children. Under the tremendous pressure of the demands of work and family, they scaled down their ideas about what their child needs. One working mother described her feelings about putting her daughter in the care of a babysitter for ten hours a day at the age of three months:

> She took long naps in the afternoon, but face it, ten hours is still a long day. When I started out, I told myself, "Don't feel guilty." But when I leave her off at my sister-in-law's, I see her perfect family (she's home all day with her children). They have a dog and a yard. I think about the fact that my mom stayed home all day with me. I wonder if I'm giving my child the foundation my mother gave me? Then I tell myself, "Don't feel guilty! Your guilt has to do with you, not the baby. The baby is fine." At least I think the baby's fine.

In each case, to resolve the conflict between work and family demands, women pursued an emotional strategy that paved the way for their course of action.

In part, the gender strategies of men paralleled those of women. In part they were different because it was not, by tradition, men's role to do housework and childcare, and men did not find themselves doing more of it, nor did they pressure their wives to share the work at home. On the contrary, men received such pressure, and often resisted. Their resistance took many forms—disaffiliation from the task at hand, needs reduction, making substitute offerings to the marriage, and selective encouragement of their wife's efforts at home. Some strategies went more against the emotional grain than others, and took more emotional preparation. Perhaps the male strategy that took the most emotional preparation was that of "needs reduction." Some men conceded that sharing was fair, but resisted increasing their labor at home by scaling down what they thought needed doing. One man explained that he never shopped because he "didn't need anything." He didn't need to shop for furniture (the couple had recently moved into a new apartment) because he didn't care about furnishing their apartment. He didn't cook dinner because cold cereal "was fine." His wife scaled down her notion of their needs with him up to a certain point, after which she gave up, furnished their apartment and cooked their meals but then resented doing it all. While some men pretended to reduce their needs, others pursuing this strategy stood by the truth of their lowered notion of needs. They actually suppressed their desires for comfort. As one man described it, "It's (working two jobs and raising small children) like being in the army. You set the comforts of home behind you."

EMOTIONAL CONSEQUENCES

Just as the emotional pathways for each line of action differ, so do the emotional consequences of the outcomes of gender strategies. Many working mothers who held egalitarian gender ideals but had husbands who refused to share housework, felt the right to feel resentful and indeed felt so. Not looking to their husband for a solution to the double day, many traditional women did not feel the right to resent non-helping husbands, and did not resent them. Under the strain, they seemed to get sick more often, to feel frustrated at things in general. Sometimes they pursued a policy of jealously guarding their sense of over-burden. If career loomed large in their identity, women who felt forced to severely curtail or relinquish their career often had to manage loss of self-esteem and depression (though not guilt). On the other hand, women who felt homemaking was important, and who cut corners at home often felt a loss of self-esteem and guilt at doing so. In general, the combination of an actor's gender ideology, and the actual result of the interplay of each partner's gender strategy seemed to determine his or her feelings about the division of labor at home.

Due to a clash between her egalitarian gender strategy and her husband's traditional one, a mother of a four-year-old, and three-month-old baby did a great deal of emotion work. Since the interplay of their gender strategies resulted in a very difficult but fairly common set of emotional sequences, I shall describe her situation in depth.

This woman, Nancy Holt, had staged a "sharing showdown" (a strategy of active change) with her husband. The issue of how to divide the housework and childcare was thick with symbolic meanings to them both and had escalated into the storm center of their marriage. For Nancy, her husband's refusal to share work at home recalled her own father, "coming home, putting his feet up, and hollering at my mom to serve him. My

biggest fear is of being treated like a servant. I've had bad dreams about it."
For her husband, Evan, Nancy's insistence felt like a form of domination.
He also suspected that Nancy's ardent desire to get him more involved in
work at home was motivated by her own desire to do less of it. His alcoholic mother had cared for her children very little; now he felt he had a
wife who was getting out of it too. The Holts fought bitterly over who
should assume how much responsibility for their domestic lives, and finally
reached an impasse. Nancy wouldn't give up wanting Evan to do half the
housework, and Evan wouldn't do half. Nancy realized she had to choose
between living up to her gender ideals or staying married. They had small
children, a network of concerned, Catholic, middle-class, family-oriented
relatives, and, aside from this great thorn in their sides, they loved each
other. So to save the marriage, Nancy backed off, adjusted to doing 90
percent of the work at home herself, and resented it.

This solution presented Nancy with a problem—how to manage her
resentment. As a feminist working the double day, she felt angry. But as a
woman who wanted to stay married to a chauvinist, she had to find a way
to manage her anger. She couldn't change her husband's viewpoint, and
she couldn't banish her deep belief that a man should share. What she
engaged in instead was a private program of anger management. So she
engaged in deep acting. She avoided resentment by dropping from view a
series of connections between his refusal to share the load at home and all
that this symbolized to her—her lack of worth in his eyes, his lack of consideration, or even love for her. She held on to sharing as a general principle that should operate in the world at large, but tucked away the
principle of sharing as not relevant in her case.

She also encapsulated her anger by dividing the issue of housework
from the emotion-loaded idea of equality. She rezoned this anger-inducing
territory so that only if Evan did not *walk the dogs* would she feel indignant.
Focusing more narrowly on the minor issue of the dogs, Nancy would not
need to feel upset about the double day in general. Compartmentalizing her
anger this way, she could still be a feminist—still believe that sharing goes
with equality and equality goes with love—but this chain of associations
now hinged more specifically and safely on just how lovingly Evan
groomed, fed, and walked the dogs.

Another plank in Nancy's emotion management program, one she
shared with Evan, was to suppress any comparison between her hours of
leisure and his. Like other women who didn't feel angry at combining full-
time work with the lion's share of the housework, Nancy narrowed her
comparison group to other working mothers, and avoided comparing herself
with Evan and other working fathers. She talked about herself as more
organized, energetic, and successful *than they.* Nancy and Evan also agreed

on a different baseline comparison between Evan and other men. If Nancy compared Evan to her "ideal" of a "liberated" husband, or to men she actually knew who did more work at home, then she grew angry that Evan did not do more. But if she confined her comparisons to Evan's father, or to her own father, or to Evan's choice of men to compare himself to, then she didn't get angry, because Evan did as much or more around the house than they.

They also spoke of their unequal contributions to the home as the result of their different characters. As Evan spoke, there seemed to be no problem of a leisure gap between them, only the continual, fascinating interaction of two personalities. "I have a lazy personality," he explained. "And I'm not well organized. I need to do things in my own time. That's the sort of person I am." Nancy, on the other hand, described herself as "compulsive" and "well-organized." Now, six months after their blow up, when discussing why Evan didn't share the housework, Nancy said fatalistically—as she had not previously—"I was socialized to do the housework. Evan wasn't." Seeing Evan's nonparticipation engraved in childhood, beyond change, lent their resolution of the matter a certain inevitability, and further buried the frightening anger each felt toward the other.

All this did not mean that Nancy ceased to care about equality between the sexes. On the contrary, she cut out magazine articles about how males advanced faster in social welfare (her field) than females. She complained about the wage gap between men and women and the deplorable state of daycare. Discrimination that was safely "out there" made her indignant, but not the not-sharing at home. She bent her beliefs around her dilemma.

Not all of these anger-avoiding ways of framing reality were Nancy's doing. Together, she and Evan developed an anger-avoidant myth. Some time after their blow up, I asked Nancy to go down a long list of household chores, packing lunches, emptying garbage . . . She interrupted me to explain with a broad wave of her hand, "I do the upstairs. Evan does the downstairs." "What is upstairs?" I asked. Matter-of-factly, Nancy explained that upstairs there is the living room, the dining room, the kitchen, two bedrooms, and two baths—basically the entire house. Downstairs is the garage, a place of storage and hobbies, Evan's hobbies. There was no trace of humor in her upstairs-downstairs view of sharing. Later I heard the same upstairs-downstairs formula from Evan. They seemed to have agreed on it. In this upstairs-downstairs account, the garage was elevated to the full moral and practical equivalence of the rest of the house. Evan is to look after the dog, Max, the car and the downstairs. The "upstairs-downstairs" formulation seemed to me a family fiction, even a modest delusional system concealing an unequal division of labor, Nancy's indignation over that inequality, and their joint fear of Nancy's anger. It seemed to me that her anger was still there—not in the sense that she acknowledged that she was angry—but in the sense that long after the crisis, her talk about the second shift evoked strong words and a raised voice. She had managed her anger by mentally partitioning anger-evoking ideas, by avoiding bad thoughts, by refocusing her attention and sustaining the upstairs-downstairs myth. But her anger seemed to persist and leak into other areas of their family anyway. Meanwhile, the myth of the upstairs-downstairs became the apparent burial ground of the very idea of the conflict and anger. It became a family cover-up that concealed a great unresolved issue in their marriage. Writ large, it concealed the conflict between an egalitarian ideology and its feeling rules on the one hand, and a traditional marriage on the other.

Many women like Nancy Holt are caught between their new gender ideology, and an old reality, her "new" rules and his "old" feelings. In the absence of basic changes in men, male culture, and the structure of work that keep up with the rapid changes in women, female emotion management smooths over the contradictions. Personal emotion work picks up where social transformtion leaves off. In this case, emotion work is the cost women pay for the absence of change in men and in their circumstances.

Since Nancy's resentment leaked out despite her emotion work, Evan paid an emotional price as well. Indeed, the most important cost of the absence of change in the social pressures on men like Evan may be the harmful ambivalence it introduces into their wives' love for them. Among the working parents I studied, the more the husband shared the load at home, the happier the marriage.

In sum, the men and women in my study pursued gender strategies, created emotional pathways for them, and experienced the emotional consequences of them. The links between gender strategies, the emotional preparation for them, and the emotional consequences of them are sketched in Table 5.1.

PATHS FOR FUTURE RESEARCH

In my research on two-job couples, I mapped out a small theoretical corner for how social actors reconcile the feeling rules that underlie their gender ideologies with how their situations make them feel. I focused on one issue—how working parents divide work at home. But men and women apply gender strategies to many other issues such as finding a mate, improving marriage, ending marriage, raising children, succeeding at work, or more generally rising up the class ladder.

My current research (1988–b) suggests that many advice books for women can be seen as recommended gender strategies for solving such problems. Attached to each gender strategy is often parallel advice on how to feel. For example, in her recent *Being Feminine*, (1988) Toni Grant advises successful thirty-year-old career women in search of a husband to "switch gears," learn to be "soft," and "submissive," and to conceive of her emotional support of her husband as a "career." The prospective bride is advised to avoid all direct expressions of anger, and to express displeasure by withdrawing emotionally—a strategy Grant ominously calls "the black madonna." On the other hand, in *Smart Cookies Don't Crumble* Sonya Friedman (1986) advises women that they will be happier with a man in the long run if they openly assert their needs and feelings.

Although fewer advice books explicitly address the relational problems of men, it would be interesting to compare those that do with advice

TABLE 5.1
Gender Ideology, Strategy, and Emotions

Gender Ideologies	Egalitarian	Traditional
	When wives work full time, men should share work at home.	Even if women work full time, it is women's job to care for the home. Women's sacrificial stance a virtue.
	Sacrifice no more natural to women than men.	
Feeling Rules	Men should want to share; no gratitude owed.	Men have a right to expect gratitude for help.
	Okay for women to enjoy status from work, identify with it.	Only women's identity at home matters.
	A man earns his own and his wife's respect when he identifies himself with activities at home.	Only what a man does at work "counts" with himself and his wife.
Distribution of Ideologies	More women egalitarian.	More men traditional.
Preferred Gender Strategies	Strategies of active change, or maintenance of equality.	Strategies of maintenance of inequality. Some strategies of passive change.
Emotional Pathways	Steel self for assertion, muster indignation.	Suppress personal needs, work ambitions.
Consequences in Emotion Management	Happier with marriage or management of disappointment and anger if husband resists sharing.	Indirect expression of discontent at strain Numbness, "I don't know what I feel."

books for women. In general we need to know more about male gender strategies, and how they apply to problems of love, parenthood, and work. For example, studies show that after divorce, many men lose touch with their children. Terry Arendell (1987) found that over half of the middle-class divorced fathers in California had not seen or called their children in the last three years. What strategies lead to this estrangement? How do fathers feel about losing contact with their children, and how do they manage their feelings?

In advice books as in real life, gender strategies may fit or scrape against the "real self." That is, who we are trying to be, and the feelings that would be useful in our attempt to be who we are trying to be may either naturally fit the self, or they may require us to continually work on our feelings.

EMOTIONAL PREPARATION FOR ETHNIC AND CLASS STRATEGIES

Just as we can speak of gender strategies so, too, can we speak of race and class strategies. Given an individual's placement in the race or class hierarchy, we can ask about what feeling rules will make sense to them, and what ways of managing emotion will seem necessary or right.

Normally, we think of race, class, and gender as stratification systems and as part of the social landscape "out there." Partly they are out there. But at the same time, intuitively, we orient ourselves to these structures. We check our available resources and the opportunities "for a person of my race," "my class," or "my gender." In light of our intuitive grasp of our location in a stratification system, certain ideologies and feeling rules gain appeal, and certain strategies of action unfold. How does the social actor deal with racial antagonism or discrimination—assimilate, retreat, or affiliate with a separate subculture? To what extent do we alter our strategy, and coordinate our emotion work to suit each different context?

In their essay, "The Hero, the Sambo and the Operator," Wellman, Weitzman and Warner (1977) point to certain "racial roles." The Sambo works through avoidance of conflict, ingratiation, and avoidance of the expression of anger, while the Operator remains detached from others. The Hero, on the other hand, confronts inequities directly, and openly expresses his feelings about them. There are analogous informal roles for women. If we conceive of these "roles" as active strategic stances toward a stratification system, we can explore the emotion management that leads to and follows from each stance, each strategy.

One unconscious emotional preparation minorities often develop for integrating with the majority group is to develop a protective sixth sense, a special sensitivity to others that highlights or filters out messages others send "to me as a black, as a gay, as an elderly person, and as a poor person." This functional "social paranoia," we might call it, allows the actor to guard against feeling hurt, or humiliated and to reframe personal insults as "X's prejudice." It is the psychological equivalent of a status shield. We need to know much more about the social categories and situations in which this protective sensitivity works.

If we move from the individual to the organization as the unit of analysis, we see that organizations provide contexts in which strategies unfold (see Kemper and Birenbaum 1988; Hirschhorn 1987.) In the Delta Airlines training program, which I studied for The Managed Heart, flight attendants were told not only how to seem but how to "see," and feel about lost, grumpy, or unruly customers, bossy pilots, or complaining co-workers. Airlines may carry explicit training in feeling rules farther than other organizations, but I believe the principle is the same in other organizations that service the public. Churches, schools, and companies (see Kleinman 1987) promote a sense of the do's and don'ts of feeling. What are these sets of feeling rules? Who are the "lieutenants" who enforce them, and who rebels against them? By what social rituals, formal and informal procedures do organizations get people to feel the "right" way?

In capitalist systems, the most powerful ideologies may be occupational (see Smith and Kleinman 1988; Smith 1988–a, 1988–b). In socialist societies, they may be political. The worker may be exhorted, not to "sell seats for Delta" or "sell yourself," but to be a "heroic worker" building a socialist future. To find out more about worker's feeling rules, we need research across cultures and political systems.

In the Managed Heart I suggested that one-third of all Americans work in jobs that call for emotional labor, a quarter of those men hold and a half of those women do. Others, too, have studied the emotional labor of service workers, for example, Smith (1988–a; 1988–b) has studied emotional labor among nurses. Tolich (1988) has studied it among supermarket checkers. But questions remain: Precisely how does the emotional labor of an executive differ from that of a secretary? How does the emotional labor of a doctor differ from that of a nurse? How does that of a male doctor differ from a female one? In addition, how do occupational cultures set the margins for hostility, jealousy, fellow-feeling in different ways? Do offices with all male employees have different emotional cultures than offices with all female workers? How does gender influence emotional labor? (see Ortiz 1988; Dressler 1987; Pierce 1988). Jennifer Pierce is presently comparing the nature of the emotional labor of men and women in three occupations: litigation attorneys (a stereotypically male profession), paralegals (in-between) and legal secretaries (a stereotypically female job).

For any worker, we can also ask to what extent a change of context from work to home requires the individual to reattune feelings? In what sense, if at all, do people carry feelings caused by experiences at home to their jobs or back the other way? Some women in my study seemed to manage the frustration of "status discrepancies" between home and work. They moved from the office where they enjoyed a status shield (Hochschild 1983; Clark 1987) to their home where they did not. A thirty-five-year-old working mother, who had been promoted from secretary to junior manager, said:

> I sit here [in the office] and I . . . meet with lawyers, and I tell consultants what to do, like a mogul. I get on the bus. I get off the bus and I'm home. I drop that personality completely. The personality I have at work is not the personality I have at home. It's frustrating to have just finished a high-level meeting on an issue involving millions of dollars and two hours later have to say to my husband, "Will you turn off the light when you come out of the kitchen." He thinks that's my job. It's very difficult making the switch those first few hours. I steam inside. The weekend—I'm fine.

In contrast, I interviewed one Chicana worker in a garment factory, a mother of four, who complained of the reverse problem. At home, she felt like a proud authority figure to her four children, but at her sewing machine in a long row of other workers, she felt like a humble worker. She wanted to avoid her children seeing her at work because she would be "too ashamed." These examples pose a further question: Who goes "up" and who goes "down" in status when they come home from work? How does this vary by race and class? Where, relatively speaking, do they feel proud, and where, ashamed? What emotion work does it take to make the transition?

To sum up, I believe one important avenue for research involves describing individual strategies of action and feeling—gender strategies, ethnic strategies, and class strategies. We can study these individual strategies as they help people face situations that arise as a result of patterns of stratification at work, in families, and in other institutional contexts. Strategies are motivated by ideologically inspired ego-ideals and feeling rules inside us. But through them we deal with the realities of stratification (ideological and structural) which are outside us. Insofar as we evoke or suppress anger, joy, sadness in order to ready ourselves for the self we have to sustain for our strategy, we lend emotion to the job of either sustaining or changing larger systems of stratification.

As a field, the sociology of emotion began by hammering a missing shingle on to the sociological house. But in the process of adding it, we are on our way to uncovering a rich store of insights about matters inside the house. With one eye on the individual, and one eye on the systems of stratification that we have always to maneuver around and between, we may begin to see more clearly what is so very social about what we feel.

REFERENCES

Arendell, Terry. 1986. *Women and Divorce.* Berkeley and Los Angeles: University of California Press.

Cancian, Francesca M. 1987. *Love in America.* Cambridge: Cambridge University Press.

Clark, Candace. 1987. "Gender, Status Shields and Humiliation: The Case of the American Elderly." Paper presented at the Southern Sociological Society, Atlanta, Georgia.

———. 1989. "Emotions and Micropolitics in Everyday Life: Some Patterns and Paradoxes of Place." (in this volume)

Dressler, Paula. 1987. "Patriarchy and Social Welfare Work." *Social Problems* 34(3):294–308.

Friedman, Sonya. 1986. *Smart Cookies Don't Crumble.* New York: Pocket Books.

Grant, Toni. 1988. *Being a Woman.* New York: Random House.

Goffman, Erving. 1969. *Strategic Interaction.* Philadelphia: University of Philadelphia Press.

Goffman, Erving. 1956. "Embarrassment and Social Organization." *American Journal and Sociology* 62:264–271.

Gordon, Steven. 1981. "The Sociology of Sentiments and Emotion." in *Social Psychology, Social Perspectives.* Edited by Morris Rosenberg and Ralph Turner. New York: Basic Books.

———. In Press. "The Socialization of Children's Emotions: Emotional Culture, Competence and Exposure." In *Children's Understanding of Emotions.* Edited by Carolyn Saarni and Paul Harris. New York and London: Cambridge University Press.

———. 1985. "Micro-Sociological Theories of Emotions." *Micro-Social Theory: Perspectives on Sociological Theory* 2:123–147. London: Sage.

Hite, Shere. 1987. *Women and Love.* New York: Knopf.

Hirschorn, Larry. 1987. "Organizing Feelings Toward Authority: Two Case Studies of Work Groups." The Wharton Center for Applied Research, Philadelphia.

Hochschild, Arlie Russell. 1975. "The Sociology of Feeling and Emotion: Selected Possibilities." in *Another Voice*, edited by Marcia Millman and Rosabeth Kanter. Garden City, New York: Anchor, pp. 280–307.

―――. 1979. "Emotion Work, Feeling Rules, and Social Structure." *American Journal of Sociology* 85:551–575.

―――. 1983. *The Managed Heart: The Commercialization of Human Feeling.* Berkeley and Los Angeles: University of California Press.

―――. 1989. "The Economy of Gratitude." In *The Sociology of Emotions: Original Essays and Research Papers.* Edited by David D. Franks and E. Doyle McCarthy. New York: JAI Press.

―――. Forthcoming. "Gender Codes in Women's Advice Books." *Beyond Goffman.* Edited by Stephen Riggins. Paris: Mouton de Gruyter.

―――. 1987. "Why Can't a Man Love Like a Woman." Review of Shere Hite's *Women and Love* (November 15) *New York Times Book Review.*

―――. 1989. *The Second Shift: Working Parents and the Revolution at Home.* New York: Viking-Penguin.

Geertz, H. 1959. "The Vocabulary of Emotion." *Psychiatry* 22: 225–237.

Kemper, Theodore. 1978. *A Social Interactional Theory of Emotions.* New York: Wiley.

―――. 1981. "Social Constructionist and Positivist Approaches to the Sociology of Emotions." *American Journal of Sociology* 87:337–362.

―――── and Arnald Birnbaum. 1988. "*Sine Ira Ac Studio?* Emotional Nexi in Weber's Ideal-Typical Conception of Organizations." Paper delivered at the American Sociological Association Meetings, Atlanta.

Lazarus, R. S. Kanner, A. D. and Folkman, S. 1980. "Emotions: A Cognitive-Phenomenological Analysis." pp. 189–218 in *Emotion: Theory, Research and Experience.* Edited by R. Plutchik and H. Kellerman. New York: Academic Press.

Mills, Trudy, and Sherryl Kleinman. 1988. "Emotions, Reflexivity and Action: An Interactionist Analysis." *Social Forces* 66:1009–1027.

Morgan, Edmund. 1944. *The Puritan Family: Religious and Domestic Relations in 17th Century New England.* New York: Harper and Row.

Ortiz, Steven M. 1988. "Emotional Life of the Athlete's Wife." Paper given at the Pacific Sociological Association, April 5–8. Las Vegas, Nevada.

Pierce, Jennifer. 1988. "Gender and Emotional Labor: An Examination of Women and Men at Work in a Corporate Law Firm." Dissertation prospectus, Sociology Department, University of California, Berkeley. Berkeley, California.

Potter, Patricia. 1988. " 'I Killed 'Em:' Comedians' Emotional Labor." Paper presented at the American Sociological Association, August. Atlanta, Georgia.

Scheff, Thomas. 1983. "Toward Integration in the Social Psychology of Emotions." *Annual Review of Sociology* 9:333–354.

——— . In Progress. *Micro-Sociology: Implication and Emotion in Discourse.*

Smith, Allen C. III and Sherryl Kleinman. 1989. "Managing Emotions in Medical School: Students' Contacts with the Living and the Dead." *Social Psychology Quarterly* 52:56–69.

Smith, Pam. 1988. "The Emotional Labor of Nursing." *Nursing Times* 84:50–51.

——— . 1988. "The Nursing Process Revisited." A paper read at the Medical Sociology Group of the British Sociological Association Conference. York, England.

Stanislavsky, Constantin. 1965. *An Actor Prepares.* Translated by Elizabeth Hapgood. New York: Theater Arts Books.

Shott, S. 1979. "Emotion and Social Life: A Symbolic Interactionist Analysis." *American Journal of Sociology* 84:1317–1334.

Schweder, R. A. and R. A. Levine eds. *Culture Theory: Essays on Mind, Self and Emotion.* Cambridge, Cambridge University Press.

Swidler, Ann. 1986. "Culture in Action: Symbols and Strategies." *American Sociological Review* 51:273–286.

Thoits, Peggy A. 1985. "Self Labeling Processes in Mental Illness: The Role of Emotional Deviance." *American Journal of Sociology* 91:221–249.

——— . Forthcoming. "The Sociology of Emotions" *Annual Review of Sociology* 15.

Tolich, Martin. 1988. "Doing Emotion Work: The Similarities and Differences Between Manual Supermarket Checkers and Hochschild's Airline Flight Attendants." Paper presented at the Pacific Sociological Association, April. Las Vegas, Nevada.

Warner, Stephen R. David T. Wellman and Lenore Weitzman. 1971. "The Hero, the Sambo, and the Operator: Reflections on Characterizations of the Oppressed." Paper delivered at the American Sociological Association, August 31. Denver, Colorado.

part four

SOCIAL CONSTRUCTION AND MANAGEMENT OF EMOTIONS

6.

Social Structural Effects on Emotions

Steven L. Gordon*

Originating in the work of Marx, Weber, and Durkheim (House, 1981), the study of social structure and personality has a proud history but an uncertain present. Many studies have examined the effects of social structure (social institutions, mode of economic production, stratification system, urbanization, societal size, complexity, and integration) on individual psychological characteristics (personality, attitudes, beliefs, identity, behavioral tendencies). Yet, recently, major reviews have concluded that the field is dormant and have called for its revival (e.g., diRenzo, 1977; House, 1981; Ryff, 1987; Turner, 1988). Interest in the field has declined because of its reliance on currently unpopular Freudian and functionalist theories and because of empirical questions about the validity of personality constructs (see reviews by Price-Williams, 1985 and by Snyder & Ickes, 1985). Research shifted from studying broad social structural effects on types of personality to research on consequences of delimited social units (e.g., family size) for particular dimensions of the person (e.g., intelligence). Current work in the field focuses mainly on cognitive factors, such as attitudinal and self-concept variables (Elder, 1974; Gecas, 1981; Inkeles, 1983; Inkeles & Smith, 1974; Kohn, 1969; Kohn & Schooler, 1983; Rosenberg, 1979).

Research on a new topic, emotion, may revitalize the analysis of social structure and personality, and social psychology generally. According to James House (1981), social psychology has split into "three faces" or separate branches: the psychological social psychology of individual outcomes, symbolic interactionist analysis of face-to-face encounters, and the social structure and personality field. Thus far the sociology of emotions has followed the path of either psychological social psychology, concerned with explaining individual emotional experience, or of symbolic interactionism, concerned with the social construction of emotions in face-to-face interactions and relationships. With few exceptions (e.g., Collins, 1975, 1984; Elias, 1978 [1939]; Gordon, 1989b; Hammond, 1986 and this volume; Hochschild, 1983), systematic consideration of large-scale social structural influence on emotion has lagged. Were the sociology of emotions to in-clude as well the social structure and personality "face" of social psychol-ogy—perhaps it would help to integrate that fragmented discipline.

THEORETICAL QUESTIONS ABOUT SOCIAL STRUCTURE AND EMOTION

To develop a research agenda, I will apply theoretical questions from the social structure and personality field to the sociology of emotions.

Effects of Social Structure and Culture. Any large-scale social phenome-non has both structural and cultural effects on the individual (House, 1981; Inkeles, 1983). "Social structure" refers to persisting patterns of social rela-tionships that establish situational contingencies and constraints, motivat-ing behavior and instigating emotion. "Emotional culture," as I term it, includes emotion vocabularies (words for emotions), norms (regulating ex-pression and feeling), and beliefs about emotions (e.g., the idea that "re-pressed" emotion is disturbing). An illustration of the parallel effects of social structure and culture is the "sophistication of sensibility," the joint emergence of family privacy and emotional intimacy among Tuscan nobil-ity on the eve of the Renaissance (de la Ronciere, 1988). The events and circumstances that established preconditions for emotions were structural: (a) the new segregation of households from outsiders, (b) the separation of family members on trade and military missions, (c) the custom of caring for sick and dying family members at home, and more. These patterns of rela-tionships produced emotional situations, for example, longing for absent family members, the joy of family reunions, and exposure to the prolonged agonies of loved ones. The quality, intensity, object, and setting of emo-tional reactions to these situations depended on emotional culture, espe-cially the growing distinction between the private and public worlds. Women were expected to be unexpressive in public but could be emotion-ally spontaneous within the household. Social "situations viewed with in-difference when they involved outsiders were here [in the household] experienced more personally and directly, with emotion and even passion" (de la Ronciere, 1988, p. 267). Social structure and emotional culture sometimes produce independent emotional effects. More research is needed, but evidence suggests that direct emotional reactions to structured relationships and events do not necessarily coincide with cultural prescrip-tions (Hochschild, 1983; Stearns, 1985; Stearns & Stearns, 1986).

Intermediary Social Structures. The major failing of social structure and personality study may be its frequent inability to explicate obtained corre-lations between specific aspects of the two levels (Elder, 1973; House, 1981;

Ryff, 1987). Effects of large-scale social structure on emotion—and of emotion on social structure—are mediated through smaller groups or institutions in which the individual participates directly (Turner, 1988). The articulation of social structure with emotion depends upon microsocial interpersonal ties—for example, marriages, childrearing relationships, social networks—through which macrosocial structures have their effects. For instance, emotions between fathers and sons have been strongly influenced throughout history by societal patterns of inheritance. Roman fathers held unlimited power over their adult sons, including the right to disinherit or even condemn them to death. Roman sons commonly hated and feared their fathers, as shown by a high rate of patricide, because of the legal and economic shaping of the father-son relationship (Veyne, 1987). Thus, intervening social relationships and groups intensify, mitigate, or even nullify the influence of the larger social order upon the person, and they also serve as mechanisms through which the individual's emotions react back upon the social structure (House, 1977).

Specification of Factors. Which specific aspects of a structural variable are relevant to its effects on emotion? The sociology of emotion should specify the proposed linkages between macro and micro constructs, and test alternative links. What is it about working in a service occupation that influences emotional experience and expression (Hochschild, 1983)? Assumptions about the quality, duration, intensity, expression, controllability, and other properties of emotions are implicit in many sociological theories. For example, Georg Simmel (1964 [1903]) asserted that urbanization leads people to become emotionally reserved because humans have a limited quantity of affect to give out. Therefore, he argued, the rapidly changing and diverse social contacts of urban life threaten to cause nervous overstimulation, against which people protect by withholding emotion from most social interactions. Simmel's hypothesis is noteworthy because it specifies the relevant, connective factors in city life and in emotional processes.

Stability of Components. Personality theorists usually distinguish between core elements that are relatively stable and have pervasive effects, and peripheral elements that are more changeable. Which emotional components are relatively dynamic, open to influence from social structure, and which are more intractable? Any emotion may be analyzed into four components: feeling, expressive gestures, relationship concepts, and regulative norms (Gordon, 1981). Some emotions appear to have a stable core of elements that appear universally, such as the fear and impulse to flee when aroused by a threat situation (however defined), or the surge of anger elicited by the interruption of an engrossing activity. Social construction is most evident in emotion vocabularies, in rules governing expression and feeling, in situational definitions of emotion-relevant meanings, and in instrumental behavior (such as courtship behavior to pursue a love partner).

Which components of any emotion are so central that a change in them produces a concomitant change in the entire emotion system? I believe that the central factor is a person's definition of a situation, which determines the direction and continuity of even innate or automatic emotional sequences. For example, when you realize that the stranger who was grabbing you from behind is actually your playful friend, your redefinition of the situation will probably transform your anger or fear to delight. Your behavioral impulses to flee or strike back will be stifled, and your subjective experience will shift from negative to positive (although you may feel residual excitement and annoyance at being surprised).

Content Versus Abstract Analytical Variables. Sociological research has focused on *content* variables, particular emotions or specific emotional relationships such as romantic love. On a larger scale, studies have concentrated on particular institutions and historical periods, such as capitalist service occupations (Hochschild, 1983), and Renaissance court life (Elias, 1978 [1939]). Little effort has been given to developing a comprehensive theory of the social processes common across emotions, such as the development of language labels for emotions. Greater advances might be made by focusing on content-independent, abstract variables (such as complexity or integration of components) that apply across particular emotions and social structures. For example do more differentiated societies produce a more refined emotion vocabulary, that is, more precise distinctions among emotions? (For a challenge to this hypothesis, see Lutz & White, 1986). The risk in abstracting general variables from content research is that across different societies, the relationship among emotional components varies (e.g., how powerfully perception evokes feeling, or how closely expression corresponds to feeling).

Relativity of Emotion Psychology. Because emotion vocabularies, norms, and expressive behaviors vary across cultures, theories of emotion developed within one society may not apply to explain emotions in other societies. Extrapolation of the Western psychology of emotion to other societies has been challenged by anthropologists who view our science as merely another "ethnopsychology," or folk belief system (D'Andrade, 1987; Levy & Wellencamp, in press; Lutz, 1985; Rosaldo, 1984; Ryff, 1987). For example, the psychoanalytic theory that unexpressed emotion becomes repressed as long lasting frustration may not apply to the Philippine Ilongot, who are reported to be able to decide to forget anger without residual tensions (Rosaldo, 1984). This challenge extends to basic conceptual distinctions in

Western psychology and sociology. For example, non-Western cultures may not distinguish between private feeling and public self-presentation (Lutz, 1982; Rosaldo, 1984).

Dynamics of Social Change in Emotions. Most research in the sociology of emotion has been ethnographic or correlational, not longitudinal or historical. Therefore, as in social structure and personality research (Elder, 1981; Ryff, 1987), the dynamics of social change in emotion are largely unexplored. The term "social structure" connotes a permanence that may obscure dynamic processes such as industrialization, social mobility, and urbanization. However classical theories contain suggestive hypotheses about emotional change. Cooley (1962 [1909]), for example, asserted that emotions in traditional society were occasional and intense, but modern emotions are frequent and mild. Abundance and choice of social contacts diffuses emotion and gives rise to new varieties of emotion, he argued. A contrasting viewpoint is held by historians who argue that although individuals in the past possessed little capacity for emotional sharing, emotional experience has become progressively richer, with more tenderness and less cruelty and indifference (see Demos, 1986, for a critique).

Any major change in social organization has implications for members' emotional experience and expression, particularly for (1) the relationships and groups in which emotions are experienced, such as family structure; (2) courses of behavior by which emotion is expressed; (3) the vocabulary by which emotions are identified; (4) the norms prescribing appropriate feeling and expression; and (5) the personal temperaments and styles of emotion that a society favors or disfavors. Structural transformations such as the transition from a blue-collar to a white-collar labor force can profoundly alter emotional experience and behavior (Hochschild, 1979, 1983; Stearns & Stearns, 1986). Change in a structural variable can have multiple emotional effects. For example, increases in parental affection toward children and in jealousy among siblings have both been attributed to the long-term reduction in family size (Stearns, 1988; Wells, 1971).

Individual Effects on Social Structure. How do emotional experiences and behavior of individuals feedback to influence social structure? Emotions have generally been examined as dependent variables. An advance in theorizing would be to examine emotions as intervening variables between one stage of social structure and the following stage in time. Emotional microrituals can reproduce the social structure (Collins, 1984). As an illustrative hypothesis, a Spanish psychiatrist suggested to me that in Catholic countries the confession ritual provides practice in expression that is generalized to other social expression of emotions and to institutions such as family and art (and contributes to the stereotype of the "expressive Latin"). Widespread patterns of individual emotion alter social structure, much as stylistic variation in performing a role can modify role expectations.

DEFINING A SOCIOLOGICAL APPROACH TO EMOTIONS

A sociological perspective reveals how seemingly individual experience and action, such as emotions, are influenced by social forces. The social significance of emotion should be explicable mainly by reference to other social phenomena, rather than by psychological variables.

The socially emergent dimensions of emotion include:

1. *Origin.* Most emotions originate in cultural definitions of human relationships, not in human biological nature. Although there are "primary" emotions composed of some universal elements (Kemper, 1987), even those emotions are subject to social definition and constraint. Fuller social construction is the case for most emotions—sympathy, sorrow, guilt, envy, humor, nostalgia, jealousy, and other sentiments.
2. *Time.* Psychological research usually investigates short-term reactions, instead of more lasting emotions—for example, love, friendship, hatred, vengeance—which are important in enduring social relationships. Sociologists understand that emotion is determined not only by present conditions, but also by cumulative properties of a social relationship based on past interactions, and by anticipations of future contacts.
3. *Structure.* The coherence of an emotion's components is maintained by psychological and social forces. A particular situation's meaning evokes specific feelings that are displayed through certain expressive gestures and instrumental actions, to which other people may respond with approval or condemnation, empathy or indifference. The nature of the particular components (e.g., which situation? what expressive gestures? what social reaction?) varies as social structural and cultural factors change. Social interaction often proceeds on the basis of what emotions seem to be present, not necessarily what is being felt. The social organization of an emotion can be partly or wholly independent of what an individual is privately experiencing.
4. *Change.* Micro-level change in emotion can be socially caused (e.g., a person transforms an emotion by adhering to expression norms), not purely psychological (e.g., the physiological arousal curve for anger or fear). Self-regulation of emotions is one answer to our theoretical question about how individuals modify or reproduce social structure. Macro-level change can result from historical trends in cultural advice about

how to reduce, intensify, or substitute emotions (Cancian & Gordon, 1988; Stearns & Stearns, 1986).

Social structural effects on emotion flow through at least three interactional processes. In emotion *differentiation*, societies and subgroups distinguish in their language and social behavior among many types of an emotion. Forms of anger can be culturally identified as annoyance, irritation, rage, fury, bitterness, jealousy, or vengeance, for example, each leading to different social interaction patterns. Through *socialization*, individuals learn to feel, attend to, express, and recognize the particular emotions identified in their society. Finally, the *management* of sentiments is the regulation of both expression and feeling according to norms of appropriateness. These three social processes link the larger social structure with the emotional experience and behavior of individuals.

DIFFERENTIATION OF EMOTIONS

A distinguishing characteristic of emotions as compared, say, to thoughts, is that emotions have been given different, common names. The verbal distinction between shame and guilt, or love and liking, is socially important. What elements form a particular emotion and differentiate it from other emotions? When lay persons and scientists describe emotions, at least these four components of experience and behavior are commonly mentioned:

1. *Bodily sensations.* Physiological feeling or arousal is usually mentioned in reports of emotion. Psychologists have focused mainly on intense emotions (anger, fear, for example), while overlooking low-arousal emotions such as gratitude or sympathy. In their theories, conscious sensations are sometimes distinguished from bodily changes of which the person is not subjectively aware. For sociologists, covert organic states may not bear much significance unless expressed in social action.
2. *Expressive gestures and actions.* An emotion's visible expression is through facial and bodily displays and instrumental actions. Although there are universal, inborn facial expressions for a set of basic emotions (anger, fear, surprise, disgust, contempt, sadness, and joy) (Ekman, 1982; Izard, 1977), these natural expressions are often masked or concealed in actual social interaction. There do not appear to be universal, innate facial expressions for most emotions; thus, there are no inborn muscle movements of eyebrows, mouth, jaw, and so forth to display jealousy, compassion, or love, although there are many culturally conventional and

personal styles. The natural prototype of facial expression is of less sociological interest than the socialized, culturally-specific form of the component that actually occurs in social interaction.

3. *A social situation or relationship.* An emotion is a reaction to a situation, usually of social origin, such as a change in a social relationship. The person responds to the situation as he/she interprets it, so this is both a cognitive and social component. The different qualities of pride, indignation, grief, enthusiasm, for example, reflect different appraisals about the meaning of social situations or relationships.

4. *Emotional culture.* For every emotion, we learn associated vocabulary, norms, and beliefs about it. Emotional culture allows members of a society to identify and discuss emotions, evaluate them as desirable or undesirable, and regulate them in line with values and norms (Gordon, 1981, 1985, 1989a). For example, to influence other people's emotional reactions, we usually employ a "naive psychology," or folk theory, about the determinants of emotion (Weiner, 1987).

Two polar positions on emotional differentiation merit attention here, defining emotions either as a universal set of innate responses, or else as culturally-specific social patterns.

Basic Emotions. Psychologists cite a list of emotions with universal, inborn facial expressions as the most basic or primary emotions (Ekman, 1982; Izard, 1977) from which all other emotions may be derived as "blends" (Plutchik, 1980). Is this approach useful for sociologists? We cannot assume human emotional nature to be infinitely malleable, and must search for any biological or psychological limiting conditions that constrain the social construction of emotions. However, some basic emotions—surprise and disgust, especially—may be environmentally adaptive but do not seem very important for social structures and relationships. Moreover, basic emotions had evolutionary value as facial signals and action cues among *prehistoric* humans. Might there be a set of "sociologically basic" emotions more relevant to social interaction in the modern era—sympathy, group loyalty, intergroup hostility, resentment, and so forth? These emotions need not be universal. Indeed they would be important precisely because they were constructed as adaptations to a particular societal type and its macrosociological characteristics—economy, stratification, urbanization, the mililtary order, and so forth.

Ethnopsychology of Emotions. Do Western sciences of emotion inevitably reflect our own ethnopsychological (folk psychology) cultural assumptions and biases? For example, public emotional displays by members of preliterate cultures often seem incongruous to Western observers: people joke and laugh during funerals, and a warrior may stop during a furious battle charge to adjust his headdress (Heider, 1984). These side involvements of emotional actors may appear to us to be insincere or an inadequate performance. Our Western assumption is that emotions are feelings and bodily sensations inside the individual, whose overt behavior should be consistent with the presumed inner state. But from a non-Western viewpoint, the referent of emotion words is mainly to social action, not inner essences. Non-Western peoples often view emotions as public performances that make a statement about a situation or social relationship (LeVine, 1980; Lutz, 1982, 1985).

There are problems in the crosscultural "translation of emotional worlds" (Lutz & White, 1986). The non-Western conception of "public social emotion" seems more compatible with a sociological perspective than is the Western psychological view of emotion as covert states. Research is needed on cross-cultural variation in the locus of emotions, examining which components are given greatest emphasis by the culture as being "the emotion." We might try to classify societies as being "feeling cultures," "expression cultures," "situation cultures," or "norm cultures," according to which component is emphasized in the cultural definition of the emotion and in collective reactions to emotion episodes.

DIFFERENTIATION AS THE LABELING OF AROUSAL

I have argued (Gordon, 1981) that emotion should be viewed as an "open system" in which the entire combination of elements is socially constructed, rather than a closed system in which society merely activates or stimulates the fixed connections (e.g., from feeling to expression). Any biological reductionism threatened to rule out the effects of social forces, a premature closure of emotion against social influences. In order to avoid an oversocialized conception of emotion, however, I also sought to integrate social influences on emotion with a physiological substrate.

The most compatible emotion theory then seemed to be psychologist Stanley Schachter's (1964) two-factor theory, in which emotions are produced by interaction between generalized feedback from physiological responses and a cognitive appraisal of what caused those responses. This theory seemed sociologically heuristic, because it said that arousal can result from a broad spectrum of different social sources, and generalized arousal could become any emotion. Finally, arousal's label could be derived from many forms of emotional culture—emotional modeling by others, situational definitions, normative expectations, and so forth.

I no longer regard the two-factor theory as a firm psychological foundation for the sociology of emotions. The original experiment's (Schachter

& Singer, 1962) design and conclusions have been challenged (Cotton, 1981; Kemper, 1978; Marshall & Zimbardo, 1979; Maslach, 1979; Reisenzein, 1983; Scheff, 1979). To summarize some of the theory's shortcomings, (1) arousal may not be necessary for emotion; a belief that one is aroused may be sufficient; (2) undifferentiated arousal of unknown origin may be experienced as negative emotion, not neutral; and (3) unexplained arousal emerges only under highly restrictive conditions and is unusual in everyday life.

An item for our agenda is to reexamine psychological theories of emotion, such as the two-factor theory, to see what can be saved for sociological use. These theories describe psychological processes through which social structure may influence individual emotion. Convincing support for part of Schachter's theory comes from studies showing that misinterpreted arousal can intensify emotional experience (Reisenzein, 1983). The misattribution process does not start an emotion but instead augments an emotion already felt (Leventhal & Tomarken, 1986; Valins, 1966; Zillman, 1978). Residual arousal can be unintentionally transferred from one emotion to another. This occurs when the individual is unaware of the true cause of the original emotion (e.g., we might forget that our body is still physically excited) and when the prior and the current emotions are similar in intensity, and in positivity or negativity. In what social structures do individuals move rapidly from one arousing situation to another? This transition probably occurs more in urban than rural settings (e.g., moving in traffic from home to job), and more in large bureaucracies that require a series of face-to-face encounters with strangers. What circumstances would obscure the true causes of arousal? Cultural feeling rules require people to align their emotions with appropriate standards; in so doing the residual arousal may remain covertly and intensify any subsequent emotions. Thus, without conceding the validity of psychological theories, we can develop their implications for analysis of emotions in social life.

VOCABULARY OF EMOTIONS

Sociologists have been interested in the cultural vocabulary of words used to identify emotions of self and others. A vocabulary is composed of labels for emotions that are (1) common experiences for many members, (2) centered on significant concerns in social interaction, and (3) sufficiently distinguished as units. Modern languages contain hundreds of emotion names (Averill, 1975). When U.S. children and adults were asked to label the feelings of actors whom they watched on TV, they used 786 different words (Storm & Storm, 1987). This profusion of terms is almost certainly greater than the range of internal sensations we can discriminate, or the variety of facial expressions we can recognize (Gordon, 1981).

Precision in Emotion Vocabulary. A vocabulary sensitizes people disproportionately to some facets of feeling, behavior, and situation. How does social structure influence the relative precision of distinctions made by a vocabulary in different areas of feeling? The emotions finely discriminated in language are probably those that are important for making subtle distinctions in socially crucial relationships and institutions—family, economy, government, religion, and so forth. Societies may develop a wealth of terms to emphasize culturally valued emotions, but also to warn against varieties of a dangerous emotion that must be controlled (Levy & Wellencamp, in press). As Arlie Hochschild (personal communication) has suggested, the naming of an emotion is a form of control in itself, acknowledging the emotion's importance and making it subject to potential regulation.

Research on vocabularies has been conducted mainly in non-Western societies, but the social origins of emotional distinctions should be investigated among our own gender, age, ethnic, regional, and occupational subcultures, such as the vocabulary that service workers use for coping with angry clients, "irates," as Hochschild (1983) reports they are called.

What problems develop in social interaction from lack of a name for an emotion, or when a broad emotional domain (e.g., sadness) is only grossly discriminated by language? We cannot assume that lack of a name necessarily prevents emotional experience, although a linguistic void would make the experience difficult to remember or talk about. Anthropologists have described "covert categories" of emotion that people do not label verbally, but which can be inferred by observers from patterns of behavior and expression (Levy & Wellencamp, in press).

Emotion Prototypes. Most emotion vocabulary studies have been horizontal, analyzing semantic distinctions across parallel categories or types of emotion. An important new approach to categorizing emotions suggests that people conceive of emotions as organized hierarchically, from a highly abstract level (e.g., "negative emotion") to a middle level ("anger, fear") to a very specific level ("alarm, panic, dread") (Shaver, Schwartz, et al., 1987; Schwartz & Shaver, 1987). The middle level is used most often, has the shortest words, and is learned earliest in childhood. People agree on emotion prototypes, the most representative examples of an emotion's typical features—when it occurs, how it feels, what you do to control it. These prototypes are used as "scripts" for interpreting our own and other's emotions in terms of typical antecedents, behavioral responses, and self-control procedures. Thus, a prototype is a micro-concept of social structure, describing relational and interactional patterns that are typical and stable. Our research agenda calls for sociological studies into how prototypes are developed in a society, acquired in socialization, employed to make sense out of experience, and used to detect deviant emotions that vary from what is typical and expected.

We also need to know how the internally consistent set of components in a prototype changes over time. As noted above in our discussion of ethnopsychology, the cultural logic of consistency between feeling and expression is often subtle or obscure to outsiders. For example, some historians contend that historical emotional experience was impoverished, on the basis of such evidence as a parent's use of strict physical punishment, or a husband's formal written greetings to his wife. Yet in that era, such behaviors were not necessarily inconsistent with genuinely warm feelings. For example, harsh punishment of a child was often a loving act, necessary to preserve the child's divine grace and salvation (Demos, 1982). Thus, a prototype's internal consistency is a culturally constructed logic.

Ordinary Language for Emotion. Most vocabulary studies have focused on formal word lists, such as nouns for emotional states. Studies are needed of ordinary conversations in which emotions (or gestures, feelings, moods, sensations, etc.) are discussed using slang, folk sayings, and other informal, technically incomplete or ambiguous language (e.g., "horny," "yucky," "pissed off"). Rom Harré's social constructionist theory (1986) assigns highest priority to the analysis of vocabulary use, narrative forms, and other language games. My work calls attention to emotional social types—names such as hothead, bully, redneck, sissy, wimp, and so forth, that are used critically to demarcate the normative boundaries of appropriate feeling and expression, labeling excesses and deficits in social emotions (Gordon, 1981, 1989b). Research is needed into other oblique ways by which people categorize and comment upon emotions in social interaction.

A RESEARCH AGENDA ON NEGLECTED EMOTIONS

Love, anger, fear, grief, and jealousy have received the most attention from psychologists and sociologists, but even these emotions remain poorly understood in their social forms. For example, anger research has concentrated on its intense variations, despite the fact that relatively mild irritation and annoyance are the most common emotional experience in everyday life (Scherer, Wallbott, & Summerfield, 1986). Of the "universal basic" emotions, disgust and surprise have received little investigation, especially with regard to their social implications. Surprise is a frequent tool in rituals of teasing and challenging other people, and is also a tactic for detecting someone's spontaneous feelings by catching them off guard. Disgust, a revulsion at certain organic substances, serves as a basis for socializing moral reactions; witness the power of epithets such as "pig," "scumbag," "shithead," "worm," and so forth. The social significance of disgust in moral stigmatization and in caste stratification systems involves the irrational belief, distinctive to disgust, that people can be contaminated by contact with a disgusting substance or even by its sight or smell (Rozin & Fallon, 1987).

The social emotions or sentiments have not been studied intensively. A research agenda should examine the social structural bases of:

- pride, hope, envy, resentment and other emotions related to success and failure in an open mobility society;
- awe, wonder, astonishment, and other reactions to novel or uncanny stimuli; are these infrequent in a "sophisticated" culture?
- patriotism and religious reverence as emotions developed by and legitimated by social institutions;
- boredom, ennui, melancholy, loneliness, and other low arousal emotions that Durkheim predicted would be common in modern society;
- regret, remorse, and emotions that serve as moral accounts;
- gratitude as a currency owed and paid socially;
- hatred, vengeance, and other persistent hostility cultivated in feuds, terrorism, and war.

ANALYZING THE SOCIAL-STRUCTURAL DIFFERENTIATION OF EMOTIONS

The study of the social-structural differentiation of emotions is rife with uncertainties, partly because of the difficulty of reliably detecting the shifting emotional patterns by which particular social relationships, feelings, expressions, and norms differentiate and recombine. Several basic questions can be raised for the research agenda. First, analysis is needed of the social structural and cultural circumstances that are prerequisite to experiencing and expressing a particular emotion. With the disappearance of what social conditions would the emotion become unknown, archaic, or incomprehensible? As Gerth and Mills noted (1964 [1953]), for example, the delicate and fainting upper status lady of the nineteenth century had leisure time for such reactions and could expect gentlemanly attention, but her maid could not afford to faint, even at the same sight or event.

Content-rich descriptions of historical or culturally-specific emotions can reveal insightfully some of the preconditions for specific emotions. An example is Rom Harré's analysis (1986) of *accidie,* a medieval emotion resulting from laziness in fulfilling one's religious duties. The emotion blended boredom with gloom and fear over losing God's grace, and thus depended upon certain religious beliefs and obligations being accepted. Similar analyses could be done of other Medieval emotions such as hubris, hauteur, and courtesie, linked to one's status in the feudal system.

The differentiation of new emotions usually affects some individuals and groups more than others. An illustration is Max Scheler's argument (1961 [1915]) that a seemingly open mobility system encourages comparisons to be made upward in class, resulting in a cumulation of repressed hatred, envy, and desire for revenge—*ressentiment*. This emotion is distributed unevenly across society, however, and is concentrated among powerless and inexpressive strivers: the lower middle class, women more than men, and oppressed minorities. Thus, the combination of components into a new emotion often occurs only at certain locations in the social structure.

Differentiation is not always the emergence of a previously unknown emotion, but can be an elaboration or altered salience of a recognized emotion. For example, marital emotions are modified by changes in a society's sex ratio (Guttentag & Second, 1983). When women are scarce, men's romantic sentiments and possessive jealousy are magnified, keeping women in essential childbearing and domestic roles. When women are in oversupply, however, men avoid romantic commitment and move among partners.

Finally, a structural transformation can produce change across a range of different emotions in a particular interactional domain. In seventeenth century Europe, the availability of rental housing (Paris) and stringent taxation on servants (Amsterdam) permitted the separation of the bourgeois dwelling from the workplace (Rybczynski, 1986). Privacy, and the feminization of the home under the wife's jurisdiction, fostered a set of emotions related to family intimacy, comfort, and domesticity, such as coziness, Gemütlichkeit, and annoyance at intruding visitors.

SOCIALIZATION OF EMOTIONS

Socialization allows the growing child to develop into a functioning member of society by acquiring the cognitive and behavioral skills to act within the emotional culture. In its original sense, socialization meant the taming of inborn human nature, making impulses and behavior fit for social life. Since the late Middle Ages, European elites have held "the civilizing process" to be a mark of their superiority as a caste or class, and later as a nation (Elias, 1978 [1939]). The boundary between the feudal lords' courtly circle and the unrefined peasantry was demarcated by *courtoisie*, a distinguishing code of behavior displayed through emotions such as shame, embarrassment, and repugnance, indicating one's heightened sensitivity to social etiquette. Later as the feudal system disintegrated and people from diverse regions came into greater contact, emotional socialization was reflected in *civilité*, a more deliberate impression management and intense self-control over emotions.

A tenet of the social structure and personality tradition was that the content of socialization corresponds to functional requirements of the society. For example, the transition of the United States from a production-oriented frontier society to a consumption-based urban society necessitated a substitution of a more flexible other-directed, shame-oriented social character in place of the inner-directed, guilt-driven character (Riesman, 1950). If innate emotions serve functions that are (or were) adaptive for group life, perhaps socially constructed emotions also fulfill adaptive functions for their society. Emotions may, for example, motivate individuals to strive for collective goals, and also promote social control of behavior through empathy, embarrassment, guilt, and shame. The content and salience of various emotions should therefore correspond to the kinship system, division of labor, stratification hierarchy, and other macrosociological patterns of a society. Socialization goals and processes should be a key link between the larger social order and the emotional experiences that motivate and regulate individuals.

SOCIALIZATION PROCESSES

The fundamental processes of emotional socialization are familiar and probably occur universally. Caregivers provide rewards to reinforce appropriate emotional behavior and administer punishments to inhibit inappropriate emotion ("big boys don't cry"). Modeling and identification also are important processes, as children imitate the emotional models set by their parents, peers, and significant others. Caregivers also label emotions for children, indicating the logic of consistency or inconsistency among components ("you don't sound as if you're sorry"). Through such references the child gradually constructs a conception of the whole emotion with its components. Facial and gestural expressions and other overt components of an emotion are probably mastered before inner feelings and situational concepts are understood—an "outward to inward" progression in emotional socialization. Caregivers' goals and techniques are guided by their ethnopsychology, particularly their standards for developing an adult emotional character and their beliefs about the emotional nature of children, such as whether children are tabulae rasae or have inborn impulses.

Cognitive and motor development set limiting conditions on the shaping of emotions by social structure. The abilities required to recognize, express, feel, and control emotions depend upon development of the self-concept, growth of empathic ability, and the decline of early childhood egocentrism. For example, as a child's role-taking ability develops, he or she can infer what others are feeling and how they feel toward him or her. Self-reflexive emotions such as pride, embarrassment, shame, and guilt develop along with self-awareness. Comprehension of the adult meanings underlying complex emotions must await advanced cognitive development. For example, young children's grief and mourning is restrained by their inability to grasp the irreversibility of death because they lack an understanding of permanence and reversibility generally (Elkind, 1979).

Children learn emotions in the course of adjusting to interaction with others. They become aware that an emotional display can serve as an interactional technique and resource. Shame and guilt, for example are learned as defensive tactics that may deter punishment. Anger can attract attention and forestall others' aggression. The social consequences of expressing an emotion become part of its meaning.

Structural change alters intervening institutions, such as the family and school, in which children adjust to emotional situations. When the workplace separated from the family household in the nineteenth century United States, the mother's prominence as an emotional model increased. Because women had traditionally been less tolerant toward anger in themselves than were men, children's anger became more controlled than when their father was more involved as an emotional role model (Stearns & Stearns, 1986).

A SOCIAL STRUCTURAL RESEARCH AGENDA ON SOCIALIZATION

Emotional Competence. Every society and subgroup (e.g., social classes, ethnic communities) direct their socialization of members according to conceptions of the knowledge and abilities required to be emotionally competent (Gordon, 1989b; Lutz & White, 1986; Saarni, 1989). For instance, the greater the division of labor between the sexes, the more women and men are socialized to have different emotional capacities (Blumberg, 1977; Collier & Rosaldo, 1981; Sanday, 1981). Thus, one's competence and social acceptance as a member of a gender depends partly on acquisition and display of emotional knowledge and abilities. Research is needed on the emotional skills, vocabulary, and social norms that permit members to feel, express, recognize, and control emotions as effective participants in group life. We also must ask critically, how closely do a society's socialization ideals correspond to the knowledge and abilities that actually are effective in social interaction?

Favored Temperament. How does temperament, or inborn emotional disposition, influence selection for differential socialization into social roles? Although empirical support for "personality types" has waned, substantial evidence still supports the existence of stable, individual differences in specific traits relevant to emotional feeling and expression. Infants differ in emotional sensitivity, activity level, quality of mood, introversion, and other emotional tendencies (Buss & Plomin, 1975; Goldsmith & Campos, 1982; Thomas & Chess, 1977). Some children's inborn temperament will fit well with culturally preferred emotional styles, and they will be socially favored as being more emotionally competent. They receive favorable attention and serve as models for other children, as in lessons in how to be friendly or display respect. Children whose temperament contrasts with the cultural ideal are regarded as emotional deviants and may be denied access to socially central roles. The majority of children are socialized to emulate the favored temperament, thereby creating the impression of a "national character," like the placid Swede or excitable Italian.

Culturally-favored types change with larger structural transformations. An economic shift in the U.S. during the 1940s and 1950s increased the importance of the managerial and service-sector economy, in which the favored emotional type was friendly and pleasing to others while restraining temper and competitiveness (Stearns & Stearns, 1986, p. 170). Advice literature on management style, and on marriage and child rearing, called for the prevention and elimination of anger. We may assume that children born with a temperament predisposed to calm and low reactivity were preferred over those who were naturally irritable and expressive.

Differential Exposure to Emotions. Exposure to an emotion—having the opportunity to experience, observe, or be told about the emotion—is an obvious precondition for being able to adapt to it and conceptualize it. A person's position in a social structure (class, gender, generational memberships, etc.) determines the type, frequency, and intensity of emotions that will be directed to the person or aroused in him or her (Gordon, 1989b). For example, Puritan children were intentionally aroused with the "terrors of separation, mortality, and damnation," and Colonial children were freely "exposed to the emotional concerns of their elders" (Stannard, 1977; Demos, 1986). To develop their competence in a mass society, modern children are exposed by their parents to public settings with demands for civility and self-control (Cahill, 1987).

The "aim of feelings" is the differential targeting of emotions across social groups and categories, whereby some individuals receive more exposure to particular emotions than do others (Hochschild, 1975). The wealthy and physically attractive must cope with envy directed at them, for example, while the poor and unattractive must adapt to disparaging humor, contempt, and moral indignation directed against them. Employees, too, find themselves exposed to demands requiring specialized emotional skills and adjustments. For example, large-scale work organizations include "emotional climate and types of emotional interchange: mutual support, subtle intimidation, periodic explosiveness, apathetic conformity, enthusiastic effort, ingratiation" (Inkeles & Levinson, 1963, p. 225). Research is needed on different emotional environments and on the adjustments required of their members through exposure to emotions.

Diverse Socialization. Individuals are socialized by various agents and groups—parents, siblings, non-family adults, peers, and mass media—who often hold contradictory views about emotions. The "marginal person" with membership in two cultures can adopt either group's perspective on a situation and often synthesizes a new one (Park, 1928; Stonequist, 1937). If we apply this social type to emotions, we may hypothesize that a marginal person feels mixed emotions about an event to which the two membership groups react differently. It may be hypothesized that these emotional responses are low in intensity (in parallel with the argument that marginal people's dual group identities both are uncertain and tentative). Effects of diverse socialization should be investigated among individuals who are mobile across different emotional subcultures of class or ethnicity, or who interact mainly with members of other subcultures (e.g., a girl who has only brothers, or a child who grows up primarily with adults). Anthropological studies have focused on small, homogeneous, and isolated communities and do not usually examine contradiction among multiple agents. Research on the effects of diversity among socialization agents should inform us about how individuals acquire a range of vocabularies, norms, and expressive styles, and how such diverse socialization becomes integrated in a person's emotional behavior and experience.

Socialization Sequence. The effects of social structural position on emotional socialization should be analyzed according to the *sequence* and *continuity* of socialization. Children develop a culturally competent understanding of some emotions before other emotions. The sequence reflects differential emphases placed upon various emotions, so that the individual receives anticipatory socialization into emotions that are of greater significance for group interaction. Research should examine how degree of *continuity* in socialization influences the internalization of emotional culture. Early socialization often differs from what is expected later in life (e.g., adults having to restrain most emotions more than do children). Emotional vocabulary, expressive techniques, and norms learned later must be substituted for, or merged with, socialization content already acquired. As abstract concepts, "sequence" and "diversity" can be employed to analyze socialization of emotions in family, occupations, and other structural settings.

Emotional socialization is an adaptation to the interactional demands of one's position in the social structure, as well as induction into the emotional culture of the society. Elsewhere I discuss in detail the effects of social class, generational cohort effects, subcultural membership, and other structural factors on sequence, diversity, and content of children's emotional socialization (Gordon, 1989b).

MANAGEMENT OF EMOTIONS

We do not simply feel emotions, but also work to create, intensify, suppress, and transform them. We manage our emotional expression by intentionally displaying gestures that differ in type or intensity from inner feeling, or by presenting a neutral expression. Our expression management may be guided by conscious self-presentation strategies to convey a particular impression of ourselves to a social audience. At other times expression is regulated by our habitual adherence to norms for appropriate emotional displays in a given situation or relationship.

The feeling component of emotion also can be managed by modifying our cognitive and somatic experience. Feeling management can be born of our sense of obligation and indebtedness to a person (Hochschild, 1979). For example, we may believe that we should feel gratitude toward an individual, or that we should suppress our impatience because of a person's status (e.g., a boss, child, elderly person, or loved one). On other occasions, we modify feelings to facilitate expressive control. For example, flight attendants may reconceptualize obnoxious adult passengers as frightened children, thereby helping to control their anger against them, while sustaining their commercial image as naturally friendly workers (Hochschild, 1983). By rethinking our interpretation of a situation or trying to alter our bodily sensations, we can influence our private awareness or feeling of emotions.

THE NATURE OF EMOTION NORMS

The most studied topic in the sociology of emotions is probably the effect of emotion norms upon experience and expression. Yet conceptual and research questions remain. For example, a model of normative influence adopted by many psychologists and some sociologists assumes that emotion norms are stated explicitly, internalized by all members of the society, and followed assiduously. The term "rule," connoting explicitness, sanctions, and obedience (e.g., "display rule"), is often used in place of "norm," which I shall use. This extreme model oversimplifies the emotion management process, obscuring important questions. For the research agenda, I suggest inquiry into the following topics.

Negotiation of Emotion Norms. Emotion norms prescribe a range of permissible feeling, not a precise point. Norms can be vague, incomplete, and contradictory. People have to fill in missing details and choose among competing norms. A research agenda should include investigation of structural factors determining whether particular norms are clear or ambiguous. The applicability of emotion norms to particular situations must be difficult for people to establish. We need studies of how people and groups debate, negotiate, and bargain over a norm's exact content and situational applicability. Research possibilities are even suggested by daily headlines, such as national debates about expressing collective guilt and remorse for historical transgressions, or intergroup negotiations about whether an "insulting" joke or remark is truly offensive, funny, inane, or a mere verbal slip.

Internalization of Norms. Norms are not always internalized deeply to motivate and direct behavior. Norms also serve as excuses, accounts, and rationalizations for behavior. What difference, if any, does it make in social interaction when emotion norm-following is either (1) consciously sincere or authentic (Hochschild, 1983), (2) automatic or habitual, or (3) half-hearted or cynical, used an an *ex post facto* excuse (e.g., to justify insulting someone by claiming "we should be honest about our feelings"). To ascertain social structural effects on emotion norms, we must recognize that norms are sometimes complex and unstable, not fixed and explicit rules.

FORMAL EMOTIONAL CULTURE

Statements of norms can be found in the formal, intellectual culture of emotions: (a) scientific publications, (b) sermons and other religious documents, (c) court records, (d) books of advice and manners and (e) other writings. However, this evidence has an uncertain status in its pertinence to actual emotional experience and expression. Emotional culture can be distant from actual emotion in some eras, and very close to it in other periods (Mechling, 1975; Stearns, 1985). When they are credible sources of evidence, documents provide detailed information about the history of emotions. Documents can have a socializing effect as self-fulfilling prophecies, shaping emotions toward the prescribed standards and thereby becoming veridical indicators of actual experience and behavior (Stearns, 1985).

Documents of emotional culture serve as an index of social structural change. For example, Francesca Cancian and I examined a sample of the advice published in U.S. women's magazines from 1900 to 1979 about the "proper" expression of love and anger in marriage (Cancian & Gordon, 1988). We found a nonlinear trend toward equating love with self-fulfillment (as a rationale for different forms of emotion management), and an increased advocacy for more open expression of anger. Normative changes appeared to reflect structural events such as the Great Depression, World War II, and the emergence of the women's movement. As shown in our research, popular sources contain more than normative prescriptions and proscriptions; also included are the rationales, counterarguments, case studies of good and bad emotion, and other details of emotional culture.

Generality of Control Across Individuals and Emotions. The classical "culture and personality" theorists believed that culture was simply the distributive aspect of personality (Benedict, 1934; Mead, 1935). In this view, all individuals in a society shared the same degree of emotional control. Anthropologists and sociologists now recognize that even in tightly-integrated communities, individuals differ in their emotional reactivity (Lutz & White, 1986). Higher social status brings the privilege of freer, more spontaneous emotional expression, but lower status requires inhibition of expression and a careful monitoring of the emotions of status superiors. High status individuals may believe that emotional candor is *owed* only to their peers, while their subordinates may receive candor, misrepresentation, or simply be ignored (Gerth and Mills suggested (1964 [1953]). Social structure therefore determines for whom emotional regulation is stringent or permissive.

Implicit in the old theories was another hypothesis, namely, that emotional constraint or freedom in a society is similar across all emotions (not just all individuals). Love, fear, anger, and shame are concealed equally in an "unexpressive culture," the argument went. This presupposition has not been challenged as incisively as that of the homogeneity of individual reactions, and in fact attracted prominent adherents. For example, Elias (1978 [1939]) argued that the civilizing process leads to increasing constraint across all emotions. A hypothesis on the research agenda is that societal emotion management is uneven across emotions. While some emotions are strongly regulated, others are freely felt and displayed. For instance, in our study of advice in women's magazines, trends in anger norms did not correlate with trends for norms about expressing love (Cancian & Gordon, 1988). Research is needed on structural factors determining which emotions are more regulated and which are openly permitted. This differential control is selective, and probably reflects the functions served by different emotions, the values implied by public emotional reactions, the stabilizing or disruptive effects of emotions on key social relationships, and the congruence of different emotional feelings and behavior with broader cultural systems such as religion.

Stability of Emotional Control. The variability over time of emotional restraint in a society is another dimension for investigation. An analysis of emotions in Europe during the Middle Ages suggests that people were both more expressive and more restrained than today (Dunning, 1987). Their emotions oscillated between polar extremes as they gave way to sudden mood swings. Their degree of control also could shift quickly from emotional release to emotional restraint. These tendencies are within human potential, and indeed are characteristic of very young children, who may, for example, laugh while tears from crying still wet their face. Whether this volatility occurs among adults and, if so, under what social structural conditions, are questions for research.

LEGITIMATION OF EMOTION NORMS

Who defines the situationally appropriate type, intensity, and target of emotions? Research is needed into the legitimation of emotions, the process by which an expression or feeling is publicly authorized as appropriate. The judgment of appropriateness sometimes carries the weight of formal authority, such as validation by legal, religious, psychiatric, or other emotional expertise. As a result, people may claim to be entitled to express and receive emotions governed by legitimate norms.

Emotional Expertise. The emergence of the emotion expert as a kind of occupation could be studied, looking, for example, at grief therapists in the funeral industry, or at how judges learn to assess a defendant's degree of remorse. Changes in the regulation of anger in the U.S. during this century were promoted by physicians, marital advisers, industrial psychologists, family sociologists, and other emotional experts (Stearns & Stearns, 1986). Family history reveals a shift from religious leaders to psychologists and doctors as primary advice-givers about marital love and anger (Cancian & Gordon, 1988). Popularized advice is produced widely after structural change has undermined the credibility of established emotion norms. In traditional societies such as the Swahili of Mombasa, people's judgments of what is shameful vary according to their social status, but of greatest influence are the judgments of prestigious role-incumbents, who act as arbiters of morality (Swartz, 1988). In modern societies, folk beliefs about emotions reflect formal scientific and intellectual ideas that filter down through popularized social science (Cancian & Gordon, 1988).

Legitimation by Ethnopsychology. Emotions are legitimated by language. By virtue of having a name, an emotion acquires a self-evident authority. Legitimation also occurs through the proverbs, wise sayings, legends and other wisdom contained in traditional ethnopsychology. This folk knowledge surrounds an emotion with beliefs that preserve the emotion's apparent reality and legitimacy. Sayings such as "true love never runs smooth," and "you always hurt the one you love," affirm that love still exists despite bad periods in a relationship. However, after a breakup, the relationship can be retrospectively interpreted as "mere infatuation," thereby preserving the possibility of "real" love next time.

Changes in Legitimation. Research is needed on the rise and fall of emotion norms as they become legitimated and de-legitimated. Research could focus on controversies over a particular emotion. In the history of Christianity, for example, debates were held over the appropriate feeling during worship—quiet reverence, ecstasy, a meditative trance, somber guilt, and other emotions. Another project would be the analysis of styles, fashions, and fads in emotions, which may change through a social class "filter down" process like other culture items in collective behavior. Examples include the diffusion of Weltschmerz ("sorrow for the world") and idealistic ennui among nineteenth century European university students, the 1960s experiment with non-jealous open marriage and that decade's psychedelic raptures, and today's nonerotic social greeting of a hug and a kiss on the cheek between cross-sex adult friends at middle-class parties. Criticism of emotional style may also be aimed upward in the struggle between social classes, as for example in the rising European bourgeoisie's published attacks on the aristocracy's discrepancy between public expression and true feeling (Vowinckel, 1988).

INSTITUTIONALIZATION OF EMOTIONS

Emotions may be legitimated by becoming attached to social institutions. When we think of a social institution, we often think of a particular emotion associated with it. Marriage means institutionalized love and sexual expression; the military means organized anger or the collective joy of battle. Plutchik (1984) suggested that universal social institutions may have developed partly to control universal emotions. For example, religion governs sadness over death and loss, while sports, games, and play systematically generate novelty leading to surprise. Institutionalization stabilizes and formalizes the occasion, expressive paradigm, and social meaning of an emotion.

The institution has authority to organize rituals arousing the emotion, to settle disputes about proper expression and feeling, and otherwise holds sovereignty over the emotion. The medieval church specified the meditational objects, rosaries, relics, and pious images aimed at producing reverence, exaltation, and other religious feelings, aided by "the intoxicating monotone of murmured prayers and confessions" (Braunstein, 1987, p. 620). What might otherwise be a random, spontaneous emotion becomes organized within the authority of an institution. Our society may view sexual jealousy as a personal option, but elsewhere its expression is a community obligation to protect property rights (Davis, 1936).

An early discussion of emotional institutionalization was Weber's analysis of the routinization of charisma, whereby a leader's personal charm for arousing excitement and loyalty was transferred to the offices of a bureaucracy. Love and friendship can become routinized to serve the purposes and ideals of institutions (e.g., military units, fraternities, etc.) (Swanson, 1965). Shared emotional experiences build solidarity while reducing variation among individuals so that they can cooperate efficiently. Collins (1975) argued that elites contend for access to a society's "means of emotional production"—the material and symbolic resources for arousing emotions. Such elites include institutions such as the government, church, and military.

Institutionalization of emotion norms is likely to occur within a particular type of social structure. A comparative analysis reports that the continuous masking of emotion (among the Pukhtun tribesmen of Pakistan) and the conscious dissimulation of emotion (in the Court of Louis XIV) both developed in relatively closed communities with a strong sense of external opposition, extensive internal competition, and a distinctly articulated, pyramidal structuring of relationships (Lindholm, 1988).

Consistency Across Institutions. Institutions often overlap in control over an emotion. Stearns and Stearns (1986) argue that standards and techniques for anger control were generalized from the workplace to the family home. Consistency resulted from the family's function in preparing children to be new workers. Institutions also may be substitutable. Men's intense personal attachment to male friends subsided as familial love became emphasized (Nelson, 1979). Sociologists should investigate the problems and solutions developed when institutions compete for authority over an emotion.

Resistance to Institutionalization. The tension between spontaneity and institutional control of emotion is a basic theme in the sociology of emotions. How do different interpretive orientations determine the relative value placed upon institutionalized emotion? The contrast between institutionalized emotion and impulsive emotion may be an important dimension in interpreting emotional experience, as it is in the locus of the self-concept (Turner, 1976). My analysis of self-reports of significant emotional episodes found that institutional emotions seem artificial, trite, and unreflective of one's true, deeper self when viewed from an impulse-based orientation (Gordon, 1989a). One respondent, for example, interpreted his outburst of anger at a neighbor as "getting in touch with my feelings" and as an expression of his true, deeper self. However, within an institutional framework, impulsive emotions seem inauthentic experiences, lapses that are uncharacteristic of who one really is. Thus, another respondent regarded his furious tirade at a girlfriend as a disturbing, atypical loss of control that did not reflect who he believed to be his deeper, real self.

De-institutionalization of Emotion. Does institutionalization of emotions increase continuously over history, or do institutionalized emotions ever become idiosyncratic again? With the breakdown of conventions and ascribed statuses of traditional society, institutionalization may be weakened (Gerth & Mills, 1964 [1953]). For instance, the emotions associated with friendship formerly were institutionalized, but friendship rituals have diminished, relegating friendship choice and interaction to personal preference within opportunities provided by propinquity (Brain, 1976).

Institutionalization and legitimation are tenuous and changeable processes. An interesting example is the ritualized anger and aggression among British working-class soccer fans, who are said to adhere to symbols, territoriality, and a conventional language of insult in their aggression (Marsh, Rosser & Harré, 1978). Although their angry displays usually are pursued within recognized limits and without much actual danger, there have been mass deaths in soccer crowds, followed by public outcries about excessive, irrational emotion and the breakdown of order. Modern sports institutionalize and legitimate a "liberating excitement" in societies where other forms of violence are highly restrained, in a "controlled de-controlling of the emotions" (Elias & Dunning, 1986). Indeed, "decontrolled" anger sometimes predominates, magnified by the large crowd assembled for institutional events, and promotes the deinstitutionalization of the emotion. The topic of the reproduction of emotional institutions brings us to our final question, how do the emotions of individuals influence social structure?

INDIVIDUAL EFFECTS ON SOCIAL STRUCTURE

The clear trend in sociology has been to explain emotions as dependent variables, viewing emotions as end-states and subjective outcomes of social interaction. Instead we should also examine emotion, like personality, as an *intervening* variable in the maintenance, modification, or disruption of society (Turner, 1988). What is it specifically that emotions do to reproduce or modify social structure? Although sociological answers have not been widely forthcoming, some functions of emotion include:

1. **Motivating Behavior.** The stem word for emotion is shared with "motivation," the Latin *emovere*, to move out or toward something. Emotion has been defined as a change in action tendency to maintain or disrupt a relationship with the environment (Frijda, 1986). Emotional culture contains assertions about motivation, such as the U.S. belief early in this century that anger should be channeled into a zeal to fuel business entrepreneurship and consumerism (i.e., by feeling irritated when one cannot have a marketed product) (Stearns & Stearns, 1986). At the level of individual behavior, being emotional may strengthen task persistence, improve memory, or increase the likelihood of acting altruistically. Does it make any difference whether social actors behave emotionally or non-emotionally? For instance, it may be that emotionally-motivated social behavior occurs more rapidly and memorably and has a stronger effect on the persistence of structural patterns of relationships.

2. **Communicating Reactions and Intentions.** Emotion has a signal function, to convey one's reactions and behavioral impulses to others (Hochschild, 1983). Facial expressions of primary emotions may have evolved as a prelinguistic, nonverbal medium for rapidly communicating messages about environmental events and one's own needs and intentions. Emotional expressions reveal one's evaluations of what was perceived and display one's allocation of attention and involvement in a social encounter. Being excited, bored, or angry indicates differential support, respect, and deference for a group or relationship and its place in the social structure. Collins (1975, 1984) argues that relations of property and authority are dependent on the emotional solidarity of the group. Repeated face-to-face interactions are the key ritual process, Collins believes, that increases or decreases the "emotional energies" of individuals and reproduces or transforms structural solidarity and hierarchy.

3. **Revealing Identities and Values.** Emotional reactions are salient cues about a person's identities (e.g., social class status, age) and the particular role or standpoint that one is taking in a social situation. For example, emotions are commonly aroused when one's expectations and values are either fulfilled (joy, surprise) or violated (anger, disappointment). A display of passion can be a strategic, rhetorical warning that

one is deeply committed to a particular expectation or value and will be intransigent, even erratic and threatening, about it (Bailey, 1983).

4. *Generalization of Emotional Temperament and Style.* Different emotional temperaments and styles can alter social structure depending upon the structural position of emotional models and their distribution across prominent statuses and roles. Some individuals become salient role models because of their power, charisma, access to mass media, and other status advantages. The rise to prominence of a prestiguous individual allows him or her to demonstrate an expressive style; a president or prime minister may react to events (e.g. national disasters) and present public appeals for support with either a sentimental and dramatic, or a coldly rational demeanor, for example. Public figures—politicians, religious figures, movie and television stars, especially—set social standards for emotional reactions, which, when emulated en masse, can change social structure. A political leader who repeatedly expresses an angry, tough stance against enemy nations, or who models compassion and pity for the unfortunate, could have a major effect upon public emotional responses, and thereby upon the military order or social policy, for example.

In addition to personal role models, the distribution of gender, age, and ethnic groups across structural roles and positions can produce widespread changes in emotional reactions. Let us assume as an illustration that women, younger people, or an ethnic group have stronger, more dramatic emotional reactions, and become the predominant incumbents of certain social roles previously held by others. Their style of emotion expression and behavior could alter the social structure by changing the functional effects of emotions—solidarity-building, motivating behavior, supporting values, and so forth.

CONCLUSION

This research agenda has proposed hypotheses but does not detail research methods for investigating them. The integration of social structure with individuals' emotions can be studied through the standard methods of social science—interviews, surveys, ethnographies, and content analysis, depending on the topic and available data sources. Models of outstanding research can be found in many of the sources cited above, and in reviews of the field (Gordon, 1981, 1985, 1989b; Kemper, 1978; Lutz & White, 1986; Scheff, 1983; Stearns, 1985; Stearns & Stearns, 1986). Perhaps the distinctive methodological characteristic of this field is that a researcher should be interdisciplinary, becoming familiar with theories, concepts, methods, and inferential approaches in psychology, anthropology, and social history. For instance, social historians of emotion may seem to interpret documents somewhat intuitively, as in studying medieval emotions (Duby, 1988), but the available diaries, correspondence, ecclesiastic chronicles, personal account books, and tax records do not lend themselves to quantitative content analyses. The intellectual task for sociologists, then, is to be able to move horizontally across disciplines and vertically through scales of analysis, in order to trace an emotion or set of emotion processes between the larger social structure and the individual level of experience and behavior.

NOTE

*My thanks go to Arlie Hochschild for her helpful comments on an earlier draft of this chapter.   •

REFERENCES

Bailey, F. G. 1983. *The Tactical Uses of Passion.* Ithaca, N.Y.: Cornell University Press.

Benedict, Ruth. 1934. *Patterns of Culture.* Boston: Houghton Mifflin.

Blumberg, Rae L. 1977. "Women and Work Around the World: A Cross-cultural Examination of Sex Division of Labor and Sex Status." Pp. 412–433 in *Beyond Sex Roles.* Edited by A. Sargent. St. Paul, Minn.: West.

Brain, Robert. 1975. *Friends and Lovers.* New York: Basic Books.

Braunstein, Phillipe. 1988. "Toward Intimacy: The Fourteenth and Fifteenth Centuries." Pp. 535–630 in *A History of Private Life: Revelations of the Medieval World.* Edited by George Duby. Cambridge, Mass: Harvard University.

Buss, Arnold H. and R. Plomin. 1975. *A Temperament Theory of Personality Development.* New York: Wiley.

Cahill, Spencer E. 1987. "Children and Civility: Ceremonial Deviance and the Acquisition of Ritual Competence." *Social Psychology Quarterly* 50: 312–321.

Cancian, Francesca M. and Steven L. Gordon. 1988. "Changing Emotion Norms in Marriage: Love and Anger in U.S. Women's Magazines since 1900." *Gender & Society* 2:308–341.

Collier, Jane, and Rosaldo, Michelle. 1981. "Politics and Gender in Simple Societies." pp. 275–329 in *Sexual Meanings*, edited by S. Ortner and H. White-
head. Cambridge: Cambridge University.

Collins, Randall. 1975. *Conflict Sociology.* New York: Academic Press.

———. 1984. "The Role of Emotion in Social Structure." Pp. 385–396 in *Approaches to Emotion*, edited by Klaus R. Scherer and Paul Ekman. Hillsdale,
New Jersey: Erlbaum.

Cooley, Charles H. 1962 [1909] *Human Nature and the Social Order.* New York:
Scribner's.

Cotton, John L. 1981. "A Review of Research on Schachter's Theory of Emotion
and the Misattribution of Arousal." *European Journal of Social Psychology*
11:365–397.

D'Andrade, Roy G. 1987. "Folk Models of the Mind." Pp. 112–148 in *Cultural
Models in Language and Thought*, edited by Naomi Quinn and Dorothy Hol-
land. Cambridge: Cambridge University.

Davis, Kingsley. 1936. "Jealousy and Sexual Property." *Social Forces* 14:395–405.

de la Ronciere, Charles. 1988. "Tuscan Notables on the Eve of the Renaissance."
Pp. 157–309 in *A History of Private Life: Revelations of the Medieval World.*
Edited by George Duby. Cambridge, Mass.: Harvard University.

Demos, John. 1986. *Past, Present, and Personal: The Family and the Life Course in
American History.* New York: Oxford University.

DiRenzo, Gordon J. 1977. "Socialization, Personality, and Social Systems." *Annual
Review of Sociology* 3:261–295.

Duby, George (editor). 1988. *A History of Private Life: Revelations of the Medieval
World.* Cambridge, Mass.: Harvard University.

Dunning, Eric. 1987. "Comments on Elias' 'Scenes from the Life of a Knight.'"
Theory, Culture and Society 4:366–371.

Ekman, P. 1982. *Emotion in the Human Face*, 2d ed. Cambridge: Cambridge University Press.

Elder, Glen. 1974. *Children of the Great Depression.* Chicago: University of Chicago
Press.

———. 1981. "History and the Life Course." Pp. 77–115 in *Biography and Society.*
Edited by D. Bertraux. New York: Sage.

Elias, Norbert. 1978. [1939]. *The Civilizing Process. Vol. 1. The History of Manners.*
New York: Pantheon.

Elias, Norbert and Eric Dunning. 1986. *Quest for Excitement: Sport and Leisure in the Civilizing Process.* Oxford: Basil Blackwell.

Elkind, David. 1979. *The Child and Society.* New York: Oxford.

Frijda, Nico H. 1986. *The Emotions.* Cambridge: Cambridge University.

Gecas, Viktor. 1981. "Contexts of Socialization." Pp. 165–199 *Social Psychology: Sociological Perspectives.* Edited by Morris Rosenberg and Ralph H. Turner. New York: Basic Books.

Gerth, Hans and C. Wright Mills. 1964. [1953]. *Character and Social Structure: The Psychology of Social Institutions.* New York: Harcourt, Brace, and World.

Goldsmith, Harold and Joseph Campos. 1982. "Toward a Theory of Infant Temperament." In *The Development of Attachment and Affiliative Systems.* Edited by Robert Emde and R. Harmon. New York: Plenum.

Gordon, Steven L. 1981. "The Sociology of Sentiments and Emotion." Pp. 551–575 in *Social Psychology: Sociological Perspectives.* Edited by Morris Rosenberg and Ralph H. Turner. New York: Basic Books.

———. 1985. "Micro-Sociological Theories of Emotion." Pp. 133–147 in *Micro-Sociological Theory: Perspectives on Sociological Theory.* Vol. 2. Edited by Horst J. Helle and S. N. Eisenstadt. London: Sage.

———. 1989a. "Institutional and Impulsive Orientations in the Selective Appropriation of Emotions to Self." Pp. 115–135 in *The Sociology of Emotions: Original Essays and Research Papers.* Edited by David Franks and E. Doyle McCarthy. Greenwich, CT: JAI Press.

———. 1989b. "The Socialization of Children's Emotions: Emotional Culture, Exposure, and Competence." In *Children's Understanding of Emotion.* Edited by Carolyn I. Saarni and Paul Harris. Cambridge: Cambridge University Press.

Guttentag, Marcia and Paul Secord. 1983. *Too Many Women? The Sex Ratio Question.* Beverly Hills, Calif.: Sage.

Hammond, Michael. 1986. "Finite Human Capacities and the Pattern of Social Stratification." In *The Knowledge Society.* Edited by G. Bohme and Nico Stehr. Dordrecht: D. Reidel.

Harré, Rom. 1986. "An Outline of the Social Constructionist Viewpoint." Pp. 2–14 in *The Social Construction of Emotions.* Edited by Rom Harré. Oxford: Basil Blackwell.

Heider, Karl. 1984. "Emotion: Inner State vs Interaction." Paper presented at annual meeting of the American Anthropological Association, Denver.

Hochschild, Arlie Russell. 1975. "The Sociology of Feeling and Emotion." Pp. 280–307 in *Another Voice: Feminist Perspectives on Social Life and Social Structure*. edited by Marcia Millman and Rosabeth Moss Kanter. Garden City, N.Y.: Doubleday/Anchor.

———. 1979. Emotion Work, Feeling Rules, and Social Structure. *American Journal of Sociology* 85:551–575.

———. 1983. *The Managed Heart: Commercialization of Human Feeling*. Berkeley: University of California Press.

House, James S. 1977. "The Three Faces of Social Psychology." *Sociometry* 40:161–177.

———. 1981. "Social Structure and Personality." Pp. 525–561 in *Social Psychology: Sociological Perspectives*, edited by Morris Rosenberg and Ralph H. Turner. New York: Basic Books.

Inkeles, Alex. 1966. "Social Structure and the Socialization of Competence." *Harvard Educational Review*, 36:265–283.

Inkeles, Alex and Daniel Levinson. 1963. "The Personal System and Social Structure in Large-Scale Organizations." *Sociometry* 26:217–230.

Inkeles, Alex and Smith, D. H. 1974. *Becoming Modern: Individual Change in Six Developing Countries*. Cambridge, MA: Harvard University.

Izard, Carroll E. 1977. *Human Emotions*. New York: Plenum.

Kemper, Theodore D. 1978. *A Social Interactional Theory of Emotions*. New York: Wiley.

———. 1987. "How Many Emotions are There? Wedding the Social and the Autonomic Components." *American Journal of Sociology*, 93, 263–289.

Kohn, Melvin. 1969. *Class and Conformity: A Study in Values*. Homewood, IL: Dorsey Press.

Kohn, Melvin and Carmi Schooler (editors). 1983. *Work and Personality: An Inquiry into the Impact of Social Stratification*. Norwood, NJ: Ablex.

Leventhal, Howard and Andrew J. Tomarken. 1986. "Emotion: Today's Problems." *Annual Review of Psychology* 37:565–610.

Levy, Robert I. & Wellencamp, Jane (in press). "Methodology in the Anthropological Study of Emotion." In *Emotion: Theory, Research, and Experience*, Vol. 4, *The Measurement of Emotions*. Edited by Robert Plutchik and Henry Kellerman. New York: Academic Press.

Lindholm, Charles. 1988. "The Social Structure of Emotional Constraint: the Court of Louis XIV and the Pukhtun of Northern Pakistan." *Ethos* 16:227–246.

Lutz, Catherine. 1982. "The Domain of Emotion Words on Ifaluk." *American Ethnologist* 9:113–128.

———. 1983. "Parental Goals, Ethnopsychology, and the Development of Emotional Meaning." *Ethos* 11:246–262.

———. 1985. "Cultural Patterns and Individual Differences in the Child's Emotional Meaning System." Pp. 37–53 in *The Socialization of Emotions*, edited by Michael Lewis and Carolyn Saarni. New York: Plenum.

Lutz, Catherine and White, Geoffrey M. 1986. "The Anthropology of Emotions." *Annual Review of Anthropology*, 15:405–436.

Marsh, Peter, Edward Rosser, and Rom Harré. 1978. *The Rules of Disorder.* London: Routledge Kegan Paul

Marshall, Gary and Zimbardo, Phillip. 1979. "Affective Consequences of Inadequately Explained Physiological Arousal." *Journal of Personality and Social Psychology* 37:970–988.

Maslach, Christine. 1979. "Negative Emotional Biasing of Unexplained Arousal." *Journal of Personality and Social Psychology* 37:953–969.

Mead, Margaret. 1935. *Sex and Temperament in Three Primitive Societies.* New York: Morrow.

Mechling, Jay. 1975. "Advice to Historians on Advice to Mothers." *Journal of Social History*, 9:44–63.

Nelson, B. 1969. *The Idea of Usury.* Chicago: University of Chicago.

Park, Robert E. 1928. "Human Migration and the Marginal Man." *American Journal of Sociology* 33:881–893.

Plutchik, R. 1980. *Emotion: A Psychoevolutionary Synthesis.* New York: Harper and Row.

———. 1984. "Emotions: A General Psychoevolutionary Theory." Pp. 197–219 In *Approaches to Emotion*, edited by Klaus R. Scherer and Paul Ekman. Hillsdale, New Jersey: Erlbaum.

Price-Williams, Douglass R. "Cultural Psychology." Pp. 993–1042 in *The Handbook of Social Psychology (3rd ed.).* Vol 2. Edited by Gardner Lindzey and Elliot Aronson. New York: Random House.

Reisenzein, Rainer. 1983. "The Schachter Theory of Emotion: Two Decades Later." *Psychological Bulletin* 94:2349–264.

Riesman, David. 1950. *The Lonely Crowd.* New Haven, Conn.: Yale University.

Rosaldo, Michelle Z. 1984. "Toward an Anthropology of Self and Feeling." Pp. 137–157 in *Culture Theory: Essays on Mind, Self and Emotion*. Edited by Richard A. Shweder and Robert A. LeVine. Cambridge: Cambridge Univ.

Rosenberg, Morris. 1979. *Conceiving the Self*. New York: Basic Books.

Rozin, Paul and April E. Fallon. 1987. "A Perspective on Disgust." *Psychological Review* 94:23–41.

Rybczynski, Withold. 1986. *Home: A Short History of an Idea*. New York: Viking.

Ryff, Carol D. 1987. "The Place of Personality and Social Structure Research in Social Psychology." *Journal of Personality and Social Psychology* 53:1192–1202.

Saarni, Carolyn I. 1989. "Emotional Competence: How Emotions and Relationships Become Integrated." *Nebraska Symposium on Motivation* 36.

Sanday, Peggy R. 1981. *Female Power and Male Dominance: On the Origins of Sex Inequality*. Cambridge: Cambridge University.

Schachter, Stanley. 1964. "The Interactions of Cognitive and Physiological Determinants of Emotional State." *Advances in Experimental Social Psychology* 1:49–90.

Schachter, Stanley and Jerome E. Singer. 1962. "Cognitive, Social, and Physiological Determinants of Emotional State."*Psychological Review* 69:379–399.

Scheff, Thomas J. 1979. *Catharsis in Healing, Ritual and Drama*. Berkeley and Los Angeles: University of California Press.

———. 1983. "Toward Integration in the Social Psychology of Emotions." *Annual Review of Sociology* 9:333–354.

Scheler, Max 1961 [1915]. *Ressentiment*. New York: Free Press.

Scherer, Klaus R., Wallbott, Harold G., & Summerfield, Angela B. 1986. *Experiencing Emotion: A Cross-Cultural Study*. Cambridge: Cambridge University.

Schwartz, Judy C. & Shaver, Phillip. 1987. "Emotions and Emotion Knowledge in Interpersonal Relations." Pp. 197–241 in *Advances in Personal Relationships*, Vol 1, edited by Warren Jones and Dan Perlman. Greenwich, CT: JAI Press.

Shaver, Phillip, Judy Schwartz, Donald Kirson, & Cary O'Connor. 1987. "Emotion Knowledge: Further Exploration of a Prototype Approach." *Journal of Personality and Social Psychology*, 52:1061–1086.

Simmel, Georg. 1964 [1903]. "The Metropolis and Mental Life." 409–424 In *The Sociology of Georg Simmel*, edited by Kurt H. Wolff. New York: Free Press.

Snyder, Mark and William Ickes. 1985. "Personality and Social Behavior." Pp. 883–947 in *The Handbook of Social Psychology (3rd ed.)*. Vol 2. Edited by Gardner Lindzey and Elliot Aronson. New York: Randon House.

Stannard, David E. (1977). *The Puritan Way of Death: A Study in Religion, Culture, and Social Change.* New York: Oxford University Press.

Stearns, Carol Z. and Peter N. Stearns. 1986. *Anger: The Struggle for Emotional Control in America's History.* Chicago: University of Chicago.

Stearns, Peter N. 1986. "Historical Analysis in the Study of Emotion." *Motivation and Emotion* 10:185–193.

———. 1988. "The Rise of Sibling Jealousy in the Twentieth Century." Paper presented at annual meeting of the American Sociological Association, Atlanta, GA.

Stearns, Peter N. (with Carol Z. Stearns). 1985. "Emotionology: Clarifying the History of Emotions and Emotional Standards." *American Historical Review* 90:813–836.

Stonequist, Everett V. 1937. *The Marginal Man: A Study in Personality and Cultural Conflict.* New York: Russell and Russell.

Storm, Christine and Tom Storm. 1987. "A Taxonomic Study of the Vocabulary of Emotions." *Journal of Personality and Social Psychology* 53:805–816.

Swanson, Guy E. 1965. "The Routinization of Love: Structure and Process in Primary Relations." In *The Quest for Self-Control.* Edited by Samuel Z. Klausner. New York: Free Press.

Swartz, Marc. J. 1988. "Shame, Culture and Status among the Swahili of Mombasa." *Ethos* 16:21–51.

Thomas, Alexander and Stella Chess. 1977. *Temperament and Development.* New York: Brunner/Mazel.

Turner, Ralph H. 1976. "The Real Self: From Institution to Impulse." *American Journal of Sociology* 81:789–1016.

———. 1988. "Personality in Society: Social Psychology's Contribution to Sociology." *Social Psychology Quarterly* 51:1–10.

Valins, Stuart. 1966. "Cognitive Effects of False Heart Feedback." *Journal of Personality and Social Psychology* 4:400–408.

Veyne, Paul. 1987. "The Roman Empire." Pp. 5–234 in *A History of Private Life, Vol. I; From Pagan Rome to Byzantium,* edited by Paul Veyne. Cambridge, Mass.: Harvard University.

Vowinckel, Gerhard. 1988. "Beautiful Souls and Political Brains." Paper presented at annual meeting of the American Sociological Association, Atlanta, GA, August.

Weiner, Bernard. 1987. "The Social Psychology of Emotion: Applications of a Naive Psychology." *Journal of Social and Clinical Psychology* 5:405–419.

Wells, Robert. 1971. "Family Size and Fertility Control in Eighteenth Century America." *Population Studies* 28:73–82.

Zillman, Dolf. 1978. "Attribution and Misattribution of Excitatory Reactions." Pp. 335–368 in *New Directions in Attribution Research*, Vol. 2. Edited by John H. Harvey, William J. Ickes, and Robert F. Kidd. Hillsdale, New Jersey: Erlbaum.

7.

Emotional Deviance: Research Agendas

Peggy A. Thoits

"Emotional deviance" (Thoits, 1984, 1985, or "affective dissidence" (Hochschild, 1979) is a relatively new concept in the sociology of emotion. I will begin by very briefly grounding it as a plausible sociological notion before moving on to discuss its research implications at greater length.

THE CONCEPT OF EMOTIONAL DEVIANCE

For sociologists, emotion is not purely a biological or psychological phenomenon, although most would acknowledge that physiological changes and cognitive perceptions are important aspects of emotional experience. For sociologists, emotion is importantly social in its origins (as well as social in its consequences).[1]

The guiding assumption that emotion is partially social in nature is supported by empirical research. Both macro- and micro-level investigations have indicated that emotional experiences are significantly influenced by social factors. Macro-level studies show that the distributions of specific emotions (e.g., grief, jealousy, love) across social groups vary systematically with changing historical, cultural, and structural forces (e.g., Stearns and Stearns, 1986; Cancian, 1987; Lofland, 1985). Micro-level studies indicate that emotional experiences, expressive displays, and attempts at emotional regulation are influenced by socialization and by prevailing situational factors (e.g., Hochschild, 1983; Pollak and Thoits, 1989; Gordon, in press; Clark, 1987; Heise, 1979; Kemper, 1978; Saarni, 1979). This research indicates that to an appreciable degree emotions are not simply automatic reactions or cognitive products, but are socially created or constructed.[2]

Because emotions justifiably can be considered social constructions, a panoply of sociological concepts can be applied to them. Of particular importance to this chapter, the concept of "norm" can and has been applied.

Hochschild (1979, 1983) and Ekman and his colleagues (1982) have defined and illustrated the concepts of "feeling rules" or "emotion norms" and "display rules" or "expression norms" (respectively interchangeable terms). Emotion norms indicate the expected range, intensity, duration, and/or targets of specific emotions in given situations. Norms are indicated most clearly by statements including the terms "should," "ought," "must," or "have a right to" in reference to feelings or feeling displays (e.g., "You should be more grateful," "You ought to be ashamed of yourself," "You must be happy about that," "You have no right to be angry"). Individuals spontaneously state such norms when discussing their own or others' emotional experiences or displays (Hochschild, 1979, 1981, 1983; Clark, 1987). Display rules also are evident when the spontaneous facial expressions of individuals in response to a stimulus dramatically change when other people are introduced into a situation (Ekman et al., 1982). Note that feeling rules or emotion norms refer to expectations regarding private or internal experience; display rules or expression norms refer to expectations governing public exhibitions of emotion.

It follows logically that just as behavior sometimes deviates from norms, so many feelings and emotional displays. In other words, emotional deviance is possible. Emotional deviance refers to experiences or displays of affect that differ in quality or degree from what is expected in given situations (Thoits, 1985). Hochschild's (1979, 1983) research clearly points to the occurrence of emotional deviance. She described numerous instances of individuals doing "emotion work" or "emotion management" in order to reduce socially inappropriate or induce socially appropriate emotions in themselves and in others.[3] Thus, emotional deviance is not just logically possible, but a concrete problem with which individuals have demonstrably grappled.

IMPLICATIONS

The concept of emotional deviance raises several interesting empirical and theoretical issues. The empirical issues are descriptive ones; Steven L. Gordon (personal communication, 1986) has referred to these as questions regarding "the epidemiology of emotions." Just how prevalent is the experience of deviant emotion—emotion that differs from that which is expected, conventional, or obligatory to feel and display? Relatedly, what are the social distributions of emotional deviance? For example, do women more frequently experience or display nonnormative emotions than men, or lower class individuals more than middle and upper class? What emotions have been regarded as especially deviant or socially problematic cross-culturally and historically (e.g., see Stearns and Stearns, 1986; Sommers, 1984a, 1984b)?

The theoretical issues are numerous. These can be subdivided into motivational, processual, and applied substantive issues. Motivationally, given that we, as social actors, are usually desirous of obtaining and maintaining social approval, how is it possible ever to experience or display deviant affect? Restating this question in researchable form, what are the conditions under which individuals will experience or exhibit inappropriate affect? Again given that social approval is usually important, under what conditions are individuals willing to endure sanctions for their unconventional reactions or even marshall the support of others to alter the rules of feeling? In other words, when and how do emotion and expression norms change?

Processually, just how is emotion work accomplished? That is, what are the techniques that people use to bring their deviant feelings and displays in line with normative requirements? Do men and women, lower, middle, and upper class people, and the young and the old use different preferred modes of emotion management? Under what conditions will emotion management attempts succeed or fail? And what do the successes and failures of these various techniques imply about the nature of emotion as a manipulatable biopsychosocial phenomenon?

These motivational and processual questions point to substantive applications of the emotional deviance concept (and to substantive applications of emotions theory more generally). At minimum, "bringing emotions back in" may further elucidate processes that are frequently studied by sociologists. Social change processes are one example. Certain subcultures, such as gay communities, swingers, and encounter groups, appear to be organized around unconventional emotions or emotional behaviors. Similarly, protest movements may be sustained by a sense of outrage or anger induced by injustice or oppression. How do subcultural and protest group members create and legitimize new emotion norms, when more powerful societal actors refuse to grant the legitimacy or rationality of the group's deviant feelings, for example, a group's feelings of outrage?

The concept of emotional deviance also has applicability in my own substantive areas, the sociology of mental health, and stress and coping processes. The concept has suggested new ways to understand how mental illness (i.e., *emotional* disturbance) may be recognized and labeled in oneself or others. It also has enabled me to reconceptualize stress as well as the coping and social support processes that are importantly involved in the etiology of mental disorder. These reconceptualizations, as I show below, lead to new research questions that may elucidate how individuals become mentally ill (and recover).

In the remainder of this chapter, I will, (a) offer some tentative hypotheses about each of the issues that I have raised above, (b) suggest some specific research strategies to pursue, and (c) point to other problems that will need attention in the future. Most of my suggested research strategies will be exploratory and qualitative in nature, because at this point we know so little about emotional deviance that quantitative survey methods are probably unwarranted.

RESEARCH QUESTIONS

DESCRIPTIVE STUDIES

The first questions I raised concerned the frequency and social distributions of nonnormative emotional experiences. However, prior to addressing these "epidemiological" issues, a key measurement question must be answered. How does one identify deviant emotions or displays?

My strategy to date has been to take the perspective of the individual. If the individual reports that his/her feelings or expressive behaviors differed from what he/she thought was expected in a situation, then that was an experience of emotional deviance. Given that feeling norms are likely to vary from one subgroup to another, this seems a reasonable way to identify emotional deviance without imposing the researcher's values on the individual's emotional experiences.

However, an intriguing alternative method is suggested by Heise's (1979, 1986, also this volume) work on affect control theory. Heise posited that the meanings of situations, actors, and behaviors are based in sentiments or affects. Every social classification has associated with it a sentiment that can be assessed on a good-bad dimension (evaluation), a powerful-weak dimension (potency), and a lively-quiet dimension (activity). Heise has had panels of college students rate various social actors (e.g., doctors, mothers, neighbors), settings (e.g., home, office, school), attributes (e.g., feminine, warm, hostile), and behaviors (e.g., cuddles, curses, instructs) on the dimensions of evaluation, potency, and activity to obtain average, or statistically normative, sentiments about those social classifications. He terms these "fundamental" sentiments; they are ratings of social objects, attributes, settings, and behaviors "out of context," or in isolation. Student panels also have rated actors, settings, attributes, and behaviors on the same three dimensions "in context," that is, when combined in statements describing events (e.g., "The old doctor soothes the anxious patient in his office"). In-context ratings are termed "transient" sentiments. When transient-sentiment ratings are virtually equivalent to fundamental-sentiment ratings, a described event is called "confirming"— it conforms affectively to what is expected, or statistically normative. When transient-sentiments in response to a described event *deviate* from fundamental expectations (e.g., "A coward and a roughneck were together in a fight, and the coward soothed the roughneck"), the event is "disconfirming." Disconfirming events are affectively motivating; they cause tension. Because affective expectations are not confirmed, a new understanding of the event must be constructed. Heise's simulation programs enable predictions of subsequent sequences of behavior that would bring transient affects back in line with fundamental affects. In short, Heise has developed computer simulations of social interaction that not only identify expected and unexpected sequences of behavior, but also *predict* subsequent sequences of behavior from prior events, using affective dynamics.

Confirming events for actors' behaviors essentially represent social norms, at least for middle-class college students. In most cases, these norms concern in-role behavior (and disconfirming events identify out-of-role behavior). However, confirming and disconfirming events for actors' emotions easily could be constructed from in-context ratings made of actors' feelings, since in Heise's previous work emotions already have been rated as fundamentals on the dimensions of evaluation, potency, and activity. Normative and deviant emotions could be identified straightforwardly by comparing transient ratings for actors' situated feelings (e.g., "The flight attendant is concerned about her passengers," "The psychiatrist is in love with his patient") to fundamental ratings. Degrees of deviation from normative situated emotion could be estimated with some precision from Heise's simulation programs.

Research such as this eventually will be necessary to map our "cultural universe" of normative and deviant feelings.[4] However, such work would only be a preliminary step, if one's goal were to assess the frequency with which deviant feelings occur in a population. Rough estimates of prevalence might be obtained without such painstaking preliminary research, if one were willing to accept subjective self-reports of affective deviance.

This was the tack I took in some recent exploratory work. I distributed an open-ended questionnaire to a sample of 200 college students (introductory psychology students at a midwestern university). The questionnaire asked students to write detailed descriptions of two important emotional episodes in their recent lives, one positive and one negative. The questionnaire also asked several follow up questions about their feelings in each situation, including whether they felt guilty or ashamed about how they reacted. They were asked why they felt guilty or ashamed, and why not, if they had not experienced these emotions. With these questions, I was attempting indirectly to elicit spontaneous statements regarding emotion norms and emotional deviance.

Preliminary analyses with 199 completed questionnaires indicated that students explicitly stated norms (such as "Boys should love their fathers" or "Emotions should be expressed") in 23.1 percent of their negative experience descriptions and 10.7 percent of their positive descriptions. Women were significantly more likely to state a norm for negative feelings than men, 30.2 percent versus 15.1 percent respectively; there were no gender differences in citing norms for positive feelings.

When I examined responses regarding guilt or shame about their feelings in each situation, I found that 46 percent felt guilty or ashamed about their negative emotional reactions; only 12 percent were guilty or ashamed about their positive reactions. Among those who were *not* guilty/ashamed of their negative feelings, 50.6 percent said this was because their emotions seemed "natural," "normal," "understandable," or "justified"; "anyone would feel this way," some said. Another 9 percent stated explicitly, "I had a right to feel the way I did." Among those who were *not* guilty/ashamed of their positive feelings, 49 percent used similar reasoning—their reactions were normal, natural, or justified; another 9 percent clearly stated that they "should" or "had a right" to feel as they did.[5]

Of those who *did* admit guilt or shame about their negative reactions, 30.7 percent explained that their feelings were too intense, too inexpressive, too uncontrolled, or simply the wrong feelings to have in the situation—in other words, that their feelings were deviant in their intensity, expression, or content (very few referred to inappropriate durations or targets of their feelings). Females were more likely than males to say that their negative reactions were inappropriate, 38 percent versus 21.6 percent, respectively (p = .10). In the positive experience episodes, 16 percent of those who felt guilty or ashamed cited the inappropriateness of their reactions; these often were "overreactions" to a competitive success. There were no gender differences in references to the inappropriateness of positive reactions.

Taking the sample as a whole, only 15.6 percent spontaneously described their feelings in the negative situation as deviant in some way, compared to 3 percent in the positive situation. So the frequency with which emotional deviance is mentioned in single episodes is relatively low, but this would be expected, since we are, after all, products of our culture. Still, deviance is appreciably present (and socially patterned), at least in this restricted age sample. Compared to positive emotions, negative emotions are more likely to elicit references to norms and to deviance, and women are more likely to make such references than men when their emotions are negative.

Note that this study focused only on two emotional episodes, one negative, one positive. Moreover, statements about norms and deviance were elicited in an unstructured fashion. A much better estimate of the prevalence of deviant feelings and displays might be obtained through the "daily diary" method of study. Representative samples of adults might be asked to keep systematic logs of changes in their feelings and expressive behaviors for a period of time and asked to identify feelings and displays that seemed wrong for the situation, too intense, too prolonged, or directed at an inappropriate target. Variations in the frequency of these occurrences by gender, age, race, marital status, and socioeconomic status also could be examined. One might expect lower-status-group members to report deviant affect or nonnormative displays more frequently, since more acts of disrespect or injustice may be directed toward less powerful societal members, and negative reactions generally are socially disapproved (Averill, 1978; Sommers, 1984b).

These examples focus only on the private emotional experiences of individuals. Similar exploratory studies might examine the frequency with which individuals have encountered emotional deviance in others and how they interpreted and handled that encounter. I have argued (Thoits, 1985) that emotional deviance may be interpreted as symptoms of psychological disorder by laypersons and psychiatrists alike, if the observed deviance occurs repeatedly or persistently. Thus, it would be important to ascertain what aspects of the target person's behavior cause respondents to attribute psychological difficulties to him or her. Presumably, the more intense, persistent, or repetitious the target person's perceived inappropriate affect, the higher the probability of attributed psychological disturbance. Alternatively, Heise's (1986) affect-control programs and data could be utilized to predict the interpretive outcomes of persistent or repeated emotional deviance, since the identities of the actors involved are likely to be reinterpreted (i.e., reclassified) as deviant following a series of disconfirming events.

STUDIES OF CONDITIONS GENERATING EMOTIONAL DEVIANCE

The second question I raised earlier was, given that we are typically well-socialized actors, how is it possible to experience emotional deviance? Actually, because it has been established that deviant affect does occur, the more appropriate question is under what conditions do individuals feel what they shouldn't, or not feel what they should? One obvious possibility is that individuals have not been well-socialized. It is clear from the developmental psychology literature that children increasingly acquire and use information about emotion and expression norms as they mature (e.g., Lewis and Michalson, 1983; Harter, 1983; Saarni, 1979; Harris et al., 1981; Mc Coy and Masters, 1985). For some children, caretakers may not have modeled, taught, and rewarded appropriate feelings and feeling displays. Consequently, such children display deviant affect in adolescence or adulthood. Although it is certainly possible not to have learned the rules (and this is clearly the case with some emotionally disturbed children [Pollak and Thoits, 1989]), relying solely on "poor socialization" as an explanation for affective deviance in older individuals is post hoc or tautological, and therefore unsatisfactory. However, this should not imply that studies of emotional socialization practices are unwarranted. Most research on children's affective development documents the *ages* at which children have acquired certain knowledge, for example, (*a*) knowledge that emotions are objects, (*b*) that several emotions can be felt simultaneously, (*c*) that others can mask their feelings, and (*d*) that emotions ought to be masked in specific situations. How children acquire that knowledge has been relatively understudied. Field studies of affective socialization in the home and in daycare settings are needed to examine the ways in which information (and misinformation) about emotion is transmitted to children. Studies of social class differences in socialization practices with male and female children also are necessary, as these social statuses are believed to powerfully influence what children learn (e.g., Bernstein, 1974; Hochschild, 1983).

In previous work I have suggested that certain aspects of emotion itself and several social structural factors could produce emotional deviations (Thoits, 1985). The aspects of emotional experience itself that may produce deviance include time, memory, and complex situational stimuli. With regard to time, emotions are sometimes slow to dissipate, so they may be carried over from one situation to another—appropriate in the first situation, but inappropriate in the next. Coming home from work in a bad mood is one example. Subsequent provocations at home may combine with undissipated physiological arousal from the previous situation to produce an overreaction to the provocation (e.g., Zillman, 1978). Memory also is a factor. By continuing to pay attention to the situation that elicited an affective state, we are likely to continue to feel or repeatedly renew the emotion (e.g., Pennebaker, 1982; Ekman et al., 1983), sometimes in subsequent situations for which the feeling is inappropriate. Finally, situational stimuli themselves can be complex and multifaceted. Consider one example from my student protocols: The student came home from college on the afternoon of her birthday to attend a party her mother was giving in her honor. She arrived early and was the first to find the body of her father in the garage—he had committed suicide. It was her birthday and he chose that day and place to kill himself. She had been estranged from her father because of her parents' divorce and had not seen him since he moved away. But he was her father, nevertheless. Her emotions were mixed—shock, horror, and sadness, which she perceived as appropriate, but also deep anger and hatred, which she perceived as inappropriate. These instances of emotional deviance may depend on specifics of the emotion or person (time, memory), or may be highly specific to the eliciting situation (complexity). More systematic social structural conditions, however, can be explored profitably.

Four structural conditions can be suggested under which self-perceived emotional deviance might be reported more frequently. These include (a) multiple role occupancy, (b) subcultural marginality, (c) normative and nonnormative role transitions, and (d) rigid rules governing ongoing roles and ceremonial rituals.

First, when a person holds multiple roles that have mutually contradictory feeling expectations, emotional deviance might be reported (for example, female doctors or professors who become "overinvolved" emotionally with their patients or students, fathers who are jealous of the attention a new baby receives from their wives, or employed parents who are worried about a sick child left at home). Second, and relatedly, when a person belongs to two or more subcultural worlds with contradictory feeling norms, emotional deviance again might occur (for example, married couples who "swing" sometimes face the problem of jealousy; the gay person "in the closet" must handle feelings of same-sex attraction in a heterosexual world). Marginal individuals and individuals holding multiple roles are aware of norms that legitimize their feelings in one role or subcultural context but may view those feelings as deviant from the perspective of another.

Third, when an individual undergoes a major role transition, or when traditional roles are in the sociohistorical process of being transformed, emotional deviations might be reported more frequently. Affective expectations for normative role transitions such as graduation, marriage, birth of a child, retirement, and bereavement tend to be simple and clear. However, the specific circumstances of the transition may generate feelings that deviate from those norms. For example, relatives who quarrel over wedding ceremony plans may make a bride and groom unhappy, although a marriage is supposed to be a happy occasion for all involved. Postpartum depression can occur for a number of reasons, including physiological imbalance, but it is viewed as a deviant reaction in a new mother. Normative role transitions are likely to be sources of affective deviance because novices are aware only of the affective ideals associated with their new roles (e.g., parents *always* love their babies). In contrast, when undergoing *nonnormative* transitions, the individual may worry less about deviation from the norms and more about lack of clarity in the norms, that is, the individual may wonder whether or not his/her feelings are actually appropriate, given the absence of normative guidance. Examples include coming out of the closet, becoming divorced, and becoming a stepparent. Sociohistorical changes are making these transitions more prevalent and thus more acceptable, yet neither behavioral nor emotional norms have crystallized for these new roles.

Finally, emotional deviance might be perceived more frequently by people in ongoing roles and ritual ceremonial situations where feeling norms are especially strong, or in other words, where there are rigid emotional constraints. Hochschild's (1983) research on flight attendants offers an example. Flight attendants are explicitly required by airline companies to smile at and sincerely care about the welfare of their passengers. But passengers sometimes are drunk, disorderly, disrespectful, or otherwise difficult to manage, generating feelings in flight attendants far different from those mandated by the airline. Parents dealing with their frustration and anger at continually crying and/or demanding babies are another fruitful example (Frude and Gross, 1981; Graham, 1981). These situational reactions conflict with strong parental norms of love and care for a child. Ceremonial occasions (birthdays, holidays, weddings, and funerals) also are likely to be times for experienced emotional deviance, because the realities of the situation do not always fit clear normative ideals. In my student protocols, there was an association between the occurrence of a ritual occasion and reports of inappropriate emotional reactions for negative experiences (28.6 percent reported inappropriate affect when the occasion was ceremonial, as opposed to 15.1 percent when the occasion was not ceremonial), but this was not a significant association due to the small number of ceremonial occasions described.

Each of the structural conditions discussed above deserves further detailed empirical attention. We know very little about the specific feeling norms involved, how much consensus there is about those norms, or the frequency with which emotional deviance occurs. Again, I would suggest exploratory research to address these questions. Intensive interviews with target samples, such as those who hold multiple roles (e.g., wife-mother-employee), those going through normative and nonnormative transitions (e.g., soon-to-be brides and grooms, the bereaved, the newly divorced, new stepparents), and those subject to strong normative emotional constraints (e.g., parents, clinical psychologists, physicians) should be fruitful. From my student questionnaires, it appears that individuals currently threatened with or undergoing role loss may constitute particularly informative target groups. Fully 48.1 percent of those who reported deviant emotional reactions were describing the serious illness, suicide, or death of a loved one;

the others described discovering a lover's infidelity, performance failure, and being rejected by a valued group. Each of these stressors involved threatened or actual role loss.

A related motivational issue I raised earlier was the conditions under which individuals are willing to accept their emotional deviations and resist the sanctions of others. Especially interesting may be members of protest groups, ranging from labor protest, nuclear protest, women's and minority group protest, to members of groups such as Mothers Against Drunk Drivers (MADD) and tenants rights groups. Protest group members are likely to be motivated by their emotional reactions to situations of injustice, oppression, or threat. Typically, too, their protests are likely to fall on deaf ears or to elicit negative sanctions from powerful others who are the perpetrators of injustice. Social support may be necessary for feelings that are deviant in the eyes of the majority to become legitimized, both for the minority and eventually for the majority. When feelings are shared and validated by others, they can become not only understandable and "normal," but also normative. Conditions under which deviant emotions can become normative may include prolonged contact between similarly affected individuals, a threshold number of such individuals, ineffective threats or incentives from powerful authorities for conformity, and perhaps a charismatic spokesperson for the group (Wasielewski, 1985). Shared deviant feelings may be crucial in the transformation of similar others into counternormative peer groups, deviant subcultures, and social movements.

To examine these issues, one would need to study a protest group from its inception, or alternatively, to rely on speeches and archival materials to reconstruct the emotional history of a movement. Further, one might be able to recreate and vary these conditions in a small-group laboratory situation to predict coalition-building and organized protest against, say, an oppressive experimental confederate. To develop such a design, one would have to look carefully at experimental studies of conflict and of coalition formation for guidance. The working hypothesis would be that without shared and validated emotional reactions among actors, an effective protest group would be unable to form or survive.

Individuals who join self-help groups may be motivated by self-perceived deviant feelings, as well (Thoits, 1986). This is especially suggested in the literature on bereavement, but may be true for single parents, children of alcoholics, victims of rape, battered women, and other individuals facing a particular stressful experience (Coates and Winston, 1983). In the bereavement literature, widows and widowers frequently note that others think that it is wrong or abnormal for them to grieve for longer than a year (Glick et al, 1974; Parkes and Weiss, 1983; Silverman, 1986; Weiss,

1976). In self-help groups, the bereaved learn that it is in fact normal (i.e., statistically normative) for mourning to go on for three years, and sometimes longer (Weiss, 1976). My impression from this literature is that American culture is perpetuating a norm for the appropriate duration of grief that is inconsistent with the actual experience of widows and widowers, and that self-help groups function, in part, to validate feelings that their members believe to be deviant. This is an important phenomenon to study. Are there other cases in which the broad social norm is simply incorrect, as measured by the modal experiences of those in the given situation? And if so, how do individuals deal with their deviant feelings, which in statistical fact may not be deviant? I suspect that differential association (Sutherland and Cressey, 1960) and social comparison processes (Festinger, 1954; Cottrell and Epley, 1977)—seeking out others who have faced or are currently facing the same circumstances, for normative comparison and guidance—may be a key way for individuals to reduce the self-condemnation that may result from self-perceptions of emotional deviance. And such studies would help to explain why social support buffers or reduces the psychological impact of major stressors (Cohen and Wills, 1985); individuals are better able to accept and thus subsequently deal with their feelings, once they are reassured that those feelings are expected. A series of participant observation studies of a variety of self-help groups would be warranted, supplemented with personal interviews to ascertain the reasons why members sought out the group and what they believe they have gained from participation. The working hypothesis is that emotional validation and emotional legitimacy are key motivators and rewards.

STUDIES OF EMOTION-MANAGEMENT (COPING) PROCESSES

Although support-seeking is one way that individuals handle emotional deviance, there are a variety of other ways, some of which have been outlined by Hochschild (1979, 1983) in her work on emotion-management. This brings us to the next set of issues raised earlier—processes of managing deviant feelings. Hochschild identifies bodily work (changing physiological sensations), cognitive work (changing the meaning of the situation or feelings), and "deep acting" (engaging in intense expression management). Recently I have expanded Hochschild's typology to outline other methods of emotion-management, or coping (Thoits, 1985, 1986). I derive these methods from a particular model of emotional experience.

Briefly, I view emotion as a subjective experience consisting of four interconnected components: (a) situational cues, (b) physiological changes, (c) expressive gestures, and (d) an emotion label that serves to identify this specific configuration of components.[6] (See figure 7.1) I have argued that children learn the associations among these components from repeatedly hearing emotion labels applied to each configuration that occurs in their experience. For example, the configuration that is culturally labeled "romantic love" might consist of the simultaneous presence of an opposite sex person (situational cue), awareness of flushing and an adrenalin rush in that person's presence (physiological changes), and an awareness of behaviors such as repeatedly looking and smiling at that person (expressive gestures). If certain configurations of components constitute particular emotions such as romantic love, then deliberately changing one element in that configuration should dampen or alter the feeling experience itself. Considerable experimental evidence indicates that changing any one emotional component in a subject's awareness can, in fact, qualitatively alter his/her reported feeling state (see Thoits, 1984, for a review). For example, experiments show that when physiological arousal is blocked with drugs, when facial expressions are posed and held, or when an emotional reaction is attributed to a nonemotional stimulus, the individual's interpretation of his/her feeling state is significantly altered (Ross et al., 1969; Schachter and Wheeler, 1962; Laird, 1984).

Not only experimenters but also individuals themselves are capable of manipulating subjective emotional experience, as numerous qualitative studies show (Mechanic, 1978; Glick et al., 1974; Hochschild, 1981, 1983; Henslin, 1970). Emotion-management, or coping, can be seen as deliberate attempts by the individual to change one or more components of his or her subjective experience in order to bring that feeling in line with normative requirements. There are two primary modes that individuals use to alter

FIGURE 7.1
A Model of Subjective Emotional Experience

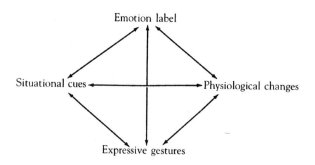

components of emotional experience: behavioral and cognitive. That is, one can target situational cues, physiological sensations, expressive behaviors, and/or emotion labels for change, and change them either behaviorally or cognitively (or both). An eight-fold table of emotion-management techniques results (with one empty cell—due to the logical impossibility of changing an emotion label behaviorally). Table 7.1 indicates a number of techniques of emotion-management that are derived from this model of emotion-management, or coping.

Through the analysis of students' written accounts of how they handled positive and negative emotional experiences, I have obtained qualitative data on the use of these (and other)methods of emotion-management. The ten most frequently mentioned techniques in handling a negative emotional experience were (in decreasing order of frequency): catharsis, taking direct action, seeking support, hiding feelings, seeing the situation differently, leaving the situation, thinking the situation through, thought-stopping, distraction, and acceptance (Thoits, 1987). The five most effective methods in the students' perceptions were (in descending order of perceived effectiveness): seeking support, seeing the situation differently, catharsis, hiding feelings, and taking direct action. In short, actions and

TABLE 7.1
Examples of Emotion-Management Techniques

Focus	Mode	
	Behavioral	Cognitive
Situation-Focused Strategies	Act, confront Seek information, advice, practical aid Withdraw, leave	Reinterpret situation Distraction Thought-stopping Accept the situation Fantasize solution, or escape
Emotion-Focused Strategies Physiology	Hard exercise Use drugs/alcohol Relaxation techniques	Biofeedback Meditation Progressive desensitization Hypnosis
Expressive Gestures	Catharsis Hide Feelings	Fantasy release Prayer
Emotional Label	(N.A.)	Reinterpret feelings

thoughts focused on the situation itself or on the expressive component of emotion were most frequently used and perceived as effective.

Other key questions to explore are whether preferred emotion-management techniques vary by gender, social class, and age; whether the methods used by individuals vary systematically with characteristics of the situation (e.g., positive versus negative, controllable versus uncontrollable, anticipated versus unanticipated situations); and whether, and when, different emotion-management techniques will be effective in lessening emotional distress. My preliminary analyses indicate that there are gender differences in the use of emotion-management strategies in negative circumstances, with women more likely to use catharsis, seeking support, hiding feelings, seeing the situation differently, and—an unanticipated, possibly cathartic method—writing about the situation (in the form of poetry, unsent letters, and journals). Men more frequently report thinking through the situation, engaging in hard exercise, and acceptance (Thoits, 1987). Similar gender differences have been reported by other coping researchers, along with age differences in the use of cognitive techniques (e.g., Pearlin and Schooler, 1978; Folkman et al., 1987). Social class differences in emotion-management are crucial to explore, as some evidence suggests that lower socioeconomic status predicts the use of less effective coping strategies (Pearlin and Schooler, 1978). The conditions under which emotion-management techniques succeed or fail to transform deviant feelings into normative ones have not been examined, but one obvious condition alluded to earlier would be the presence or absence of social support (i.e., emotion-management assistance) from others who have been similarly affected in the past (Thoits, 1986).

Such exploratory research ultimately may result in more rigorous hypothesis-testing in laboratory situations or in field experiments. For example, my preliminary impressions from the student data suggest that uncontrollable situations (such as death, a parent's divorce, being laid off, being rejected by a lover) more frequently are managed cognitively—that is, the individual looks for the "silver lining," has a realization that allows acceptance, or compares him/herself to someone worse off. If this is the case, then one would expect that subjects exposed to an uncontrollable stressor in a laboratory situation would be less distressed if an experimenter or confederate suggested a way to reinterpret the meaning of the stressor, rather than advocated some other emotion-management method (such as distraction, feigning calm, or practicing deep breathing) (see Speisman et al., 1964). One could systematically vary the nature of the laboratory stressors and the emotion-work advice that is given in order to identify what types of coping methods are most effective in what types of situations. Results of such testing would have some practical implications in the long run for developing interventions for distressed groups.

SUBSTANTIVE APPLICATIONS

Some of the most obvious theoretical applications of the emotional deviance concept have been discussed above: experienced feelings, feeling and display rules, and emotional deviance are important and currently neglected topics in social change and in stress and coping processes. Attention to affective dynamics in protest-group formation and in stress management could elucidate substantive issues in each area *and* reveal more about the properties of emotions themselves. To illustrate these latter points, I will draw examples from studies of stress.

One puzzling substantive problem in the stress field is the apparent nonspecificity of the impacts of stress exposure. Some individuals become physically ill while others become psychologically disturbed after undergoing major stressful life changes. A closer reading of the literature indicates that positive *or* negative life changes can produce physical illness, while only negative life changes produce psychological disturbance, often with accompanying physical complaints (see Thoits, 1983, for a review). But why should this be? Why should positive events predict physical illness but not psychological disturbance? Attention to emotion could further specify the conditions under which stress exposure will result in physical as opposed to psychological disorder. It is important to note that stress reactions are *emotional* reactions to perceived threat to the self—feelings of anxiety, tension, frustration, upset, and despair. The physiological arousal accompanying such emotional reactions can overtax bodily resources, for example, immunological responses to infectious agents are impaired under stress (Jemmott and Locke, 1984). Because *any* stressor, positive or negative, can produce emotional and thus physiological arousal, physical illness is a risk during periods of positive as well as negative life change; risk of psychological disturbance is minimized because desirable changes have positive implications for self-esteem. In contrast, because negative events are both physiologically arousing and threatening to self-esteem, both physical and psychological disturbance are health risks. Researchers might profit theoretically from conceptualizing stress reactions explicitly as emotional reactions. By acknowledging the physiological components of emotion as well as their psychological or sociocultural meanings, psychosocial stress researchers might better specify and explain the conditions under which stress exposure produces physical versus psychological disorder.

Further properties of emotion also might emerge from substantive research. For example, deviant emotions appear to be manipulatable only up to a point; individuals often report unsuccessful outcomes of their emotion-management attempts (e.g., Hochschild, 1981, 1983). Evidence in the emotional socialization literature suggests that the connections among some components of emotion are stronger than others, for example, situational stimuli and facial expressions seem to be more strongly associated with each other and with particular emotion labels than they are with discernible physiological states (Pollak and Thoits, 1989; Gordon, in press). Thus, attempts to change feelings by manipulating an existing physiological state may be relatively unsuccessful in transforming a deviant or undesirable emotion because physiological states are only weakly linked to other emotional components. If research consistently shows certain emotion-management strategies to be unsuccessful, then further evidence for the relatively weak or strong relationships among the elements that comprise emotional experience could be deduced. Thus, substantive research could reveal further properties of emotions per se.

The concept of emotional deviance also can be applied more generally within the substantive field of deviance. It seems especially applicable to the recognition and labeling of mental illness (and perhaps as well to the labeling of other problems involving feelings states such as addiction, homosexuality, and child and spouse abuse). I have argued elsewhere (Thoits, 1985) that a large subset of mental disorders described in the Diagnostic and Statistical Manual, Third Edition, or DSM-III (APA, 1980) are essentially defined by the presence of deviant emotions or deviant expressive behaviors. My informal analysis of the diagnostic criteria indicates that 46 percent of the 210 disorders described in DSM-III are identified by the presence of inappropriate or socially undesirable emotional states or affective displays. A more systematic analysis with interrater-reliability coding of the diagnostic criteria still needs to be done. However, it seems clear from this preliminary analysis that the "residual deviance" that Scheff (1966) claimed to identify mental illness is, in an important subset of cases, *emotional* deviance (e.g., anxiety disorders, affective disorders, adjustment disorders). In short, clinicians and laypersons alike may recognize and label mental illness when emotional deviance is observed to occur persistently, repeatedly, or with intensity.

That laypersons' attributions of psychiatric disturbance are based at least in part on observed emotional deviations has been shown in a preliminary study by Pugliesi (1987). Similar systematic studies are needed to verify this finding. The use of vignettes seems particularly useful for this research question (see Lam and Thurman, 1985, for an excellent example of the use of this method). The symptoms of a described target person can be systematically varied in vignettes or short case histories and then assessed by samples of judges. The working hypothesis would be that persistent or intense inappropriate feelings or displays will be judged by samples of laypersons *and* clinicians to be indicators of psychiatric impairment much more frequently than will symptoms involving inappropriate cognitions or inappropriate behaviors. If this hypothesis is confirmed, a foundation for further work on the causes and consequences of psychological disturbance as emotional deviance will have been laid.

Substantive attention to emotion-management processes and emotional deviance enables the development of a theory of the social etiology of mental illness. To summarize the argument to which I have alluded at various points in this chapter, structural conditions (role conflict, role strain, marginal status, normative and nonnormative role transitions) can produce emotions that deviate from those that are socially expected in given situations. Desirous of maintaining social approval, the individual will likely engage in emotion-management attempts to bring feelings in line with expectations. Under certain conditions, such as persistent structural strain and the lack of emotion-management assistance from others, emotion-management attempts will fail (or in some cases miscarry, as when a specific technique is overused to the exclusion of others). Failures will result in continued or recurrent emotional deviance, which in turn may be interpreted by the individual himself or herself or by others as symptoms of mental disorder. Once this deviance has been labeled as a psychological problem by the individual, by observing laypersons, or by clinicians, certain consequences follow, among them, voluntary or involuntary treatment for disorder. However, unlike other labeling theorists, I argue that labeling does not necessarily transform the individual's identity to mental patient nor is the individual's disorder necessarily sustained through differential treatment by others (see Scheff, 1966).

Because psychiatrists and psychologists are in the business of providing emotion-management assistance,[7] the willing participant in treatment may be able to convert his/her emotional deviance to emotional "normality." When feelings have been transformed successfully, psychological disturbance no longer exists. (See Thoits, 1985, for a more detailed explication of this argument.) Note that this explanation of mental illness etiology (and of therapeutic outcomes) has translated a set of concepts and processes from stress theory into the language of emotion. Structural conditions produce emotional deviations (reactions to stress); the individual attempts to manage (cope with) these deviant feelings; when emotion-management assistance from others (social support) is unavailable, emotion work is more likely to fail, resulting in persistent or recurrent emotional deviance (psychological disturbance). Professional emotion-management assistance (psychotherapy) can help to transform deviant affect into normative affect. Emotions theory helps integrate what have been treated as distinct substantive topics in stress and mental health research: stress, coping, social support, and psychological disorder. Moreover, attention to affective processes points to new hypotheses for research in mental health. For example, if social support is conceived as emotion-management assistance, then forms of support (or even psychotherapy) that legitimize and reinforce the individual's own preferred emotion-management strategies ought to be more effective in transforming deviant feelings than support attempts (or therapeutic modes) that differ from those that the individual prefers. This is the substantive promise of emotions theory and emotional processes, more generally: old notions can be reconceptualized and new hypotheses developed to better explain how important sociological phenomena such as deviance are created, maintained, and/or terminated.

This chapter has suggested a number of difficult, but, I hope, intriguing issues that need to be explored in the future. The concept of emotional deviance is a rich one, with implications for a number of substantive areas—social problems, social deviance, social movements, and, of course, stress, coping, and mental health. Exploratory research into some of the issues that have been raised here should further refine our understanding of the emotional underpinnings of problems that have preoccupied the sociological imagination for some time.

NOTES

1. The social consequences of emotional expression tend to be explored less frequently.

2. However, debates have focused on the degree to which emotions are socially constructed (and physiologically undifferentiated) as opposed to socially determined (and physiologically distinct) (e.g., Kemper, 1980, 1981, 1987; Shott, 1979, 1980).

3. I have pointed out (Thoits, 1984) that emotion work is similar to coping, since through coping individuals try to change problematic situations that induce unwanted emotions or try to change the problematic emotions themselves.

4. See also Rossi and Berk (1985) for alternative methods of identifying norms, including estimates of the degree of normative consensus.

5. Notice the "taken for granted" nature of emotion in these replies; conventional emotional reactions are viewed as "normal" or "justified." In a very real sense, emotion norms may be "residual norms," in Thomas Scheff's (1966) terms—recognized and acknowledged only when deviance has occurred.

6. Expressive gestures (facial expression, body posture, tone of voice, expressive behaviors) are not necessarily observable during a subjective emotional experience. This is due to the considerable control individuals can exercise over the public display of affect. However, individuals are often privately aware of the sup-

pression or control of such gestures, so even when suppressed, they remain an important and distinguishable component of subjective experience.

7. Another important topic for research would explore the degree to which this claim about psychotherapy is valid. Certain schools of therapy appear to advocate particular emotion-management methods. Behavioral therapy advocates changing the situation or expressive performances; cognitive therapy advocates changing the meaning of stressful situations; biofeedback and progressive desensitization, changing physiological reactions through cognitive means, and so on. A careful analysis of the methods of emotion-management promulgated by these different schools would be useful. Assuming that individuals have preferences for certain emotion-management strategies over others, a further hypothesis regarding early termination of treatment might be examined: those who stay in treatment of a certain type prefer the emotion-management method being advocated; those who terminate prematurely have experienced a mismatch between their preferred coping strategy and the strategy advocated by the therapist.

REFERENCES

American Psychiatric Association. 1980. *Diagnostic and Statistical Manual of Mental Disorders, 3rd Edition.* Washington, DC: APA.

Averill, James. 1978. "Anger." Pp. 1–80 in *Nebraska Symposium on Motivation, Vol. 26,* edited by H. Howe and R. Dienstbier. Lincoln, NB: University of Nebraska Press.

Bernstein, Basil. 1974. *Class, Codes and Control.* London: Routledge & Kegan Paul.

Cancian, Francesca M. 1987. *Love in America: Gender and Self-Development.* Cambridge: Cambridge University Press.

Clark, Candace. 1987. "Sympathy Biography and Sympathy Margin." *American Journal of Sociology* 93:290–321.

Coates, Dan and Tina Winston. 1983. "Counteracting the Deviance of Depression: Peer Support Groups for Victims." *Journal of Social Issues* 39:169–94.

Cohen, Sheldon and Thomas A. Wills. 1985. "Stress, Social Support, and the Buffering Hypothesis." *Psychological Bulletin* 98:310–57.

Cottrell, Nickolas B. and Stephen W. Epley. 1977. "Affiliation, Social Comparison, and Socially Mediated Stress Reduction." Pp. 43–68 in *Social Comparison Processes: Theoretical and Empirical Perspectives,* edited by Jerry M. Suls and Richard L. Miller. Washington, DC: Hemisphere.

Ekman, Paul, R. W. Levenson, and Wallace V. Friesen. 1983. "Autonomic Nervous System Activity Distinguishes among Emotions." *Science* 221:1208–10.

Ekman, Paul, Wallace V. Friesen, and Pheobe Ellsworth. 1982. "What Are the Similarities and Differences in Facial Behavior across Cultures?." Pp. 128–43 in *Emotion in the Human Face, 2nd Edition*, edited by Paul Ekman. Cambridge: Cambridge University Press.

Festinger, Leon. 1954. "A Theory of Social Comparison Processes." *Human Relations* 7:117–40.

Folkman, Susan, Richard S. Lazarus, Scott Pimley, and Jill Novacek. 1987. "Age Differences in Stress and Coping Processes." *Psychology and Aging* 2:171–84.

Frude, Neil and Alison Goss. 1981. "Maternal Anger and the Young Child." Pp. 52–63 in *Psychological Approaches to Child Abuse*, edited by Neil Frude. Totowa, NJ: Rowman & Littlefield.

Glick, I. O., Robert S. Weiss, and C. M. Parkes. 1974. *The First Year of Bereavement*. New York: Wiley.

Gordon, Steven L. (in press). "The Socialization of Children's Emotions: Emotional Culture, Competence, and Exposure." In *Children's Understanding of Emotion*. Edited by Carolyn I. Saarni and Paul Harris. Cambridge: Cambridge University Press.

Graham, Hilary. 1981. "Mothers' Accounts of Anger and Aggression toward Their Babies." Pp. 39–63 in *Psychological Approaches to Child Abuse*, edited by Neil Frude. Totowa, NJ: Rowman & Littlefield.

Harris, Paul, Tjeert Olthof, and Mark Meerum Terwogt. 1981. "Children's Knowledge of Emotion." *Journal of Child Psychology and Psychiatry* 22:247–61.

Harter, Susan. 1983. "Children's Understanding of Multiple Emotions: A Cognitive-Developmental Approach." Pp. 147–94 in *The Relationship between Social and Cognitive Development*, edited by Willis F. Overton. Hillsdale, NJ: Lawrence Erlbaum.

Heise, David R. 1979. *Understanding Events: Affect and the Construction of Social Action*. Cambridge: Cambridge University Press.

———. 1986. "Modeling Symbolic Interaction." Pp. 291–309 in *Approaches to Social Theory*, edited by Siegwart Lindenberg, James S. Coleman, and Stefan Nowak. New York: Russel Sage.

Henslin, James M. 1970. "Guilt and Guilt Neutralization: Response and Adjustment to Suicide." Pp. 192–228 in *Deviance and Respectability: The Social Construction of Moral Meanings*, edited by Jack D. Douglas. New York: Basic.

Hochschild, Arlie R. 1979. "Emotion Work, Feeling Rules, and Social Structure." *American Journal of Sociology* 85: 551–75.

——— . 1981. "Attending to, Codifying, and Managing Feelings: Sex Differences in Love." In *Sex and Gender: A Reader.* Edited by L. W. Richardson and V. Taylor. New York: Heath.

——— . 1983. *The Managed Heart: The Commercialization of Human Feeling.* Berkeley, CA: University of California Press.

Jemmott, John B., III and Steven E. Locke. 1984. "Psychosocial Factors, Immunologic Mediation, and Human Susceptibility to Infectious Diseases: How Much Do We Know?" *Psychological Bulletin* 95:78–108.

Kemper, Theodore D. 1978. *A Social Interactional Theory of Emotions.* New York: Wiley.

——— . 1980. "Sociology, Physiology, and Emotions: Comment on Shott." *American Journal of Sociology* 85:1418–23.

——— . 1987. "How Many Emotions are There? Wedding the Social and Autonomic Components." *American Journal of Sociology* 93:263–85.

——— . 1981. "Social Constructionist and Positivist Approaches to the Sociology of Emotions." *American Journal of Sociology* 87:336–61.

Laird, James. 1984. "The Real Role of Facial Response in the Experience of Emotion: A Reply to Tourangeau and Ellsworth and Others." *Journal of Personality and Social Psychology* 47:909–17.

Lam, Julie A. and Quint C. Thurman. 1985. "Sorting Out the Cuckoo's Nest: How Do We Know Who is Crazy?" Presented at the American Sociological Association, Washington, DC, August.

Lewis, Michael and Linda Michalson. 1983. *Children's Emotions and Moods: Developmental Theory and Measurement.* New York: Plenum.

Lofland, Lynn. 1985. "The Social Shaping of Emotion: Grief in Historical Perspective." *Symbolic Interaction* 8:171–90.

McCoy, Charles L. and John C. Masters. 1985. "The Development of Children's Strategies for the Social Control of Emotion." *Child Development* 56:1214–22.

Mechanic, David. 1978. *Students Under Stress: A Study in the Social Psychology of Adaptation.* Madison, WI: University of Wisconsin Press.

Parkes, C. M. and Robert S. Weiss. 1983. *Recovery from Bereavement.* New York: Basic Books.

Pearlin, Leonard I. and Carmi Schooler. 1978. "The Structure of Coping." *Journal of Health and Social Behavior* 19:2–21.

Pennebaker, James W. 1982. *The Psychology of Physical Symptoms.* New York: Springer-Verlag.

Pollak, Lauren Harte and Peggy A Thoits. 1989. "Processes in Emotional Socialization." *Social Psychology Quarterly* 52:22–34.

Pugliesi, Karen L. 1987. "Deviation in Emotion and the Labeling of Mental Illness." *Deviant Behavior* 8:79–102.

Ross, Lee, Judith Rodin, and Phillip G. Zimbardo. 1969. "Toward an Attribution Therapy: The Reduction of Fear through Induced Cognitive-Emotional Misattribution." *Journal of Personality and Social Psychology* 12:279–88.

Rossi, Peter H. and Richard A. Berk. 1985. "Varieties of Normative Consensus." *American Sociological Review* 50:333–47.

Saarni, Carolyn. 1979. "Children's Understanding of Display Rules for Expressive Behavior." *Developmental Psychology* 15:424–29.

Schachter, Stanley and Ladd Wheeler. 1962. "Epinephrine, Chlorpromazine, and Amusement." *Journal of Abnormal and Social Psychology* 65:121–8.

Scheff, Thomas. 1966. *Being Mentally Ill.* Chicago: Aldine.

Shott, Susan. 1979. "Emotion and Social Life: A Symbolic Interactionist Analysis." *American Journal of Sociology* 84:1317–34.

———. 1980. "Reply to Kemper." *American Journal of Sociology* 85:1423–6.

Silverman, Phyllis R. 1986. *Widow to Widow.* New York: Springer.

Sommers, Shula. 1984a. "Adults Evaluating Their Emotions: A Cross-Cultural Perspective." Pp. 319–38 in *Emotion in Adult Development,* edited by C. A. Malatesta and C. E. Izard. Beverly Hills, CA: Sage.

———. 1984b. "Reported Emotions and Conventions of Emotionality among College Students." *Journal of Personality and Social Psychology* 46:207–15.

Speisman, J. C., R. S. Lazarus, A. M. Mordkoff, and L. A. Davison. 1964. "The Experimental Reduction of Stress Based on Ego-Defense Theory." *Journal of Abnormal and Social Psychology* 68:367–80.

Stearns, Caroline Zisowitz and Peter N. Stearns. 1986. *Anger: The Struggle for Emotional Control in America's History.* Chicago: University of Chicago Press.

Sutherland, Edwin H., and Donald R. Cressey. 1960. *Principles of Criminology,* 6th Ed. Chicago: J. B. Lippincott.

Thoits, Peggy A. 1983. "Dimensions of Life Events that Influence Psychological Distress: An Evaluation and Synthesis of the Literature." Pp. 33–103 in *Psychosocial Stress: Trends in Theory and Research,* edited by Howard B. Kaplan. New York: Academic.

————. 1984. "Coping, Social Support, and Psychological Outcomes: The Central Role of Emotion." Pp. 219–38 in *Review of Personality and Social Psychology, Vol. 5.* edited by Phillip Shaver. Beverly Hills, CA: Sage.

————. 1985. "Self-Labeling Processes in Mental Illness: The Role of Emotional Deviance." *American Journal of Sociology* 92:221–49.

————. 1986. "Social Support as Coping Assistance." *Journal of Consulting and Clinical Psychology* 54:416–23.

————. 1987. "Gender Differences in Coping with Emotional Distress." Paper presented at the American Public Health Association, New Orleans, October.

Wasielewski, Patricia. 1985. "The Emotional Basis of Charisma." *Symbolic Interaction* 8:207–22.

Weiss, Robert S. 1976. "Transition States and other Stressful Situations: Their Nature and Programs for Their Management." Pp. 213–32 in *Support Systems and Mutual Help: Multidisciplinary Explorations,* edited by Gerald Kaplan and Marie Killilea. New York: Bruce & Stratton.

Zillman, Dolf. 1978. "Attribution and Misattribution of Excitatory Reactions." Pp. 335–61 in *New Directions in Attribution, Vol. 2.* Edited by John H. Harvey, William Ickes, and Robert F. Kidd. Hillsdale, NJ: Lawrence Erlbaum.

part five

EMOTIONS AND SOCIAL MICRO PROCESSES

.

8.

Social Relations and Emotions:
A Structural Approach

Theodore D. Kemper

There are many points of entry into the sociology of emotions. Here the approach is relational. Emotions are seen to result from events that happen in episodes of social interaction with family, friends, coworkers, organizational superiors and subordinates, and so on. Undeniably we experience fear, anger, joy, sadness, pride, guilt shame, nostalgia, hope, hate, desire, contempt, and other emotions in consequence of what our interaction partners do to us and what we do to them. The only advance that a sociologist can hope to make over this common sense understanding is to systematize what we know about how social relations produce emotions. A systematic formulation permits us to explain with a plausible certainty why certain emotions are felt, as well as to predict with some confidence which emotions are likely to emerge in specified conditions. This is much like the theory that explains the motion of a ball rolling down an inclined plane. One doesn't need to be a physicist armed with the concepts of gravity, mass, and friction to tell what will happen. But the physical theory provides a systematic explanation of why it does happen.

First, I will review the work that affords systematic knowledge about the relational precursors of emotions. This will show that there is substantial evidence for plausible hypotheses about many relational conditions and their probable emotional outcomes. But every theory is incomplete. In order to explain anything, it must omit the pretense of explaining everything. Thus, there are always unanswered questions: (*a*) challenges from other theories, (*b*) from disconfirming findings, and (*c*) from possible failures of internal logic. In the latter part of this chapter, I will examine these issues. They invite a research agenda of work that needs to be done to establish a relational theory more firmly.

A LOGIC FOR A SCIENCE OF SOCIAL RELATIONS

Let us grant that the social world is mysterious and challenging. Is it also inherently unknowable? Some social scientists, who are presumably dedicated to learning about the world, take this view. This means, for them, that no systematic knowledge about the social world is possible. It means also that for them descriptive typologies and category schemes are arbitrary constructions of little value. It means that all efforts to sort human conduct into meaningfully coherent classes are doomed from the outset because human agency and human freedom defy and invalidate such schemes.[1]

An opposed view operates on the philosophy of "as if" (Vaihinger, 1965). Whether or not the world is fundamentally mysterious and unknowable, is itself unknowable. If it is true, how can we know it in advance of very strenuous efforts to prove otherwise? Indeed, the history of social science is so brief that it can hardly be said to have had a fair chance to show what it can accomplish. Perhaps, comparatively, we are only in *our* days of alchemy. But, if this is the case, it is well to remember that alchemy was the precursor of scientific chemistry. Indeed, the whole issue is philosophical, not scientific, for science must proceed "as if" knowledge is possible. And if not today, then tomorrow. To rule out the possibility a priori may make sense philosophically, but not scientifically.

Now, to be anti-scientific, though it goes against a strong tenet of the modern ethos, is no crime. And there is, perhaps, some merit to such a position, or at least to a view that reserves some judgment. Indeed, the Frankfurt School of social philosophers (e.g. Horkheimer, 1976; Marcuse, 1964) raised many serious questions in their critique of the spirit of scientific rationality in our age. If one accepts the validity of their indictment, one does not engage in scientific inquiry as it has been conventionally understood, namely, a rigorous empirical search for universal laws of conduct, through the use of quantitative methods. Yet, the spirit of scientific inquiry, though susceptible to warp, distortion, and ideology, also holds out an optimistic hope in the face of pessimistic alternatives, that whether or not the social world is inherently knowable, it is worth making the effort to find out. This is the position taken here and in the social relational approach to the understanding of emotions.[2]

Within the sociology of emotions there is a variant of the anti-positivist position that is known as "social constructionism." Its fundamental premise is that social life is created by actors in the process of interaction, guided in some sense by social norms. The construction of social life includes also the emotional responses to interaction. Taken very seriously, this means that there are no natural emotional reactions to stimuli. Indeed, there are no stimuli, in an objective sense, but simply individually guided interpretations of what is perceived, which is itself—to take the argument to a radical conclusion—formed by interpretation (Heelas, 1987). Hence, if we say that it is "natural" to experience fear or anger or satisfaction, and so forth in certain situations, this violates the social constructionist canon with respect to: (1) the presumed nonnaturalness of emotions; and (2) that "situations" are in any sense universal, definable in the same way for everyone.

The upshot of these views is that it is not possible to predict emotions. The further consequence is that the sociology of emotions must rest content with a post-hoc descriptive understanding rather than a causal explanation of its phenomena. The relational approach demurs at this, and seeks, per contra, to establish adequate causal explanation of emotions at the social level.

Although the relational approach is espoused here, there are serious questions of theory and metatheory that are contained in the social constructionist challenge. These questions will be examined in the latter section of the chapter. At this point, the stage is set for presenting the relational approach.

SOCIAL RELATIONS AS POWER AND STATUS

What goes on between human actors? What do they actually do to, with, by, for, against each other? Indeed, an infinite number of concrete actions may be observed. No conceivable act can be omitted from a complete catalog. But there would be relatively little value in knowing the infinite set of behaviors that are possible. What to do? Indeed, we must do what is done in any science, namely, taxonomize, create classes of behaviors that somehow fit together and are more or less surrogates for each other, thus reducing the infinite variety of possible behaviors to a few manageable classes. For example, in semantics we have classes of *synonyms*, namely, words that mean essentially the same thing. Clearly, this is a useful concision. The class label, or concept, references the whole set of verbal behaviors and meanings that it stands for. Can the same be done for other behaviors? Indeed it can. But the stakes change, for the interest is not merely in efficiency, but also in necessity.

Now the question is: What is the least number of classes necessary to describe social behavior? It is certainly a basic scientific question, and as such, any answer to it must necessarily be tentative, tested by its usefulness according to the usual canons of science, namely, that it suggests productive lines of research and provides satisfying explanations of the phenomena to which it is applied.

A major reason for seeking the least number of classes to describe behavior is that a good answer augurs completeness, namely, that one has got hold of all the important terms of the theory that explain the matters at hand. Now, completeness is a chimera in science. If ever it were attained, it would signify the end of inquiry. This has not yet happened in the history of any science, and is not likely to. The pursuit of knowledge is open-ended. Each answer produces new questions. Indeed, the history of science has been called "the history of human error." This is because each advance in knowledge is superseded by new advances that show how the previous understanding was inadequate, wrong, incomplete, or otherwise flawed. But, and this is crucial, the prospect of error should not deter scientific forward motion. Indeed, it is only by proceeding onward with the answers we have that we can learn their defects and obtain better ones.[3] Although this is more easily done in some sciences than others, in principle it applies in all pursuits of knowledge. Albeit we must guard against the hubris of believing that we have attained completeness at any state of scientific work, at every stage we must proceed "as if" we possessed it.

Now there are several ways to get at the least number of dimensions of social interaction. One, and historically the longest enduring, is simply to think them up. Indeed, this is what social theorists—mainly philosophers—have done for several thousand years. They—we—try to understand matters from a general point of view. We ignore some distinctions in order to embrace the whole set of possibilities under a comprehensive rubric. For many purposes, we think better with general rubrics. There are fewer specifics to clutter the analysis, and we can reason to more general conclusions. Every time we say "that *kind* of thing," "those *sorts* of people," "under *certain* circumstances," we are reasoning with general rubrics. Granted that any particular things, people, or circumstances are never precisely the same as others in their class, it is still exceedingly useful for many purposes to ignore the minor differences. Therefore, we do it. We refine, or redefine, our classes when we see that they do not work.

In the domain of modern scientific analysis, we still proceed as philosophers have for several millennia and as ordinary people do in everyday life. But we also have other methods. They include systematic observation and statistical analysis of the observations. If done right, they are rigorous and are both valid and reliable. Validity means that we are actually observing what we set out to observe, and not something else. Reliability means that other observers would also see what we see, and that the observations are stable over time. The name given to this empirical-statistical approach to obtain the least number of dimensions of social behavior is "factor analysis." Of considerable interest for what is to come is that in the domain of social behavior, the mental method of ancient philosophers and the factor-analytic method of modern social science are in fundamental agreement on the least number of dimensions of social behavior and what they mean. This is a remarkable convergence, wholly unexpected, but highly gratifying to workers in this area. In addition, as will be detailed below, other domains of investigation—from semantics to ethology—also support the factor analytic findings about social interaction. First, the factor analytic research.

In by-now dozens of studies involving observations of ad hoc discussion groups, husbands and wives, parents and children, teachers and students, children at play, labor and management negotiators, military teams, supervisors and subordinates in corporations and other bureaucracies, intimates in love relations, clients and therapists in psychiatric interviews, and in numerous other interactional settings, two significant dimensions of social relational behavior have emerged. They are variously named by the investigators but they signify the same underlying notions. [4]

The first dimension contains behaviors that are oriented toward control, dominance, coercion, threat, punishment, and assertion of self over others. I call this "power," since it reflects Weber's (1946) idea of power as the ability to realize one's will even over the opposition of others. The others do not like it, but they comply because resistance will bring consequences and costs they are not prepared to pay, for example, pain, incarceration, loss of benefits, psychic wounds and the like, to themselves or to those they care for. Everyone has experienced power in one or another way, to one or another degree of intensity. In general, we do not like it. Equally, everyone has used power against others. In general they do not like it. Some use power when they do not have to. Others do not use it when perhaps they should in their own defense. We may say in general that power is a major mode of human social behavior, one that is frequently manifested in relations between individuals.

The second factor analytic dimension comprehends behaviors that are understood as supportive, giving, friendly, congenial, affectionate, rewarding. I call this dimension "status-accord" (status, in brief) because it reflects the kind of voluntary deference and compliance that is the mark of true systems of status, sociologically conceived (see Zelditch, 1968). In these, individuals receive rewards and benefits, but not on the basis of threat, compulsion, or punishment, as in power relations, but rather because the givers authentically want to accord their respect, cooperation, good feelings, and intimacy to the other. In this model, the ultimate level of status-conferral is love, where, in principle, one person offers unlimited benefits to the other. We have all experienced status-conferral (in varying amounts) from others—parents, friends, intimate acquaintances, spouses, bosses, teachers, et al. Sometimes we have received less status from them than we thought we deserved. And sometimes they have received less from us than they thought they deserved.

Keeping in mind now the perils of claiming completeness in a scientific model, I want to assert that on the basis of the many factor-analytic results, the power and status dimensions characterize social relations sufficiently well for a large number of purposes, and especially for understanding emotions. This means that when we observe the many concrete actions of persons relating to each other—arguing, kissing, grabbing, pushing, caressing, agreeing, pointing at, eyeing, touching, turning away from, shouting, cooing, frowning, striking, smiling, and so forth—underlying these observations are the operating dimensions of power and status—some behaviors reflecting one factor, some the other. Concrete social relations are composed of different mixes of power and status behaviors. Sometimes these are fairly stable over time and we can speak of a "social structure"—a pattern of social relations that we expect to occur again and again. Sometimes the power-status mix varies considerably from occasion to occasion—indeed it can vary from moment to moment as power and status behaviors produce emotions of anger, fear, chagrin, guilt, shame, hate, or of gladness, love, pride, astonishment, and so forth. Indeed, emotions are among the primary effects produced by power and status behaviors, both within ourselves and in others. Before we turn to the emotions, two tasks remain. One is to compare the factor-analytic results with the mental reflections on the problem of the least number of dimensions of social behavior. The other is to examine evidence from other domains in support of the power-status formulation.

Dimensions similar to power and status were first recorded twenty-five centuries ago in the work of the Greek pre-Socratic philosopher Empedocles (c490–430 B.C.). He proposed the two dimensions out of a need to introduce dynamism into his essentially static physical model, which consisted of the four elements earth, air, fire, and water. As did many thinkers, both of his own and later times, Empedocles considered these to be the basic constituents of matter in the universe. In order to allow for the obvious changes of state manifested by the four elements, he introduced two dynamic principles, namely, "love" and "strife."

In a manner not entirely clear to us today, since much of Empedocles' work was lost, love and strife enabled the four elements to interact and to change, hence, corresponding with what was empirically known of them. Our best understanding (see Wright, 1981) is that for Empedocles love engendered bonding, closeness, and solidarity, while strife represented dissolution and destruction. What is most engaging about Empedocles' application of love and strife to the transformations of the material world is that he apparently derived the two dimensions from his observations of social life, thus generalizing in the direction opposite from that which is most frequently employed, and criticized by many, today. Notwithstanding the passage of time and the difference in culture, Empedocles' love and strife are incontrovertibly recognizable as the status and power dimensions, respectively. This correspondence between ancient thought and modern scientific analysis is remarkable and augurs well for social science, in that the fundamental principles of human conduct may not be as arcane, hidden, or difficult to discern as some suppose, in the way, for example, that the true properties of the atom are (the domain of particle physics). [This idea, that we know more about social life than we suppose, was put well by Virginia Woolf in her novel *Jacob's Room*.

The strange thing about life is that though the nature of it must have been apparent to everyone for hundreds of years, no one has left any adequate account of it. The streets of London have their map; but our passions are uncharted.[5]

Indeed, the basic forms of social life may be readily apparent. If this is so, an important mission of modern social science would be to choose carefully among the insights that have been offered to us and to examine them with the tools of systematic observation.[6] Whether or not this proves to be the case, the convergence between Empedocles and the factor-analytic method is a landmark in the history of social science discovery.

Empedocles' surmise has found resonance in other formulations over the years (see Kemper, 1978; 1987, for other instances). Most directly, Freud (1937, pp. 349–50) referred to Empedocles as "my great predecessor," because of the obvious parallels between love and strife and Freud's two instinctual principles of Eros and Thanatos.

Although the power and status dimensions are valuable in themselves as comprehensive descriptors of social relations, they are also important as "theoretical constructs" (Willer and Webster, 1970). Theoretical constructs are relatively abstract conceptions that are not tied to specific instances found empirically, but, via rules of correspondence or translation equations, contain all pertinent empirical instances as exemplars. This means that we do not ever see "power," as such, but we do see the kinds of acts—threatening, punishing, depriving, and so forth—that we understand to be connected, conceptually and empirically, to what we have agreed to call power. According to Willer and Webster, sociological theory has failed to cumulate and to attain its proper level of generality because it has not, by and large, operated at the level of theoretical constructs. Hence, for example, it tends to examine specific actions, for example threatening, punishing, depriving—or specific categories of actors—males and females, whites and blacks, teachers and students—instead of theoretical constructs, for example, power relations in the case of the actions listed, and higher and lower status groups in the case of the pairs of actors. Willer and Webster point out that in the mature sciences, specific instances are ignored in the service of the construct level of abstraction. They claim that were sociological theory to be specified at the construct level it would have a fair chance of attaining the same theoretical stature as the mature sciences.

For some this will be read as hubris or wrongheadedness. Indeed a widely prevalent view in contemporary sociology, stemming from the *Geisteswissenschaft* approach of Dilthey (1965), is that sociology can never attain the status of a generalizing science, hence, any search for theoretical constructs is a *fata morgana*. Admittedly, the problems are great. But the search for theory at the construct level has not proceeded at anything like the pace required of it. This, indeed, was Willer and Webster's point.

As sociologists, our main concern is with the applicability of the power-status model to social phenomena, and here, particularly, to emotions. However, it is encouraging that, in one form or another, the self-same model has emerged in a number of other disciplines in the life sciences. Broadly speaking, there appear to be two main systems of relations, structures, or processes—depending on discipline—that are connected with the power and status dimensions and are either parallel to them at different disciplinary levels, or articulate with them as one moves from level to level. Indeed, although we must be sensible to the difficulties involved, there is clearly evidence for a comprehensive biosocial model of human interaction and its outcomes across a broad span, from emotion-related physiological processes in organisms to macrostructures of stratification in society. I turn now to evidence for this.

EVIDENCE FOR POWER AND STATUS FROM OTHER DOMAINS

The power-status model appears to be general, emerging in a number of disciplines in the life sciences, as behavior, as structure, or process. Here I will review evidence from cross-cultural studies, semantic analysis, learning theory and other psychological approaches, parent-child relations, personality development, autonomic and neurophysiological structures and processes, and behavior among infrahuman primates. These additional materials should strengthen confidence in the validity of the power-status dimensions.

Cross-Cultural Studies. A common method of establishing the panhuman validity of a concept is to demonstrate its cross-cultural universality. For example, in recent years researchers in the area of facial expressions of emotion have demonstrated the universality of certain expressions in this way. Reviewing the available studies of social interaction in various cultures, Triandis (1972) concluded that two relational factors called "superordination-subordination" (power) and "intimacy" (status)—are "the fundamental dimensions of human social behavior [that] are obtained with different methods of human investigation" (*The Analysis of Subjective Culture*, p. 270). Subsequently, White (1980) was able to repeat the finding with Melanesian and Indian data, using descriptors of personality that reflect social interaction. Employing multidimensional scaling, Lutz (1982) found that emotion words used by the people of Ifaluk Atoll in the Western Pacific fall along two scales that reflect the power and status dimensions.

Semantic Analysis. The two dimensional model receives strong support from the analysis of semantic meaning, both within and between societies. Using the method of the Semantic Differential, Osgood, Suci, and Tannenbaum (1957) found three fundamental dimensions of meaning: (*a*) potency, (*b*) evaluation, and (*c*) activity.[7] Potency is clearly identifiable with power, and evaluation, reflecting "goodness," with status. These results have been replicated recurrently, and have been found to constitute the fundamental dimensions of meaning cross-culturally as well (Osgood, May, and Miron, 1975).

It has sometimes been argued (D'Andrade, 1965) that results such as these are inevitable, in as much as we are conceptually imprisoned in a certain meaning space. That is, we "see," so to speak, what is already in our head (as conceptual apparatus expressed in language) and no other results are possible. Hence, we view the phenomenal world in the terms of our conceptual structure. A priori linguistic meaning and our models of interaction must thus coincide.

This argument is fundamentally self-defeating. Either it is wrong, in which case language and conceptual structure are not prisons that constrain our observations of the world; or the argument is fundamentally correct, but the effect of this is nil, since, if it is correct, there is no way for us to get at the "real" world in any case. That is, any real world that is different from our conceptual world could never be apprehended. Therefore, it appears that we are left with what has been found semantically, cross-culturally, in observations of human and also, as will be seen below, infrahuman, interaction. Orienting the semantic results sociologically, Heise (1979, and this volume; and see Smith-Lovin this volume) has formulated a set of equations that allow predictions of outcomes of interaction, both behaviorally and emotionally based on the potency (power) and evaluation (status) valences of common language terms that describe interaction.[8] For example, it would be possible to predict the outcomes of such interactions as: The young woman insulted the old man, or the unhappy father picked up the crying baby. Results from this work show good correspondence with predictions of emotion derived by Kemper (1978).

Learning and Other Psychological Theory. Learning theory is a mainstream tradition in Psychology. There is clearly a very close correspondence between the two central dimensions of that theory, rewards and punishments, and status and power, respectively. However, some reconstruction of perspective is necessary to accommodate the two positions. In psychological analysis, punishment and reward refer only to the experience of the actor who receives the stimulus, that is, does it feel bad (punishment) or does it feel good (reward). This is not suitable for sociological analysis, which requires interaction. Yet interaction and experience can be connected by understanding that power has the intent and, if successful, the effect of punishment, and status, similarly, of reward.

Leaning theory has a bad name, so to speak, among some humanistically oriented sociologists; they view it as a soulless technique for manipulation. Therefore, for some, the correspondence between learning theory dimensions and what is proposed here may redound to the disadvantage of the two-dimensional model. Therefore it is useful that the power and status modes are found also in Bakan's (1966) humanistic clinical analysis. Bakan adopted the terms "agency" and "communion" to characterize "two fundamental modalities in the existence of living forms. . . . Agency manifests itself in self-protection, self-assertion, and self-expansion; communion in the sense of being at one with other organisms. . . . Agency manifests itself in the urge to master; communion in noncontractual cooperation" (*The Duality of Human Existence:* pp. 14–15). The correspondence with the power and status dimensions should be overwhelmingly clear.

Parent-Child Interaction and Personality Development. In the domain of child development and socialization, the power and status equivalents are frequently called "control" and "affection" (Becker, 1964; Sroufe, 1979), respectively. The two dimensions are seen by many investigators as the way parents are oriented behaviorally and attitudinally to their children and, in turn, are the relational conditions the children experience. Pearce and Newton (1969) impart a special urgency to the relational conditions in so far as they generate two central dimensions of personality, which they name "security system" and "integral personality." The former reflects distortions of power relations and the consequent warping of personality in the direction of self-protection and defence (power-oriented), while the latter reflects the healthy, open self (status-oriented) that is grounded on a sufficiency of loving care (status-accord).

Autonomic and Neurophysiological Bases. Contemporary sociology may be said to have a "cognitive" bias. This suits the temper of the times in social science, since the same is also true for contemporary psychology. In sociology the cognitive tendency is fostered through the popularity of Symbolic Interactionism, which is oriented to "mind," "meaning," and "symbols"— cognitive elements all. G. H. Mead (1934), of course, is the inspiration for this perspective in sociological analysis.

Yet this is to do some violence to Mead's work, as has been pointed out (McPhail and Rexroat, 1979). Mead, who expatiated on cognitive aspects of mind, was also fully committed to the bodily referents of role-taking. The abandonment of the body in contemporary studies claiming descent from his approach omits a large part of what Mead, as a self-designated "social behaviorist," found relevant. The recent emergence of emotions as a widespread topic both in psychology and sociology reflects an ebbing of the view that the only part of the body that counts for these two fields lies between the hairline and the eyebrows.

Yet, it is admittedly difficult for sociologists, to do more than peer from afar at physiological scholarship as it may pertain to sociological interests. Therefore, the following, elaborated in Kemper (1978; 1984), is only meant to suggest the possibilities that await thorough interdisciplinary investigation.

There is evidence for a heuristic surmise about an important degree of integration between the social (expressed as power and status relations), the psychological (expressed in terms of specific emotions that are instigated in power and status relations—to be described in the next section), and the neurophysiological and autonomic structures and processes that accompany emotions. Funkenstein (1955), whose work has given rise to what is called the "Funkenstein hypothesis," and Gellhorn (1967; 1968) have provided evidence of hormonal and hypothalamic structures and processes that accompany specific emotions that articulate with specific power and status relational outcomes.[9]

The dimensional and processual parallelism between the three levels—social, psychological, and physiological—suggests an important degree of integration of social and physiological processes. Indeed, these systems must necessarily be integrated, or the person, qua organism, would be unable to engage in social relations. A future field of sociophysiology, with more than its bare handful of current practitioners (Barchas 1976; Mazur 1973, 1985; Brinkerhoff and Booth 1984; Ellis, 1986; Udry and Billy, 1987) awaits development. For present purposes, it is important to recognize the degree of articulation that even present-day knowledge allows between the two-dimensional model of social relations and both emotions and physiological structures and processes.

Infrahuman Primates. Perhaps even more tenuous for sociologists than physiological evidence are data from other species. We only rarely examine social behavior among infrahumans, leaving this important domain to ethologists, who begin with a biological orientation and, we may even say, bias. However, the field is theirs by omission. (See Mazur, 1973, for an exception.) Somehow it may seem that for a sociologist to dabble in such work is to endorse the sociobiological premise. However, this does not follow, as I will discuss below.

The case for the two-dimensional model is greatly strengthened by the discovery of its applicability to the social behavior of other primates. Working independently of any sociological scholarship on the subject, Chance (1976; 1980; 1985) also fixed on the two dimensions, referring to them as "the two modes" and calling them "agonic" and "hedonic," for power and status, respectively.

Derived from observations of infrahuman primate societies, the agonic and hedonic forms characterize different patterns of social cohesion in those groups. In the agonic, the focus of attention is toward a central, dominating animal or small set of such animals. Behavior is generally undertaken with reference to the possibility of aggression from the dominant(s). Ordinarily, relatively low amounts of actual aggression take place. The group has achieved a power structure, hence, the active processual display of power is obviated, though it may emerge at any time.

By contrast, in hedonic groups, social organization is a flexible mix of attention to more dominant animals, combined with indifference to them. The group may disperse widely for a time, hence, dominance itself is only occasional. Even when dominance is manifested, it is not with strictly power-based threat or aggressive behavior, but with "displays" that the less dominant animals reflect back with displays of their own. In hedonic groups, there is also a good deal of grooming and hugging, the analogues of status-conferral in these infrahuman groups.

Chance (1985) has also extended to human studies the implications of the two-mode attentional structure, finding in the observations of children's leadership-followership patterns in play by Montagner et al. (1970) close variants on the agonic and hedonic styles of primate social attention structure. Chance has further advanced our understanding by noting the compatibility of the two modes with the personality model posited by Pearce and Newton (1969), presented above, and also one by Vaillant (1977). Chance, (1980; 1985) too, has recognized the important parallelism between the two modes and the autonomic and neurophysiological theory of Gellhorn (1967; 1968), also discussed above.

In conclusion, it can be seen that developments in a number of separate fields, and in the work of many independent investigators, have converged on two dimensions that can be used to characterize social behavior, or related processes. Furthermore these dimensions articulate in important ways with systems at different biological levels. The evidence supports serious consideration of the power and status dimensions as central to social behavior.

However, as sociologists, there is a last issue that we must confront, particularly in light of the extensive claims made in behalf of sociobiology (Wilson, 1975). Although there appears to be phylogenetic continuity in the power and status modes between human and infrahuman forms, and despite the fact that the two modes of relationship are articulated with neural and physiological support structures—as of course they must be, otherwise no power or status behavior would be possible—it must not be assumed that these elements are under genetic control. It is easy to see that all species face problems of adaptation that are similar in important respects, therefore, certain gestures and emotions are adaptive, for example, offering a threat when one is about to be attacked or deprived of some benefit; or responding with care to the cries of one's offspring, and so forth. Learning, by modeling and association, can explain a good deal of what we observe in actual behavior. Harlow's (1962) studies of imprinting have shown that simple genetic control does not exist even in so fundamental a species requirement as reproduction. My conviction is that while power and status are the important analytic dimensions of social behavior, and in this sense reflect phylogentic continuity, social organization and ideology, not genetic constitution, determine what particular mix of power and status relations will prevail in any human group.

RELATIONSHIPS IN THE POWER AND STATUS SPACE

If power and status are the important dimensions of social relations, then it follows, heuristically, that social relationships can be represented in a space formed by the two dimensions. Because the power and status factors were produced by orthogonal (right-angle) rotation of the factor axes, a two dimensional space with power as ordinate and status as abscissa can be used to represent the factor-analytic results. Any social relationship can be located in the space so formed.

We see in figure 8.1 some relationships that are discursively defined. The 1-1 relationship may be understood under the heading of master-slave, or victor-vanquished. Neither actor accords the other voluntary compliance or benefit (i.e., status). But one of the actors has a great deal of power over the other, while the second is entirely powerless.

The 2-2 relationship can stand for any parties engaged in intense conflict. As in 1-1, neither gives any benefit (i.e., status) to the other voluntarily, but each is engaged in efforts to coerce the other.

FIGURE 8.1
Some Relationships Depicted in the Power-Status Space

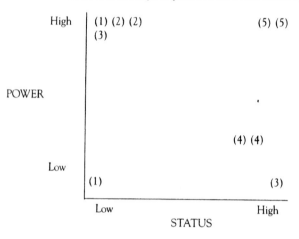

Types of Relationships:

1 = 1   Master-slave
2 = 2   Parties in intense conflict
3 = 3   Parent-infant
4 = 4   Friendship
5 = 5   Romantic love

The 3-3 relationship can be seen as representing parent and infant. The infant, in the lower right corner, receives all the status, that is, all the benefit necessary to maintain the infant's health and life. But the infant ordinarily has little power to coerce the parent. On the other hand, the parent, who receives no status from the infant, has enormous power over the infant, indeed the power of life and death. This is say that the parent has the actual ability to coerce and dispose of the infant how he or she wills.

Relationship 4-4 can be understood as one between two good friends. They mutually accord each other considerable status, but they both are low in power. Indeed, friends rarely coerce each other. This type of relationship approaches, but does not reach the end of the status scale. Hence, it differs from love, as indeed most, though not all, friendship differs from love.

Finally, relationship 5-5 is a full-blown love relationship, since it accords with the definition provided earlier, namely, at least one actor giving unlimited status to the other. Here both are mutually according this extreme amount of status. But in this particular love relationship both actors have a great deal of power as well. It is a type of love relationship in which there is full recognition of one's dependency on the other, hence, that one is vulnerable to the power of the other, should the other choose to use the power. (See Emerson, 1962, for discussion of power-dependence relations.) Few love relationships avoid this stage (see Kemper, 1978, for a description of seven types of love relationships, and their sequential connections).

Although the relational space has been presented in terms of independent (i.e., geometrically orthogonal) dimensions, it should be apparent there is a dynamic relationship between the two dimensions. There is strong evidence (see summary in Kemper, 1978) that power behavior is ordinarily met with counterpower behavior. Thus, once begun, aggressive action tends to develop an autonomy that leads to an escalating round of power acts until one actor departs or is defeated, or desists from the use of power from fear or from conscience; or there is an intervention from outside the system.

In general it appears, too, that actors in relationships that do not provide sufficient status (according to their judgment) are prone to leave those relationships as long as there are no constraints to prevent this. Similarly, whether or not there is sufficient status, actors are prone to leave relationships in which they are (excessively in their judgment) subject to the power of the other.

In these two statements, we encompass a large amount of what can be understood relationally about divorce, runaway children, job changes, the vagaries of friendships, alliances, and political coalitions that bloom and decline, and so forth. The essential point is that if power and status are useful dimensions for descriptive and analytic purposes they should also be useful in accounting for social processes in which relationships are the focus. However, in the dynamic interplay between power and status emotions are the energizing factor. I turn to these now.

POWER, STATUS, AND EMOTIONS

Most human emotions result from outcomes of social interaction. This suggests that we would understand emotions better if we knew how to describe outcomes of social interaction. The discovery of the power and status dimensions assist this effort considerably. If the model is valid, it means that interactional outcomes can be characterized in power and status terms, and in dyadic interaction, these are relatively simple: One's own power can increase, decrease, or remain the same; one's own status can increase, decrease or remain the same. Similar results can occur in the other actor's power and status. This paradigm sums to twelve possible outcomes, only four of which will actually occur. That is to say, each episode of interaction will produce an outcome in one's own power and status in some way and in the power and status of the other. What are the emotional consequences of the possible power and status outcomes?

In broad outline (details are in Kemper, 1978; 1987), the following will ordinarily result: elevation of one's own power will lead to a greater sense of ease and *security*, as will decline in the power of the other. Elevation of the other's power will lead to *fear/anxiety*, as will a decline in one's own power. The effect of no change in power for either self or other is complicated by the state of ancipatory emotions (Kemper, 1978). For example, if one anticipated increase in one's own power (or decrease in the other's power) and it did not occur, this should instigate *fear/anxiety*. On the other hand, if one anticipated that one's own power would decrease (or that the other's power would increase), and it did not, this should enhance feelings of ease and *security*.

Turning to the status dimension, increase in status obtained from the other will lead to *satisfaction* or *happiness*, while decrease in status will lead to *anger*, or *shame*, and/or *depression*. Status loss or deprivation is a complex situation, and the specific emotion depends on whether the other is seen as arbitrarily withdrawing the status, in which case the emotions is likely to be *anger*. If self is seen as responsible for the loss of status, the emotion is likely to be *shame*—one has not acted so as to confirm the right to the status others have normally accorded. However, if the agent of the status loss is conceived of as some irremediable element, for example, Fate, Life, Nature, God, the emotion is likely to be *depression*. Indeed, all of these may be experienced in a case of status loss, depending on how agency is perceived. If status does not change, the resulting emotion depends on what was anticipated: if an expected increase in status occurs, then some extra *satisfaction* may result from the confirmation of the expectation. If the expected increase does not occur, then *disappointment* plus (depending on agency, as described above) *anger*, *shame*, and/or *depression* is likely. If one anticipated that one's status would fall and it either rises or remains the same, the emotion should be strong *satisfaction*. But if the expectation for a decrease is confirmed, the likely emotion is again either *anger*, *shame* and/or *depression*, depending on the agency of the status loss.

The case of increase in other's status, that is, one is giving status to the other, leads to *satisfaction* for oneself. When the status of the other decreases, that is, we withdrew status from the other, the emotional outcome depends on whether or not we desired to reduce the other's status: if so, this ought to evoke *satisfaction*, and perhaps some *fear* of retaliation from the other. If we denied the other status although we desired to give it, or we believed we ought to have given it, the emotional outcome for us would be *guilt* and/or *shame*. In the case of guilt, we believe we have wronged the other by the failure to confer the status that was due. In the case of shame, we believe that by failing to accord the status, we have ourselves acted unworthily (Kemper, 1978; 1987). Indeed, in the given situation, we could experience both emotions.

This brief summary does not address the full complexity of the issues involved in relating power and status outcomes to emotions, but gives some notion of the manner in which this can be done (see Kemper, 1978; 1987 for extensive analysis and supporting evidence for the hypothesized outcomes). What should be apparent is that there is ample ground for supposing that emotions result from outcomes of power and status relations.

A RESEARCH AGENDA FOR THE SOCIAL RELATIONAL APPROACH TO EMOTIONS

As will all theories, the social relational approach to emotions relies upon a set of assumptions that require testing. Three of these are crucial to the validity or the scope of the theory. The first assumption is that the propositions of the theory are valid in all social and demographic groups. This means that when the theory says that a particular emotion (e.g., anger) results from a particular social relational outcome (i.e., status loss), this is assumed to hold true for men and women, higher and lower class, older and younger, and so forth. I call this the "Universality" assumption.

The second assumption is that, for sociological purposes, social structure (i.e., power and status outcomes of social relations) rather than culture (i.e., norms and expectations), is the prime determinant of what emotion one experiences. For example, this means that status loss instigates anger and culture cannot convert it into something else, for example, satisfaction or glee. This assumption is at the heart of the disagreement between the positivist and social constructionist approaches to the sociology of emotions (Shott, 1979; 1980; Hochschild, 1979; 1983; Kemper, 1978; 1980; 1981). I call this the "Social Structural" assumption.

The third assumption is that there is truly an important degree of integration of the social, the emotional, and the physiological, as hinted at by the Funkenstein hypothesis, discussed above, and extended by Kemper (1978; 1987). This assumption is important in the explanation of the particular form of linkage between the social determinants of emotion and the physiological components. A complete sociology of emotions must at least address the question, which speaks to the degrees of freedom, so to speak, available to the social, however conceived, in the determination of emotion. I call this the "Sociophysiological Integration" assumption.

In each case, were the assumption refuted, the social relational theory would require major restructuring. On the other hand, if the assumptions are shown to be valid, the theory would be strongly supported. I will discuss the broad theoretical framework that underlies each assumption, in order to suggest where the research focus might best be directed.

The Universality Assumption. The fundamental theoretical proposition of the social relational approach to emotions is that the power and status outcomes of social interaction produce emotions. These can be real, recollected, or imagined interactions. Implied here is that the biosocial structure of human experience has given us the capacity to feel certain basic emotions that have high survival value. These are the primary emotions of fear, anger, depression, and happiness (Kemper, 1987). They require, in this view, relatively little social or cultural priming, since they have pan-human value, as indicated by the indentity of their cross-cultural indicators (e.g. facial expressions [Ekman, 1973]). They are also differentially wired in the autonomic nervous system, and this gives us further confidence that they are a basic set of emotions. Additional emotions such as guilt, shame, pride, love, nostalgia, schadenfreude, and so forth, are also produced as outcomes of social interaction, but these (secondary) emotions require considerable cultural shaping of their cognitive components to link them to underlying autonomic mechanisms. Notwithstanding the important cultural influences in the construction of these *as* emotions (see Kemper, 1987), like the four primary emotions, they are also triggered by the outcomes of social relations in power and status terms.

A basic assumption of the social relational approach is that the power and status propositions about emotions apply universally across the spectrum of social and demographic categories, for example, gender, race, ethnicity, social class, and so forth. Unfortunately, although many propositions in the theory are empirically grounded (see the review of studies in Kemper, 1978), the work falls within a relatively narrow population range (mainly college students), a problem shared with much of contemporary social psychology.

Remarkably, most psychologists who work on emotions are not concerned with this issue. Ordinarily, they assume that the processes they study are universal, therefore, what they find out about cognition, intellect, motivation, emotion and the like in one population is constant across all populations. Sociologists generally demur from this view, in as much as they are highly conscious of the important differences frequently found between different age, sex, social class, ethnic, and other groups. Therefore, it must be seriously examined whether the group differences extend to the domain of emotions, and specifically to the relationship between power and status outcomes and the emotions hypothesized here to ensue from them. Heuristically, it is plausible that at least the primary emotions are connected in the same way to social relations in all human social categories and groups. This position is based partly on the communication or signal function of emotions (Buck, 1984). Were the primary emotions to vary in their relational precursors, considerable social ambiguity would result. It would be hard to understand the social state and feelings of a person in a different social category from one's own, and this would make problematic what emotion may, in an evolutionary sense applying to all humans, have emerged to make clear. In addition, it would confute one of our best understandings of why emotion is expressed to a great extent by the face and in visible body movements.

Another reason to support the universality assumption is that virtually everyone has multiple memberships and identities, hence, is a member of overlapping social categories, for example, a lower-class Italian white male, a middle-class English black female, and so forth. Were the emotional effects of power and status outcomes to vary by social category, the problem would arise of reconciling the possible differences in the effect of the different categories on the experience of emotion in given relational situations.

But what about within-category differences? Males versus female? White versus black? Middle versus lower class? Old versus young? And so on. This is a more complex issue, but the universality principle is still assumed to hold. Indeed, if within-category differences were to be found, I hypothesize that they will relate *not* to differences in the association between power-status outcomes and emotions, but rather to sub-category differences in the phenomenal indicators of power and status and of gain and loss of power and status. For example, a male may experience a significant rise in anger if someone withdraws status from him by calling him a coward, but he may not become angry if he is called unkind. Per contra, a female may respond in exactly opposite fashion, deflecting the accusation of cowardice and bristling at the charge of unkindness. Such findings would not violate the universality assumption, because in each case, although the indicators of status withdrawal differ, it is the withdrawal of status that induced anger. Although the case for universality seems clearer for the primary emotions, the same principles are hypothesized to hold for the secondary emotions, for example, shame, guilt, pride, and so forth.

Some within-category differences are immutable, for example, male-female, white-black. Others can change, either developmentally (e.g., age), or by achievement (e.g., social class). The universality assumption is expected to hold even for within-category identities that can change. If differences are found, I hypothesize that they will result, as discussed above, from a change in the phenomenal indicators of power and status. For example, what inflamed the youth is often unremarked in older years. The experience simply does not signify status-loss any more.

Alternatively, age change may lead also to a change in the concept of agency. As detailed above, status-loss leads to anger only if the other, having acted arbitrarily, is viewed as the agent responsible for the loss. With increasing age, there may be a shift in perspective, so that, given the same act, *self* is now viewed as the effective agent of the status-loss (e.g., one is now less resolute; one is no longer so formidable; in earlier years "they wouldn't have dared" . . . and so on). Or there may be a sense of irremediability in the situation, for example, a recognition of the inevitability of declining vigor and mastery—it happens to all of us, and we must all suffer it. In such cases, the identical status-loss would produce, not anger, but shame and/or depression. Crucially, despite these potential transformations in perspective, if agent *is* viewed as other, status-loss should still lead to anger. In research on these questions, it is important to recognize modal shifts with increasing age (in this case), or with any shift in social affiliation.

Another, related, problem in the investigation of the universality assumption involves its applicability at different social structural levels of power and status. Persons at different power and status levels may interpret the meaning of power and status interaction outcomes differently (see Kemper, 1978, chapters 3 and 5). At a low structural status level, even a small loss may be viewed as large, while at a higher structural status level, the same loss may perhaps not even be noticed. Conversely, long habituation to a low structural status level, may breed apathy and resignation, hence, status-loss is viewed, somehow, as "just," the way things are (this is again a case of irremediability), hence, it is not as emotionally provoking as it would be to someone of higher status, for whom such a loss was inconceivable and could portend a reversal of previous good fortune. Clearly, what is at issue here is *relative*, as opposed to *absolute*, status-loss. What must be compared are the marginal utilities of gain or loss at different social structural levels of power and status. The universality assumption can well afford this kind of modification, should the data show it to be necessary.

Also somewhat problematic in the research on the universality assumption is the matter of coping and expression of emotion. This bears on the way emotion is measured. Under the universality assumption, arbitrary status-loss should produce anger regardless of the actor's power and status level. But while an actor at a high level can, with considerable impunity, express the anger, someone at a lower level may need to suppress the expression for fear of the consequences. This does not mean that anger is not felt, only that its expression is suppressed. Hochschild (1983) has argued that this may manage the emotion out of existence. The position taken here is that, suppressed or not, the initial emotional result of status-loss is still anger, regardless of any succeeding psychic states or emotions that may ensue from differences in management or coping.

Social Structural Assumption. The social structural assumption is that emotions result from outcomes of power and status relations, *naturally*. At least this is assumed to be true for the four primary emotions: fear, anger, depression, and happiness. This means that if, as presented above, one believes that the other has more power, one feels fear; if the other has unjustly or arbitrarily deprived one of status, one feels anger; if the other has deprived one of status in an irremediable way, or one has effectively caused the loss of one's own status, one feels shame and/or depression; and if the other has accorded status, one feels happiness.

Nevertheless, is it possible for society, acting through cultural prescriptions to evoke other emotions for the same set of power and status outcomes? For example, can society engender happiness when there is status-loss, anger when there is status-accord, and so on? Indeed, societies occasionally attempt to enforce what might be called "unnatural" emotions. Some of these are well-intended, some are ideological, some are clearly wrongheaded. Let us discuss some examples.

Our universal fate is to die, leaving a gap in the lives of those we have loved and those who loved us. In relational terms, this is irremediable status-loss for them. All we gave when we lived is now lost to them. The loss is material, symbolic, and emotional. In all societies, this loss has emotional consequences, namely, sadness, depression, grief, enacted in a variety of ways, but recognizable as grief. Yet, while society countenances grief for a while, it sets a limit on what it deems seemly (see discussion in Thoits, this volume), or on degrees of mourning that do not damage societal interests in productivity, security, and so forth. Therefore, social prescriptions for grief are usually very explicit: (a) length of mourning period, (b) permitted demeanor and decor, (c) the manner of the ingathering of kin. In addition, there may be symbolic representations of an afterlife: the deceased has gone to "heaven," to the "happy hunting ground," to Valhalla, to reincarnation, or to ultimate resurrection. Or, it is proposed that the dead person is now free from the turmoil and suffering of existence, therefore, better off than when he or she was alive. All of these representations can be understood as consolations to the living, to help them restrain their grief over both their loss and the potential harm that death may have brought to their loved one. Thus, culture opposes what it defines as "too much" grief. Does it work, in the sense that, by cultural fiat, people can feel happy rather than sad? This is an exceedingly important question for the social relational theory of emotions.

Let us consider another example of cultural prescription in the face of social structural reality. In capitalism, the principle of labor power as a factor of production is well established. Adam Smith (1937) proposed that pay be in proportion to such criteria as difficulty and agreeableness of the work, risk of failure, and steadiness of employment. These tenets emerged in somewhat different form in the more recent Functionalist theory of stratification (Davis and Moore, 1945; Parsons, 1954). According to these views, workers would be more or less content with the wages they were offered as long as they were in proportion to their supposed contributions and the costs they incurred in making them. Indeed, with the rise of industrialism, it was necessary for employers and ideologists of industry to propose that workers, given their "scant" contributions to the manufacturing process compared to the contributions of their employers, must be content with their lot. These lessons were propounded not only at the factory gate, but also from the pulpit. The cultural prescription, as delivered from the authoritative nuclei of society, was to be content with one's wages.

But, in the history of the labor movement, pay and working conditions have been "contested terrain" (Edwards, 1979). Why should this be, when the cultural prescriptions would have it otherwise? According to the structural position on emotions, not cultural prescriptions, but the actual social relational evidence of low power and low status—namely, poor pay and employer's unresponsiveness to pleas for better working conditions—produced in workers the anger and energy to organize and, ultimately to transform, the market place for labor.

A final example of cultural overweening is that as part of the same industrial ideology that sought to foster workers' contentment with wages, a relatively rigid sexual code of conduct emerged in the nineteenth century in Western Europe and the United States. Applied to factory workers, its object was to focus attention on work responsibilities instead of pleasure, and to ensure punctuality and concern for duty. In Marcuse's (1955) term, this pattern of sexual regulation constituted "surplus repression," applied in the interest of generating "surplus value." In the middle class, the object of the rigid sex code was to ensure not only the principle of legitimacy in the transmission of wealth and fortune to the next generation, but also that one's children would not mix their fortunes with social inferiors. Every society knows the power of sexual attraction. Every culture has at least some cautionary tales to tell about it. Every culture puts at least some brake on it through incest taboos, marriage rules, and a sexual code. But what has come to be known as Victorian sexual morality took these societal interests to relatively extreme lengths (see Gay, 1984). The effect of Victorian cultural prescriptions in the domain of sex was not merely to suppress sexual expression, but also, for at least some, to repress sexual feelings. The rigid sexual code also induced a (perhaps) new form of neurosis in both men and women, tied to their repressed sexuality (Kaplan, 1974). Thus, we see that cultural prescription can work on feelings as fundamental as the sexual, but can only divert them, not substitute for them. In this respect, Freud's notion of sublimation was at least partly flawed.

Given these three instances of culture in opposition to social structure, the task must be to examine the question more closely, to choose instances where it may be possible to measure the contrary impulses from social relations and from normative prescription. In doing so, one must examine emotion as soon as possible after the instigating social relational episode, because coping and emotion management can come into play very early in the sequence, shortcircuiting an emotion that social relations instigated. Even prior to the experience of a particular emotion (see Thoits, this volume), one can decide to avoid it by putting oneself in a social relational situation that does not evoke the proscribed emotion, but rather, spontaneously and naturally, instigates a culturally preferred emotion. While this demonstrates the efficacy of cultural prescription—against which I am arguing here in particular—it does so only distally. Proximally, social relations in the new situation still give rise to the particular emotion one sought. Cultural prescription has simply directed the individual away from one social relational matrix to another. Indeed, while culture can thus specify which emotions are desirable, it is still social relations that determine, in the proximal sense, which emotions will be felt.

Even if culture is able to supervene and abort an emotion, it may be doing so at a price. Prematurely terminated expressions of grief may emerge as the inability to form new intimate relationships. Workers who adopt pacifying and stultifying ideologies may fail to experience the pride of autonomy and self-empowerment. In the case of stringent sexual moralities, the casebooks of psychiatry are replete with instances of a variety of maladies and failures of relationship.

It is not that society cannot impose an emotional yoke on its members contrary to what might be thought of as "natural." It is somewhat like the outmoded Chinese custom of binding the feet of girls. It can be done, but it deforms their bones and injures their ability to stand or walk. Indeed, there can be "social construction," in this sense. But society, or at least some of its members, pays a price for the emotional footbinding that culture may impose in opposition to natural emotional outcomes. The social structural assumption therefore rests on a notion of "natural" emotional outcomes of power and status relations. Culture can't ordinarily change these very much, except at some cost. Nor is this to deny that some culturally sponsored modifications do occur and that they may be beneficial. Freud (1951) argued the case best in *Civilization and its Discontents*, proposing that the price of an orderly society was some degree of control over sex (desire) and aggression (anger). But, he only argued the need for the *moderation* of these motives, not their transformation into something else. Indeed, culture may moderate the intensity of the natural connections between power and status outcomes and emotions, but not substitute arbitrarily any emotion it chooses for the natural one.

What we may expect to find in research directed to these questions is often a tension between social structure and culture, with each pulling in a different direction. Here the claim is that the difference cannot be too great, otherwise the human material—the individuals who must bear the emotional effects of social relations and of culture—could not long endure.

Sociophysiological Integration. One of the most interesting results of the social relational approach to emotions was the possibility of uniting the social and the physiological grounds of emotion. Although sociologists of emotions are not required to explore physiological questions, they also must see the merit of any approach that makes possible some articulation between the two domains. Indeed, sociologists of emotion have not only not turned their back on physiology, they have leapt to embrace it, provided it was convenient to do so. And, indeed, it can be said that in some respects, it has been made too convenient by the much disputed psychophysiological theory propounded by Schachter and Singer (1962). In their view, emotions rest on a foundation of undifferentiated physiological arousal, with the particular emotions then specified by situational or cultural definitions of what it was appropriate to feel. At its most extreme, physiological arousal produced by whatever means, could be put at the service of any emotion. In the version espoused by Walster and Berscheid (1971), the physiological arousal of horror at a public hanging could be transferred easily to feelings of love!

For some sociologists of emotion, this undifferentiated arousal position suited quite well, since it accorded to situational definition and cultural prescription alone the ability to define the emotion specifically. On the other hand, the social relational view relies more on the view that social relations and physiological substrate are connected in a more differentiated way, more as key and lock, in which certain relational patterns trigger specific physiological processes (Kemper, 1978; 1981).

The research required here is normally outside the competence of sociologists and, to be accomplished at all, will necessitate interdisciplinary collaboration, with all the problems and perils that entails. The principal difficulty would be to find a psychophysiologist who cares enough about a sociologist's questions in the domain of emotions to enter into a cooperative endeavor. The invidious ranking of the sciences, in which sociology is relatively low in the view of laboratory based disciplines, is a barrier that is not easily breached. Ordinarily, to get the work under way, requires that the sociologist go more than half way. Actually, this is ironic, for while the psychophysiologists generally view a sociological perspective with disdain (for an exception see Gale and Edwards, 1983) they have a good deal to learn from it. Even a casual inspection of the social parameters of much laboratory based psychophysiological work reveals that important conclusions about emotions are being missed because the investigators ignore the social aspects of their experimental paradigms. The social relational theory of emotions has a good deal to contribute to the comprehensive sociophysiological understanding of emotions, but its own understanding of the integration of the two domains must be tested. Indeed, the empirical and theoretical articulation of the social and physiological aspects of emotion must be settled some time.

CONCLUSION

The social relational approach to understanding emotions takes what could be called a "standard sociological social-psychological" approach to the question, namely, social independent variables (social interactional outcomes) are used to predict dependent variables (emotions). I assume that actors interpret the situations they are in to make sense of them, just as Mead or Blumer or Stryker would say, but that ultimately all interpretation comes down to seeing the situation in terms of power and status outcomes. Of course, most individuals do not use these terms, which are sociological jargon (and useful notwithstanding), but a natural language that is conventional to the particular group(s) of which the individuals are members. Yet, the central theme here is that regardless of particularities of language, social relations are fundamentally about power and status. Furthermore, the structure of the human organism, evolved over time, contains enough prewiring to produce physiological and behavioral responses to the power-status outcomes. Together, then, the cognition of the power-status outcome, the physiological response and the behavior constitute the emotion.

Though culture has a role in this model of social relations and emotions, it is not omnipotent. Culture specifies the actions and situations that signify different levels of power and status, and the meaning of different actions as power and status outcomes. Culture may also attempt to impose emotions upon individuals, sometimes even with success, but sometimes at a price. One of the important issues in the developing field of the sociology of emotions is to examine the tension between, and respective territories of, social structure and culture. Both the universality and the social structural assumptions are implicated in this large question.

Of equal interest for a complete theory of emotions, in which the sociological contribution receives its full due, is the connection between the social and the physiological. Although individual sociologists may shun preparation that would enable them to engage physiological questions from a sociological vantage point, they must recognize that eventually sociology must meet the challenge. This is in line with the idea that ultimately there will be one human science. Perhaps, as Comte (1975) dreamed, sociology will indeed be preeminent in that comprehensive science. If so, the emergence of sociological interest in the emotions, even down to the physiological ground of them, is a significant step forward.

Notes

1. Some instances of this view are found in the symbolic interactionist approach of Blumer (1969), although others (e.g., Stryker, 1980) oppose Blumer's radical antagonism to scientific apprehension of the social world; and in the work of a number of contributors to the volume edited by Harré (1987).

2. The search for laws and the use of empirical and quantitative methods places this approach under the rubric of what is ordinarily called "positivism" (Camic, 1987).

3. Here, to proceed, means that the available knowledge be tested for its validity and generality. To the degree the model fails such tests, it indicates a degree of incompleteness, therefore, requiring revision.

4. For an early discussion of the commonality of results of different investigators, see Carter (1954). For more recent discussions of problems of interpretation and resolution of differences between different investigators, see Kemper (1973; 1978). For recent additions to the literature of factor analytic results, see Kemper (1987).

5. I thank Thomas Scheff (1986:433–34) for having used this as an epigraph to his review of a book by Tuan (1984) entitled, Dominance and Affection, or in present terms, power and status.

6. Modern social science has more to do than this, since present-day societies have invented forms and formulae of social organization that are different from

those available to the ancients. But even these may be but a small proportion of the total mass of phenomena, compared with that of the physical sciences, that needs to be understood.

7. The activity dimension is sometimes found in another form in some factor analytic results, for example, Carter, 1954. This third factor is frequently understandable as "technical activity," referring to the task that group members are together to do. Task behavior (e.g., building a house, playing an instrument in an orchestra, etc.) is analytically distinct from relational behavior (e.g., dominating, approving, etc.), which deals with what the actors do to and with each other, over and above the task. In some cases, task and relational activity overlap (e.g., in making love), but this does not affect the analytical distinctness of the two. In some work with the Semantic Differential (Heise, 1969), activity merges with potency to form a single dimension.

8. Following the Osgood, Suci, and Tannenbaum model, Heise and Smith-Lovin also included the activity dimension in their equations.

9. For terminological purposes, Gellhorn called the two important structural features linking neurophysiological and autonomic processes the "Ergotropic and the Trophotropic." They are the integrated organismic responses to specific outcomes of power and of status relations respectively (see Kemper, 1978, 1987) for details.

REFERENCES

Bakan, David. 1966. *The Duality of Human Existence: An Essay in Psychology and Religion.* Chicago: Rand-McNally.

Barchas, Patricia. 1976. "Physiological Sociology: Interface of Physiological and Biological Processes." In *Annual Review of Sociology,* Vol 2. Palo Alto, Calif.: Annual Review, pp. 299–333.

Becker, Wesley C. 1964. "Consequences of Different Kinds of Parental Discipline." Pp. 169–208 in *Review of Child Development.* Vol. I. Edited by Martin L. Hoffman and Lois W. Hoffman. New York: Russell Sage Foundation.

Blumer, Herbert. 1969. *Symbolic Interaction.* Englewood Cliffs, N.J.: Prentice-Hall.

Brinkerhoff, David, and Alan Booth. 1984. "Gender, Dominance, and Stress." *Journal of Biological and Social Structures* :159–77.

Buck, Ross. 1984. *The Communication of Emotion.* New York: Guilford.

Camic, Charles. 1987. "The Making of a Method: A Historical Reinterpretation of the Early Parsons." *American Sociological Review* 52:421–39.

Carter, Launor F. 1954. "Evaluating the Performance of Individuals as Members of Small Groups." *Personnel Psychology* 7:477–84.

Chance, Michael R. A. 1978. "Social Attention: Society and Mentality." Pp. 315–33 in *The Structure of Social Attention*. Edited by Michael R. A. Chance and Ray R. Larsen. London: Wiley.

––––––. 1980. "An Ethological Assessment of Emotion." Pp. 81–111 in *Emotion: Theory, Research, and Experience*, Vol. 1. Edited by Robert Plutchik and Henry Kellerman. New York: Academic.

––––––. 1984. "A Biological Systems Synthesis of Mentality Revealing an Underlying Functional Bimodality (Hedonic and Agonic)." *Man-Environment Systems* 14:143–57.

Comte, Auguste. 1975. *Auguste Comte and Positivisim: The Essential Writings*. Edited by Gertrud Lenzer. New York: Harper and Row.

D'Andrade, Roy G. 1965. "Trait Psychology and Componential Analysis." *American Anthropologist*. Part 2. 67:215–28.

Davis, Kingsley, and Wilbert E. Moore. 1945. "Some Principles of Stratification." *American Sociological Review* 10:242–49.

Dilthey, Wilhelm. 1962. *Pattern in History*. Edited by H. P. Rickman. New York: Harper.

Edwards, Richard. 1979. *Contested Terrain: The Transformation of the Workplace in the Twentieth Century*. New York: Basic.

Ellis, Lee. 1986. "Evidence of Neuroandrogenic Etiology of Sex Roles from a Combined Analysis of Human, Nonhuman Primate and Nonprimate Mammalian Studies." *Personality and Individual Differences* 7:519–52.

Emerson, Richard. 1962. "Power-Dependence Relations." *American Sociological Review* 40:252–57.

Freud, Sigmund. 1959 (1937). "Analysis Terminable and Interminable." In *Collected Papers*. Edited by Joan Riviere. New York: Basic.

––––––. 1951 (1937). *Civilization and Its Discontents*. London: Hogarth.

Funkenstein, Daniel. 1955, "The Physiology of Fear and Anger." *Scientific American* 192:74–80.

Gale, Anthony, and J. Edwards. 1983. "Psychophysiology and Individual Differences: Theory, Research Procedures, and Interpretation." *Australian Journal of Psychology* 35:361–79.

Gay, Peter. 1984. *The Bourgeois Experience*. New York: Oxford.

Gellhorn, Ernst. 1967. *Principles of Autonomic-Somatic Integration: Physiological Basis and Psychological and Clinical Implications*. Minneapolis: University of Minnesota.

————. 1968. "Attempt at a Synthesis: Contribution to a Theory of Emotion." Pp. 144–53 in *Biological Foundations of Emotion: Research and Commentary.* Glenview, Ill.: Scott, Foresman.

Harlow, Harry F. 1962. "Development of Affection in Primates." In *Roots of Behavior.* Edited by E. L. Bliss. New York: Harper.

Harré, Rom. 1987. (Ed.) *The Social Construction of Emotions.* London: Blackwell.

Heelas, Paul. 1987. "Emotion Talk Across Cultures." Pp. 234–66 in *The Social Construction of Emotions,* edited by Rom Harré. London: Blackwell.

Heise, David. 1969. "Some Methodological Issues in Semantic Differential Research." *Psychological Bulletin* 72:406–22.

Hochschild, Arlie R. 1979. "Emotion Work, Feeling Rules, and Social Structure." *American Journal of Sociology* 85:551–75.

————. 1983. *The Managed Heart.* Berkeley: California.

Horkheimer, Max. 1976 (1937). "Tradition and Critical Theory." Pp. 206–24 in *Critical Sociology.* Edited by Paul Connerton. New York: Penguin.

Kemper, Theodore D. 1973. "The Fundamental Dimensions of Social Interaction: A Theoretical Statement." *Acta Sociologica* 16:41–58.

————. 1978. *A Social Interactional Theory of Emotions.* New York: Wiley.

————. 1980. "Sociology, Physiology, and Emotions: Comment on Shott." *American Journal of Sociology* 85:1418–23.

————. 1984. "Power, Status, and Emotions: A Sociological Contribution to a Psychophysiological Domain." Pp. 369–83 in *Approaches to Emotion,* edited by Klaus R. Scherer and Paul Ekman. Hillsdale, N.J.: Erlbaum.

————. 1987. "How Many Emotions Are There? Wedding the Social and The Autonomic Components." *American Journal of Sociology* 93:263–89.

Lutz, Catherine. 1982. The Domain of Emotion Words on Ifaluk." *American Ethnologist* 9:113–28.

Marcuse, Herbert. 1955. *Eros and Civilization.* Boston: Beacon.

————. 1964. *One-Dimensional Man.* Boston: Beacon.

Mazur, Allan. 1973. "A Cross-Species Comparison of Status in Small Established Groups." *American Sociological Review* 38:196–205.

————. 1985. "A Biosocial Model of Status in Face-to-Face Primate Groups." *Social Forces* 64:377–402.

McPhail, Clark, and Cynthia Rexroat. 1979. "Mead vs. Blumer: The Divergent Methodological Perspectives of Social Behaviorism and Symbolic Interactionism." *American Sociological Review* 44:449–67.

Mead, George H. 1934. *Mind, Self, and Society.* Chicago: University of Chicago.

Montagner, H., J. C. Henry, M. Lombardot, A. Restoin, D. Bolzoni, M. Durand, Y. Humbert, and A. Moyse. 1970. "Behavioral Profile and Corticosteroid Excretion Rhythms in Young Children. Part 1. Non-verbal Communication and Setting up of Behavior Profiles in Children from 1 to 6 years." Pp. 207–28 in *Human Behavior and Adaptation.* London: Taylor and Francis.

Osgood, Charles E., George J. Suci, and Percy H. Tannenbaum. 1957. *The Measurement of Meaning.* Urbana, Ill.: Illinois.

Osgood, Charles E., W. H. May, and M. S. Miron. *Cross Cultural Universals of Affective Meaning.* Urbana, Ill.: Illinois.

Parsons, Talcott. 1954. "A Revised Analytical View of Stratification." In *Essays in Sociological Theory.* Rev. Ed. Glencoe, Ill.: Free Press.

Pearce, Jane, and Saul Newton. 1969. *The Conditions of Human Growth.* New York: Citadel.

Schachter, Stanley, and Jerome Singer. 1962. "Cognitive, Social and Physiological Determinants of Emotional State." *Psychological Review* 69:379–99.

Scheff, Thomas J. 1986. Review of *Dominance and Affection,* by Yi-Fu Tuan. *Contemporary Sociology* 15:433–34.

Shott, Susan. 1979. "Emotion and Social Life: A Symbolic Interactionist Analysis." *American Journal of Sociology* 84:1317–34.

———. 1980. "Reply to Kemper." *American Journal of Sociology* 85:1423–26.

Smith, Adam. 1937 (1776) *The Wealth of Nations.* New York: Random House.

Sroufe, L. Alan. 1979. "Socioemotional Development." Pp. 462–516 in *Handbook of Infant Developments,* edited by Joy D. Osofsky. New York: Wiley.

Stryker, Sheldon. 1980. *Symbolic Interactionism: A Social Structural Version.* Menlo Park, Calif.: Benjamin/Cummings.

Tuan, Yi-Fu. 1984. *Dominance and Affection.* New Haven: Yale.

Triandis, Harry. 1972. *The Analysis of Subjective Culture.* New York: Wiley.

Udry, J. Richard, and John O. Billy. 1987. "Initiation of Coitus in Early Adolescence." *American Sociological Review* 52:841–55.

Vaihinger, Hans. 1965 (1911). *The Philosophy of 'As If'.* London: Routledge & Kegan Paul.

Vaillant, George. 1977. *Adaptation to Life*. Boston: Little, Brown.

Walster, Elaine, and Eleanor Berscheid. 1971. "Adrenaline Makes the Heart Grow Fonder." *Psychology Today* 5:47–55.

Weber, Max. 1946. "Class, Status, and Party." Pp. 180–96 in *From Max Weber: Essays in Sociology*. Edited by Hans H. Gerth and C. Wright Mills. New York: Oxford.

White, Geoffrey. 1980. "Conceptual Universals in Interpersonal Language." *American Anthropologist* 82:759–81.

Willer, David H., and Murray Webster, Jr. 1970. "Theoretical Constructs and Observables." *American Sociological Review* 35:748–57.

Wilson, Edwin O. 1975. *Sociobiology: The New Synthesis*. Cambridge: Harvard.

Wright, M. R. 1981. *Empedocles, the Extant Fragments*. New Haven: Yale.

Zelditch, Marvin. 1968. "Social Status." Pp. 250–57 in *International Encyclopedia of Social Sciences*, edited by David Sills. New York: MacMillan.

9.

Emotion as the Confirmation and Disconfirmation of Identity: An Affect Control Model

Lynn Smith-Lovin [*]

One goal of sociologists who study emotions is a powerful, general model of how people understand and react emotionally to social situations. To accomplish this goal, we need a model that combines the insights generated by both qualitative and quantitative research. We seek a representation that will capture the valence and strength of affect generated by events, phenomena that quantitative researchers often try to measure. But we also want to model the qualitative differences that come from differing definitions of a situation. Our understanding of social events around us affects our emotional reactions. A sociological model will recognize that how events affect us emotionally depends on how we see ourselves and others, and how we define the events that occur. And since emotions also influence people's judgments and actions, we require a theory that represents the normative aspects of emotional display. The model should show how nonnormative emotions lead to qualitative changes in our view of reality (like labeling or reinterpretation of events).

A sociological theory of emotion should link emotional response also to other aspects of social action like identity, role, ideology, and culture. Ideally, sociologists of emotion will produce a parsimonious model that emphasizes the fact that emotional responses are an integral part of social interaction, rather than generating separate theoretical statements for specific emotions. From this view, an adequate model of emotional life will necessarily be a theory of social action; our emotional reactions are affected by social events around us, and mobilize us to further action.

The goal of a general theory linking emotion and social action may seem overly ambitious at this stage of our development. However, I am encouraged by the fact that our knowledge about affect and emotion is deepening rapidly as sociologists, anthropologists, psychologists, linguists, biologists and even economists concentrate on the area.[1] What we need is a framework within which to fit the pieces of the puzzle that are being developed by researchers with more specialized interests.

In this chapter, I describe a theoretical model that begins to attempt this task. Affect control theory (Heise 1977, 1979, 1986; Smith-Lovin and Heise 1988) provides a model of social action incorporating the basic assumptions of symbolic interactionism. It also implies a sociological model of emotion that captures some relationships among social institutions, emotion, and social action. Below, I summarize the theory and discuss its view of emotional life. Then I relate affect control processes to the insights generated by other research traditions in the sociology of emotion. Finally, I outline the questions that the affect control paradigm generates for future research.

THE AFFECT CONTROL MODEL

Heise (1977, 1978, 1979) developed affect control theory from symbolic interactionist ideas and from empirical work on the psychology of impression formation. The theory is based on the proposition that people perceive and create events to maintain the meanings evoked by their definition of a situation.

When people enter a situation, they occupy identities like Host or Guest, Doctor or Patient.[2] Institutions and their physical settings heavily support some definitions (a lecture hall supports the identities of Professor and Student) (Goffman 1959:1, 124; 1963:18, 20; 1974:1–2; Gonos 1977). Other identities may be less formal and less setting-specific, as when two Lovers conduct their romantic relations in mundane sites like a city street. Through their chosen identities, actions and physical props, individual actors may transform the relations among others; for example, a person with a gun can transform a bank setting with Managers, Tellers, and Customers into a robbery scene with a Robber and Hostages (Goffman 1974:447).

People recognize social events (like the Host is Ignoring me, his Guest) within their definition of the situation. The interpretation of behavior (i.e., its cognitive categorization or label) determines its affective impact: we might approve of a Mother Disciplining her Child but would be unlikely to condone Abusing. As with the definition of the situation, individual variation in event interpretation may occur, but is not without limits. We might argue about spanking as discipline or abuse, but cigarette burns and skull fractures would be physical events that allowed little dispute about interpretation.

The labels we use to characterize self, others and social actions carry important meanings—fundamental sentiments about how *good*, how *powerful* and how *lively* such people and behaviors are. A key feature of affect control theory is that it conceptualizes "meaning" in a specific, measurable way. The fundamental sentiments of goodness, powerfulness and liveliness correspond to the three dimensions of affective meaning (evaluation, potency, and activity) that Osgood and his colleagues (1957, 1975) discovered. These dimensions underlie reactions to many types of concepts in a variety of linguistic and national cultures. (See Heise's technical appendix, this volume, for a more complete description of scales, and their use in measurement of affective meaning.)[3]

Such meanings are a part of our culture. Despite widely varying backgrounds, we largely agree that Mothers are nicer than Mafiosi, that Physicians have more power than Patients, and that Children are livelier than Cripples. Table 9.1 contains the average ratings of a few social identities and behaviors on the three dimensions. Studies on topics ranging from word connotations to occupational prestige to severity of criminal acts find surprising agreement across social strata in the affective meanings associated with social identities and behaviors (Gordon et al. 1963; Heise 1966; Reiss 1961; Osgood 1962; Rossi et al. 1974).

TABLE 9.1

Ratings of Selected Identities and Behaviors on Evaluation (E: good/bad), Potency (P: powerful/weak), and Activity (A: lively/quiet) Dimensions (from Smith-Lovin [1979] and Heise and Lewis [1988])[*]

Stimulus	Male				Female			
	E	P	A	N	E	P	A	N
Mother	2.52	1.50	−0.13	25	2.33	1.90	0.04	28
Mafioso	−1.78	2.09	0.31	19	−1.57	1.80	0.21	14
Physician	1.90	1.85	−0.36	27	1.57	1.68	−0.46	26
Patient	0.07	−1.72	−0.78	28	0.26	−1.55	−0.97	25
Child	1.42	−1.48	2.31	23	1.94	−1.10	2.52	27
Cripple	−0.14	−1.62	−1.03	26	0.32	−1.04	−1.13	26
Love	2.87	2.62	0.50	27	2.89	2.67	0.48	27
Hate	−2.50	0.38	0.77	26	−2.77	0.09	0.77	28
Rescue	2.77	2.78	2.03	27	2.41	1.76	1.22	26
Nag	−1.81	−0.72	0.76	27	−1.54	−0.17	0.59	26
Tease	−1.01	−0.02	1.48	27	−0.46	0.14	1.68	24
Soothe	1.73	1.09	−1.26	26	2.00	1.49	−1.02	28

[*]Scales range from +4 to −4, with a zero midpoint indicating neutral. Good, powerful and lively are the positive ends of the scale. More information on the scales and data collection are available in the technical appendix here, Smith-Lovin (1979), Smith-Lovin and Heise (1988), and Heise and Lewis (1988).

Obvious exceptions occur when subcultures develop unique meanings for identities central to the group (e.g., homosexual identities in a gay church [Smith-Lovin and Douglass forthcoming] or law enforcement identities within their professional subculture [Gilchrist project reported in Heise 1979:100–21]). Often, though, such subcultures develop a new set of identities (in effect, a new vocabulary) to reflect their differences from the mainstream society; gang members may share the mainstream ideology's view of Police Officer, but be more likely to use slang words like Pig that carry a more negative and less potent connotation.

Affect control theory focuses on the goodness, powerfulness, and activity dimensions of meaning for four reasons: (1) they can be used to characterize many significant elements of social situations, including identities, actions, emotions, and settings; (2) they are widely shared and represent important cultural information; (3) they correspond to important social features of identities and behaviors like status, power, and expressivity (see review in Kemper 1978:26–42); and (4) we can measure people's reactions on these dimensions. Furthermore, our measurements of affective meaning allow us to link the qualitative features of situational definitions to the quantitative processes of impression-change and control.

Social events may change impressions of people, making them seem better or worse, stronger or weaker, livelier or quieter than they were expected to be. For example, suppose I attend a party and think that the Host is Ignoring me, her Guest. Hosts and Guests normally are viewed as pleasant people, with the Host adjudged somewhat more powerful and lively than the Guest. When rated by female undergraduates on a scale ranging from −4 to +4, Host has an evaluation (goodness) of 1.5, a potency (powerfulness) of 1.2 and an activity (liveliness) of 0.5; Guest has an evaluation of 1.7, potency of 0.0 and activity of −0.2 (Heise and Lewis 1988:97, 98). The unpleasant and inappropriate act of Ignoring (with an evaluation of −1.8, potency of −0.2 and activity of 0.2) damages the reputation of both Host and Guest. A Host who has Ignored a Guest loses goodness and power, though not liveliness.

Affect control theory uses impression-change equations, estimated from large numbers of such events, to predict the outcome (Smith-Lovin 1987a; see the technical appendix for more detail about the equations, their estimation and use). Calculations using the input sentiments above and impression-change equations predict that such a Host will lose 2.2 units of evaluation and 0.7 units of potency; but she will gain slightly (0.2 units) in liveliness. One might think of an identity as a point in a three-dimensional space; an event, when recognized and processed by someone, has the capacity to move the person in that identity from its original, culturally given location to a new position.[4]

The Host suffers because she has done a bad act to a good person, namely, the Guest. The equations capture notions of equity with an inter-action term that represents the traditional balance effect (Smith-Lovin 1987a: 47–9). That is, good unto bad and bad unto good damages one's reputation while doing good to the deserving and punishing the villains increases the evaluation of the actor.[5] The Guest, too, suffers from the perception of being Ignored. The victim of a negative act loses evaluation, as the impression-change equations capture the derogation of the victim effect (Smith-Lovin 1987a:50–1). Power is lost too, by being the object of another's inappropriate, unpleasant action (Smith-Lovin 1987a:55).

When events create transient impressions that differ from our funda-mental understandings of what people and behaviors are like, we are likely to generate new events that restore these fundamental sentiments.[6] In other words, people construct new events to *confirm* fundamental senti-ments about self and others; they manage social life in ways that *control* their feelings about reality. The maintenance of meaning is accomplished by creating a new event that, when processed, will move the identities of actor, behavior, and object back to their original positions in the three-dimensional space.

In the example above, the Host and Guest have both lost status as a result of the Ignoring. The theory suggests that this event is unlikely, since it does not maintain and support the identities of the interactants. But such a behavior might be produced accidentally (if the Host is busy with other party arrangements, or if the Guest comes in a back way) or because of some mood left over from another interaction (the Host is depressed because of a rejection by her boyfriend) or because the Host temporarily defines the Guest as Obnoxious. If the Guest points out the event as Ignor-ing and the Host accepts this account of what has transpired, the Host is likely to produce a restorative act: a behavior that, when processed, will move impressions back in line with fundamental meanings. Or she may expect the Guest to repair the situation with such an act. Possibilities for the Host include Appreciate, Soothe, and Apologize To; the Guest might Excuse or Caution the Host to restore her view of the occasion.

The theory produces these predictions about impression-change and behavioral reactions with a computer simulation program called "INTER-ACT" (Heise and Lewis 1988). The program contains the formal structure of the theory and empirical estimates of its parameters. Specifically, the program consists of equations that show how impressions change on the three meaning dimensions (evaluation, potency and activity or EPA) for actor, object-person, and behavior (Smith-Lovin and Heise 1988).[7] It uses a mathematical transformation to represent the proposition that people maintain fundamental meanings: the program solves for the three-number

EPA profile of possible behaviors that would return the identities of the actor and object closest to their positions before the event was processed. The program contains the current form of the theory—the equations and the mathematical transformation—and allows us to link verbal descriptions (identity and behavior labels defining the situation) to their numerical values in EPA terms.

Program INTERACT can model more than behavioral reactions. Sometimes events affect us so deeply that no new event could possibly restore our original sentiments about the participants in the scene. In our studies, the event of the Grandfather Rapes the Granddaughter is an example of an incident that produces massive impression-change. No action is sufficient to restore our original view of the relationship. Transient impressions that cannot be restored to fundamental sentiments through action may lead to redefinition of the situation.

In such cases, actions that are uninterpretable within a given set of identities may lead to a search for identities that they do confirm. In effect, we search for a view of the situation that "makes sense" of the events. INTERACT solves for a new identity EPA profile, rather than a three-number behavior profile. A Grandfather who Rapes a Child may be many things, but he no longer fits into our cultural view of what a Grandfather is. He may be a Rapist instead, or a Child Molester; both are identities that are nasty and lively enough to do such a heinous thing.

Reidentification also can occur in less criminal circumstances. A Wife announces she is divorcing her Husband—that creates substantial deflections from her EPA profile. It leads to questions like: "How could she do this to me, her good, loving husband? What kind of a person would do such a thing?" INTERACT simulations suggest identities that could resolve the dilemma. They suggest that the rejecting Wife might be a Lesbian ("she must be gay!"), a Psychotic ("she must be crazy!") or a Bitch ("I hate her. Good riddance!"). A more introspective Husband, who was willing to change his own identity, might consider the possibility that his Wife wants to divorce someone she considers to be a Creep.

Affect control theory is mathematical in form, but both qualitative and quantitative in its predictions. Although it is based on empirical equations and their mathematical transformations (Smith-Lovin 1987a, 1987b; Heise and MacKinnon 1987; Heise 1987), and we use computer simulations to explore the theory's implications (Heise 1978; Heise and Lewis 1988), the computer program works with natural language descriptions of the social situation and what is happening in it. And it produces natural language outputs showing how people might interpret the situation and how they might respond. Our hope is that the theory will be accessible for research by both mathematical sociologists who are interested in the formal representation (e.g., Heise 1985, 1987), and by those who wish to consider the ideas in more general terms and to explore their implications for social relationships.

THE AFFECT CONTROL MODEL OF EMOTION

Although early versions of affect control theory (Heise 1977, 1978, 1979) were based on affective processing and on social actors' maintenance of fundamental sentiments, the theory modeled only behavioral responses and labeling. It did not deal explicitly with emotional reaction. Later work developed the empirical base necessary to describe emotions within an affect control framework (Averett and Heise 1987; Smith-Lovin and Heise 1988).

Affect control theory assumes that emotions provide signals about how well events are maintaining social meanings. Events may produce transient impressions that vary from our fundamental notions of how good, how powerful, and how lively we, or others, are, or ought to be. Emotions are the "code" for representing the degree and kind of confirmation or disconfirmation of identities that is occurring. If someone Insults us while we are operating in a positive, institutionalized identity like Student, we may feel momentarily put down (unpleasant and bad). We have been deflected away from a fundamentally good, pleasant identity by a negative act. Specifically, Student has an EPA profile of 1.2, -0.1 and 1.7 (female ratings from Heise and Lewis 1988:99); being Insulted by a fellow Student leads to a loss of 2.2 on the evaluation dimension. (Potency and activity change only marginally, increasing 0.3 and 0.1 respectively.)

In our model, emotion words describe feelings that characterize the combination of a fundamental EPA profile (that is, the person's original identity in a situation) and the transient profile produced by an event. A female Student Insulted by a fellow Student might feel Flustered, Embarrassed and Shook Up (predictions from INTERACT simulations). The emotion thus captures the disconfirmation of the Student identity resulting from the insult. The Student who does the insulting would be affected too. Assuming that she saw the event in the same light, she would fell Spiteful and Bitchy.

The emotional reactions and the behaviors produced by INTERACT are, in effect, hypotheses derived formally from the theory. If people define the situation as we posed it (two Students), and view the action as we expressed it (Insulting), then the behavioral predictions should correspond to what people would normally expect of the interactants (and, within physical limitations, their actual behaviors). The emotions, too, should be the ones that are expected and actually experienced.[8]

IDENTITY AND EMOTION

Averett and Heise (1987) have estimated how emotions and moods combine with identities to form impressions of emotion—identity composites (e.g., a Sad Friend). The emotion model uses these equations to describe how identities and impressions from events imply emotion. The equations reveal that emotion is a function of (1) the transient impression created by an event and (2) the difference between the transient impression and the fundamental meaning (Averett and Heise 1987:124–8). Not unexpectedly, nice events lead to positive transient impressions and create positive emotions, while nasty behaviors lead to negative emotions. That is true in general. But a transient impression that is nicer than one's identity fosters an especially positive emotion. If one occupies very high status, positive identities, one simply expects the nice things that are directed toward oneself. If one's identity is more neutral, the positive event causes elation. An Apprentice glows from a compliment that an Expert takes as his due (see also Kemper 1978:72–79).

If people interpret events and act to maintain their transient states near fundamental meanings, then affect control theory points to an interesting conclusion, that the character of one's emotions is sharply determined by his or her identity (Averett and Heise 1987: equations 19, 20, and 21). Maintenance of positive identities in the kinds of roles one normally occupies creates positive emotions.[9] Maintenance of a negative identity (for example, in some type of deviant role) normally fosters negative emotions.

We expect people in powerful identities to feel deep, high-potency emotions like Pride and Fury, while people in powerless positions will experience emotions of impotency like Fear, Anxiety, and Depression.[10] People inhabiting less lively, older identities are prone to quieter emotions (like Contentment or Remorse) while those who take on younger, more lively identities are inclined toward emotions like Euphoria, Fury, and Passion. From our computer simulations, we find that in normal, identity confirming circumstances a Boyfriend would typically feel Happy, a Grandfather would feel Kind, a Maiden would be Agreeable, an Old Timer would be Calm, a Racketeer would feel Extravagant, a Tightwad would feel Smug, a Braggart would be Dissatisfied and a Loafer would feel Disappointed (Heise 1982).

Obviously, occupying stigmatized identities requires people to feel negative emotions, *if* they remain a part of the dominant culture. Indeed, we have many examples of such "proper" deviants. Mentally ill people often incorporate society's negative view and have lowered self-esteem (Marks 1965). Many times, powerless people—those most likely to be stuck with stigmatizing labels by society—often share normal people's view of their worthlessness. Delinquent youth often report anxiety and distress associated with their negative identities (Rains 1982).

Although negative emotions can be the mechanism by which deviants are reclaimed to normal society (Rains 1982; Glassner 1982), they may undermine one's commitment to the dominant ideology. We might expect this value shift when no avenues for identity-change are available. Thus, deviants may create or search for a subculture where they are offered positive feelings through a competing ideology. Many studies show how deviants assemble to generate their own definitions. They develop an ideology that makes their emotional life tolerable, even fulfilling. A gay church did exactly this (Smith-Lovin and Douglass forthcoming). The church transformed homosexual identities and behaviors into positive, powerful meanings that engage religious ritual positively. As a result, the gay members experience the pleasant, potent emotions of worship.

SITUATIONS LEADING TO DISCONFIRMATION AND EMOTIONAL RESPONSE

Affect control theory also alerts us to situations where events fail to confirm identities. Since disconfirmation (the deflection of a transient identity from fundamental meaning) is experienced as an emotional response, the theory indicates the types of situations that are likely to lead to this kind of emotional arousal.

Disconfirmation of identity is likely when people differ in their definition of a situation—I know I'm a Professor but a Student who sees me in the department office thinks I'm a Secretary. In such cases, actors will intend and expect events that confirm differing views of the interaction. Actions that are confirming for one will be disconfirming for the other. In this example, the behaviors that a Student directs at a Secretary will not be deferential enough for a Professor. (Notice that this confusion of institutionally based identities can be corrected by direct comment as soon as it is noticed. Such corrective action may not be feasible in the case of informal identities: he thinks he is a Sophisticate, but I think he's a Bore.)

Disconfirmation of identity also occurs when people come from differing subcultures and have different meanings for identities and behaviors. Two people may agree on the definition of the situation (e.g., Professor and Student), but different cultural backgrounds may entail different EPA profiles for those identities. As a Professor from the relatively egalitarian U.S. educational system, I expect lively, collegial interaction with Graduate Students (including acts like Challenge, Question, and Josh). It is sometimes difficult to deal with the quieter, more deferential behaviors directed at me by Asian students who (I presume) see Professors as less nice but more pow-

erful and who see Students as quieter than I do. Culturally different fundamental meanings for Professor and Student make confirming events from
one person's viewpoint disturbing for the other. Affect control researchers
have collected extensive data on affective meanings of common identities
and behaviors from U.S. undergraduates (Heise 1978; 1979; Smith-Lovin
and Heise 1988; Heise and Lewis 1988), Canadian undergraduates
(MacKinnon 1983) and Catholic adolescents in Belfast, Northern Ireland
(Smith-Lovin, Heise and Willigan 1983).[11] By simulating interactions
where members of two cultures meet, we can predict when disconfirmation
of identity will occur, and the resulting emotion. For example, Wife and
Husband are seen as very nice, powerful and lively identities among U.S.
undergraduates; to confirm and support such identities, marital partners are
expected to Entertain, Desire-sexually, and Play-with one another in a
lively, companionable, sexual relationship. However, among Catholic adolescents in Belfast, the same identities show a much larger difference in
power, especially as defined by the young men. They rate the Husband
identity 1.9 units more powerful than the Wife. (The difference is 0.4 units
for females.) The Husband is also substantially less lively than the Wife in
Catholic Northern Irish families. Therefore, the predicted behaviors for a
Husband to a Wife in that culture are calmer, more directive acts like Encourage, Compliment, Assist, and Treat. However, the Wife is still expected to behave in a lively, companionable manner (Entertain, Amuse,
Delight).

Note that the Wife's behavior is similar in both cultures, while the
Husband's is quite different. Thus, in a couple comprised of a Belfast Catholic wife and a U.S. husband we predict that their relationship will be
similar to that of a couple from the U.S., and will confirm the husband's
view of the Husband and Wife identities. The Belfast born wife, on the
other hand, might see him as somewhat cavalier about their relationship
and find herself trying to calm him.

In contrast, in a couple with a U.S. wife and a Belfast Catholic husband, he will produce behaviors that seem less playful and more directive
than she expects. Our simulation suggests deflection of transient from fundamental values to produce the emotions of Touched, Contented and At-
ease for the U.S. Wife, rather than the more exciting emotions that are
normative for a U.S. couple (Friendly, Cheerful, In Love, Affectionate,
Warm).[12]

For a more extreme contrast, consider a couple combining an older
Japanese Wife (of marriage age during World War II) and a younger U.S.
Husband. Meanings collected in a student project (Okuyama 1984) indicate that such women view the Wife identity as much more passive (lower
potency and activity) than the typical U.S. respondent. Ideal role behav-

iors for a Husband in traditional Japanese culture include Console, Explain, Forgive, Pray-for, and Teach. The Wife is expected to Need, Ask-about, and Admire a Husband. Such behaviors, producing emotions for the Husband like Contented, Touched, and Charmed, would fail to confirm the lively, sexy comradery expected by an American partner—Lighthearted, Warm, Affectionate are the feelings predicted for the Husband in a normative U.S. relationship.

Notice that all emotions in the marital relationships above are positive—deflection of meaning away from our fundamental conception of an identity does not automatically imply anguish. Pleasant marriages are possible between those from different cultures. Only a very unusual subculture (like perhaps an abusive family group) could create Husband/Wife identities that are not positive in evaluation.[13] As long as the identities are fundamentally positive, the expectations will be for pleasant behaviors and emotions. Still, the variations in power and expressivity in the national cultures lead to substantial differences in normative emotional climates, with lighthearted affection predominating in the view of U.S. undergraduates, and calm contentment the expectation of more traditional Japanese women.

The situations described above produce identity disconfirmation because interaction partners come into association with differing views (either because they disagree about the relevant identities or because they hold different meanings for the same identities). Notice, however, that situations can produce disconfirmation (and emotion) without such full scale disagreement. Events can push impressions away from fundamental meanings simply because few actions can perfectly confirm all identities and behaviors in a complex situation. Many situations require us to operate simultaneously in multiple identities of varying salience (Burke, 1980). Acts that confirm one identity may disconfirm another. (A devotion to work that reaffirms my identity as a Scholar may do violence to my view of myself as a Wife or a whitewater Paddler.) Some settings have identity conflict built into them; Thoits (1985:228–9) points out that these are likely occasions for strong emotion. When a Father remarries after divorce, his Son is dealing with a Stepmother whom the Father views as Wife (a more pleasant, powerful and lively identity). The Son may have to do considerable emotion work (Hochschild 1979, 1983) to produce the appropriately positive reactions to the wedding.

DISCONFIRMATION AND EMOTION

When disconfirming events do occur, emotions signal the character of the deflection. When especially good fortune strikes, affect control theory predicts positive emotions: a Child that is Treated feels Delighted and Light-Hearted; the Mother who provides the Treat is Happy and Pleased. Negative events cause negative emotions for both the actor and object. Parents who Punish a Child feel Annoyed, Disturbed and Pained. Only people with very negative, deviant identities are glad when evil prevails.

EMOTION AND LABELING

Affect control theory reveals interesting affective dynamics for the object of a negative act. While victims may be blameless in principle, they suffer negative consequences beyond material damage (Ryan 1971). The tendency to derogate victims is strong and it shows up in our equations. Victimization may require that the object feel (and express) negative emotion in order to confirm the vileness of the act and show that it was truly inappropriate for the object.[14] A victim who leaks a display of positive emotion invites being labeled and stigmatized—seen as someone who got what he deserved. By signaling a positive deflection, he shows that he views himself as occupying a negative identity—an appropriate object of evil. On the other hand, if one feels and displays the proper distress to signal the unfairness and inappropriateness of the act, one is then free to engage in constructive acts of recovery. This is what people ordinarily do. But of course, recovery acts imply a certain amount of power over circumstances, and unfortunately victimizations are most likely for those with least power. The poor, the elderly, and other low-status groups are more likely to be victims of crime and oppression, but they also have fewer resources for regaining a sense of control in their lives. The negative consequences of victimization—unresolved negative feelings or permanent stigmatization by self and others—are greatest in these groups without power and privilege.

Displays of appropriate emotion cues are used by actors to avoid labeling during self-disclosure of negative information. Lazowski (1987) pointed out that negative information typically has high information value in interpersonal interactions; it leads to firm impressions and to dislike. But if we become close to others and disclose much information to them, some of this information must be negative. How is it that people sometimes like us anyway? Lazowski suggested that nonverbal expressions of emotion moderate listener's reactions to negative self-disclosure content. Her experimental results showed that sadness on the speaker's part led listeners to form more positive impressions of someone who admitted harming another. Anger also had this effect (although to a lesser degree), primarily because it was perceived by observers to be self-directed anger or shame.

Affect control theory has a ready explanation for this mitigating effect of emotion (Heise 1989). We show through our sadness (or sometimes anger, if it appears to be self-directed) that we recognize the negative character of our behavior. Perhaps more importantly, we show that our self-concept or identity is fundamentally positive. Our emotion signals that the negative behavior that we have described has caused negative deflection. In one condition in Lazowski's experiment where no emotional reaction was shown, the viewer must infer that the negative behavior produced no deflection (or even positive impression-change). Since only bad people are expected to do bad things and feel neutral or good about them, the inference is that the speaker must be a fundamentally bad person. To avoid this inference, we display negative emotion when revealing our shortcomings to others. Such emotions often are played to and for an audience (Averill 1980:323) to authenticate identities and to mitigate the effects of negative information that is revealed through circumstance or self-disclosure.

Others' emotional displays help us infer the character of actions or actors in ambiguous circumstances. For example, suppose that when visiting a foreign culture you do behavior X and a native expresses horror. That emotional reaction tells you that X is immoral or dangerous in the culture, even if it's not bad or malignly powerful in your own. In another example, a child asks a man for coin change and the man is seen to cheat the child. You look to the faces of observers. Seeing disgust, you infer that the man must have a normal respected identity. Seeing cynical amusement, you know that the man has an identity that led them to expect his behavior, something like a Scrooge. Seeing surprised relief—that he did not do worse—you know the man is a powerful, evil character, like a Dictator or Mafioso. You can infer the man's identity from the event and the observer's emotional reactions—in affect control terms, you have solved for an affective profile that makes sense of the peoples' reactions, then searched for a language label that corresponds to the goodness, power and liveliness of the identity. After this inference, you are ready to generate further expectations for the man in realms other than interaction with the child.

AFFECT CONTROL AND OTHER RESEARCH TRADITIONS

Readers familiar with the sociological literature on emotions have doubtless noticed that many affect control theory "predictions" correspond to important insights by other researchers. This pleases us. If our model suggested outcomes that didn't dovetail with the knowledge we've cumulated so far, we'd worry. But notice that our predictions come only from numerical calculations on three-number profiles that represent the goodness, powerfulness and liveliness of identities, behaviors and emotion words. INTERACT's knowledge of human emotions is derived only from these affective inputs, the impression-change equations, and the theoretical model (provided by the affect control proposition that people act to reduce the deflection of transient feelings from fundamental sentiments).

We hope this parsimonious model can add to the sociology of emotion by creating a formal apparatus for predicting which emotion occurs in which circumstances. It provides a framework for integrating and interpreting findings in a wide range of research traditions. While a comprehensive review of the literature is beyond the scope of this chapter, this section will outline the connection of affect control ideas with a few major insights by other researchers.

Since it is based on symbolic interactionist principles, affect control theory is closely linked to traditional theorists within that perspective. For example, Shott (1979) and Denzin (1983) argue that situational definitions are critical factors in the definition of emotion. Affect control theory also asserts that what we feel depends on who we are and how we view a situation. Stryker (1987) points out that emotions are not only shaped by social situations, but that they also importantly affect future commitment to roles and network connections. Our approach is compatible with his view; redefinition of a situation (i.e., changing an identity label) signals a different future for a relationship.[15] However, our model differs from more traditional interactionist approaches in that it specifies the types of meaning that are evoked by situational definitions and maintained by interaction. The major dimensions of affective meaning linked to these cognitive categorizations are evaluation, potency, and activity. The use of these three dimensions to describe social relationships and emotional reactions to them coincides with a large body of literature on the dimensionality of emotion terms (Fehr and Russell 1984; Ortony and Clore 1981; Morgan and Heise 1988) and of facial expression (Cuceloglu 1970; Osgood 1966; Ekman 1982).

Within the sociology of emotions, the affect control approach is most closely linked to that of Kemper (1978). He also argues that the basic dimensions of social relationships are status (regard, liking or goodness), power, and technical activity.[16] More importantly, Kemper views emotions as outcomes of interaction. His "structural" emotions parallel the affect control predictions about the influence of identity on emotion when confirming events occur. What Kemper calls "consequent emotions" are analogous to the deflection or disconfirmation aspect of the affect control view (Kemper 1978:49). Both Kemper's structural theory and affect control theory share an imagery of people moving through a multidimensional space, with their emotional experience determined both by their absolute position in the space and by their direction of movement.

Since both Kemper's work and affect control theory are formal models of emotional response, perhaps their correspondence is not surprising. Links to more qualitative traditions of research also are strong, however. Perhaps the clearest link is to scholars in the Goffman tradition. Goffman (1956, 1959, 1963a, 1964, 1967) focused attention on feelings of embarrassment and shame. Occupying "soiled identities" can' be the source of shame; the interaction of "normal" people with these stigmatized others can produce negative emotion (Goffman 1964:120). This discussion is similar to the effect of identity on emotion in affect control theory. Negative identities typically lead to distressing emotional lives; the evaluation standing of one interaction partner tends to rub off on the other during events that join them.[17]

Goffman (1967:105) noted that embarrassment results from unfulfilled expectations. Given their social identities and settings, participants sense what sort of conduct should be maintained. Since Goffman concentrated primarily on interaction or identity "failure" and the resulting stigma, he inevitably treated the negative emotions that result from lowered evaluations and from the use of interactional power. However, in his discussions of occasions, he noted that occupants can be too quiet (as at a party), or too lively (as in a sacred place) (Goffman 1963b;11–9, 173–4). He recognized, as affect control theory does, that deflection can be deviant in both positive and negative directions and can entail not only the dimensions of evaluation and power, but activity as well.

Recent research in the Goffman tradition also analyzes events in terms of evaluation, power, and movement. Clark (1987) pointed out that to give sympathy is a signal of positive regard after bad things happen to good people. Even minor losses will make us sympathetic toward our friends, while only major disasters will elicit sympathy for our enemies. We get sympathy when events happen to us that are worse than we *deserve*. Affect control principles highlight that these emotions and actions will occur when events are bad enough to cause negative deflection from our current identity.

But Clark (1987:308–9) points out that giving sympathy involves the dimension of power as well. It sends a dual message: it is a sign of caring and of the superiority of the donor. If we seem too powerful, we will not receive sympathy (Clark 1987:308–9). On the other hand, we can deflect someone else's power downward if we give sympathy where it is not wanted (e.g., Clark's [1987:317] example of a professional woman putting down her boss by giving sympathy). Such dynamics can be analyzed in the affect control paradigm by analyzing the effects of behaviors like Sympathize With and Pity.

EMOTION NORMS

Other theorists, notably Collins (1975; 1981) and Hochschild (1978, 1983), emphasize the normative, ideological aspect of emotion. Ritual sequences of behavior can create powerful, predictable emotional outputs to support and reaffirm identity and meaning. This ritual means of emotion production is a potent tool for groups that contest for power and legitimacy. Emotions are not just reactions to events; they also sustain and validate the norms, values and expectancies that are the blueprint for their construction. Thus, one of the surest ways for a religious or political convert to affirm the validity of a new system of beliefs is by experiencing (and displaying) the emotions considered authentic by the group (Averill 1983:1158). Conversely, Hochschild (1979:567) points out that one can defy an ideological stance by inappropriate affect; lax emotional management is a clue to a lapsed or rejected ideology.

Affect control theory articulates with the ideological interpretation of emotions because it claims that emotion is a direct outcome of the sentiments held for the actor, behavior and object in an event. Once a group reaches agreement on what happened—who did what to whom—then the participants' emotions directly signal whether or not their sentiments correspond to the group's interpretation of events. At first, ideological deviance instigates attempts to correct and resocialize sentiments into conformity; success is assessed by a display of "appropriate" affect from the violator. If that fails, the deviant is stigmatized and expelled from the group. Thus, a display of inappropriate affect—signifying ideological nonconformity—leads the violator either to strengthen the legitimacy of sentiments that originally were contrary to his own, or else to give up the benefits of status in the group. One can see why group dynamics revolve centrally around the process of attaining leaders and coalitions that express one's own values (Bales 1971, 1980; Bales and Cohen 1979). Reward and fulfillment in a group depend mainly on whether one's own value direction monopolizes the judgment of events and feelings.

The affect control view of the emotion behavior—norm relationship is similar to that proposed by Kemper (1981:346): "First comes the social relationship, with its concrete behavior pattern and its characteristic emotions. Only later does a rule emerge to guard the relational pattern by guarding the emotions it evokes." Those who hold the sentiments associated with a dominant ideology and culture experience the proper emotions without regard to feeling rules or norms. Feeling rules are a means of controlling those who do not maintain the ideologically appropriate meanings.

In a sense, all of affect control theory's predictions about emotions define norms since they are the responses generated by consensually held meanings. They will also be predictions for individual response for members who share the definition of a situation and who share the culture. When members of differing subcultures meet, or when definitions of situations differ, or when people bring idiosyncratic meanings to interaction, emotion norms will be violated.

When such violations occur, interactants who wish to continue their relationship (or "pass" as an adherent to an ideology they have not yet thoroughly incorporated) may engage in emotion management to produce the desired affective displays (Hochschild 1978, 1983; Thoits 1984, 1985). One may relabel an emotional display ("I'm not angry, just surprised") of self or other. Alternatively, one could "re-think" the situation in different terms. Affect control theory would suggest that changing the identities and/or behaviors could lead to an authentic display of appropriate emotion. Hochschild (1983) reported that flight attendants manipulated their emotional life in this way by imagining that Passengers who Belittle them are actually recent Widowers from whom negative behavior would be expected. The older Japanese Wives could produce the appropriate behaviors and emotions for U.S. culture if they began thinking of themselves as occupying some livelier, more powerful identity within their own cultural system (a Co-worker in the enterprise of family, perhaps?).

EMOTIONS AND LABELING

One implication of the normative view of emotional display, developed by Thoits (1984, 1985) and supported by affect control theory, is that emotional deviants are at risk for labeling. When we observe inappropriate emotional response in others, we may surmise that either the person is not who we thought he/she was (i.e., we have labeled him/her with an incorrect identity), or he/she does not share our view of the situation (the actor, object and behavior labels we have used to characterize it cognitively), or he/she does not share our sentiments about the evaluation, potency and liveliness associated with the situational definition. When our own feelings fail to match our expectations, we may be sensitized to competing identities or may even begin searching for new ways to characterize the self. Segregating settings (e.g., not taking work home from the office) or ritual behaviors may help to restore appropriate feelings. In cases of extreme and repeated deviation from appropriate emotional response, Thoits (1985) pointed out that we may doubt our sanity and relabel ourselves as mentally ill. Such relabeling processes, whether carried out by self or others, are represented in affect control theory as "re-identification." If emotion management does not work, we then ask the question: What kind of person could I be, to react in such a way?

Clearly, much knowledge already produced by sociologists and psychologists is consistent with, and helpful to, the affect control perspective. Therefore, the theory may serve as a useful paradigm with which to organize information produced by scholars from widely varying traditions. But a powerful model should also be able to guide future work. We now turn to this.

THE RESEARCH AGENDA

TESTING THE MODEL

One of the first things we need to do is to test the predictions of the INTERACT simulations. They seem roughly correct and they agree with previous research, but we need more systematic work to see whether the emotions that the model produces are actually what people expect and feel in real situations. Although our intention is not to describe research design, it may be useful to suggest a few lines of attack on the difficult business of verifying a simulation result. The possibilities are (at least) threefold.

First, one could make use of naturally occurring experiences and try to recreate those experiences using the affect control dynamics. Qualitative researchers have traditionally asked their respondents about situations that provide telling examples of the phenomenon under study (e.g., Clark 1987 or Thoits, this volume). Scherer and his colleagues (1986) systematically surveyed samples in five European countries to find the antecedents of memorable instances of joy, sadness, fear, and anger. The respondents described features of the antecedent situations as well as the intensity and duration of the emotions. A researcher could attempt to match the data from this study (or from similar self-report frames) to affect-control generated sequences of behavior and emotion. The fact that the data are descriptions from one person's point of view is not problematic; affect control theory predicts that the respondent's labeling of actors, behaviors, and emotional productions are what will affect his or her emotional response.

However, matching simulations to reported experiences is difficult. In practice it becomes an interpretive process in which several simulations of the situation must be tried out in order to reproduce the action sequence and emotional production (e.g., did the friend see the put down as a Tease or an Insult?).[18]

A second strategy is to present a scenario, and ask people what they expect as emotional response. Affect control theory predicts differences in emotional reaction based on behaviors and identities. Since INTERACT produces both natural language labels and quantitative values for how good, powerful and lively a person will feel after an event, the responses could take the form of (1) an open-ended description of the anticipated emotional state; (2) a fixed choice from a set of emotion labels (where the response from INTERACT is one of the alternatives); or (3) a rating of how good, potent and lively such a person would feel after experiencing the event. (This procedure is similar to the one used by Wiggins and Heise [1987:153–158] to test the model's behavioral productions.)

Similarly, one could describe events and emotional responses, then ask if the emotion was normative or deviant. Pugliesi (described in Thoits 1985:224–5; and this volume) used this technique to study emotion norms and imputations of mental illness. Affect control analyses could refine the predictions of deviance, since the difference between the normative emotional response (the one generated by INTERACT) and the deviant emotion described in the scenario can be expressed as a numerical value (the difference between the evaluation, potency, and activity profiles of the normative and deviant emotions).

Since affect control processes also model the labeling of people who show deviant emotions, we can study labeling simulations in the same way. For example, INTERACT predicts that a Man who Kisses a Woman, then looks Cheerful could be labeled a Sweetheart, a Pal or a Mate; a Man who appeared Nervous after the same act would risk being labeled a Clod or viewed as mentally ill (a Psychotic) (examples from Heise, 1989). We can present subjects with scenarios that vary the emotional response and have them choose among the labels for the actor.

Ultimately, readers will want to compare the theory's efficacy not only to verbal descriptions of past events and to judgments about hypothetical scenarios, but also to behavior in real social situations. Here, ethical concerns will be serious. Since the model suggests that emotion will occur with disconfirmation of identity, we must take care not to create harmful feelings or permanent self-labeling.

One way to avoid ethical dilemmas is to observe or film naturally occurring interactions. Deflections generated by the model should be correlated with the facial expressions that indicate emotional response to the events.[19] One problem with the approach is that the theory hypothesizes that most interaction will confirm people's identities. This would limit the range of emotions available for observation and filming.

Experiential sampling techniques also have potential for studying the influence of identity on typical emotion in normal, identity-maintaining settings. Burke and Franzoi (forthcoming) had students carry beepers for several days. The beeper would go off at random times; when it did, subjects described the situation they were in, the identity they were occupying, and how they were feeling. If affect control theory is correct, we could predict the average quality of these respondents' emotional experiences from their identities.

Experiments dealing with self-concept can also be used for testing affect control principles. When people with varying levels of self-esteem (a fundamental evaluation of a self-identity) enter experimental situations, we expect differential emotional and behavioral responses to experimental manipulations. People with relatively negative self-images will find negative information, insults, and failure self-confirming; people with positive self-images will experience more deflection of their feelings from fundamental meanings when faced with these negative events. Affect control should model both the emotions and the behavior that result when people undergo such manipulations. (Examples of experiments in this vein are Swann's [1987b] on identity-maintenance vs. self-enhancement and Baumeister and Tice [1985] and Baumeister et al. [1985] on self-esteem and responses to success and failure.) In fact, one could use affect control simulations to reanalyze almost any study that measured self-esteem before an experiment, manipulated an interpersonal event, then measured affective variables after the manipulation.

We can study the use of emotional cues for labeling by extending the experimental paradigm developed by Lazowski (1987). Affect control theory suggests that emotional displays will modify the connection between behavior and labeling: people who do bad things don't look so bad if they're torn up about it, while people who do good things are still suspect if they show inappropriately negative affect (Heise 1989). Our experimental manipulation can consist of information about events combined with affective display (like Lazowski's videotaped self-disclosures or faked "transcripts"). Then we can ask subjects what they think of the person they've seen or read about. Again, affect control theory generates both quantitative EPA values and labels (e.g., we could predict specific numerical ratings on the evaluation, potency and activity dimensions, or that the subject would pick the situation-produced label "Hothead" out of a list of alternative labels).

Finally, we do not want to limit our tests to conventional methods like survey or experimental work. We need considerable creativity in the relatively new enterprise of evaluating the simulation model. For example, archival materials may prove useful. Jury trials are examples of situation defining tasks: was it murder or self-defense, rape or consensual sex? By examining the court record for instances of descriptive testimony that mention emotional reaction, we can study the attempts of prosecution and defense to define the situation for the jurors. If our hypotheses about emotional displays and labeling are correct, emotion should be used as evidence. Furthermore, we should be able to predict what types of cues will be mentioned by the prosecution and the defense in their attempts to create the image of Criminal and Victimized Citizen, respectively.

All of the suggestions above focus on testing the theory by matching the productions of the simulation program to other data. However, this necessary task represents only a small part of our research agenda. More exciting is the work we can do if we are willing to assume that affect control processes are a useful way to view emotional phenomena. Ultimately, it is the fruitfulness of these applications and the insights that they provide into areas of substantive concern that will determine the theory's worth.

NEW SUBSTANTIVE DIRECTIONS

One new application of the theory is in the study of culture and subcultures. Several studies show that the processing of affective information is highly similar in different cultures (Smith-Lovin 1987a:60–65; MacKinnon 1983). This result implies that we can represent differences between cultures using only the EPA meanings of identities, behaviors, emotions, and settings. These meanings are easy to measure. We already have "dictionaries" of these cultural values for U.S. undergraduates, Canadian English-speaking undergraduates, and Catholic adolescents from Belfast Northern Ireland. Smaller studies, focusing on specific domains, exist for Metropolitan Community Church (a gay congregation, surveyed about religious and homosexual identities) and Unitarian groups (religious and homosexual identities), Japanese immigrants (marital and religious identities), and North Carolina State Troopers (law enforcement and criminal identities).

The time is ripe for large, cross-national data collection. Scherer et al. (1986) provided an excellent model in their study of emotional productions in eight countries. A major affect control study in a non-English speaking culture would also be very useful. The theory offers an efficient model for generating and exploring the cultural practices, emotion norms, and labeling behavior of any society.

For subcultures, it is reasonable to assume that the meanings of most behaviors and non-salient identities are shared with the encompassing culture (Heise 1966). Therefore, a researcher need concentrate only on identities and behaviors that are central to the subculture (e.g., religious identities in a church group, gay slang within a cohesive segment of the homosexual community, or occupational roles in a professional subculture). After a simple data collection task, one can examine (1) the emotion norms within the group (by simulating the emotions implied by identities), (2) socialization into the subculture (by comparing outsiders, initiates and oldtimers), (3) conflict between the subculture and the mainstream ideology (by stimulating interactions between outsiders and members, and examining the emotional productions), and (4) rituals used to produce emotional products within the subculture (with simulations using the identities and behavior patterns involved).

Studies in our own culture can concentrate on areas likely to cause strong emotions. Simulation studies can show what combinations of identities will produce role strain. When the behaviors required to sustain one identity lead to strong negative emotions for another simultaneously held identity, affective disturbance is likely. Similarly, researchers and clinicians can use affect control theory to isolate areas where differences in the definition of the situation or in subcultural meanings are likely to produce emotional distress. For example, one could examine sexual harassment in the workplace by looking for emotional displays that lead to mislabeling Employer and Employee as occupants of sexual identities, and explore the emotional distress that the misidentification and/or inappropriate behavior causes.

THEORETICAL QUESTIONS

In addition to testing and applying the current theory substantively, computer simulations have suggested several interesting questions that need further work. One aspect of this theory of emotions is counter-intuitive— emotions are not motivational in the sense that we usually think. Emotion is a signal about fundamental identity and deflections from it—the very things that shape the next action. But the relation of the emotion to the next action is reflective rather than directly causal. For example, suppose an event occurs that makes a Father momentarily angry and he interacts with his Son. Affect control theory predicts Comforting and Soothing behavior. The angry Father does *not* act angrily. If anything, the model predicts that he acts nicer and calmer than usual. In affect control theory, subsequent behaviors compensate for emotions. Since behaviors are chosen to reduce deflection and to maintain meaning, the behaviors must, in general, be opposite to deflections (and therefore, the emotion labels). Psychologists have observed this process to some degree, but it is still counter-intuitive. We normally think of people as acting out their emotions, and assume that they try to maximize positive emotion. Per contra, because it is *control* theory, our approach posits that we behave so as to maintain identities for ourselves and others. Hence, instead of reflecting our feelings, our actions may belie them, when the feelings are generated by disconfirming events.[20] An alternative approach, but still within the model, is to assume that emotions get attached to identities, as moods of some duration, thus forming a composite identity. This attachment would alter fundamental meanings in the situation, and suggest that the person (at least temporarily) differs in character from the typical person in that role. In this case an Angry Father is not merely experiencing a flash of emotional feeling; he is more fundamentally altered—he would produce acts that would sustain, confirm, and communicate the Angry Father status. The predicted behaviors of such an Angry Father toward a Son who has Disobeyed include Halt, Catch, and Oppose. These behaviors are more aggressive than a Father's usual affectionate, protective self. This new type of behavior would communicate to observers (even to the Father himself) that he is an Angry Father—his past negative acts are explained by this definition of the situation and future negative acts are motivated by this new identity. Returning to nice, normal parental behavior would require a reidentification back to normal; it would require noticing that the mood had ended.

Viewed as moods, emotions do produce and explain out-of-role behavior in affect control theory. When emotion is transformed from a transient condition to a temporary trait—a component of identity—then behaviors are controlled by the mood and serve to maintain it. But this also raises an important question—when do emotions exist as a quick flash of feeling and when do they get absorbed into identity as a situationally stable mood? My guess is that it would depend on the nature of the event that causes the transient impressions. Perhaps if I unintentionally engaged in out-of-role behavior, and then recognized it as such,[21] then I would experience an emotional response, but not incorporate it into my identity. But if another actor directed unexpected and inappropriate behavior at me (especially if this were repeated, as it would if our definitions of the situation clashed) I would be more likely to respond with a mood: Irritated, Angry or Elated, depending on the impressions created. This reaction would be especially likely if the institutitonal supports for the situation are such that I could not easily label (i.e., re-identify) the other. There is a nice parallel to this in psychological attribution research—we can see the "accidental" nature of *our* mistakes but assume more intentional behavior when others err (Ross and Fletcher 1985)

Another difficult issue raised by simulations is the emotional response of a bystander or observer. In affect control theory, disconfirmation of identity produces emotion. Unless they have been involved in an event that changes the evaluation, potency, and activity levels of their relevant identity, people are not predicted to have strong emotional reactions. Clearly, however, people *do* react affectively to seeing others mistreated or exalted. We do not actually have to play in the game to feel the thrill of victory, or lose our spouse to experience the pain of grief. Sometimes the reaction may result from standing by without taking suitable action (e.g., one of the reasons we feel miserable about seeing a Mother Slap her Child is that we Ignore the Injured Child and our self-esteem is damaged by the nonintervention). However, we often react affectively to films and to social situations where intervention is not an issue. Clearly, some type of cognitive processing or identification is occurring that allows us to experience vicariously the identity deflections of other persons. We take the role of the other spontaneously in a wide variety of circumstances, and experience the emotions of others vicariously. Eventually, we will need impression formation studies that predict impression changes for bystanders as well as event participants. A clear statement of these processes—when they occur and how they produce deflection--is necessary for a fuller application of affect control theory to emotional life.

A final research area where some exciting questions are raised involves attempts to link the affect control dynamics with models of rational action called "production systems." Production systems are grammars for social action; they specify a system of rules by which role occupants generate appropriately organized sequences of action in relation to current conditions. Typically, such systems are composed of "if-then" rules and a priority structure that indicates which action will be taken when the conditions for more than one action are met. Fararo and Skvoretz (1984; Skvoretz and Fararo 1979; Fararo 1986) pointed out how production systems are linked to institutional action. In their view, institutions are sets of role-grams (or production systems) that fit together to maintain higher-order institutional forms (e.g., in a restaurant, the major goal is to serve customers food in exchange for money). Heise (forthcoming) has developed a new program called "ETHNO" that can use the production system idea to elicit and encode qualitative, ethnographic information. Carley (1988) has worked on making production system models more *social* by combining them with the affect control model.

The link between affective processing and rational action (as represented by production systems) is an important one for both perspectives. On one hand, affect control theory currently describes behavior at a very general level: a Waitress might Serve a Customer, but the details of the service, the coordination of multiple customers, and other institutionalized routines would be impossible to anticipate. We might predict the negative emotion that would result if the Waitress Ignored the Customer, but we would not know that it was the cook's fault for letting the order sit too long. Production systems handle such problems admirably.

In return affect control theory may contribute solutions to some core problems in the production system approach. Affective processes may help us to explain the creation of behavioral goals, the impetus to achieve them, and the commitment to carry them out. Affective meanings are the values that provide stability to institutional systems. Emotions are signals about how well they are being maintained, and what type of work needs to be done to restore disturbed relations. I agree with Minsky (1986:163), a well-known artificial intelligence researcher, when he says, "The question is not whether intelligent machines can have any emotions, but whether machines can be intelligent without any emotions." If machines, like people, had the ability to alter their own capabilities (one definition of artificial intelligence), they would have to have all sorts of complex checks and balances to guide their self-development. I think emotional life plays this role for human actors.

Based on interpretative principles, affect control theory contains the impact of both cultural values (through the fundamental sentiments) and individual thought (through the definition of the situation and its maintenance). It is specific enough to be falsifiable (i.e., the theory can be tested). That is why the research agenda that I have outlined above is so important; it will tell us whether we are fundamentally correct in our view of emotions as signals of identity confirmation and disconfirmation. And, if we are, it will show us how the model needs to be elaborated to reflect the emotional complexities of social life.

Notes

*Some of the ideas included here were originally presented in a paper, "A Quantitative Model of Affect Control," at the American Sociological Association meetings in Chicago, 1987. The author thanks Mitch Abolafia, Steve Barley, Ronald Breiger, Carolyn Ellis, John Freeman, David Heise, Theodore D. Kemper, David Krackhart, Miller McPherson, Beth Rubin, and David Weakliem for helpful comments on this paper.

1. Excellent reviews of the work by sociologists are available in Gordon (1981) and Scheff (1983). A new assessment for *Annual Review* is under preparation by Peggy A. Thoits. Lutz and White (1986) review the work in anthropology. Psychologists made few references to emotion in their major review volume, *The Handbook of Social Psychology*, perhaps because emotion is not viewed as a primarily social phenomenon in that discipline. Luckily, two recent books by European authors provide useful summaries as introductions concentrating on empirical research (Frijda 1986; Scherer et al. 1986). Isen (1984) gives a helpful review of the relationship between affect and cognition. Ortony and Clore (1981) and Kemper (1987) give

brief reviews of relevant linguistic and biological work, respectively. Frank (1988) describes economists' preliminary thrusts from the rational world into the realm of passion.

2. I use capitalized words in the text of this chapter to indicate words that describe identities, social behaviors, emotions, traits, or personal characteristics, and settings that one could use to define situations. These capitalized words come from a corpus of terms that can be used when running simulations of social events and emotional reactions using the INTERACT program (Heise and Lewis 1988; see also the technical appendix to this chapter).

3. See Morgan and Heise (1988) for a description of how the semantic differential dimensions relate to other aspects of meaning and to dissimilarity ratings for emotion words.

4. In the example here, the Host moves from the good, potent, lively corner of the space downward in evaluation and potency, but increases somewhat in activity. The equations predict the three numbers (EPA) that specify the new location. We call the squared distance moved "deflection."

5. Carolyn Ellis (personal communications) points out that social workers help criminals and ministers work with sinners without damaging their reputations. The impression-change equations indicate that these positive professional identities are maintained by the positive evaluation of the acts they direct at negative objects (like Rehabilitate and Pray For). Conversations with such practitioners also indicate some desire to distance themselves from the negative acts of their clients (creating other events like the Minister Criticizes the Sinner) and to stress the positive nature of their actions for the public (allowing a more positive object for some events: the Social Worker Aids the Probation Officer).

6. Heise (1979; 1986) uses the term "sentiments" to refer to fundamental meanings on the evaluation, potency and activity dimensions.

7. Extensions of the program described in later sections add consideration of emotions, personal traits and settings to the program.

8. The distinction between experienced emotion, expressed emotion and feeling rules (or emotion norms) is implicit in affect control theory at this stage in its development. The INTERACT program predicts what people will feel, given their definition of the situation and the EPA meanings associated with the identities and behaviors. Their expression of that emotion may be managed, since they recognize that their emotional reaction will provide information about the identity they occupy and their view of the situation (e.g., if I am Insulted but I want my Supervisor to believe that I interpreted his action as Teasing, then I will not display my flustered anger).

9. In affect control theory, a role is an identity taken in relationship to another identity. For example, Mother is an identity and is a role (with a corresponding set of behavioral predictions) when viewed in the context of the Mother-Son relationship.

10. Notice that a negative rating on the potency dimension does not imply that these emotions have little impact on the person experiencing them. Rather, they imply that the person experiences a sense of powerlessness or lack of control.

11. The most recent U.S. undergraduate study (Smith-Lovin and Heise 1988; Heise and Lewis 1988) and the Canadian study (MacKinnon 1983) also contain ratings of emotion and trait terms. The U.S. study includes social settings as well.

12. These simulations use impression-change equations from the U.S. data since analyses indicate few cultural differences in the *processing* of affective information (Smith-Lovin 1987a:60–65; 1988). They use emotion and behavior profiles for the U.S., since the primarily U.S. readership will want labels corresponding to their cultural view of the actions and emotions produced. (Also, emotion meanings are available only for the U.S. and Canada.) In each analysis, male meanings are used for the Husband and female meanings are used for the Wife.

13. Note that in such situations, negative emotions need not imply break-up of the marriage. If negative identities are being confirmed, these abusive situations can be unfortunately stable (see above discussion of the effect of identity on emotional experience).

14. Alternatively, Heise (personal communication) suggests that victims may mask emotion and appeal more directly to ideology by pointing out the evil character of the behavior.

15. For example, if interactions with a child produce very negative emotion, the child may eventually be re-labeled as occupant of some other identity (Drug Pusher) and no longer viewed as Child. This disowning of the kinship relation obviously has serious implications for the future interaction: the parent will no longer try to engage in rehabilitative acts to restore the positive Child identity, but will instead reject and avoid the stigmatized offspring.

16. Those readers familiar with Kemper's work will recognize that his category of technical activity, a much less central part of his model than status and power, is elevated in this discussion to a full-fledged third dimension. I do not wish to imply that he agrees with this new importance attached to activity/liveliness.

17. In affect control terms, the evaluation of the actor affects the evaluation of the object-person after an event during the impression-change process; similarly, the evaluation of the object-person affects the outcome for the actor in the event (Smith-Lovin 1987a:48–51).

18. Note that this necessity for shaping the INTERACT representation of an event is not an indication that the model is incorrect. Rather, it is an acknowledgment that even straightforward events (and descriptions of them) are multifaceted and capable of multiple interpretations. The fact that a good fit *can* be found, given a reasonable representation of the event, is strong evidence for the model.

19. Research using unobtrusive observation will benefit from the extraordinary body of research on the coding and cross-cultural interpretability of facial expressions of emotion (Ekman 1982).

20. This maintenance principle does not imply that people who are deflected upward (who feel very good) will necessarily act in a nasty manner. For example, if a Father is Rescued by his Son, he feels very good (although somewhat weakened by being the recipient of such a strong act). His predicted behaviors toward the Son are Befriend, Honor, Back, Assist and Congratulate. These acts restore his power and maintain the positive identities.

21. Someone may call it to my attention and define it for me, or I could recognize it myself either through self-observation or through observing the effects of my actions on others.

References

Averett, Christine, and David R. Heise. 1987. "Modified Social Identities: Amalgamations, Attributions and Emotions." *Journal of Mathematical Sociology* 13, 1-2:103-32.

Averill, James R. 1980. "A Constructionist View of Emotion." Pp. 305-339 in R. Plutchik and H. Kellerman (eds.), *Emotion: Theory, Research and Experience.* New York: Academic Press.

———. 1983. "Studies on Anger and Aggression: Implications for Theories of Emotion." *American Psychologist* 38:1145-60.

Bales Robert F. 1970. *Personality and Interpersonal Behavior.* New York: Holt, Rinehart and Winston.

———. 1980. SYMLOG *Case Study Kit.* New York: Free Press.

Bales, Robert F., and Stephen P. Cohen. 1979. SYMLOG: *A System for the Multiple Level Observation of Groups.* New York: Free Press.

Baumeister, Roy F., Jeremy P. Shapiro, and Dianne M. Tice. 1985. "Two Kinds of Identity Crisis." *Journal of Personality* 53:407-24.

Baumeister, Roy F., and Dianne M. Tice. 1985. "Self-Esteem and Responses to Success and Failure: Subsequent Performance and Intrinsic Motivation." *Journal of Personality* 53:450-67.

Burke, Peter J. 1980. "The Self: Measurement Requirements From an Interactionist Perspective." *Social Psychology Quarterly* 43 (March) 1:18-29.

Burke, Peter J., and S. L. Franzoi. Forthcoming. "Situations and Identities: An Experiential Sampling Study." *American Sociological Review.*

Carley, Kathleen. 1988. "Emotions and Artificial Intelligence." *Sociology of Emotions Newsletter,* 3 (2):6.

Clark, Candace. 1987. "Sympathy Biography and Sympathy Margin." *American Journal of Sociology* 93 (2):290–21.

Collins, Randall. 1975. *Conflict Sociology: Toward an Explanatory Science.* New York: Academic Press.

——— . 1981. *Sociology since Midcentury: Essays in Theory Cumulation.* New York: Academic Press.

Cuceloglu, D. M. 1970. "Perceptions of Facial Expressions in Three Different Cultures." *Ergonomics* 13:93–100.

Denzin, Norman K. 1983. "A Note on Emotionality, Self and Interaction." *American Journal of Sociology* 89:402–9.

Ekman, Paul (ed.). 1982. *Emotion in the Human Face.* 2d ed. London: Cambridge University Press.

Fararo, Thomas. 1986. "Action and Institution, Network and Function: The Cybernetic Concept of Social Structure." *Sociological Forum* 1:219–50.

Fararo, Thomas, and John V. Skvoretz. 1984. "Institutions as Production Systems." *Journal of Mathematical Sociology* 10:117–82.

Fehr, Beverly, and James A. Russell. 1984. "Concept of Emotion Viewed from a Prototype Perspective." *Journal of Experimental Psychology: General* 13:464–68.

Frank, Robert. 1988. *Passions within Reason.* New York: Norton.

Frijda, Nico H. 1986. *The Emotions.* London: Cambridge University Press.

Glassner, Barry. 1982. "Labeling theory." Pp. 71–89 in M. M. Rosenburg, R. A. Stebbins, and A. Turowitz (eds.), *The Sociology of Deviance.* New York: St. Martin's Press.

Goffman, Erving. 1956. "Embarrassment and Social Organization." *American Journal of Sociology* 62:264–71.

——— . 1959. *The Presentation of Self in Everyday Life.* Garden City, NY: Doubleday.

——— . 1963. *Behavior in Public Places: Notes on the Social Organization of Gatherings.* Glencoe, IL: Free Press.

——— . 1964. *Stigma: Notes on the Management of Spoiled Identity.* Englewood Cliffs New Jersey: Prentice-Hall.

——— . 1967. *Interaction Ritual: Essays on Face-to-Face behavior.* Garden City, NY: Doubleday and Co., Anchor Books.

————. 1974. *Frame Analysis: An Essay on the Organization of Experience*. New York: Harper and Row.

Gonos, G. 1977. " 'Situation' versus 'Frame': The 'Interactionist' and the 'Structuralist' Analyses of Everyday life." *American Sociological Review* 42:854–67.

Gordon, Robert A., James F. Short Jr., Desmond S. Cartwright, and Fred Strodbeck. 1963. "Values and Gang Delinquency: A Study of Street-Corner Groups." *American Journal of Sociology* 69:109–28.

Gordon, Steven L. 1981. "The Sociology of Sentiments and Emotion." Pp. 562–92 in M. Rosenberg and R. H. Turner (eds.), *Social Psychology: Sociological Perspectives*. New York: Basic Books.

Heise, David R. 1966. "Social Status, Attitudes and Word Connotations." *Sociological Inquiry* 36, 2:227–39.

————. 1977. "Social Action as the Control of Affect." *Behavioral Science* 22:163–77.

————. 1978. *Computer-Assisted Analysis of Social Action*. Chapel Hill, NC: Institute for Research in the Social Sciences.

————. 1979. *Understanding Events: Affect and the Construction of Social Action*. New York: Cambridge University Press.

————. 1982. "Emotions as Signals of Self Confirmation or Disconfirmation." Paper presented to the Society for Experimental Social Psychology. Nashville, IN. October 1982.

————. 1986. "Modeling Symbolic Interaction." Pp. 291–309 in S. Lindenberg, J. S. Coleman and S. Novak (eds.), *Approaches to Social Theory*, New York: Russell Sage Foundation.

————. 1989. "Effects of Emotion Displays on the Assessment of Character." *Social Psychological Quarterly* 52:10–21.

————. Forthcoming. "Modeling Event Structures." *Journal of Mathematical Sociology*.

Heise, David. R., and Elsa Lewis. 1988. *Introduction to Interact*. National Collegiate Software Clearinghouse, Box 8101, North Carolina State University, Raleigh, NC 27695.

Heise. David R., and Neil J. MacKinnon. 1987. "Affective Bases of Likelihood Judgments." *Journal of Mathematical Sociology* 13 (1–2):133–52.

Hochschild, Arlie Russell. 1977. "Emotion Work, Feeling Rules and Social Structure." *American Sociological Review* 85:551–75.

————. 1983. *The Managed Heart*. Berkeley: University of California Press.

Isen, Alice M. 1984. "Toward Understanding the Role of Affect in Cognition." Pp. 179–236 in R. Wyer and T. Srall (eds.), *Handbook of Social Cognition*. Hillsdale, NJ: Erlbaum.

Kemper, Theodore D. 1978. *A Social Interactional Theory of Emotions*. New York: Wiley.

———. 1981. "Social Constructionist and Positivist Approaches to the Sociology of Emotions." *American Journal of Sociology* 87:336–62.

———. 1987. "How Many Emotions are There? Wedding the Social and Autonomic Components" *American Journal of Sociology* 93 (2):263–89.

Lazowski, Linda E. 1987. *Speakers' Nonverbal Expressions of Emotion as Moderators of Listeners' Reactions to Disclosure of Self Harm and Social Harm*. Unpublished doctoral dissertation, University of California, Santa Barbara.

Lutz, Catherine, and Geoffrey M. White. 1986. "The Anthropology of Emotions." *Annual of Review of Anthropology* 15:405–36.

Marks, I. M. 1965. *Patterns of Meaning in Psychiatric Patients: Semantic Differential Responses in Obsessives and Psychopaths*. London: Oxford University Press.

Minsky, Marvin. 1986. *The Society of Mind*. New York: Simon and Schuster.

Morgan, Rick L., and David R. Heise. 1988. "Structure of Emotions." *Social Psychology Quarterly* 51(1):19–31.

Okuyama, Ikuko. 1984. *Japanese American Intermarriage: An Affect Control Analysis*. Master's Thesis. University of South Carolina, Columbia, SC.

Ortony, Andrew, and Gerald L. Clore. 1981. "Disentangling the Affective Lexicon." *Proceedings of the Third Annual Conference of the Cognitive Science Society*. Berkeley, CA.

Osgood, Charles E. 1962. "Studies on the Generality of Affective Meaning Systems." *American Psychologist* 17 (January):10–28.

———. 1966. "Dimensionality of the Semantic Space for Communication via Facial Expressions." *Scandinavian Journal of Psychology* 7:1–30.

Osgood, Charles E., W. H. May and M. S. Miron. 1975. *Cross-cultural Universals of Affective Meaning*. Urbana, IL: University of Illinois Press.

Osgood, Charles E., George C. Suci, and Perry H. Tannenbaum. 1957. *The Measurement of Meaning*. Urbana, IL: University of Illinois Press.

Rains, Prue. 1982. "Deviant careers." Pp. 21–41 in M. M. Rosenberg, R. A. Stebbins and A. Turowitz (eds), *The Sociology of Deviance*. New York: St. Martin's Press.

Reiss, Albert J. Jr. (editor). 1961. *Occupations and Social Status*. New York: Free Press of Glencoe.

Ross, Michael, and Garth J. O. Fletcher. 1985. "Attribution and Social perception." Pp. 73–122 in Gardner Lindsey and Elliot Aronson (eds.), *The Handbook of Social Psychology, Vol. 2*. 3rd ed. New York: Random House.

Ryan, William. 1971. *Blaming the Victim*. New York: Pantheon.

Rossi, Peter H., Emily Waite, Christine E. Bose and Richard E. Berk. 1974. "The Seriousness of Crimes: Normative Structure and Individual Differences." *American Sociological Review* 39:224–237.

Scheff, Thomas. 1983. "Toward Integration in the Social Psychology of Emotions." *Annual Review of Sociology* 9:333–54.

Scherer, Klaus R., Harold G. Wallbott and Angela B. Summerfield (eds) 1986. *Experiencing Emotion: A Cross-Cultural Study*. London: Cambridge University Press.

Shott, Susan. 1979. "Emotion and Social Life: A Symbolic Interactionist Perspective." *American Journal of Sociology* 84:1317–34.

Skvoretz, John, and Thomas Fararo. 1979. "Languages and Grammars of Action and Interaction: A Contribution to the Formal Theory of Action." *Behavioral Science* 25:9–22.

Skvoretz, John V., and Thomas Fararo. Forthcoming. "Action Structures and Sociological Action Theory." *Journal of Mathematical Sociology*.

Smith, Eliot R., and James R. Kluegel. 1982. "Cognitive and Social Bases of Emotional Experience: Outcome, Attribution and Affect." *Journal of Personality and Social Psychology* 43:1129–1141.

Smith-Lovin, Lynn. 1987a. "Impressions from Events." *Journal of Mathematical Sociology* 13 (1–2):35–00.

——— . 1987b. "The Affective Control of Events within Settings." *Journal of Mathematical Sociology* 13 (1–2):71–102.

Smith-Lovin, Lynn, and William T. Douglass. Forthcoming. "Modeling Emotions in Religious Ritual: An Affect Control Analysis of Two Religious Groups." In David R. Franks and Viktor Gecas (eds.), *Social Perspectives on Emotion Vol. 1*. JAI Press.

Smith-Lovin, Lynn, and David R. Heise. 1988. *Analyzing Social Interaction: Advances in Affect Control Theory*. New York: Gordon and Breach Science Publishers.

Stryker, Sheldon. 1987. "The Interplay of Affect and Identity: Exploring the Relationships of Social Structure, Social Interaction, Self and Emotion." Paper presented at the American Sociological Association meetings, Chicago, IL.

Swann, William B. Jr. 1987a. "Self-Verification and the Cognitive-Affective Cross-fire." Paper presented at the American Sociological Association meetings in Chicago, Il.

———. 1987b. "Identity Negotiation." *Journal of personality and Social Psychology* 53:1038–51.

Swann, William B. Jr., John J. Griffin Jr., Steven C. Predmore and Bebe Gaines. 1987. "The Cognitive-Affective Crossfire: When Self-Consistency Confronts Self-Enhancement." *Journal of Personality and Social Psychology* 52 (5):881–9.

Thoits, Peggy A. 1984. "Coping, Social Support and Psychological Outcomes: The Central Role of Emotion." Pp. 219–38 in Philip Shaver (ed.), *Review of Personality and Social Psychology, Vol. 5.* Beverly Hills, CA: Sage.

———. 1985. "Self-Labeling Processes in Mental Illness: The Role of Emotional Deviance." *American Journal of Sociology* 91 (2):221–49.

Wiggins, Beverly, and David R. Heise. 1987. "Expectations, Intentions and Behavior: Some Tests of Affect Control Theory." *Journal of Mathematical Sociology* 13 (1–2):153–69.

10.

Affect Control Model
Technical Appendix

David R. Heise

This appendix briefly reviews some of the technical aspects of affect control theory and shows how the theory fosters computer analysis of social interaction.

QUANTITATIVE ASPECTS

Affect control theory is grounded in quantitative measurements on the Evaluation (good/bad), Potency (strong/weak), and Activity (active/passive) dimensions of the Semantic Differential (Osgood, May & Miron, 1975). Measurements are made with bipolar rating scales defined by adjectives at each end. Ratings on one side are coded plus, ratings on the other side are coded minus, and the midpoint is coded zero. The scales range from about -4.0 to $+4.0$ with suitable intermediate steps.

The quantitative model is based on empirically-derived equations that predict how people respond to events. Impression-formation equations are obtained by presenting a sample of events to respondents, who record their impressions of event elements on EPA rating scales. For example, respondents might be asked to use the Evaluation scale to rate a Mother who hurt her child, the Child who was hurt by the mother, and the act of Hurting when a mother hurts her child. Respondents also rate the same elements—a Mother, Child, Hurting someone—out-of-context.

Equations for predicting outcome impressions are obtained by regressing in-context measurements on out-of-context measurements. Interaction effects turn out to be important, so products of out-of-context variables also are included. This procedure produces empirical impression-formation equations like the following:

$$A' = -.43 + .39A + .48B + .15BO$$

This says that the perceived goodness (A') of the actor in an event is a function of the initial level of good/bad attitude toward the actor (A), the morality or goodness, of the behavior (B), and an interaction effect (BO) obtained by multiplying goodness of act by goodness of object to which the act is done, for example, doing bad to a bad person is good. This particular equation accounts for 86 percent of the variance in impressions of goodness/badness of outcome (Gollob, 1968).

Impression-formation equations have been obtained to describe the post-event goodness, powerfulness, and activation of four elements: (a) actors, (b) behaviors, (c) objects, and (d) settings. Actual equations in use are more complex than the one above, with more interaction terms and cross-dimensional effects, for example, it has been found that behavioral inhibitedness (the activity dimension) affects impressions of actor goodness (the evaluation dimension).

Proaction equations (predicting what actors will do) are derived mathematically from the reaction equations, by assuming that people construct events that confirm their fundamental sentiments about event elements. For example, a normal mother would not Hurt her child because the act disconfirms the fundamental goodness of Mother and Child; instead she would more likely choose an act like Assist, which reinforces the meanings of Mother and Child.

The analytic problem is to obtain a quantitative specification of behaviors that would confirm the identities of a given actor and object. Pre-event feelings about the actor and object are assumed to be known. Although the specific behavior is unknown, it is constrained theoretically to minimize deflections of outcome impressions from fundamental sentiments. Algebraic expressions are set up to represent the differences between outcome impressions and fundamental sentiments, employing the reaction equations that contain only pre-event quantities. The expressions are differentiated by the method of calculus to find their minima, resulting in equations that define the required proaction behavior in terms of pre-event information about the given actor and object.

The proaction equations thus obtained define the acts in terms of the required levels of goodness, potency, and activation. These quantitative specifications are translated into qualitative results using dictionaries of EPA profiles. For example, the equations might specify the values 0.4, 1.2, 1.3 on evaluation, potency, and activity, respectively, and this profile would translate into the behaviors "initiate" or "debate with."

The calculus minimization logic also is used for another event construction problem—redefining people who are involved in problematic events. In this case, the analytic problem is to obtain a quantitative definition of the kind of actor who would be confirmed by a given event. Applying the same procedures as before results in event reconstruction equations that define the required actor in terms of pre-event information about the given behavior and object. (Another solution provides the optimal object for an event involving a given actor and act.)

Another line of research supports Affect Control Theory's treatment of modified identities, attributions, and emotions. In this case, impression-formation equations are obtained by presenting a sample of modifier-identity combinations to respondents who record their impressions of the combinations on EPA rating scales. For example, respondents might be asked to use the evaluation scale to rate an Angry Mother. Respondents also rate the same elements out-of-context—that is, being Angry and Mother. Prediction equations are obtained by regressing the ratings of combinations on the ratings of components.

The results are equations like the following: (Heise & Thomas, 1988).

$$C_e = -.32 + .69M_e - .36M_p + .47I_e - .07I_a + .12M_e I_c$$

This says that the evaluation of a combination depends positively on evaluation of the modifier (M_e), inversely on the potency of the modifier (M_p), positively on the evaluation of the identity (I_a), and positively on the interaction between the evaluation of the modifier and evaluation of the identity ($M_e I_e$). An effect of the interaction is that people with stigmatized identities are judged bad regardless of how happy they feel, and people expressing unpleasant emotions are condemned even if they have prestigious identities.

These equations can be solved for the EPA profile of the modifier that would relate a particular outcome impression to a particular identity. The resulting equations have two applications. First, they can define how someone's identity has to be modified in order to form a new fundamental sentiment profile that accounts for that person's participation in a recent event. The equations provide a model of attributional processes when applied this way. Second, the equations can define the emotion that describes the relation between a person's identity and transient impression of the person that has been generated by the recent event. In this application, the equations provide a model of emotion.

INTERACT

INTERACT is a program for carrying out computer simulations of social interaction in the framework of Affect Control Theory. Simulation analyses begin with natural language specifications of a social situation and produce natural language predictions concerning the behaviors, emotions, and reconceptualizations that might occur. The program transforms words into EPA profiles; applies equations; and then transforms numerical results back to verbal form.

The program translates back and forth between the verbal and quantitative levels by using dictionaries of EPA profiles constructed from surveys of several thousand undergraduates in the United States mainly from the South (Smith-Lovin, 1979; Heise & Lewis, 1988). These dictionaries provide archival data for 750 social identities, 600 social behaviors, 400 emotion and trait terms, and 200 social settings. (A complete set of Canadian dictionaries is available from Neil MacKinnon at Guelph University.)

Here is an example of how the program can be applied to analyze some relationships that are central to one identity—an Evangelist. I report INTERACT analyses conducted with EPA profiles obtained from males, and I show only selected portions of the computer output. Heise and Lewis (1988) provide a tutorial covering all aspects of the program.

I assume the Evangelist is a male and his relational partner is a female. The Evangelist presumably sees himself as an Evangelist, and let us say he sees the other as Sinner. For purpose of illustration, the other is assumed to see things the same way: Evangelist and Sinner.

INTERACT retrieves EPA profiles for these identities as follows.

	E	P	A
Evangelist	0.0	0.6	0.8
Sinner	−1.6	−0.8	1.1

The evaluation of Evangelist is 0.0—neither good nor bad—which is somewhat disreputable for an authority figure (e.g., a Minister is evaluated at +1.2, a Father +1.8). An Evangelist is slightly potent at 0.6, which is lower than the potency of other authority figures (e.g., a Minister's potency is 1.5, a Father's +2.1). An Evangelist is slightly active at 0.8, and this also is unusual because authority figures usually are more inhibited (e.g., Minister at −0.5 and Father at −0.7).

On the other hand, a Sinner is quite bad (−1.6), slightly weak (−0.8), and somewhat lively (1.1).

The program computes the ideal EPA behavior profile for each actor and lists specific behaviors that fit, presenting the results as follows.

From the Evangelist's perspective:
The Evangelist might criticize [−0.3 0.6 0.8] the Sinner (or contradict, bluff, bewilder, affront, fool, deter her).
The Sinner should mock [−1.0 −0.7 1.6] the Evangelist (or mimic, chatter-to, tease, wheedle, annoy, deride him).

(The phrase "From the Evangelist's perspective" means that these are the results based on the Evangelist's male sentiments. Similarly, the word "should" appears in the second sentence to signal that the results define expectations of a male.)

The numerical profiles indicate the kinds of behaviors that might be expected of an Evangelist and a Sinner were they to interact with each other. The Evangelist's behavior toward the Sinner should have some negative tone −0.3)and be slightly potent (0.6) and slightly active (0.8). The Sinner's acts toward the Evangelist should be slightly bad (−1.0), slightly weak (−0.7), and quite activated (1.6). The listed behaviors are the actions from the EPA dictionary that best correspond to these ideals: behaviors in a list taken from the dictionary are ordered by how closely their EPA profiles fit the ideal profile.

Thus, maintenance of the Evangelist and Sinner identities requires that the Evangelist act antagonistically and the Sinner disparagingly.

INTERACT, which contains all the principles of Affect Control Theory, allows an event to be implemented at this point, and the choice is up to the analyst. I selected the word "criticize": the Evangelist Criticizes the Sinner. INTERACT computed how this event would change impressions of the two parties:

	E	P	A
Evangelist	−0.4	0.6	0.9
Sinner	−1.0	−0.8	0.8

Criticizing a Sinner makes the Evangelist look a bit crueler, weaker, and more lively than he should be in order to maintain his identity perfectly, but the discrepancies are so small that we can say this kind of action suits him extremely well. The encounter with the Evangelist makes the Sinner look too nice (and a bit too quiet) for proper confirmation of the Sinner role.

INTERACT translates these changes in state into predictions about the emotions each party would feel.

The Evangelist feels [0.3 0.6 0.9] emotional, lighthearted, charmed, anxious, satisfied, moved.
The Sinner should feel [0.2 −0.3 0.3] awestruck.

The numbers 0.3, 0.6, 0.9 define the ideal EPA profile for an adjective that can be combined with Evangelist in order to produce the transient impression of −0.4, 0.6, 0.9 (see above), and INTERACT reports the emotion adjectives that would accomplish this. Theoretically, these words define the kinds of feelings the Evangelist might have as he criticized the Sinner. The emotions are mainly positive, confirming the notion that the action is appropriate to his role. ("Anxious" is rated slightly positive by college males, as in "anxious to do something.")

Similarly, the numbers 0.2 −0.3, 0.3 define the emotion that interprets the impression of the Sinner created by the event relative to the Sinner's identity. The appropriate feeling is essentially one of neutrality, as reflected by the paucity of retrieved emotion words. The Sinner feels unmoved.

Next INTERACT recomputes behavior profiles. The results are not precisely the same as the first time because the next event has to transform impressions created by the first event in order to get to impressions that fit identity sentiments.

> The Evangelist might bluff [−0.1 0.5 0.7] the Sinner (or contradict, butter up, criticize, patronize, bewilder, order her).
> The Sinner should mock [−1.0 −0.5 1.8] the Evangelist (or tease, chatter-to, annoy, taunt, wheedle, pester him).

I selected "mock": the Sinner Mocks the Evangelist, and INTERACT reported the following emotions.

> The Evangelist feels [−0.1 −0.2 0.4] awestruck.
> The Sinner should feel [0.3 −0.0 0.7] awestruck, anxious and emotional.

The next round of behavior predictions were:

> The Evangelist might bewilder [−0.4 1.0 0.8] the Sinner (or affront, criticize, contradict, divert, confound, indoctrinate her).
> The Sinner should chatter-to [−0.9 −0.8 1.9] the Evangelist (or mock, mimic, tease, annoy, wheedle, taunt him).

And I implemented the event "the Sinner Taunts the Evangelist," whereupon INTERACT reported the following emotions:

> The Evangelist feels [−0.6 −0.1 0.2] fearful, self-conscious, apprehensive, lovesick, flustered, shook-up, uneasy.
> The Sinner should feel [0.1 0.4 1.2] emotional, anxious, lighthearted, restless, carefree, angry, charmed.

(The somewhat odd retrieval, lovesick, is a word that seems to be used little by college males and therefore may have been rated incorrectly.)

Theoretically, the first deprecating act from the Sinner leaves the Evangelist unmoved but the second creates distress. The reason is that the events cumulate: a barrage of unanswered deprecation leaves the Evangelist feeling weakened. Similarly, the Sinner feels only a bit active after her first deprecating act but quite active after the second, because the second act compounds with the first and leaves her feeling good, potent, and very expressive relative to her Sinner identity.

Now suppose that the Evangelist tried to comprehend the situation by reidentifying the woman. I instructed INTERACT to predict answers to the question: what kind of person would Taunt an Evangelist? The INTER-ACT results were as follows.

That the Sinner would taunt the Evangelist makes the Evangelist think:
The Sinner is [−1.4 −0.2 1.8] a tease, hussy, hotshot; or [0.0 0.6 2.1] a rebellious, lustful, horny sinner.

The first set of numbers is the EPA profile for the kind of actor who would be best confirmed by the event, and the nouns are social entities that are close to this profile. The second set of numbers is the ideal EPA profile for a modifier that would combine with the profile for Sinner and produce the outcome impression of −1.4, −0.2, 1.8; the words are the best-fitting adjectives.

It is interesting that the Evangelist might interpret what is happening to him in erotic terms (i.e., tease, hussy, lustful, and horny): this is a complex outcome of how Southern male culture defines evangelists, sinners, and sexuality.

Now consider the Evangelist's relationship with God. This is set up in INTERACT by defining the female partner as God (disregarding the evangelist's probable astonishment at Her gender): the Evangelist sees himself as an Evangelist and the other as God, and I assume God sees things the same way. Thereby events have to confirm a fundamental sentiment about God which measures at 3.0, 3.6, −0.5: She is extremely good, infinitely powerful, and a bit quiet.

Once again, INTERACT computes the behavior profiles for acts that would best confirm the identities of each actor, arriving at the following predictions:

The Evangelist might [0.9 −0.3 2.2] josh God (or kid, spoof, jest her).
God should [2.2 2.5 −0.6] forgive the Evangelist (or educate, teach, pray for, thank, aid, guide him).

The Evangelist's predicted behaviors toward God are much nicer and more active than toward a Sinner. Indeed, they seem too lively, which suggests either something interesting about evangelists' relations with God or else that the theoretical model falters in some way in this particular analysis. The predictions for God, however, are appropriate (except for "pray for" which is illogical for God).

I had God "forgive" the Evangelist, and INTERACT predicted emotions as follows:

> The Evangelist feels [1.1 −0.1 0.0] at ease, contented, moved, calm, relieved, grateful, touched.
> God should feel [1.9 1.4 −0.1] generous, secure, compassionate, affectionate, warm, forgiving, kind.

The Evangelist's emotional experience as a result of being forgiven by God is pleasant and soothing. Thus, the Evangelist might invoke his private relationship with God in order to experience positive emotions that provide blessed relief from unpleasant worldly encounters, such as being taunted by sinners.

Although much more can be done with INTERACT to analyze the range of action and emotional experience for the Evangelist, this example illustrates some of the possibilities of using the program in order to examine emotional relationships.

RESOURCES

The program for analyzing social relationships is available along with another program for making EPA measurements on microcomputers (Heise, 1988). The development of impression-formation equations for dealing with events is described in detail by Heise (1978), Heise and Smith-Lovin (1981), Smith-Lovin and Heise (1982), and Smith-Lovin (1987a, 1987b). The derivation of proaction equations from impression-formation equations is discussed by Heise (1979; 1985; 1987). The development of impression-formation equations for dealing with modifier-identity combinations is discussed in Averett and Heise (1987), Heise (1987), and Heise and Thomas (1989); and the same sources also provide more details on the models of attribution and of emotion.

References

Averett, C. P. and Heise, D. R. 1987. Modified Social Identities: Amalgamations, Attributions, and Emotions. *Journal of Mathematical Sociology* 13:103–132.

Gollob, H. F. 1968. Impression Formation and Word Combination in Sentences. *Journal of Personality and Social Psychology* 10:341–353.

Heise, D. R. 1978. *Computer-Assisted Analysis of Social Action.* Institute for Research of Social Action. Chapel Hill, N.C.

Heise, D. R. *Understanding Events: Affect and the Construction of Social Action.* New York: Cambridge University Press.

Heise, D. R. 1985. Affect Control Theory: Respecification, Estimation, and Tests of the Formal Model. *Journal of Mathematical Sociology* 11:191–222.

Heise, D. R. 1986. Modeling Symbolic Interaction. In *Approaches to Social Theory.* Edited by S. Lindenberg, J. S. Coleman, and S. Nowak. New York: Russell Sage Foundation p. 291–309.

Heise, D. R. 1987. Affect Control Theory: Concepts and Model. *Journal of Mathematical Sociology* 13:1–33.

Heise, D. R. 1988. Programs INTERACT and ATTITUDE. Durham, NC: National Collegiate Software Clearinghouse, Duke University Press.

Heise, D. R. and E. M. Lewis 1988. *Introduction to INTERACT.* Durham, NC: National Collegiate Software Clearinghouse, Duke University Press.

Heise, D. R. and Lynn Smith-Lovin 1981. Impressions of Goodness, Powerfulness, and Liveliness from Discerned Social Events. *Social Psychology Quarterly* 44:93–106.

Heise, D. R. and N. MacKinnon 1987. Affective Bases of Likelihood Judgments. *Journal of Mathematical Sociology* 13:133–151.

Heise, D. R., and L. Thomas 1989. Predicting Impressions Created by Combinations of Emotion and Social Identity. *Social Psychology Quarterly* 52:10–21.

Osgood, C. E., W. H. May, and M. S. Miron 1975. *Cross-Cultural Universals of Affective Meaning.* Urbana: University of Illinois Press.

Smith-Lovin, L. 1979. Behavior Settings and Reactions to Social Scenarios: The Impact of Settings on the Dynamics of Interpersonal Events. Ph.D. Dis., Department of Sociology, University of North Carolina, Chapel Hill, N.C.

Smith-Lovin, L. 1987a. "Impressions from Events." *Journal of Mathematical Sociology* 13:35–70.

Smith-Lovin, L. 1987b. The Affective Control of Events within Settings. *Journal of Mathematical Sociology* 13:71–101.

Smith-Lovin, L., and D. Heise 1982. A Structural Equation Model of Impression Formation. Pp. 163–221 in *Multivariate Applications in the Social Sciences.*

Edited by Nancy Hirschberg and L. G. Humphreys. Hillsdale, NJ: Lawrence Erlbaum Associates.

Smith-Lovin, L. and Heise, D. R. 1988. *Analyzing Social Interaction: Advances in Affect Control Theory.* New York: Gordon and Breach Science Publishers. (Reprint of a special issue of the *Journal of Mathematical Sociology.* Vol. 13.)

11.

Socialization of Emotions:
Pride and Shame as Causal Agents

*Thomas J. Scheff**

In this chapter, I explore the role of shame in the socialization of emotions. Although it has long been taken for granted that shame is a rare emotion in adults, I will discard that premise, as did Piers and Singer (1953). There is another tradition suggesting that shame is the primary social emotion, found in theorists as diverse as Darwin (1872), McDougall (1908), Cooley (1922), Lynd (1958), Goffman (1967) and Lewis (1971).

In *The Expression of Emotions in Men and Animals*, Darwin (1872) devoted the last substantive chapter to blushing and its relation to shame. He stated his thesis quite simply: "[Blushing is caused by] shyness, shame, and modesty, the essential element in all self-attention" (p. 325). For present purposes, the important proposition comes next, where he explained "self-attention": "It is not the simple act of reflecting on our own appearance, but the *thinking what others think of us*, which excites a blush." (p. 325 italics mine) His discussion suggests that blushing may be caused by perceptions of evaluation of the self whether positive or negative.

Darwin's argument about the relationship between blushing and "self-attention" can be restated as two propositions connecting blushing with emotions, on the one hand, and social perception, on the other. First, *Blushing is caused by shame* (as will be discussed below, "shyness" and "modesty," Darwin's two other causes of blushing, can be considered to be shame variants [Lewis, 1971] or cognates [Wurmser, 1987]). Second, and more important, shame is caused by the *perception of negative evaluations of the self*. Since blushing is only one of many visible markers of overt shame, it is not a primary concept for my discussion. The second statement, however, contains the basic proposition: shame is the social emotion, arising as it does from the monitoring of one's own actions by viewing one's self from the standpoint of others.

Shame as a crucial emotion for adults is prominent in the thought of William McDougall (1908). He thought of shame as one of the "self-regarding sentiments," perhaps the most important one. "Shame is the emotion *second to none* in the extent of its influence upon social behavior" (p. 124). Like Darwin, he seems to have understood that it arose as a result of self-monitoring. He also pointed out that although shame undoubtedly has a biological basis that we share with other higher mammals, the human emotion of shame in adults is considerably more elaborate and complex (p. 56). Since self-consciousness is enormously developed in humans and largely absent in other creatures, the ramifications of human shame are likely to be vast.

LOW-VISIBILITY PRIDE AND SHAME

Cooley (1922) considered pride and shame to be the crucial "social self-feelings." At some points, he seemed to regard as a self-feeling *any* feeling that the self directs towards itself. His passage about the extraordinary importance of the self-feelings in human behavior appears to be in this key (p. 208):

> . . . [With] all normal . . . people, [social self-feeling] remains, in one form or another, the *mainspring of endeavor and a chief interest of the imagination throughout life* (italics mine).

Cooley continues:

> As is the case with other feelings, we do not think much of it [social self-feeling] so long as it is moderately and regularly gratified. Many people of balanced mind and congenial activity scarcely know that they care what others think of them, and will deny, perhaps with indignation, that such care is an important factor in what they are and do. But this is illusion. If failure or disgrace arrives, if one suddenly finds that the faces of men show coldness or contempt instead of the kindliness and deference that he is used to, he will perceive from the shock, the fear, the sense of being outcast and helpless, that he was living in the minds of others without knowing it, just as we daily walk the solid ground without thinking how it bears us up.

Although neither pride nor shame is mentioned in this passage, they are implied, especially the almost continuous presence of *low-visibility pride*. Could Cooley have thought of pride and shame as the crucial self-feelings?

This possibility is confirmed when we examine his concept of "the looking-glass self," his description of the social nature of the self. He saw self-monitoring in terms of three steps (p. 184):

As we see our face, figure, and dress in the glass, and are interested in them because they are ours, and pleased or otherwise with them according as they do or do not answer to what we should like them to be; so in imagination we perceive in another's mind some thought of our appearance, manners, aims, deeds character, friends, and so on, and are variously affected by it.

A self-idea of this sort seems to have three principal elements: the imagination of our appearance to the other person; the imagination of his judgment of that appearance, and some sort of self-feeling, such as pride or mortification.

In this passage, he restricts self-feelings to the two he seems to think are the most significant, pride and shame (considering "mortification" a shame variant) To make sure we understand this point, he mentions shame three more times in the passage that follows (184–85, italics mine):

> The comparison with a looking-glass hardly suggests the second element, the imagined judgment, which is quite essential. The thing that moves us to *pride or shame* is not the mere mechanical reflection of ourselves, but an imputed sentiment, the imagined effect of this reflection upon another's mind. This is evident from the fact that the character and weight of that other, in whose mind we see ourselves, makes all the difference with our feeling. We are *ashamed* to seem evasive in the presence of a straightforward man, cowardly in the presence of a brave one, gross in the eyes of a refined one, and so on. We always imagine, and in imagining, share, the judgments of the other mind. A man will boast to one person of an action—say some sharp transaction in trade—which he would be *ashamed* to own to another.

What is oddly unappreciated about the supposedly familiar looking-glass self is that Cooley is implying that *society rests upon a foundation of pride and shame*. His analysis of the social nature of the self can be summarized in terms of two propositions:

1. In adults, social monitoring of self is virtually continuous, even in solitude. (We are, as he put it, "living in the minds of others without knowing it" (p.208).
2. Social monitoring always has an evaluative component, and gives rise, therefore, to either pride or shame.

When taken together, these two propositions suggest a puzzle. If social monitoring of self is almost continuous, and if it gives rise to pride or shame, why is it that we see so few manifestations of either emotion in adult life? One possible solution to this puzzle would be that either pride or shame is always present, but with such low-visibility that we don't notice, giving rise to a third proposition:

3. Adults are virtually always in a state of either pride or shame, usually of a quite unostentatious kind.[1]

This proposition suggests a step toward a theoretically grounded operational definition of a concept that until now has been undefined, namely, a *level of self-esteem*. Self-esteem would be a summary measure, representing the balance between pride and shame states in a person's life, taking into account not only duration but also intensity. This definition is still very crude, but has heuristic value. It implies that self-esteem involves how one *feels* about one's self, a primitive concern that seems to precede thoughts, perceptions, and behaviors. Perhaps because self-feelings are usually denied and disguised, as implied in Cooley's discussion, they have been omitted from most scholarly discussions of self-esteem.

Possibly Cooley's most dramatic analysis of shame, one that brings him closest to the position taken here, involves his use of an excerpt from Rousseau's autobiography (p. 291, italics mine):

> Social fear, of a sort perhaps somewhat morbid, is vividly depicted by Rousseau in the passage of his Confessions where he describes the feeling that led him falsely to accuse a maid-servant of theft which he had himself committed. "When she appeared my heart was agonized, but the presence of so many people was more powerful than my compunction. I did not fear punishment, but I dreaded *shame*: I dreaded it more than death, more than the crime, more than all the world. I would have buried, hid myself in the centre of the earth: invincible *shame* bore down every other sentiment; *shame* alone caused all my impudence, and in proportion as I became criminal the fear of discovery rendered me intrepid. I felt no dread but that of being detected, of being publicly and to my face declared a thief, liar, and calumniator.

Rousseau's phrase, "invincible shame," will stand us in good stead below. Notice also that Cooley suggested this instance as an example of "morbid", (i.e., pathological) rather than normal, shame. I will use a similar distinction in my discussion. Cooley's emphasis on the role of self-monitoring in the make-up of the self clearly invokes pride and shame as the basic social emotions.

THE RECURSIVENESS OF UNACKNOWLEDGED SHAME

In modern societies, adults seem to be "uncomfortable" about manifesting either pride or shame. The emotions of *shame and pride often seem themselves to arouse shame.* (This proposition explains Darwin's observation that both positive and negative evaluations can give rise to blushing.) In adults, shame may be recursive, acting back on itself. If shame is evoked but not acknowledged, the possibility arises that one may react emotionally to one's initial emotional reaction, then react again to the second reaction, and again and again, ad infinitum.

For example, one might be ashamed of being ashamed, creating a shame-shame spiral, or angry because one is ashamed, then ashamed because one is angry, creating a shame-anger spiral. If I am (1) humiliated by my father's innuendo, then (2) angry at my father, then (3) ashamed of my anger [What a monster I am! Angry at my own father when he is only trying to help me!], the next step might be (4) to be angry at myself, and (5) to be ashamed of myself because I was so upset about what I might think of as "nothing." Even if each link in this chain lasts only a few seconds, several thousand such links would add up to hours of what might be experienced as "helpless anger," a mild form of the shame-anger chain reaction, or, in its more intense form, "humiliated fury" (Lewis, 1971).

The recursive potential of unacknowledged shame may give rise to a phenomenon that is rare in nature, a chain reaction with no natural limit to its duration or intensity. One cannot harm oneself by holding one's breath; before any damage can occur, the body takes over by fainting. But the spiraling of shame seems to have no inner or outer regulator. Perhaps a biological analogy will clarify this point. Like normal shame, the immune reaction is usually life enhancing. But under certain conditions, the body reacts to itself as alien, setting up a runaway cycle that can result in permanent injury or death. Emotions that arise in a shame context can result in endless destruction.

To this point the discussion has concerned the inner recursion of unacknowledged shame. In a social context, however, a much greater potential for intense arousal occurs. Emotions can spiral not only *within*, but also *between* parties in social interaction. What I have called a "triple spiral" forms a cycle complete in six steps: (1) A insults B who (2) is ashamed, then (3) almost instantaneously angry. As a result, (4) B insults A, who (5) is ashamed, then (6) is angry. At this point, the cycle can begin again. One can think of this chain as three spirals: one within A, one within B, and one between them (Scheff, 1987).

As reported by Retzinger (1988) in her analysis of videotapes of marital quarrels, the shame-anger cycle can be completed so quickly so as to be almost invisible when the tape is run at normal speed. For example, in the first minute of trying to agree on which of their recurring arguments they are to discuss, one of the couples have what they refer to as a "little bristle." By repeatedly observing the verbal and nonverbal gestures in slow-motion during this moment, Retzinger was able to demonstrate four full shame-anger cycles in the first thirty-four seconds. When observed in this way, an ordinary conversation phrased with seemingly polite words can be seen to be packed with hostile innuendo, mutual insult, and revenge.

If the two parties are individuals, the conflict can last as long as a lifetime; mutual hatred would seem to involve the intermittent replaying of triple spirals of shame and anger. If the two parties are groups, the sequence can last longer than a life-time, since the antagonism can be transmitted from generation to generation. The recursive potential of unacknowledged shame may provide an explanation why humans alone among living creatures have an unlimited potential for destructiveness. I will return to the issue of recursiveness below.

LOW-VISIBILITY SHAME

If, as I have suggested, shame has a strongly recursive character, then we would expect that most shame and pride would have low/visibility. Even if they were widely prevalent, persons who were proud or ashamed might be ashamed of their state, and therefore hide it from others, and from themselves. If pride and shame are usually hidden, how can one study these emotions?

I know of no systematic studies of pride, but methods for detecting low-visibility shame were developed independently by Gottschalk and Gleser (1969) and by Lewis (1971). The Gottschalk-Gleser method is rudimentary, since it is atheoretic and deals only with verbal texts. Their procedure involves lists of sentences containing words they consider to be shame markers. These sentences are listed under five categories (I provide a few samples under each category, pp. 49–52):

1. Shame, embarrassment: I feel funny . . . . I had behaved improperly . . . (And other sentences using terms such as "disconcerting, self-conscious, degrading, nonsense, shy, disreputable, discredit, or unworthy.")
2. Humiliation: I don't know what was wrong with me letting myself go like that, (And other sentences involve such terms as "humbling, degrading, or little self-respect.")
3. Ridicule: He twitted me about being fat. I really feel utterly ridiculous in a situation like that. They stared at me and laughed.
4. Inadequacy: Where was I when brains were passed out? I feel stupid . . .
5. Overexposure of deficiencies or private details: I don't even know how to wipe my ass. I didn't want to talk about such personal things.

Although Gottschalk and Gleser do not discuss the matter, or refer to any of the shame theorists discussed above, only a few of the sentences contain explicit references to shame. Instead, most of their examples assume what the shame theorists posited to be the basic context for shame, perception of negative evaluation of the self, even if the negative evaluation is indirect. The absence of theory and direct validation makes the Gottschalk-Gleser method seem arbitrary.

In her pioneering analysis of clinical dialogues, Lewis (1971) treated the issue of shame markers much more explicitly and broadly that Gottschalk and Gleser. Her work is both theoretical and empirical, since she connected theory, method, and concrete episodes of behavior. For this reason she is the heir to Darwin, MacDougall and Cooley. However, she advanced further than either the original theorists, or the more recent advocates, Lynd (1958), Tomkins (1963), and Goffman (1967), since they all used concrete episodes only in an *illustrative* way.

Lewis's basic empirical study (1971) is not merely illustrative. She conducted a systematic analysis of shame content in complete episodes of real social interaction, entire clinical sessions. Her laborious word-for-word analysis of these sessions led her to the discovery of what she called "unacknowledged" shame, the low-visibility shame implied by my explication of Cooley. She showed that in the hundreds of clinical sessions she examined, most shame episodes were virtually invisible to the participants; they were acknowledged by neither the patient nor the therapist. She divided episodes of unacknowledged shame into two basic types: (*a*) overt, undifferentiated shame, and (*b*) bypassed shame.

Overt, undifferentiated shame involves *painful feelings* that are not identified as shame by the person experiencing them. Rather they are labeled with a wide variety of terms that serve to disguise the shame experience, for example, feeling foolish, stupid, ridiculous, inadequate, defective, incompetent, low self-esteem, awkward, exposed, vulnerable, insecure, helpless, and so on. Our culture provides a very large number of these codewords. Many of them project the inner feeling of shame onto the outside world. For example, instead of saying "both of us were embarrassed," we say "it was an awkward moment," that is, it was not I who felt shame, but the situation that was awkward. Our very language betrays us into denying sham.

Lewis classified all the terms listed above as shame markers because they occurred only in a certain context, and only in association with a specific type of nonverbal marker. The context always involved perception of self as negatively evaluated, either by self or other(s), that is, the basic context for shame. In this context, Lewis always found a change in the patient's *manner*, characterized by such nonverbal markers as: (*a*) speech disruption (stammering, repetition of words, speech "static" like "well", "uhhhh", long pauses, etc.); (b) lowered or averted gaze, blushing, and especially noticeable, a sharp drop in the loudness of speech, even to the point of inaudibility.

Both the verbal and nonverbal markers of overt shame can be characterized as forms of *"hiding" behavior:* the words hide shame under a disguising label; the nonverbal forms suggest physical hiding: averting or lowering the gaze to escape the gaze of the other, and speech disruption and oversoft speech hiding the content of one's speech and thoughts.

At times, but not always, the ideation of the person undergoing overt shame may also involve hiding (I wanted to disappear; I wished that the earth had opened and swallowed me). Since Lewis's work was based on audiotapes, her markers for shame are limited to verbal and paralinguistic cues. In a study (Scheff, 1985; Scheff and Retzinger, 1989) of videotapes of the "moment of truth" in *Candid Camera,* we found striking nonverbal markers of overt shame.

When the subjects learned they had been caught on camera in what they thought was a private moment, some of them show extreme hiding behavior, they not only covered their face with both hands, but also simultaneously turn away from the camera, and in some cases, even attempt to escape completely. (One man crawled beneath a desk). We also observed gestures that we interpreted as hiding behavior, but in what Tomkins (1963) characterized as a "miniaturized" form. At the moment of truth, many subjects began to bring one or both hands up to their face in a manner that suggests that they wished to cover it. However, instead of covering the face, they ended up only touching it. The relation of face-touching to shame has been independently validated by a study with a very different methodology. Edelman and his associates (1987) surveyed five European countries on the experience of embarrassment. Along with various other gestures the subjects associated with that emotion, face-touching was mentioned in all five countries, with the size of this response ranging from a low of 2% in Greece to a high of 16% in Russia. An examination of the gestures accompanying "coyness behavior" in photographs taken in small traditional societies (Eibl-Eibesfeldt, 1975) suggests that embarrassment and hiding behavior, especially gaze aversion, are universally linked. To summarize: overt, undifferentiated shame occurs when one (1) feels the self negatively evaluated, either by self or other; (2) manifests "hiding" behavior, and/or (3) labels or associates the painful feeling with undifferentiated terms such as those listed above. In these instances, the negative evaluation of self appears to cause so much pain that it interferes with the rapid production of thought and/or speech, but the pain is mislabeled.

Like the overt pattern, *bypassed* shame always begins with a perception of the negative evaluation of self. However, unlike the markers of overt, undifferentiated shame, which are often flagrant and overt, those of bypassed shame may be subtle and covert. Although thought and speech are not obviously disrupted, they take on a speeded-up but repetitive quality that Lewis refers to as *"obsessive."*

Typically, patients repeated a story or series of stories, talking rapidly and fluently, but not quite to the point. They appear to be unable to make decisions because of seemingly balanced pros and cons ("insoluble dilemmas"). Patients complained of endless internal replaying of a scene in which they felt criticized or in error. Often they reported that when they first realized the error, they winced or groaned, then immediately began obsessing about the incident. The mind seems to be so involved with the unresolved scene that one feels in adequately involved in the present, even though there is no obvious disruption. One is distracted.

The two patterns of shame appear to involve opposite styles of response. In overt shame, the victim *feels* emotional pain to the point that it obviously disrupts thought and speech. In bypassed shame, the victim *avoids* the pain before it can be completely experienced, through rapid thought, speech or actions.

The two types of shame appear to correspond to my distinction between under and over-distanced emotion (Scheff, 1979). Overt, undifferentiated shame is under-distanced, since the intense pain of embarrassment or humiliation is experienced. What G. A. Mead (1934) called the "I" phase of the self, the "biologic individual," predominates in consciousness. One becomes overly "subjective," in the style that is referred to in psychiatry as "hysterical." Bypassed shame is over-distanced. One avoids the pain by stepping outside of self, into the "me" phase of the self, as if the pain were not occurring. One learns to ignore the pain, turning off the sensations by entering the verbal realm of rapid thought and/or speech. One is overly "objective", in the obsessive style.

Adler's (1956) theory of human development anticipated Lewis's discovery of the two basic types of unacknowledged shame. Although he did not use the term shame, a cognate, "the feeling of inferiority," played a central role in his theory. He argued that children's primary need is for love [for what Bowlby (1969) calls a "secure attachment"]. If love is not available at crucial points, the child can proceed along one of two paths: either develop an "inferiority complex", that is, become prone to overt, undifferentiated shame, or compensate by seeking power, that is, avoid feeling shame by bypassing it, through incessant thought, speech, and/or actions.

Although the two formulations are compatible, Lewis's work marks an immense advance over Adler's. His theory, true to the psychoanalytic genre, uses concepts that are static and highly abstract. For this reason his propositions, though provocative, are virtually untestable. Neither he nor anyone else has envisioned the observable markers of feelings of inferiority, the inferiority complex, or the compensatory drive for power. Nor has the process implied by this theory been spelled out in sufficient detail so that it could be falsified by observations if it were not valid. Through what concrete steps does deprivation of love cause either an inferiority complex or the drive for power? Adler's theory is couched in concepts that are only "black boxes." The wiring within and between these boxes is not specified. His theory is not contestable as it stands.

By contrast, Lewis's formulations provide the foundation for a testable theory, since they describe or at least strongly imply observable markers for the major concepts, and for the events in the causal chain that connects them. Her work points to the events in social interaction that can be characterized as evidence of either a secure, threatened, or severed attachment, that is, the amount of love in a relationship. (See the discussion of infant- and child-caretaker interaction below.) By describing the observable events in shame and shame-anger sequences, she also specifies the behavioral manifestations of Adler's structures, to the point that their presence or absence can be detected in actual episodes of social interaction. To my knowledge, Lewis's is the first general theory of human behavior that has these desirable characteristics.

Although overt and bypassed shame present a very different appearance, the difference is one of outer style, since the appearances mask an underlying similarity. Both the slowed-down pattern of overt shame and the speeded-up pattern of bypassed shame are disruptive; both involve rigid and distorted reactions to reality. Both kinds of shame are equally invisible, since one is misnamed, the other ignored. These two basic patterns explain the puzzle of how shame might be ubiquitous, yet usually escape notice.

Lewis's analysis of shame also converges with Freud's early work on *repression*, and with Tomkins's[1] on grief, but extends both. In his first book (1897), with Breuer), Freud argued that hysteria was caused by repressed emotion, "strangulated affect," as he called it. He based his conjecture on the observation that patients improved when they expressed until then forgotten emotions, for example, by crying or uttering heated words, a rudimentary theory of catharsis (Scheff, 1979).

Tomkins (1963) approached repression from a very different direction, through surmises about the fate of grief that did not result in catharsis (crying). This approach led him to describe the outer signs of low-visibity grief, the miniaturizations, defenses and transformations that have already been mentioned above. Lewis's (1971) concept of "unacknowledged" emotion is very useful here, since it subsumes two different types of affect, types sometimes confounded in Tomkins's work. He describes both conscious concealment, for example, the maneuvers of the patient in the dental chair to avoid crying, and the type of denial that is often virtually automatic and outside awareness, for example, the masking of grief with anger. Only the second type is unconscious, a manifestation of repressed emotion.

Lewis extended the concept of repression both theoretically and empirically. Using the kind of shuttling back and forth between deductive and inductive methods that C. S. Peirce called "abduction" (Scheff, 1990), she laid the groundwork for the shame construct, the description of the context and markers for unacknowledged shame, and its role in the genesis and maintenance of compulsive behavior. Most of the shame episodes she reported appeared to be not only out of awareness, but also not available to it. Her work therefore confirms not only the second proposition I derived from Cooley above, (the one about shame), but also confirms and expands Freud's (1897) central hypothesis, that neurosis is caused by strangulated affect. Yet her work goes beyond Freud's in suggesting the origins of all compulsive behavior in unacknowledged shame, and in formulating this thesis in a way that allows it to be tested empirically.[2]

SHAME IN OTHER THEORIES OF EMOTION

In order to relate the shame construct outlined here to the existing literature on emotion, it is necessary to review earlier analysis by three theorists, Tomkins, Goffman, and Kemper. All three had important and perceptive things to say about shame, but none of them assigned it a central role in human behavior. I will argue that their formal analyses were too specialized in terms of discipline and method. Tomkins's formal analysis was overly psychological, Goffman's and Kemper's, overly sociological. Tomkins and Kemper overemphasized formal concepts and evidence, avoiding the intuitive analysis of extended examples. Goffman used only the latter method, avoiding formal concepts and evidence. In order to understand the role of shame, it is necessary to utilize both psychological and sociological perspectives, and both formal and informal approaches.

Next to Lewis's (1971), Tomkins's is the most extended analysis of shame (he called it "humiliation"). He devoted almost all of the second volume of *Affect/Imagery/Consciousness* to this emotion, about four hundred pages. But his treatment at the conceptual level is highly specialized, dealing almost entirely with the internal, psychological side of shame. Tomkins conceived of all emotion, including shame, as arising out of sudden changes. With respect to shame, his basic formulation concerns its relation to "interest or joy" (1963, II, p. 123):

> The innate or activator of shame is the incomplete reduction of interest or joy.

Tomkins's approach to emotions has given rise to considerable discussion, debate, and even to research programs. However, his basic formulations appear to be somewhat circular. If shame is activated by the incomplete reduction of interest or joy, what caused this incomplete reduction, and what activated the interest or joy? He did not provide a single conceptual answer to the first question; instead he described many different types of situations that may give rise to shame (pp. 184–251). His types are at different levels of abstractness. He did not show the interrelations between these types, because he had no typology of the social contexts that produce shame (pp. 184–251). He did however, state that *interest* is activated by "optimal rates of increase of stimulation density" (V.I, p 341), and joy by "steep reduction of the intensity of stimulation or neural firing" (V.I, p. 371).

Tomkins's discussion avoids dealing with the context in which emotions arise. Interest and joy are explained in physical, rather than contextual terms, "stimulation density and neural firing." Although his discussion of the sources of shame invokes interpersonal and social elements, it is descriptive and atheoretic. Even if his propositions were completely and exactly true, they still would comprehend only a few relatively simple links in what is probably a long and complex causal sequence. This sequence appears to be highly dependent on social events, as suggested in this paper and by the work of Goffman and Kemper.

It is ironic that Tomkins places such importance on shame, yet ignores its connection with social events. The dominant paradigm in behavioral science exactly reverses his emphasis. The behaviorist approach contains the social link, since it involves reinforcement through punishment and reward, not only by the physical environment, but also by the social environment. But it usually ignores pride and shame as reinforcers.

The classic social psychological studies of conformity, if reinterpreted, can be seen as exceptions to this criticism. For example, my (Scheff, 1988) reanalysis of the Asch study (1956), suggests that pride and shame are very powerful reinforcers, giving rise to large effects. Asch conducted laboratory studies of social influence, showing the effect of a unanimous but erroneous majority on subjects who thought they were alone in their correct judgments. 75% of the subjects yielded to the majority judgment at least once, even though it contradicted the evidence of their own senses. Some of the subjects yielded at every opportunity. Only a quarter remained completely independent. Although pride and shame are not mentioned, Asch's comments on his results and the remarks by the subjects can be understood in terms of these emotions.

Large effects were also reported in the conformity studies by Sherif, Milgram, Zimbardo, and many others. Like Asch, however, none of these researchers carry out a causal analysis, focusing instead on the dependent variable: yielding (in the Asch study) and the autokinetic, obedience, and compliance effects in the others. Just as shame goes unacknowledged in real life, it is also unacknowledged in social and behavioral science studies. (For a similar point with respect to the vast corpus of research on self-esteem, see Scheff, et al, 1989.) Tomkins's work provides access to shame as a causal agent in social events, but in a format that severs the connection to those events. As in current behaviorism, his format denies a causal role to pride and shame.

Goffman came closest to describing a model of the interaction between deference and emotion in his analysis of "interaction ritual." His assumptions form the basic elements in my model of socialization, to be outlined below: protection of "face" is the dominant motive in social life, interactants are exquisitely sensitive to the exact amount of deference extended and received, and avoiding embarrassment is the goad that drives "face work." But Goffman stopped short of a model of the interaction between inner and outer events. He stated explicitly that he was to deal only with the outer, social aspects of interaction, avoiding the inner ones, restricting his purview in order to provide a purely sociological analysis.

Kemper (1978) is more interdisciplinary than Tomkins or Goffman, since he included social, psychological, and biological concepts and evidence. But like Tomkins and Goffman, Kemper's formal analysis is organized by discipline; he placed the causes of emotion arousal entirely in social structure, namely, in power and status. Because of Kemper's social emphasis, his analysis at times runs parallel to mine. As in my analysis, and unlike most others, he called attention to pride as an important emotion in its own right (he referred to "justified pride", p.280) Similarly, he recognized that shame may be an ingredient of punishment (pp. 255–257). He also called attention to shame-anger sequences, acknowledging the possibility that it may be shame, rather than anger that is the causal agent in aggression, (pp. 261–62), a crucial implication of the shame construct.

In the main, however, Kemper's framework, like those of Tomkins and Goffman, falls short of a comprehensive model of the role of shame in behavior. Like the behaviorists, he recognized the social link, but slights shame and pride as reinforcers. His treatment of "justified pride" is virtually in passing, since it is mentioned as only one of a long list of other positive

emotions. Similarly, although he recognized that shame may be an ingredient of punishment, he reduced its importance by making it one of a group
of emotions—depression, guilt and anxiety—which may also figure in punishment (pp. 257–269). His treatment of shame-anger sequences is similarly brief, to the point of being incidental to his main analysis, the effect
of social structural variables on emotions.

Tomkins and Kemper both try to construct formal theories, but their
attempts are so abstract that they are unable to specify the major causal
sequences for a model of emotions. Both resort tö reified explanations of
causation. Tomkins's analysis reifies physical processes (stimulation and
neural firing) but treats social structure only descriptively. Kemper's analysis errs in the opposite direction, reifying social structure as power and status variables, but slighting the internal aspects of emotion. Each theorist
decided, a priori, that one element in the individual-environment relationship is causal, instead of granting them parity.

The a priori restrictions in both Tomkins's and Kemper's theories
both have the same relation to my analysis. In their formal analysis, both
theorists deny, in effect, the role of pride and shame as causal agents. They
emphasize, instead, what they consider to be more "objective" causes, internal physical processes for Tomkins, (stimulation and neural firing) and
for Kemper, social structure (power and status). The causes they emphasize
seem more objective to them, perhaps, because pride and shame do not
seem real in a shame-denying culture.

Most formal theories of human behavior are biased toward rational or
material models of causation, because emotion and mood do not seem real
in our civilization. Mood, in particular, is usually seen as evanescent and
therefore unimportant in serious discussions of human behavior. The one
exception to this stricture occurred in discussions of elementary collective
behavior, describing the actions of crowds, mobs, and publics. In this limited area, the importance of emotion and mood have long been acknowledged (Lofland, 1981). But the idea that mood and emotion could
dominate institutionalized behavior has been virtually absent from social
and behavioral science (Hochschild, 1975, also made this point).

Mood, a complex biosocial psychological phenomenon, may dominate many kinds of social events, in addition to elementary collective behavior. Lewis (1971) demonstrated that unacknowledged sequences of
shame and anger sharply curtail the effectiveness of psychotherapy. She
also argued (1981) that such sequences may be the causal agents in mental
illness. My analyses of cases of what I call "interminable quarrels" (Scheff,
1986, 1987, 1988a) provide support for both of her contentions.

Recent work on crime, physical and verbal violence implicates
shame/anger sequences as causal agents (Lansky, 1987; Katz, 1988; Retz-

inger, 1988). In addition to these studies, my own have suggested that un-acknowledged shame/anger spirals may be the causal agents in conflict between groups, even nations, leading to lengthy and destructive cycles of revenge, humiliation and counter-revenge (Scheff, 1987, 1988a and 1990). Laypersons, researchers, and governments deny the importance of emotions, seeking more dignified kinds of motives. The propensity to reify the kinds of "causes" that seem real and dignified, and to ignore those that do not, may lie at the root of our failure to solve the most fundamental problems facing our civilization.

A RESEARCH AGENDA: SOCIALIZATION OF EMOTIONS AND LEARNING

One implication of my argument is that shame, even though its manifestations are almost universally disguised and denied, may be nevertheless crucial in the socialization of emotions. It can be argued that basic emotions such as grief, fear, anger, and shame are unproblematic in themselves, since there appear to be both biological and social mechanisms for expressing and resolving them. Bowlby (1969) and many others have argued that grief is the normal reaction to loss, and is discharged by crying, both grief and crying being natural biological mechanisms. Similarly, it might be argued that ceremonies of mourning and bereavement are social mechanisms that have evolved for dealing with the biological inevitability of loss, grief, and crying. Similar arguments can be made for the emotions of fear, anger, and shame (Scheff, 1979).

However, if any of these emotions, including shame, are aroused in a context that gives rise to shame about them, either in the person initially aroused or in others, then resolution may fail to take place. Instead, shame may serve to inhibit resolution, and, under some conditions, give rise to intense and/or lengthy chain reactions, as when one is angry that one is ashamed, and then ashamed that one is angry, and so on.

Given this possibility, shame in the caretaker in response to children's emotions could be of extraordinary significance. Children whose emotion were socialized in this way, if the shame model outlined here is accurate, might view their own emotional arousal as having the potential of becoming an infinitely painful experience, (a chain reaction involving the initial emotion alternating with shame). Perhaps this model could be used to explain what otherwise has been a mystery in psychoanalytic theory, the origin and process of *repression*. Lewis (1971) suggested that momentary blankness is almost always caused by bypassed shame. If she is right, it might be possible to extend her reasoning to explain all repression.

Parental shame responses to children's emotions can be flagrant and overt, for example, physical violence, or harsh verbal chastisement involving rage, contempt and/or disgust. However, since shame seems to be a biologically-based, mammalian response, small children might also be genetically programmed to be extremely sensitive even to mild or disguised reactions in the caretaker, for example, withdrawal, silence, and/or embarrassment. A caretaker might inadvertently pass on to the child his or her own unrecognized patterns of shame, because of embarrassment over the child's manifestation of emotions for which the caretaker had been shamed as a child. Perhaps disruptions of psychosexual functions could be explained in this way.

Part of the difference in the ability of men and women to achieve orgasm might be traceable to disruptions of women's psychosexual functioning. Sexual orgasm is instinctive in men and women, yet many women, perhaps a majority, appear to need instruction in order to be orgasmic. Parents may be more embarrassed about female sexuality than male sexuality. If this were the case, and this embarrassment were inadvertently transmitted to girls, their understanding of their own sexuality would be more repressed than that of boys.

There is evidence that men and women's emotions are socialized somewhat differently. Lewis (1977) and others have suggested that women are usually more *field dependent* (prone to overt shame) and men usually more *field independent* (prone to bypassed shame). Perhaps field dependence is caused by socializing techniques involving overt shame, and field independence, bypassed shame, for example, silence and withdrawal. This pattern takes on considerable significance if it is related to Adler's theory of development, as was done above: persons prone to overt shame have chronic feelings of inferiority, but those prone to bypassed shame compensate by a drive for power. Perhaps a finegrained analysis of the occurrence of shame and embarrassment in the socialization of children could explain characteristic personality problems in both male and female development, as well as common difficulties in adult male-female relationships, such as the misunderstandings and quarrels that are common in romantic relationships.

The shame construct could be used to revive the interest in childrearing that was so prominent in the research on child development in the 1950s and 1960s. These studies traced the difference in effects of discipline by physical punishment and discipline by "the removal of love" (Maccoby, 1980). In the light of my discussion, perhaps a new direction would be needed to go beyond the findings of the earlier studies. The crucial distinction would not be between physical and emotional punishment, but would concern the *manner* that accompanied punishment. That is, a respectful manner of punishment would not be shaming, and would not cause resentment, regardless of whether the punishment was physical or emotional

(Scheff, n.d.). A respectful manner would be less likely to evoke shame in the child, and therefore less likely to damage the relationship with the parent.

The *absence* of shaming may be a prominent feature in one specific area of childhood socialization, the acquisition of language. It has been widely remarked how complex language is, and how quickly and easily young children learn their native tongue. The understanding and use of natural language requires an extraordinary level of intelligence, but by the age of six or seven, most children can understand sentences they have never heard before, and within a few years, invent new sentences as they are needed. It is particularly interesting to contrast the ease of language acquisition with learning in other areas, for example, mathematics. Although even the most complex mathematics is much simpler than natural language, many children experience intense difficulties even with elementary arithmetic.

A possible explanation arises from my discussion of the shame construct. Children are taught their mother tongue largely by their parents, who are self-confident experts in the subject. The teaching of language is virtually continuous from birth, highly interactive, and builds upon the child's spontaneous utterances through a process of positive reinforcement and shaping. All of these conditions favor a moratorium on shaming as a technique. The expertness of the teachers might be particularly crucial in removing shame from learning. The parents, native speakers themselves, understand the subject matter, language, from the inside, not just as definitions and rules. They are also able to give continuous demonstrations of correct language use in context, serving as models for the child. These conditions favor the absence of shame in both child and parent.

Consider how different the situation may be in the teaching of elementary mathematics in grade school. Unlike the parent, the teacher is a relative stranger who comes to the child late, say in the eighth or ninth year, with a panoply of abstractions and rules for the manipulation of numbers. Rather than beginning with the child's spontaneous interest in enumeration, as is done in the Montessori method, the elementary school teacher seeks to impose an alien system of symbols and rules. Most important, the teacher is usually not an expert mathematician, who grasps the subject "from the inside." Rather, many teachers seem to teach subject matter as they were taught. (That was my experience as a student in the calculus courses I took as an undergraduate.)

All these conditions may combine to make shame a pervasive and disruptive influence in the teaching of mathematics, or any other academic subject. Since both teachers and students may feel incompetent, and therefore ashamed, the contagion of embarrassment and shame might come to be widely prevalent in classrooms. Perhaps if academic subjects were taught in the way that the mother tongue is, most children could reach the same level of genius in them as they do in their mother language. Or, to consider the reverse, if we taught our own children our mother tongue the way we teach academic subjects, most of them might never learn it. (Goodman, 1969).

STUDY DESIGNS

Videotape recording has been used very successfully over the last fifteen years to study the moment-by-moment interaction between infants and their caretakers. I propose to build upon this format, but expand it in such a way as to test a hypothesis concerning the role of excessive shaming in producing compulsive behavior. My expanded format involves comparing contexts in which excessive shaming may be frequent, to contexts which it may be infrequent. One such context, as already suggested, is children's acquisition of their mother tongue.   •

I hypothesize that the socialization of language in infants and very young children will be virtually free of excessive shaming in almost all families. However, in certain areas, for example, the socialization of the cry, body functions, genital touching, and disputes, I hypothesize two different kinds of family settings: (1) one in which the frequency of intense shaming and embarrassment is low, and (2) one in which it is high. Before spelling out the details of the design of the study, I will first review some of Skinner's contributions to our understanding of effective instruction which I think are relevant to my proposal.

In his discussion of programmed instruction, Skinner (1984) has shown that following certain principles leads to accelerated rates of learning:

1. Clear goals of instruction
2. Student is allowed to move at his/her own pace.
3. Student is often right and quickly told that he/she is right.
4. Punitive sanctions are avoided as much as possible.

He cited studies showing that programs based on these principles lead to learning at twice the rate as that which occurs in conventional instruction.

Although emotions are not mentioned in Skinner's analysis, I believe that they are implied by three of the four principles. (The first, clear goals, is cognitive.) By concentrating his attention entirely on the stimulus side of instruction, describing only the reinforcement schedule, Skinner avoids naming the actual rewards and punishments implied by his system. The remainder of the principles (2, 3, and 4) imply that effective instruction rewards learning with feelings of pride. For this reason, students are highly motivated to learn. A further implication is that conventional instruction alienates students because punitive sanctions cause shame, leading to low rates of learning.

Perhaps language acquisition by infants and children offers an even more powerful example of rapid learning, since language is much more complex than even the most advanced mathematics. Natural language involved myriad terms that are all ambiguous; it is an *open system*, that is, understanding natural language in context requires instantaneous part/whole analysis, relating each part in an expression to the whole of the language. Mathematics, on the other hand, is a closed system, as are most games. There are only a few terms, and each is defined unambiguously. One can have an understanding of closed systems that is purely "local." Since such systems do not require part/whole analysis, they allow the possibility of idiot savants, as is the case with mathematics, music, and chess expertise.

How is it possible for children to learn the extraordinarily vast and complex part/whole analysis that natural language requires so quickly and effortlessly? This problem is so mysterious that many linguists have posited a built-in genetic mechanism for language. This purported mechanism is only hypothetical, however; no evidence has been advanced that attests to its existence.

The shame construct described in this paper suggests an alternative hypothesis, a moratorium on shaming children in their attempts to learn their mother tongue. In the family setting, adults and older siblings usually seem encouraging or at least tolerant of the child's efforts to master language. Often parents react with pride even to the child's mistakes. If in a first attempt he calls a ball a "bawk," the father is unlikely to say "You didn't get it right! And if you can't say it right, don't say it at all!" He is more likely to say, "Wow! Did you hear that? That kid is *talking!*" A study designed to contrast socialization in language, where I expect shaming to be rare, with areas where shame and embarrassment are prevalent might bring socialization practices and their results into high relief.

Four areas where high levels of shame and embarrassment might be expected are (a) the socialization of the infant's cry, (b) its body functions, (c) genital touching, and (d) disputes. The recording of infant-caretaker interaction in the first three areas could begin very early in the infant's life, even during the first month. The arousal of shame or embarrassment in the caretaker might be of low intensity, requiring careful analysis of facial expression and other nonverbal markers.

Because shame arousal in the caretaker is likely to be subtle, the comparison between caretaker expressions in these areas with those that occur during language acquisition is very important. We can expect that infants would be sensitive not only to the *presence* of emotional arousal in the caretakers, but also to its *absence*. That is, if the caretaker is affectionate and responsive to the infant's vocalizations, but withdrawn and/or embarrassed during crying spells, changing of diapers or genital exploration, the contrast between the caretaker's behavior in the two instances may strongly impress itself on the infant (Personal communication from Joseph Campos, 1988).

A second study would explore the possibility that rigid patterns for socializing emotions are transmitted from generation to generation. The study would compare dispute tactics within and between three different generations. Such a design would require moment-by-moment analysis of disputes between parents and their children, between the parents (husband and wife) and between parents and grandparents (parents and their parents). The design would be psuedo-longitudinal. If similar dispute tactics are found to be characterize conflict at all three levels, the hypothesis of social transmission would be supported.

To facilitate the videotaping of disputes, the technique that Gottman (1979) used to study marital quarrels could be adapted to this intergenerational design. Gottman used couples who volunteered to be videotaped for 45 minutes. He divided this time into three equal segments. In the first, the couple was asked to talk about the events of their day (neutral). In the second, they were asked to discuss a topic of frequent argument (conflict). Gottman reports that this second period always resulted in an actual quarrel. Retzinger (1988) reports the same finding. In the last segment, the couple was asked to discuss activities they enjoy doing together (positive). The last segment serves as a cooling down period.

This identical technique could be used at the husband-wife and parent-grandparent level, but would need some modification at the level of parent-child disputes. Perhaps it could be used in a similar way with older children, but with very young children the method could be adapted by arranging to videotape interactions in which the parent reports the most conflict, for example, eating, going to bed, separation, meeting strangers, or other situations of recurring conflict.

The socialization model outlined here suggests that some of the parents would socialize the child's emotions during disputes with virtually the same tactics that were used by the grandparents in similar situations when the parent was a child. A child's expression of overt anger might be met by parental anger, contempt and disgust, on the one hand, or by silent disapproval, on the other. The first type of response might give rise to the child developing a style of overt shame about its feelings of anger, and the second, a style of bypassed shame about its feelings of anger. Since these tactics are compulsive and ordinarily outside awareness, the probability that the child or the parent's dispute tactics would change would be low.

However, other parents might be more tolerant of the child's anger. Parents whose anger was tolerated by their parents might also tolerate their children's anger. This issue is subsumed by the distinction that Bowen (1978) made between families that allow "individuation" and those that don't. In the latter, the ways in which a child is different from the parents may be perceived as signs of disloyalty. In the former, the child's differences may be tolerated, or even encouraged as signs of uniqueness or growth. If the theory outlined here provides an accurate account of socialization, then it would explain both effective and disrupted learning with a single model. The agenda outlined here might carry forward the current surge of interest in emotions into many new areas of research.

NOTES

*Some of the sections of this chapter are based on an earlier article (Scheff, 1988) and on a paper presented at NICHD, Washington, D.C., April 1988. It has benefited from extensive comments by Theodore D. Kemper and Suzanne M. Retzinger. For the theoretical basis connecting shame with the social bond, see "Human nature and the social bond", Chapt. 1 in Scheff, 1990.

1. Tomkins (1963, p.56) noted a puzzle concerning grief parallel to my discussion of pride and shame:

> The reader must be puzzled at our earlier affirmation that distress is suffered daily by all human beings. Nothing seems less common than to see an adult cry. And yet we are persuaded that the cry, and the awareness of the cry, as distress and suffering, is ubiquitous.

His conjecture (p.56) also parallels the one I have suggested:

> The adult has learned to cry as an adult. It is a brief cry, or a muted cry, or a part of a cry or a miniature cry, or a substitute cry, or an active defense against the cry, that we see in place of the infant's cry for help.

2. In a parallel finding, Volkan (see Volkan and Josephthal, 1979 for a list of citations) discovered the syndrome of pathological grief, and its cure, a cathartic treatment, "regrief therapy."

REFERENCES

Adler, Alfred. 1956. *The Individual Psychology of Alfred Adler.* New York: Basic Books.

Asch, Solomon. 1956. "Studies of Independence and Conformity: 1. "A Minority of One against a Unanimous Majority." *Psychological Monographs* 70:1–70.

Bowen, Murray. 1978. *Family Therapy in Clinical Practice.* New York: Jason Aronson.

Bowlby, John. 1969. *Attachment and Loss.* 3 Vol. New York: Basic Books.

Campos, Joseph. 1988. Personal communication.

Cooley, Charles H. 1922. *Human Nature and the Social Order.* New York: Scribners.

Darwin, Charles. 1872. *The Expression of Emotion in Men and Animals.* London: John Murray.

Edelman, Robert J. 1987, et. al. "Self-reported Verbal and Nonverbal Strategies for Coping with Embarrassment in Five European Cultures." *Social Science Information,* 26:869–93.

Eibl-Eibesfeldt, Irenaeus. *Ethology.* 2d ed. New York: Holt, Rinehart and Winston.

Freud, Sigmund, and Josef Breuer. 1987. *Studies of Hysteria.* New York: Avon. (1966).

Goffman, Erving. 1967. *Interaction Ritual.* New York: Anchor.

Goodman, Paul. 1969. *New Reformation.* New York: Vintage.

Gottschalk, Lewis A., and Goldine C. Gleser. 1969. *Manual of Instruction for Using the Gottschalk-Gleser Content Analysis Scales.* Berkeley, Calif: U. of California Press.

Gottman, John. 1979 *Marital Interaction.* New York: Academic Press.

Hochschild, Arlie Russell. 1975. "The Sociology of Feelings and Emotions." In *Another Voice.* (M. Millman and R. Kanter, Editors). Garden City, New Jersey: Doubleday and Co.

Katz, Jack. 1988. *The Seductions of Crime.* New York: Basic Books.

Kemper, Theodore D. 1978. *A Social Interactional Theory of Emotions.* New York: Wiley.

Lansky, Melvin. 1987. "Shame and Domestic Violence." In *The Many Faces of Shame.* Edited by D. Nathanson. New York: Guilford.

Lewis, Helen B. 1971. *Shame and Guilt in Neurosis*. New York: International Universities Press.

———— 1977. *Psychic War in Men and Women*. New York: New York University Press.

Lofland, John, 1981. "Collective Behavior: the Elementary Forms". In *Social Psychology: Sociological Perspectives*. Edited by M. Rosenberg and R. Turner. New York: Basic Books.

Lynd, Helen M. 1958. *Shame and the Search for Identity*. New York: Harcourt Brace.

McDougall, William. 1908. *An Introduction to Social Psychology*. London: Metheun.

Maccoby, Eleanor. 1980. *Child Development: Psychological Growth and the Parent-child Relationship*. New York: Harcourt Brace.

Mead, G. H. 1934. *Mind, Self, and Society*. Chicago: U. of Chicago Press.

Piers, Gerhart, and Milton B. Singer. 1953. *Shame and Guilt: A Psychoanalytic and Cultural Study*. New York: Norton.

Retzinger, Suzanne, 1988. "Marital Conflict: The Role of Shame." Ph.D. dissertation, University of California, Santa Barbara,

Rousseau, J. J. 1736. *Confessions*. New York: Modern Library (1950).

Scheff, Thomas J. 1979. *Catharsis and Healing in Healing, Ritual, and Drama*. Berkeley, Calif.: University of California Press.

———— 1985. "The Primacy of Affect." *American Psychologist*. 40: 849–850.

———— 1986. "Microlinguistics and social structure: a theory of social action." *Sociological Theory*. Vol. 4, pp. 71–83.

———— 1987. "The Shame/Rage Spiral: Case Study of an Interminable Quarrel". In *The Role of Shame in Symptom Formation*. Edited by H. B. Lewis. Hillsdale, New Jersey: Lawrence Erlbaum, pp. 109–50.

———— 1988. "Shame and Conformity: the Deference/Emotion System". *American Sociological Review*, 53: 395–406.

———— 1988a. "Cognitive and emotional components of anorexia: a reanalysis of a classic study". *Psychiatry* 52: 148–163.

———— (n.d.) "Studies of self-esteem: a critique."

———— 1990. *Micro-sociology: Discourse, Emotion and Social Structure*. Chicago: U. of Chicago Press.

Scheff, Thomas J., and Ursula Mahlendorf. 1988. "Emotion and False Consciousness: Analysis of an Incident from *Werther.*" *Theory, Culture, and Society* 5:57–79.

Scheff, T. J., Retzinger, S. M., and Ryan, M. T. 1989. Crime, Violence, and SelfEsteem. In A. Mecca, N. Smelser, and J. Vasconcellos (Editors) *The Social Importance of Self-Esteem.* Berkeley: U. of California Press.

Scheff, T. J. and S. M. Retzinger. 1989. "Hiding Behavior: Toward Resolving the Shame Controversy." Paper presented at Annual .Meeting of the American Sociological Association, San Francisco, Cal.

Shibutani, Tamotsu. 1961. *Society and Personality.* Englewood Cliffs, New Jersey: Prentice-Hall.

Skinner, B. F. 1984. "The Shame of American Education." *American Psychologist.* 39: 947–954.

Tomkins, Silvan S. 1963. *Affect/Imagery/Consciousness.* Vol. 1 and 2. New York: Springer.

Volkan, Vladimir and Daniel Josephson. 1979. "Brief Psychotherapy in Pathological Grief: Regrief Therapy." In *Specialized Techniques in Psychotherapy.* Edited by T. B. Karasu and L. Bellak. New York: Brenner/Mazel pp. 102–52.

Wurmser, Leon. 1981. *The Masks of Shame.* Baltimore: Johns Hopkins University Press.

12.

Emotions and Micropolitics in Everyday Life: Some Patterns and Paradoxes of "Place"

Candace Clark

Micropolitics, like all politics, has to do with the creation and negotiation of hierarchy: getting and keeping power, rank, standing, or what I will call "social place"[1] (Goffman, 1951:297). In everyday, face-to-face encounters and relationships, we constantly monitor the shifting micropolitical balance. We want to know where we stand, relative to others, at a given moment. And we want to have a say in negotiating our standing.

Emotions, by virtue of the fact that they define and alter people's social place, play an important part in micropolitics. In this chapter, I will consider how a self-targeted [or, to use Kemper's (1978) term, "introjected"] emotion like awe, shame, or pride can produce a felt sense of place in one's psyche and soma. Such an emotion serves as information about where one stands—a "place marker."

Next, I will argue that emotions can serve as "place claims," messages about where one wants to stand. Once displayed, an other-targeted ("extrojected") emotion such as anger, love, or sympathy can make a claim to a place one chooses or desires to occupy.

Because emotions both mark and claim place, people can use their own emotions and elicit emotions from others in a variety of micropolitical strategies. I will describe five strategies in which an actor attempts to trigger others' emotional place markers with place claims in order to assert, maintain, usurp, upset, or deny a social placement.

Along the way, I will propose a research agenda centered on the assumptions, paradoxes, and problems to be sketched here. Systematically pursuing this agenda will lead to greater understanding of what Collins calls the "emotional interactional substrate" (1986:1349) of everyday social life. And, recognizing the interplay between social place, on the one hand, and emotions and emotional strategies, on the other, will give us greater insight into the phenomena of hierarchy.

THE CONCEPT OF SOCIAL PLACE

One of the most interesting paradoxes of social existence is that while we share group life together, we are also separated and divided by hierarchies based on gender, race, social class, age, ethnicity, occupation, beauty, intelligence, competence, interpersonal skills, and so forth. We find hierarchy virtually everywhere, permeating the social structure and everyday interaction.

In the micro-hierarchy of a given encounter, one person has higher standing or a higher place than others, even if all are ostensibly peers or intimates. We imply as much when we say: "Know your place," "She put him in his place," "Who does he think he is?" (read: "What place does he think he occupies?"), or "It's not my place to . . . " The gap between one person's place and another's can vary greatly, from immense (as between Southern white corporate executive and black typist) to almost imperceptible (among friends). To use Stephen Potter's (1948) term, person A can be "one-up" or even two- or three-up on B. As long as people agree upon a certain distance between them, they may interact freely, frequently, and almost "intimately" without altering the place configuration.[2]

As I see it, place is to everyday interaction what social status is to social structure. That is, while a status is a socially agreed upon, macro-level position (Merton, 1957:368, 381–384), a place is a less well defined, micro-level position such as follower, leader, star, supporting character, or the One with the Upper Hand. The concept of place encompasses differences in what sociologists have variously called power, prestige, face-to-face status, and social distance (or intimacy). Those occupying higher place have more esteem and privilege. They have more and different interactional rights, including the right to evaluate others, ask personal questions, give advice, point out flaws, have their opinions count, be late, have something more important to do, ignore the other, and so on. Of course, social statuses affect one's micro place, but the relationship is not perfect.

Social actors are often uncertain about the abstract concept of place as well as their concrete place in a specific encounter. Part of the reason is that places are situational, overlapping, and changeable. First, we move among many places in the course of a day, occupying at least one in each of our relationships or encounters. Second, when many actors are present we may occupy several social places at once. Sometimes (as with boss and worker who are also friends) one can simultaneously be in two or more place relationships with a single person. Third, place configurations are unstable. In an instant, the gap between the parties can widen or narrow, or superior can become inferior. (This instability also creates difficulty for the sociologist trying to capture configurational subtleties.)

Further, at the same time that others try to place us, we place others and ourselves. There are, then, multiple perspectives on a given person's place: the "objective" (other-constructed) and the "subjective" (self-constructed). Objective placement is not where people wish to stand or think they stand, but the place that others ascribe through their attention, esteem, deference, honor—or lack thereof. Objective place affects the subjective sense of "where I stand in this relationship" but is not altogether determinate.

Consider, for example, Person A, who feels ordinary and equal but whom others look up to as dominant and superior. If group members ask A to solve a problem, she/he may work hard to warrant their trust and support and an elevated place. Also consider a business meeting in which Person B puts forth an idea he/she expects others to follow. Person B could be placing himself/herself highly: "I should be an important personage here, the leader." If the others accept Person B's suggestion (and the premise about place), B's subjective and objective place coincide. But the others may criticize, laugh at, or ignore Person B's suggestion and, in so doing, refuse to accept the place claim. In turn, Person B can modify his/her sense of place to agree with the group's or reject it and try to elevate him/herself or lower the colleagues. We can see that, in the span of a few minutes, objective and subjective place may shift from concordance to discordance and back again.

It seems reasonable to suggest that the self-concept affects subjective sense of place and vice versa. We can see subjective place as an impermanent adjunct to self. Self, the sum of all one's thoughts and feelings about oneself, is created through interaction but takes on a life of its own. It is a somewhat enduring understanding of "who I am" and the corollary "how I can act." Sense of place, in contrast, arises only in interaction (or imagined interaction). It is the *momentary* consciousness of "who I am and how I can act at this moment in this encounter," or part of the situated self.

Many sociologists have asked how people know their place. The traditional answers have focused on combinations of cognitive and behavioral factors: what people assume about their statuses, how they read cues from (and into) others' behavior, the messages they receive from the self-concept, and how they act. Discussing the effects of class status on everyday interaction, Goffman (1951) noted that class-specific etiquette, vocabulary, dialect, and overall demeanor act as "status reminders." Henley (1977) catalogued the many studies showing that differences in status and power, as well as intimacy, are communicated by nonverbal cues, for example, touching, eye–contact while listening and while speaking, taking up space, interrupting, and the like. Schwartz (1973) demonstrated that monopolizing others' time by making them wait reflects and reinforces power differences. He also described power-messages inherent in gift giving (1967), for example, "My expensive gift shows that I have more wealth than you" or "I know what gift is good for you."

More recently, expectation-states theory has been applied to issues of face-to-face status. Ridgeway, Berger, and Smith (1985) explained that people's performance expectations (for themselves) affect the kinds of cues they send in interaction and, in turn, the interaction outcome itself. In experiments with task groups, subjects with "dominant" ascribed statuses, who expected to be better or stronger, talked first and maintained gaze longer than subjects who expected to be inferior. In consequence, the "dominant" actors dominated the interaction.

Although abundant evidence shows that these sorts of interaction cues reflect and reinforce differences in power, prestige, and intimacy, this explanation of how people know their place is incomplete. We have not shown exactly how status reminders remind, how intimidation intimidates, or how esteem gratifies. One explanation, that people "internalize" or "incorporate" objective placements into the subjective, is somewhat magical. We almost never bother to ask what it means to internalize social norms and cues, let alone how place messages get into the sense of self. Neither do we understand what happens when status reminders *fail* to remind, when intimidation *fails* to intimidate, or when esteem *fails* to gratify, nor why some relationships (for example, worker-boss or marriages) are more hierarchical than others. Further, we know little about why some people resist the place others define for them, while some accept it.

I believe we will understand more about how social actors generate micro-hierarchy if we pay attention to emotion.[3] After all, people constantly experience and elicit emotions in interaction (Kemper, 1978). Are these emotions mere epiphenomena? It seems more reasonable to assume that they do something significant.

EMOTIONS AND PLACE

People assemble place configurations with the glue provided by emotions. Constructing a sense of one's relative place involves self-evaluation and comparison, and these activities evoke feelings, for example, pain, shame, and belittlement, or pride, pleasure, and empowerment. Sending a place message can evoke some of these feelings in the other. The emotion conveys information about the state of the social ranking system: it informs us where we stand and tells others where they do or should stand.

Consider the remarks of a student who wanted her professor to confirm or deny her potential as a graduate student—her future place.

> I showed Prof. X the ideas I had put together for my term paper. . . .
> He doesn't do anything to intimidate me, but I'm intimidated anyway. I guess
> I care a lot about what he thinks of me.
>   Anyway, I showed him the paper . . . he started reading it out loud. It
> sounded so pretentious and dumb. . . . I could hardly talk. I certainly
> couldn't look him in the eye. He kept apologizing, but . . . it even made me
> more embarrassed. Embarrassed *because* I was embarrassed. . . . Of course, he
> didn't do a thing to make me feel that way. I did it to myself by making his
> opinion count so much. (Free-writing, 1988)[4]

Here we can see a blend of self-targeted emotions (hope, anxiety, and embarrassment) and other-targeted emotions (respect and admiration) that combined to create the young woman's inferior self-placement. This sense of place affected how she acted, how she read the professor's cues, the emotions she produced in him (e.g., discomfort or guilt), how he acted, and both parties' sense of own and other's place. In short, emotions played a major part in creating place.

Because of emotions, felt social place can persist over time and across settings. For example, a manager who is demoted may continue to feel disdainful of former underlings. A student who graduates and becomes the colleague of formerly revered professors may have difficulty shifting to the new place, and they may have difficulty letting him or her do so. Habitual emotional stances sustain the former place relationship.

Some emotions are uniquely relevant to issues of place. When subjective and objective place are aligned, emotions such as satisfaction, pride, and exultation record this comfortable state (see Smith-Lovin; and Heise, this volume). But when they diverge, certain emotions (e.g., anxiety, resentment, or indignation) record the fact and, if the emotions are visible, convey it to the other actors present.

As we will see in the discussion of strategy 3 below, the act of displaying emotion can affect place. For example, experts who make errors may reveal embarrassment; as much as erring, revealing the emotion puts them (temporarily at least) one-down; and members of the audience, no matter how uncomfortable about it, are one-up.

In many ways, then, emotions relate people to place. Below I will discuss in greater detail an *intra*personal dynamic, the place-marking function of emotions, and an *inter*personal dynamic, the place-claiming function of emotions. Neither has been systematically studied.

EMOTIONS AS PLACE MARKERS

First, emotions relay messages—sometimes physically unmistakable messages—to self about one's place in an encounter. At the boss's withering stare, Person A feels hurt, shamed, and lowered. Or A's feelings of resentment and indignation mark A's refusal to accept the implied message. Person B adores Person C, and C's consequent ecstasy elevates him or her (most people apparently experience ecstasy as extremely empowering [Morgan and Heise, 1988:22–23]). Person D offers help to Person E in a patronizing way, and E feels humiliated. Social role-taking emotions such as humiliation, disgust, shame, gratitude, and admiration can serve to let people know their place. From the examples above in which behavior denotes place and elicits "consequent" emotions (Kemper, 1978:49), we may conclude that *place reminders remind when they evoke emotions.*

These examples illustrate cases in which one actor experiences consequent emotions in response to cues from another. However, emotional place markers can involve more than consequent emotions. For instance, if Person B is awed at the prospect of meeting Person A, B's emotion has marked B's place. A's elevated status characteristics or A's past dominance of B may have come into play. But it is the full complement of B's other- and self-emotions, not only A's characteristics or B's shared history with A, that mark B's inferior place.

Our awed subject might experience any of several emotional combinations.[5] In one, he/she might feel awe, fright, self-disgust, and embarrassment. Another could be awe, satisfaction, safety, and contentment. The reader can see that these two emotional blends would mark different places for the actor, the former probably lower than the latter. Jealousy provides another example. A jealous person who experiences anger and disgust feels differently placed from one who experiences fear and loss of self-worth (Ellis and Weinstein, 1986). These examples only hint at the subtlety and complexity of emotional blends and the wide range of consequent self-placements.

To date, the most relevant research on emotions as place markers comes from studies of "inferiors" who have submitted to extreme oppression and violence, for example, political prisoners, racial minorities, and battered women. Among the most striking findings of this body of research are the cases of some hostages, slaves, and concentration-camp inmates whose feelings of inadequacy vis-à-vis their oppressors led them to feel they deserved a subordinate place (Bettelheim, 1943; N.Y. Times, 1985:A7). Coles (1967) found that, before the Black Power movement of the 1960s and 1970s, feelings of inferiority and self-contempt pervaded the self-portraits of many black children in the South. The slogan Black Is Beautiful was aimed to counteract such feelings.

Women who are the targets of emotional and physical violence may feel shame, guilt, and even self-disgust—marking for them their "rightful" place (see e.g., Dobash and Dobash, 1979; Ferraro and Johnson, 1983; Denzin, 1984). Consider the following:

> I couldn't believe it. It hadn't happened in the first couple of years, and then one day, Wham! My first thought was that I had done something wrong, I wasn't good enough. I tried to get everything just right, the house, the meals, and all. And everything was okay for a few weeks and then, wham, it happened again. . . . I sort of *know* most of the time it's not my fault, I didn't do anything wrong. But I still *feel* like I must be defective or dirty. (Field notes, 22-year-old conservatory student and night-club singer)

These comments evidence some "identification with the oppressor" (Bettelheim, 1943) or partial "role fusion" (Franks, 1989) in which victims of violence cannot steadfastly cling to positive self-assessments and self-emotions. For years after leaving her abuser, she may feel about herself as he does (see, e.g., Ferraro and Johnson, 1983:334). According to Denzin (1984:507), to remove herself from a violent relationship, the battered woman must "restructure her relationship with herself" and reclaim a sense of the accuracy of her own positive self-judgments. Failing this, her emotions place her abuser in a superior place, herself in an inferior one.

We can also see emotions serving as place-markers in cases provided by respondents in a pilot study of humiliation among the elderly (Baillif and Clark, 1987). When embarrassment or humiliation occurred, people wanted to "become invisible" or "sink through the floor" [see also Scheff and Retzinger (1988) on hiding behavior associated with shame]. Some withdrew mentally from interaction, "pretending nothing had happened" but remaining silent. An eighty-seven-year-old widow who was incontinent reported her experience of mortification and hurt since she had moved in with her son and daughter-in-law.

> I'm only allowed to sit on one chair. . . . Nobody talks to me all day except to yell at me. I've never been so humiliated in my life. I just want to die.

This woman *felt* as worthless, helpless, and lowly as others treated her.

There are several other ways in which emotional processes can mark place. Some battered women, for instance, respond to extreme or prolonged emotional abuse with "numbing," a condition in which one pushes feelings of anger and resentment below conscious awareness (Mills and Kleinman,

1988). Emotional numbing marks inferior standing among battered women as it did among flight attendants in Hochschild's (1983:129) study who shifted into a mental state they called "robot." It may be "natural" for the victim of abuse to react with anger (Kemper, 1978:128), but only if she admits being abused; sometimes this reaction is just not *possible* (Thibaut and Kelley, 1959). Numbing permits people to stay in dangerous or unpleasant situations. It also denies the worth and substance of one's own feelings (see also Hochschild, 1983, pp. 172–174; Denzin, 1984; Franks, 1989). The other's feelings take precedence. One becomes emotionally invisible, unentitled, not only to the other, but also to oneself, and thus justifiably allocated to a lower place.

Battered women also may develop emotional habits that limit their emotional repertoire and, therefore, continually remind them of inferior standing. Accustomed to smiling ingratiatingly (Henley, 1977) or to feeling guilt, shame, and humiliation, some women may not be able to call forth the more powerful emotions of resentment or anger. It may take coaching and practice to recondition their emotional responses (Ferraro and Johnson, 1983:333; Denzin, 1984:507).

Further, negative self-emotions can incapacitate role performance (Gross and Stone, 1964) and create the objective conditions for inferior status. Because they cannot conceive of appropriate counter-actions to block abuse, battered women report "freezing."

> [Y]ou're sitting there in a cold sweat waiting on whatever else is going to happen. I couldn't talk. My mouth was shut. I would just sit . . . (Dobash and Dobash, 1979:117).

Less severe outcomes are also common. Those who are embarrassed or humiliated, for instance, sometimes run from the interactional arena, abdicating their place. *Candid Camera* victims often tried to hide or avoid making eye-contact (Scheff and Retzinger, 1988). Students asked to recite or answer questions in the classroom may worry about their competence and remain mute (Karp and Yoels, 1976).

Indeed, anyone required to perform before an important or powerful audience may develop self-doubt and stagefright (Lyman and Scott, 1970:159–188), which sets up a self-fulfilling prophecy. Questioning one's own standing or the rightfulness of one's claims to a place can lead to agitation. Unable to regain composure, the person may *become* inferior—incompetent, ridiculous, or deficient.

It is precisely the creation of "fluster" that Stephen Potter (1948; 1950) proposed as a major technique of "lifemanship" and "gamesmanship." "The object is to create a state of anxiety, to build up an atmosphere of muddled fluster" (1948:20–21) in which the other experiences "distrust, uncertainty and broken flow" (1950:xvi). The gamesman may throw off his or her victim, Potter explains, by appearing to scoff at the other's stance toward the game. Wearing the "wrong" clothing, "clothesmanship," is one strategy: if the opponent is likely to appear in appropriate sporting costume, wear old clothes; if the opponent generally wears old clothes, dress up. "If you can't [play], wear velvet socks. . . . " Potter, 1948:23–24). The opponent, vaguely flustered, feels and becomes less adequate.

Similarly, members of many occupational groups (sociologists included) may purposely try to create superior place by using mystifying jargon and insider language, prominently displaying imposing certificates and diplomas, or deliberately obfuscating straightforward matters (see, e.g., Freidson, 1970; Collins, 1982:81–84). Their audiences, for example, car buyers, patients, and students, may feel bewildered and inadequate in the face of such mystification, readily submitting to the "expert."

So far, I have given examples of how negative self-emotions may mark inferior places. However, positive self-emotions may also mark inferiority. In Japan, the emotion of *amae*, a delighting or basking in a superior's doting attention and kindness (Morsbach and Tyler, 1986), can mark an inferior place in some respects. Some self-emotions may mark one's refusal to be placed or removed from one's place by another. For example, pride and self-righteousness may help people cling stubbornly to preferred positions that others challenge.

We have barely begun to ask, let alone answer, questions about emotions as markers of social place. How aware are actors of the effects of their own and others' emotional place markers on interaction? I suspect that most people pay little conscious attention to them. Would greater awareness lead to more effective lines of action in one's everyday encounters and/ or to more cynical role performance and manipulation?

How persistent are people's emotional place markers? Do "inferior" self-emotions, as literature on the "marginal man" [sic] (Wittermans and Kraus, 1964; Potter, 1965) suggests, play a part in keeping the lower class, racial and ethnic minorities, women, and others from seeking or accepting upward social mobility? Do "superior" self-emotions protect the powerful? That is, do emotional place markers serve to reproduce the stratification system?

We might also explore variations in emotional place markers among social groups with different forms of stratification. In paternalistic systems (e.g., feudal Europe, the antebellum South, and the traditional Western family) those in superior positions felt and acted in protective (but demeaning) ways toward their inferiors (Weber, 1947; Genovese, 1969; van den Berghe, 1978). By contrast, competitive stratification arrangements (e.g., modern capitalism) seem to foster different emotions of superiority, for example, contempt, disdain, and disgust toward inferiors. In consequence, the reciprocal emotions of inferiority in these two types of systems probably differ, the former involving more awe and deference and the latter more rage and despair.[6] Thus, more than one combination of emotional place markers can sustain hierarchy. Which combinations make for more self-perpetuating systems, and which contain the seeds of change?

Studying these and similar questions about emotional place markers should increase our understanding of both micro- and macro-stratification processes and the links between them.

EMOTIONS AS PLACE CLAIMS

In addition to serving as intrapersonal place markers, emotions may be used interpersonally as place claims. In the course of interaction people may actively and intentionally instigate emotions in each other and themselves. They do so to shape definitions of situations and of self. Often they want affirmation of their standing. Having no place, or feeling "out of place," can be more painful even than having an inferior place. Sometimes actors negotiate their place, trying to move (usually up, sometimes down), reminding and counter-reminding each other of their proper place with "emotion-cues."

In general, people seem to know that one's extrojected emotion is often matched by the other's reciprocal introjected emotion. There are some "logical" couplings: Person A's anger or disgust can arouse Person B's embarrassment, shame, or fear; Person C's admiration can evoke Person D's happiness, liking, or pride. Since people often expect emotional gears to mesh in these ways, they may act as if they can successfully predict the effect their own emotions will have on others. That is, people sometimes act manipulatively, targeting emotions at each other to elicit specific emotional effects.

One person's feelings about another are important interaction cues that can in turn evoke the other's place-marking emotions. Emotion cues may be used to enhance one's power (e.g., Napoleon Bonaparte's mock rages in the presence of ambassadors of nations he sought to cow); to put one in another's good graces (e.g., the lover's swoons in the presence of someone he is trying to win); to indicate the limits of one's deference (e.g., the flash of anger in the "uppity" servant's eyes); or to minimize inequalities (e.g., the boss's hearty laughter at a subordinate's joke).

Further, emotions such as awe or anger or even gratitude or sympathy project their own assumptions. For example, if Person A expresses hatred for Person B, A is doing more than merely displaying his or her internal feeling state. Person A is conveying evaluations of both B's moral worth and his or her own, thereby claiming a superior place.

It is not only *negative* other-emotions that can transmit claims to superior standing. *Positive* other-emotions may do so as well, although they often serve as claims of equality or inferiority—"I like you" may translate into "I want to be close to you" or "I admire you" translates into "You are better than I am." As Henley (1977) found, we usually think of touching as making a claim for equality or intimacy, but it sometimes makes a claim for power. Adding to Henley's argument, in certain circumstances one can make *both* claims at once; in effect a touch can mean, "I have the power to initiate closeness with you"—as many victims of sexual harassment can attest. Because of the several possible meanings, this type of place claim can confuse the recipient. If we add to this the fact that an emotional display can be insincere or cynical, we see how complex interpretation problems can be.

In general, we tend to ignore the place-claiming function of positive emotions. When a displayed emotion is positive—a "gift," a social reward—rules of reciprocity and exchange come into play (Simmel, 1950; Schwartz, 1967; Clark, 1987; Camerer, 1988). The act of giving may underscore or enhance the donor's social worth. It may also obligate the recipient to repay the social debt.

Further, by giving an emotional gift, perhaps a smile or a look of concern, the donor gets to impose his or her definition of what the other wants or needs. Both the content of the gift and the fact that it is given are important. If the gift is accepted, the other is agreeing to be "altercast" (Weinstein and Deutschberger, 1963) and is accepting the donor's definition of the situation as well as the donor's right to define it—that is, the donor's superior place (Schwartz, 1967).

We can recognize positive-emotion place claims most clearly when parties disagree about a place one of them is claiming. The donor of the positive emotion probably feels that the recipient *should* feel rewarded and *should* be obligated because the gift is valuable; but the recipient may not concur. Consider the following case involving gratitude. A sociologist remarked on an unsettling occurrence after a conference of emotions researchers:

> A psychologist said to me, "Others here may not appreciate sociological work, but I'm really grateful that you sociologists are helping us out." That really rankled. It shows how much they think of us.

The psychologist's gratitude was, the sociologist felt, genuine; but the sociologist reported feeling belittled and unappreciated. The emotional "gift" carried the donor's place claim: "I am an expert, and I'm also nice." The unacceptable corollary place message was: "We are not equals. I am the central and important figure in this work, and you are a mere helper."

To summarize the assumptions I have made to this point, let me set forth some postulates.

- Interaction is often a process of negotiation with each party trying to construct—to arrive at, and at the same time influence—a definition of the situation.
- People define situations, that is, construct reality, in order to confirm "who they are" and know how to act.
- The definition of the situation includes an assessment of each party's relative standing, or "place."
- People arrive quickly at preliminary judgments of their rank, but place must be continually negotiated.
- In order to define a situation, a person processes a host of verbal and nonverbal cues (that may evoke emotions).
- Some of these cues are "emotion-cues," information about one's own and the others' emotions.
- Many emotion-cues relate, often in complex ways, to place.

EMOTIONAL MICROPOLITICS

Micropolitics involves lines of action designed to get and keep place in face-to-face interaction. Because emotions mark places and make place claims, *emotional* micropolitics are possible. People may use their own emotions strategically to elicit emotions in others in order to mark and claim place.

These emotions may be spontaneous reactions to situations. They may also result from conscious and unconscious molding, managing, and shaping in "deep" and "surface" acting, or "emotion work" (Hochschild, 1979, 1983). People generally know and use a variety of techniques to work on their emotions (Thoits, 1985; and this volume). For example, one can try to change the *physiological* part of an emotional experience with drugs, alcohol, cigarettes, food, exercise, or catharsis (Scheff, 1979). One can *cognitively* alter a cultural label, construing love as infatuation or anger as impatience. Or, one can argue with oneself about, say, the merits of feeling shame or guilt. Emotion work is a means to generate the emotions that may put us in the places we prefer.

We can work on our own emotions, and we can work on others' emotions, as Hochschild (1983) demonstrated in her study of flight attendants' "emotional labor." In our everyday encounters and relationships, we often express emotions (whether sincerely or cynically) to instigate emotions in others and, in turn, help resolve (or provoke) questions of relative social place. These are the ploys of emotional micropolitics.

Here I wish to consider some micropolitical strategies in detail. I do not suggest that people are *always* aware that they are using these strategies, but that they are *sometimes* aware. Nor do I assume that all people are equally good at knowing what strategies will work or at carrying them out. I will focus on cases involving two people who, to some degree, contest their places.

If two people do not agree on their relative standing, what happens? How do they jockey for position? How can Person A try to "knock Person B down a peg or two"? One person's ploy, if it is strong enough, may end the contest. But it may also evoke a counter-strategy and so on in an escalating power struggle. The struggle tends to provoke both emotions and emotion work. One type of evidence indicating the contest is over and how it came out is the resulting emotions.

I will suggest five interaction strategies and counter-strategies that involve displaying and/or evoking emotions to negotiate place in contests between A and B. People normally use these strategies to enhance place, whether the place is initially inferior or superior. Person A's intention may not be to move one-up above B, but to move one-more-up or only to be one-less-down. Often people use more than one of these strategies in the same encounter. I will now discuss these strategies in turn.

STRATEGY 1: EXPRESSING NEGATIVE OTHER-EMOTIONS

The strategy of using negative emotions is one of the most obvious and understandable—and the least polite. Person A displays disdain, contempt, disgust, hate, exasperation, impatience, anger, or doubt toward Person B. These emotions all comment on B's negative attributes—he or she is unworthy, contemptible, disgusting, nasty, stupid, ridiculous, inept, clumsy, and so on.

We can also include in this category cases in which A refuses to honor B's claims to respect, admiration, and so forth. In a study of humiliation among the elderly (Baillif and Clark, 1987), for example, a woman reported saying "Good morning" to a friend who did not answer. The lack of response, whether intentional or not, carried a negative emotional message that put the woman down.

A negative strategy "works" if Person A manages to reduce B's standing, if A raises his or her own standing, or if both occur. To have an effect, the negative emotion (or lack of positive emotion) must "reach" the target, as it did with the elderly woman above. Depending on A's emotion, B feels lowered, shamed, humiliated, embarrassed, or degraded. Or, B may feel respect, awe, fear, or envy toward A. If B accepts A's place claim, he or she feels reduced in consequence and exhibits signs of it; A is elevated. (Of course, B may respond with anger or resentment, in which case we could say the strategy failed.)

We can turn again to the family-violence literature for examples of the negative strategy. Denzin's (1984) description of men who heap emotional and physical abuse and even torture on their spouses indicates the vicious nature of this category of emotional micropolitics. Denzin (1984:499) argued that while child abuse usually starts out as discipline, the initial goal of wife abuse is to degrade. In his words, "The victim's moral worth is denied, suspended, deemed irrelevant, or judged to need a physical attack so that it will become more worthy . . . (1984:501)." Violent men, Denzin claimed, feel they deserve more *voluntary submissiveness* (what Kemper, 1978, called "voluntary compliance") from their partners than they are getting—they want to be treated as guests in their own homes. But, because the men have used violence to claim their place, they can never achieve their goal (1984:489). Their feeling of being cheated *grows* rather than diminishes, and a spiral of violence ensues.

Many violent men apparently never recognize that they have "won" at reducing their target's power and sense of worth and, according to Denzin, continue to seek the place they have "lost" (p. 488). Cultural and structural factors associated with patriarchy, including men's role-taking inabilities (see Thomas, et al., 1972), conspire to render such men incapable of seeing the woman's "invisible" emotions (see also Hochschild, 1983:172–174). Denzin's account points to a vicious case of self-righteous place claims coupled with misperception of their emotional consequences for their victims. Whether abusers are aware of it or not, abused women often feel inferior. It is probable that chronically abused women always feel inferior relative to their abusers.

In seeking to understand the use of negative emotion to claim place, we need more description of how and in what circumstances people put each other down. Is it more likely to occur in some ethnic, social class, or age subcultures than others? We do not know if put-downs are more common in face-to-face primary-group interaction or in formal, secondary-group "degradation ceremonies" (see e.g., Garfinkel, 1956). Is the superior usually acting within or apart from a social role such as parent or prison guard? Put-downs sometimes occur between two people in private (in the principal's or boss's office), sometimes in the presence of an audience (at the dinner table, on the drill field, at a convicted criminal's sentencing hearing, or during a theatrical performance). What conditions encourage and discourage the use of negative emotions in such settings? Given the cultural prohibitions on putting others down and the potential for recrimination, it is likely that something in the setting or situation protects the negative emoter. In private encounters, this may be a social status such as parent, husband, or teacher. In public scenes, for example, when construction workers yell epithets at female pedestrians, the presence of an audience may offer further protection (Gardner, 1980).

Structurally, some categories of people are apt to inflict degradation while others receive it. Hochschild's concept of "status shields" is relevant here (1983:163, passim). She argued that norms covering interaction between unequals shield people who occupy more powerful positions (e.g., men and customers) from others' (e.g., women and service workers) scorn and anger. The norms also allow the powerful to vent their negative feelings and ignore the emotional consequences for inferiors. Superiors have a right to have their feelings "count"; inferiors' emotions are discounted or invisible (see also Scully and Marolla, 1984, for similar beliefs of some rapists about their victims). We should expect to see superior standing associated with a greater tendency to claim place through use of negative emotions. Alternatively, we might find the direction of the relationship to be the reverse; that is, regardless of status, people who use a "powerful" strategy like expressing negative emotions may create their own protective shields. For example, one of my male informants contended,

> Women have to understand men. The best way for a woman to get rid of a man in a come-on situation is to humiliate him. It's all politics; take something away from him. It doesn't have to be blatant. Do it in some small way. Point out a small flaw. He'll be deflated and leave the woman alone.

As important as the issues of how and where this strategy works is the question of when and why it fails. Sneers and derision may *not* evoke the other's emotions of inferiority. Thus, we may ask under what conditions negative emotions "work."

Kemper (1978) suggested one explanation: people who receive fewer rewards than they believe they deserve will feel shame if they accept responsibility for the paucity of rewards and anger if they think it is the other's fault. Thus, one's assignment of blame affects outcomes. It is important to discover why some people blame themselves and some blame their degraders and why some expect much and others expect little.

Research on self-concept and self-esteem suggests that most people tend to "defend" their self-concepts, using a variety of devices including "interpersonal selectivity, selective imputation, selective causal attributions, selective interpretation, selective attention to facts, terminological selectivity, selective social comparisons, and selective comparison levels"

(Rosenberg, 1979:276). On the other hand, principles of self-consistency may motivate a person with a negative self-picture to use selectivity devices to choose social cues and interpretations that fit that negative picture (Lecky, 1945). The success of a degradation attempt may depend as much on the target's initial self-concept and subjective sense of place as on the degrader's performance.

We should also examine the emotion-work strategies (Hochschild, 1983; Thoits, 1985) people use to deal with the degradation attempts of others. Strategies vary in their capacity to protect one from being reduced in place. For instance, pretending that nothing happened or turning humiliation into anger are, respectively, more self-protective and self-assertive than strategies such as fleeing the situation or crying and trembling in public (Baillif and Clark, 1987). Social roles include prescriptions for proper emotion-work strategies. If gender roles are any guide, I suspect that superior roles call for emotion-work strategies that are most likely to preserve superiority (see Lever, 1976; Gilligan, 1982).

Although being the target of another person's negative emotions is not pleasant, virtually everyone experiences episodes of derision or ridicule. If these are prolonged, is it possible to develop special skills at combating attacks on self? Can one learn emotion-work strategies that preserve self and place in inhospitable circumstances? Gross and Stone (1964) suggested that adolescents' embarrassment rituals—including "doing the dozens"—serve as toughening trials. It would be useful to study what emotion-work strategies successful resistors of dis-placement use and when and how they work.

Finally, many people—the medical worker conscious of the patient's embarrassment or the loan officer concerned with the shame of the financially strapped—often handle potentially degrading situations in a kindly fashion. Why do some people try not to display negative other-emotions when they have the chance? Are they upholding social rules for "niceness" (see Weinstein, 1965, for examples of "nice" put-downs)? Are they deliberately trying to be deferential and self-effacing? Are they more empathic and sympathetic than others? Are they more likely to be women than men (see Hochschild, 1983:167–170)?

STRATEGY 2: EXPRESSING POSITIVE OTHER-EMOTIONS INDICATING OWN INFERIORITY OR EQUALITY

This positive strategy centers on gaining another's acceptance by displaying respect, admiration, liking, love, and similar other-emotions (or by withholding criticism). An example from a college professor points up the emotional and political dimensions of such flattery.

> A soon-to-be graduate student said, "I saw your name all through our textbook." While I knew he was exaggerating, I felt proud. The pride . . . stayed with me even after I arrived home that night.
> Later I volunteered to do an independent study with this student. He accepted. Then I offered him an out: "This topic is not really in my area though. So perhaps you should work with someone else." He said, "I will make whatever project I do fit your interests somehow. I'll do anything to work with you." That was what I had hoped to hear. The way I felt told me, as much if not more than what the student said, that I had "arrived." (Freewriting, 1988)

The professor agreed to award the student a new and higher place, to intensify the relationship, as a result of the pride his admiration engendered in her.

When flattery is insincere, its strategic aspect becomes more apparent. "Buttering up" the boss and "apple polishing" with the teacher are common tactics for self-gain. If the other cooperates by "fishing" for compliments, the micro-politician's job is even easier. If the other suspects insincerity, the flatterer's credibility may be reduced and the ploy may fail, but it may work. As Rosenberg (1979) argued, there seems to be a strain toward perceiving the reactions of others as flattering even when they are not. The target's self-protective perceptual processes may assist the flattering micropolitician.

Although strategy 2 is also fairly obvious, we have as little empirical research on it as on strategy 1. How common is it? What sorts of people are most likely to use it and use it effectively? Is it primarily a tactic for the impersonal world of secondary groups, or do primary-group members engage in it too? What kinds of emotion work does it require? What costs does it impose on the tactician? How do people know whom to use it on, when to stop, and when it is backfiring? Can it be used effectively in combination with other strategies to gain place?

STRATEGY 3: CONTROLLING THE BALANCE OF EMOTIONAL ENERGY

I have suggested that people can display negative and positive other-emotions to enhance their place in an encounter. *Evoking* another's emotions while controlling one's own can also enhance place and create "superior" self-emotions. We can readily see this result among those who elicit others' liking or love. As Waller [(1930) 1963] long ago asserted in his "principle of least interest," the person who loves least usually maintains more power in a relationship (see also Blau, 1964). A less obvious tactic for gaining place is evoking another's anger, ridicule, or other negative emotions. In general, those who can elicit more emotion from others than they invest exercise control over the interaction.

Take, for instance, "getting a rise" from someone. That a person shouts angrily does not inevitably elevate the shouter's place; sometimes it reduces it. Indeed, with this knowledge in mind, some may finesse others' shouts. Thus, what might appear to an outsider to be a degradation ceremony could be a quite different affair to the participants. For instance, the teenager who has taunted or goaded a parent into a display of anger may feel gleeful rather than debased; the parent who loses his or her "cool" and blows up at the child is one-down compared to the previous moment.

> I would refuse to respond to my mother on purpose. She would say, "Clean up your room," and I would keep quiet. Then she'd say it louder, and I'd say, sarcastically, "Sure, Mom," and keep on doing what I was doing. Finally she'd be yelling, and I'd smirk and walk out the door. (Interview, 1988, college financial aid worker)

Here, as with many of the husbands whom Hite's (1987) respondents described, the target of wrath refuses to respond "normally" (i.e., with emotional engagement) to the other's anger. When Person A gets angry or laughs at Person B, B is normally supposed to be fearful or ashamed. But if B can get A to expend the emotional energy and yet refuse to respond "appropriately," B wins doubly.

We can see elicitation of another's negative emotion coupled with studied aloofness as a "passive" strategy to gain place. A's place-claiming effort to engage B's negative extrojected emotions thrusts the issue of hierarchy more centrally into the participants' consciousness. It is no longer a taken-for-granted feature of the interaction. Either it will be re-established, or altered. Perhaps this is why it seems that "getting a rise" is often a strategy of those who are one-down.

Of course, the target of this passive strategy—the person being "ignored"—may also remain passive. He or she can refuse to get rattled, ruffled, unhinged, or "bent out of shape." For example, a frustrated parent can take a deep breath, count to ten, and break the emotional line of action in midstream. The unflappable, imperturbable person shows him– or herself to be truly *self*-possessed rather than other-possessed. The collected individual also upholds norms of politeness and propriety, which in itself adds to one's standing.

A more "active" tack for evoking negative emotions to enhance place occurs among stand-up comedians (see Potter, 1988). Comics like Joan Rivers or Rodney Dangerfield, who invite others to laugh at their appearance, class background, or other failings, may not feel embarrassed or humiliated, but effective. They have taken away others' ability to use strategy 1; that is, they have defused a potential source of hurt or diminution by putting themselves down first. By laughing at themselves, they are refusing to respond to others' negative emotions "normally."

Place strategies that involve balancing emotions alert us to the question of cost: What does feeling or displaying emotions cost the emoter? Anger, derision, laughter, sympathy, patience, and love all cost energy and may reveal information that makes the emoter vulnerable. If Person A gets Person B to experience more emotion than A, A is "ahead of the game."

In sum, to be an effective micro-politician one must walk a fine line between displaying and controlling other-targeted emotions. Withholding contempt, ridicule, or love can signify inferiority and put us one-down, and displaying them can do the same. We do not know how people learn where the fine line is, what emotion work they must undertake to walk it, how conscious they are of their "active" and "passive" emotional strategies, or which sorts of people are successful in what situations.

STRATEGY 4: ELICITING OBLIGATION

Sociologists often use the language of reciprocity and exchange to explain the give-and-take of everyday interaction. One "owes" gifts, emotions, time, energy to others. We rarely ask *why* people feel they owe something to others, what the "ligament" is that connects people, or what the *feeling* of owing or obligation consists of.

I propose that obligation is an emotion or an emotional blend, although everyday language usage does not reflect this fact. We tend to see "an obligation" as a "thing" imposed from outside, and for this reason obligation has acquired a bad reputation in our culture. In the U.S., at least, people believe they should act because they "want to," not because they "have to," and we often regard those who act because they feel they should as being untrue to themselves. To the extent that we think of obligation as a feeling, we tend to focus on it as imposition.

This way of thinking about obligation obscures its physiological and cognitive push, the sense of urgency, the feeling of wanting to act, the "impulsion from within on moral grounds" (Webster, 1967). Obligation can make people *want* to behave in certain ways toward others—or toward the society as a whole (see Durkheim, 1951:221–223; Parsons, 1950). I speak here not merely of fear of dishonor or a kind of proto-guilt, although these may be present, nor of the relief, pride, or satisfaction that comes when a duty is done. I want to point also to a *feeling* of responsibility, an account to self that includes affect surrounding the cognition: "This is my duty. I have to do this for X." Many of us, much of the time, sincerely fulfill our felt obligations.

If our language and sociology have largely overlooked the emotional content of obligation, people have not. Relying on this to enhance their standing, everyday micro-politicians often remind others of their place by invoking a feeling of obligation. The message is: "Your place has rules. The rules are bigger than both of us. God/society/everyone knows that people in your place should. . . . " For example, parents should take care of their children, wives should prepare dinner, husbands should earn enough money to pay the bills, secretaries should not make typos, friends should help out when needed, and citizens should defend their country.

Alter-casting is one technique for reminding people of their obligations. In alter-casting, one person refers to a particular status of the other to make a role expectation more salient. One might say, "John, *old friend*, surely you can lend me $20." A less flattering version (after a refusal) might be: "And you call yourself a friend?" If John accepts the status of friend, he may also accept the emotional obligation the role entails.

Other tactics that serve as obligation reminders are both more subtle and complex. The practice of "loaning" in the Mississippi Delta plantation region provides an example (Clark and Robboy, 1981). In the Delta social system, planters are mainly upper class, educated, and white, while farm workers are poor, uneducated, and black. A version of the "company store" arrangement still exists. Laborers often ask their boss for loans of $10 or $20 or $50, even though the planters charge them as much as 100 percent interest per week. Given that wages are low and weather-dependent, it is extremely hard for workers to repay these loans. Planters usually deduct loans and interest from the next week's pay, which makes for further borrowing, thus leaving the worker perpetually in debt. Why, then, do laborers ask for loans? And why do planters give them?

Poverty and abundance are only part of the answer. Planters feel obligated by the patriarchal tradition to provide workers and their families advice, medical treatment, retirement benefits, and extra cash (although some complain, as one planter did, "I'm always having to be a mother to these people!"). On the other hand, a worker who obtains a loan knows that he will probably not be dismissed until the loan is repaid. The loan provides the worker with both money and a sense of place—job security. Even laborers who are not needy borrow to assure their bosses' obligation to them and to insure their employment.

Although little attention has been directed to the matter of inducing obligation, clearly much sociological theory about group and societal cohesion—functionalist, exchange, interactionist, and even conflict theory—assumes that people feel obligated to each other. If we look specifically at the emotional aspects of obligation (as Hochschild, in this volume, does among married couples), we may understand more about variability in social cohesion, especially cohesion under conditions of inequality. Settings to explore might include work groups, sports teams (see Adler and Adler, 1987), and any other groups requiring coordination of effort and affect. We might discover how feelings of obligation develop and are channeled by taking a longitudinal look at dating and love relationships or at the graduate school experiences of students entering professions.

STRATEGY 5: EXPRESSING POSITIVE OTHER-EMOTIONS INDICATING OWN SUPERIORITY

Expressing positive emotions to others can serve nicely to establish place, either elevating oneself or, paradoxically, reducing the standing of the other. For instance, a middle-aged professional woman reported in a 1985 interview:

> I remember that I once used sympathy on purpose to try to knock someone down a peg. I had a boss who was always doing and saying things to put me down in a semi-nice way. . . . I got tired of it, so I turned it around on him. I was in his office, and I said, "Oh, Mr. Wall, look at all those reports you have to get done. I feel so sorry for you. I wouldn't want your job for the world." He changed colors, and I could see he was mad. He just said, "Oh, I can get this done in a snap. Nothing to it!" and edged me out the door. Normally he would have chatted a while. So I really got in a good zinger. (Clark, 1987:317)

Here we see a sympathy donor purposely pointing out another's problem. The other may not want to admit to a problem, because it acknowledges failure to control either oneself or the environment. If he publicly acknowledges vulnerability, the boss moves one-down.

In reflection, people often work up sympathy for threatening or powerful others. Several interviewees (Clark, 1987) reported that, in their own minds, they had changed their place with bosses, customers, or spouses by turning fear and anger into sympathy. Changes in modes of interacting followed. "The pitied other seems to threaten or to intrude into one's consciousness less; his or her power to disrupt one's equilibrium is diminished."

(Clark, 1987:318). Giving sympathy symbolically or in reality can protect both self and place.

In another interview, a sympathy *recipient* described reactions that point to its micro-political effects. A young college professor met with a student from her course on death and dying. After sympathizing with the young man's recent loss, the professor found herself the proposed object of sympathy.

> He wanted me to start telling him all my problems. I thought to myself, "I don't want to get any closer to you. I don't want to tell you any more about myself. And what makes *you* think *you* can help *me*?" . . . I knew what I was doing: trying to preserve my position as professor (Clark, 1987:318)

The young man may not have intended to bring the professor closer to his level, but she was alert to the possibility. This case also illustrates that the parties' original places in the hierarchy affect the meaning they attribute to the same emotional display.

Because it is predicated on others' problems, is sympathy uniquely suited to emotional micropolitics? Or can other positive emotions be used micropolitically? We saw above that gratitude can work this way if the donor casts the other in an inferior role. So, I believe, can patience, liking, love, and other emotions that we think of as marking closeness or equality. Patience, for instance, can signify Person A's understanding and concern; it can also convey the message that Person B is deficient or slow, and A is resisting using strategy 1 by being very nice not to point out the deficiency in a more hurtful way.

We have come again to the emotions and the emotional strategies and uses of "niceness"—genuine niceness and cynical, ironic, and damn-with-faint-praise varieties. Researchers could learn more about the place-functions of niceness by focusing on people in crisis situations—disaster victims, the ill, the bereaved, or divorcing couples—to see whose sympathy, advice, and patience they accept and whose they find themselves resenting or rejecting. How are acceptable and unacceptable emotional gifts offered? Which specific words, tones of voice, gestures, or material goods are comforting and which demeaning? How do people respond to these gifts and their givers?

We must also recognize that positive emotions may be given cynically or insincerely. How important is the issue of sincerity? What are the consequences of receiving sincere versus insincere sympathy, patience, and so forth, for an actor's self-concept and subjective sense of place, for the ongoing interaction, and for the future of the relationship? I contend—and recent research on the effectiveness of critical vs. praising managerial styles

(Baron, 1988) bears out—that insincere sympathy and faint praise are better than none at all. That is, one's place is reduced farther by others' negative emotions or detachment than by positive but superior ones. We could test this contention experimentally by comparing individual subjects' and groups' reactions to a variety of positive- and negative-emotion treatments. Whether genuine or not, positive other-emotions of superiority carry place messages. Increasing our understanding of their hidden meanings and consequences should tell us more about reciprocal emotions such as admiration and deference. In fact, much interaction among unequals may revolve around Person A's use of strategy 5 and Person B's use of strategy 2. Understanding these place-motives should provide useful insights into the variety of interpersonal conflict disguised as affability.

SUMMARY AND CONCLUSION

Social place is a product of the social structure, the interaction order, the individual's self-concept, and emotions. Emotions mark place in the self, and they serve to make place claims. Because emotions function in these ways, and because people can do emotion work, we are able to display and elicit emotions to enhance place. The micropolitical strategies I have outlined include expressing negative other-emotions, expressing positive other-emotions (to curry favor, promote own self-worth, and diminish others), controlling the balance of emotional energy, and eliciting a sense of obligation. Empirical research into the emotional components of hierarchy will no doubt lead to refinements of these formulations, and future researchers will uncover still more strategies.

A further issue related to the ideas outlined here concerns the degree to which sensibility or emotionality—the very emotions people experience and their attitudes toward them—depends on social placement in both macro- and micro-hierarchies. Throughout society, we may discover many emotional subcultures associated with social place. That is, people located in particular gender, social-class, racial, occupational, age, and ethnic statuses may experience unique combinations of self- and other-emotions, employ some micropolitical strategies more than others, and even develop emotional realities at odds with what we take to be the mainstream. For instance, even emotion labels, like "humiliation" or "belittlement," may mean one thing to white women, another to black or Hispanic men, and yet another to white men.

In one of the first studies of an emotional subculture, Dodd (1987) found that social placement set the parameters for emotionality in the California ghetto he investigated. For poor urban blacks, he maintained, feelings are capital—perhaps the only valuable resources some people have. His respondents put considerable effort into learning about, managing, and manipulating their own and others' emotions. Even small children were master emotional tacticians, using first one place strategy, then another to suit the audience. Paramount reality for this group is not cognitive, but emotional.

It is important that sociologists of emotions undertake more systematic study of emotional subcultures and their values, beliefs, rules, and place strategies. These emotional subcultures may be smaller and more specific to people in particular place constellations than we have imagined. Are the sensibilities of white, suburban, teen-age girls like those of middle-aged, male salesmen or engineers who may be their fathers? What about middle-class black men compared to middle-class black women or to the ghetto blacks whom Dodd described? How does social place affect the emotions and strategies of, say, female clerical workers or elderly, working-class, Jewish men or Hispanic housewives? If we do not begin to compile accounts of emotional subcultures, we run the risk of projecting our own place-conditioned emotions on others, who may remain as invisible to us as battered women are to their abusers.

NOTES

1. I greatly appreciate the helpful comments and suggestions of Mary Dassing, David J. Dodd, Carolyn S. Ellis, David D. Franks, Arlie Russell Hochschild, Theodore D. Kemper, Sherryl Kleinman, Mario E. Kravanja, Eve C. LaMonte, Jay H. Livingston, Patricia A. Potter, Howard Robboy, and Paul R. Williams.

2. See, for example, van den Berghe (1978:25–34) on the role of racial etiquette in maintaining hierarchy among people in close interaction in the southern U.S. and South Africa.

3. Following Thoits (1985:232), I define emotion as an awareness of some combination, but not necessarily all, of the following elements: (1) external situational cues, (2) changes in physiological sensations, (3) expressive gestures, and (4) a cultural label.

4. What have been called revolutions of rising expectations may reflect shifts in the emotional bases of hierarchy, as perhaps with the feminist movements of the nineteenth and twentieth centuries.

5. Some of the illustrative cases cited here, including this one, come from respondents' free-writings (Elbow, 1973). Free-writing consists of nonstop writing on an assigned topic without regard for spelling, word usage, organization, sentence structure or any rules that inhibit word flow. Many free-writers comment on the

value of the practice for uncovering thoughts and feelings they were previously unaware they had. Tapping into this source of information on inner life seems especially appropriate for the sociology of emotions. It provides data at least as valid as those we gain from interviews and should be a useful tool for encouraging introspection (Ellis, 1987).

6. This case illustrates that emotions tend not to come up neatly, one at a time. A person may feel a series or a mixture of other- and self-emotions at once. Sometimes remembered or re-evoked emotions belonging to another time and setting mix with or even fuel "current" emotions. Rosenfield (1988) suggested that memory itself works via emotions; the emotional component of an event is what makes it literally "remember-able."

REFERENCES

Adler, Peter, and Patricia Adler. 1987. "The Social Construction of Organizational Loyalty: A Sociology of Emotions Model." Paper presented at the annual meetings of the American Sociological Association.

Baillif, Dianne Stannard, and Clark, Candace. 1987. "Gender, Status Shields, and Humiliation: The Case of the Elderly." Paper presented at the annual meetings of the Southern Sociological Society.

Baron, Robert. 1988. "Negative Effects of Destructive Criticism: Impact on Conflict, Self-Efficacy, and Task Performance." *Journal of Applied Psychology* 73:199–207.

Bettleheim, Bruno. 1943. "Individual and Mass Behavior in Extreme Situations." *Journal of Abnormal Social Psychology* 38:417–452.

Blau, Peter M. 1964. *Exchange and Power in Social Life.* N.Y.: Wiley.

Camerer, Colin. 1988. "Gifts as Economic Signals and Social Symbols." *American Journal of Sociology* 94 (Supplement):S180–S214.

Clark, Candace. 1987. "Sympathy Biography and Sympathy Margin." *American Journal of Sociology* 93:290–321.

————, and Howard Robboy. 1981. "Elites and Changing Race Relations: The Mississippi Delta Plantation Owner." Paper presented at the annual meetings of the Southern Sociological Society.

Coles, Robert. 1967. *Children of Crisis: A Study of Courage and Fear.* Boston: Little, Brown.

Collins, Randall. 1982. *Sociological Insight: An Introduction to Non-obvious Sociology.* New York: Oxford University Press.

————— . 1986. "Is 1980s Sociology in the Doldrums?" *American Journal of Sociology* 91:1336–1355.

Denzin, Norman K. 1984. "Toward a Phenomenology of Domestic, Family Violence." *American Journal of Sociology* 90:483–513.

Dobash, Emerson R., and Russell Dobash. 1979. *Violence Against Wives.* New York: Free Press.

Dodd, David J. 1987. "Feelings as Capital: The Existential World of Black America." Paper presented at the annual meetings of the Southern Sociological Society.

Durkheim, Emile. 1951. *Suicide: A Study in Sociology.* Translated by John A. Spaulding and George Simpson, edited by George Simpson. New York: Free Press.

Elbow, Peter. 1973. *Writing without Teachers.* New York: Oxford University Press.

Ellis, Carolyn S. 1987. "Systematic Sociological Instrospection and the Study of Emotions." Paper presented at the annual meetings of the American Sociological Association.

————— , and Eugene Weinstein. 1986. "Jealousy and the Social Psychology of Emotional Experience." *Journal of Social and Personal Relationships* 3:337–357.

Ferraro, Kathleen J., and John M. Johnson. 1983. "How Women Experience Battering: The Process of Victimization." *Social Problems* 30:325–339.

Franks, David D. 1989. "Power and Role-Taking: A Social Behaviorist's Synthesis of Kemper's Power and Status Model." In *The Sociology of Emotions: Original Essays and Research Papers.* Edited by David D. Franks and E. Doyle McCarthy. Greenwich CT: JAI Press.

Freidson, Eliot. 1970. *Profession of Medicine.* New York: Dodd, Mead.

Gardner, Carol Brooks. 1980. "Passing By: Street Remarks, Address Rights, and the Urban Female." *Sociological Inquiry* 50:328–56.

Garfinkel, Harold. 1956. "Conditions of Successful Degradation Ceremonies." *American Journal of Sociology* 61:420–424.

Genovese, Eugene. 1969. *The World the Slaveholders Made: Two Essays in Interpretation.* New York: Pantheon.

Gilligan, Carol. 1982. *In a Different Voice: Psychological Theory and Women's Development.* Cambridge, Mass.: Harvard University Press.

Goffman, Erving. 1951. "Symbols of Class Status." *British Journal of Sociology* 2:294–304.

Gross, Edward, and Gregory P. Stone. 1964. "Embarrassment and the Analysis of Role Requirements." *American Journal of Sociology* 70:1–15.

Heise, David. 1989. "Affect Control Theory Technical Appendix." In Theodore D. Kemper, ed., *Research Agendas in the Sociology of Emotions*. Albany, NY: SUNY Press.

Henley, Nancy M. 1977. *Body Politics: Power, Sex and Nonverbal Communication*. Englewood Cliffs, New Jersey: Prentice-Hall.

Hite, Shere. 1987. *Women and Love: A Cultural Revolution in Progress*. New York: Knopf.

Hochschild, Arlie Russell. 1979. "Emotion Work, Feeling Rules and Social Structure." *American Journal of Sociology* 85:551–575.

———. 1983. *The Managed Heart: The Commercialization of Human Feeling*. Berkeley: University of California Press.

Karp, David, and William C. Yoels. 1976. "The College Classroom: Some Observations on the Meanings of Student Participation." *Sociology and Social Research* 60:421–439.

Kemper, Theodore D. 1978. *A Social Interactional Theory of Emotions*. New York: Wiley.

Lecky, P. 1945. *Self-Consistency: A Theory of Personality*. New York: Island Press.

Lever, Janet. 1976. "Sex Differences in the Games Children Play." *Social Problems* 23:478–87.

Lyman, Stanford M., and Marvin Scott. 1970. *A Sociology of the Absurd*. New York: Appleton, Century, Crofts.

Merton, Robert K. 1957. *Social Theory and Social Structure*. New York: Free Press.

Mills, Trudy, and Sherryl Kleinman. 1988. "Emotions, Reflexivity, and Action: An Interactionist Analysis." *Social Forces* 66:1009–1027.

Morgan, Rick, and David Heise. 1988. "The Structure of Subjective Emotions." *Social Psychology Quarterly* 51:19–31.

Morsbach, H., and W. J. Tyler. 1986. "A Japanese Emotion: Amae," In *The Social Construction of Emotions*. Edited by Rom Harré. London: Blackwell.

Parsons, Talcott. 1951. *The Social System*. Glencoe, IL: Free Press.

Potter, Patricia. 1988. "I Killed 'Em: Comedians' Emotional Labor." Paper presented at the annual meetings of the American Sociological Association.

Potter, Stephen. 1948. *The Theory and Practice of Gamesmanship, or the Art of Winning Games without Actually Cheating*. New York: Henry Holt.

————. 1950. *Some Notes on Lifemanship*. New York: Henry Holt.

Potter, Thomas H., Jr. 1965. "Evaluation of the Marginal Man Concept in Industrial Sociology." *Social Science* 40:11–21.

Ridgeway, Celia L., Joseph Berger, and LeRoy Smith. 1985. "Nonverbal Cues and Status: An Expectation States Approach." *American Journal of Sociology* 90:955–978.

Rosenberg, Morris. 1979. *Conceiving the Self*. New York: Basic Books.

Rosenfield, Israel. 1988. *The Invention of Memory: A New View of the Brain*. New York: Basic.

Scheff, Thomas J. 1979. *Catharsis in Healing, Ritual, and Drama*. Berkeley: University of California Press.

————, and Suzanne M. Retzinger. 1988. "Hiding Behavior: Toward Resolving the Shame Controversy." Paper presented at the Conference on Shame Research, Asilomar, Calif.

Schwartz, Barry. 1967. "The Social Psychology of the Gift." *American Journal of Sociology* 73:1–11.

————. 1973. "Waiting, Exchange, and Power: The Distribution of Time in Social Systems." *American Journal of Sociology* 79:841–870.

Scully, Diana, and Joseph Marolla. 1984. "Convicted Rapists' Vocabulary of Motive: Excuses and Justifications." *Social Problems* 31:530–563.

Simmel, Georg. 1950. *The Sociology of Georg Simmel*. Edited by Kurt Wolff. New York: Free Press.

Smith-Lovin, Lynn. 1989. "Emotion as Confirmation and Disconfirmation of Identity: An Affect Control Model." In Theodore D. Kemper, ed., *Research Agendas in the Sociology of Emotions*. Albany, New York: SUNY Press.

Thibaut, John W., and Harold H. Kelley. 1959. *The Social Psychology of Groups*. New York: Wiley.

Thoits, Peggy A. 1985. "Self-Labeling Processes in Mental Illness: The Role of Emotional Deviance." *American Journal of Sociology* 91:221–249.

Thomas, D. L., D. D. Franks, and J. M. Calonico. 1972. "Role-Taking and Power in Social Psychology." *American Sociological Review* 37:605–614.

van den Berghe, Pierre. 1978. *Race and Racism: A Comparative Perspective*. 2nd ed. New York: Wiley.

Waller, Willard [1930] 1963. *The Old Love and the New: Divorce and Readjustment*. Carbondale, Ill.: Southern Illinois University Press.

Weber, Max. 1947. *The Theory of Social and Economic Organization*. Translated by A. M. Henderson and Talcott Parsons. New York: Oxford University Press.

Webster's New Collegiate Dictionary, 7th ed. S. V.

Weinstein, Eugene A. 1965. "The Applied Art of One-Downsmanship." *Transaction* 2:36–38.

——— and Paul Deutschberger. 1963. "Some Dimensions of Altercasting." *Sociometry* 26:454–466.

Wittermans, Tamme, and Irving Kraus. 1964. "Structural Marginality and Social Worth." *Sociology and Social Research* 48:348–360.

Contributors

CANDACE CLARK, Professor of Sociology, Montclair State College, Upper Montclair, New Jersey.

RANDALL COLLINS, Professor of Sociology, University of California at Riverside, Riverside, California.

NORMAN K. DENZIN, Professor of Sociology, University of Illinois, Urbana, Illinois.

STEVEN L. GORDON, Professor of Sociology, California State University at Los Angeles, Los Angeles, California.

MICHAEL HAMMOND, Professor of Sociology, University of Toronto, Toronto, Ontario, Canada.

DAVID R. HEISE, Professor of Sociology, Indiana University, Bloomington, Indiana.

ARLIE RUSSELL HOCHSCHILD, Professor of Sociology, University of California at Berkeley, Berkeley, California.

THEODORE D. KEMPER, Professor of Sociology, St. John's University, Jamaica, New York.

THOMAS J. SCHEFF, Professor of Sociology, University of California at Santa Barbara, Santa Barbara, California.

LYNN SMITH-LOVIN, Professor of Sociology, Cornell University, Ithaca, New York.

PEGGY A. THOITS, Professor of Sociology, Indiana University, Bloomington, Indiana.